CRIME ANALYSIS THROUGH COMPUTER MAPPING

Editors: Carolyn Rebecca Block, Margaret Dabdoub
and Suzanne Fregly

Police Executive Research Forum

These essays were commissioned by the Illinois Criminal Justice Information Authority; Loyola University–Chicago; the Innovations in State and Local Government Program of the J.F. Kennedy School of Government–Harvard University; and the Ford Foundation. The opinions expressed herein are those of the authors and do not necessarily reflect those of PERF's members.

Police Executive Research Forum, Washington, D.C. 20036

Printed in the United States of America

Library of Congress Catalog Number 94-70186

ISBN 1-878734-34-2

Cover by Marnie Deacon

Contents

Exhibits, Figures, Maps, and Tables

Chapter 17

Chapter 18

Chapter 19

Chapter 20

Chapter 21

Chapter 22

Introduction

More Than Just a Pretty Map: How Can Spatial Analysis Support Police Decisions?

George F. Rengert
Department of Criminal Justice
Temple University

Law enforcement personnel have been conducting spatial analysis since the beginning of modern policing. Much of this analysis has been carried out in the brains of seasoned detectives. These days, however, more and more of this analysis is conducted on desktop computers. Rather than have seasoned officers pass down techniques to their colleagues by word of mouth and example, we now house this knowledge in the memory of a computer. This change is important not only because it supplements the expertise of an experienced police officer, but also because the knowledge and techniques accumulated over the years do not retire with a veteran detective. They are there for others to build on.

The development of computer techniques of spatial analysis useful to police is in its infancy. Law enforcement personnel have borrowed many of these techniques from geography, regional science and economics. For example, they use real estate house-hunting models to describe the spatial search behavior of residential burglars. They use shopping models to explain the spatial behavior of shoplifters. They use nearest-neighbor analysis developed in ecology to analyze the spatial clustering of crime sites. Only a few scholars have developed new models of spatial analysis of criminal activity. There will be many more in the future.

What should these new models of criminal activity be like? First, they should have a clear, logical structure. That is, *A* leads to *B* because of *C*. "Because of *C*" is the most important part. It is the explanation. Too often, crime researchers stop with "*A* leads to *B*." For example, one finds studies that conclude that residential burglars exploit the same area again and again, which is termed *spatial persistence*, or studies that conclude that crime tends to cluster spatially. These studies are mere description, as they provide no explanation for why the spatial clustering of crime sites occurs.

Second, models must be operational. Officers must be able to measure the model's components. Otherwise, they are just taking someone's word for why something occurs. Scholars in the 1960s grew dissatisfied with the "expert witness" type of science. They demanded proof in their scientific investigations. In other words, the factors in their studies had to be measurable.

Third, and most important, the models of criminal spatial activity should make sense based on real-world experience. The best models will explain what is already known to be true. If the models and techniques of spatial analysis do not make sense to an experienced police officer, they are probably faulty. This may be true even if they fit statistically.

One of the tools used to develop spatial models is maps. Police officers examine maps for a variety of reasons. For one, maps are a source of evidence that may help them learn about the phenomenon represented and the processes responsible for generating it. Quite often, police get ideas about the locational behavior of criminals from such maps. Secondly, police examine maps if their knowledge of a phenomenon is rudimentary. Information gained from analyzing a map may enable them to acquire some initial insights into the phenomenon. In all cases, analysis should be practical and support police officers' decision-making ability.

All ranks of police officers make spatial decisions. High-level administrators make deployment decisions concerning how many officers to assign to each police division and district. Beat patrol officers decide where the trouble spots are likely to be at different times of the day. Detectives try to solve serial cases with point-pattern analysis of crime sites. Many of these techniques are highlighted in the chapters that follow.

Chapter 1

Strategic Crime Patterning: Problem-Oriented Policing and Displacement

D. Kim Rossmo
School of Criminology
Simon Fraser University
Vancouver Police Department

INTRODUCTION

As North American policing moves from a professional to a community-based model, it is timely for communities, governments and police agencies to consider the nature and role of the policing function.

> If . . . the policing institution is guided through the change . . . the public will be better served, policymakers and police administrators more effective, and the profession of policing revitalized (Kelling and Moore 1988:14).[1]

Perhaps the most critical point that needs to be addressed is the development of some form of consensus on the issue of where should policing go from here (Goldstein 1977:chap. 1). Implicit in this discussion is an appraisal of where policing can go—in other words, we need to delineate the limitations to our social control mechanisms.

When August Vollmer spearheaded the development of the professional policing model, he sought to raise standards, reduce corruption, increase efficiency, and improve effectiveness through the use of modern management techniques, the latest technology and scientific investigative techniques (Douthit 1983; Goldstein 1977:228–229). But along the way, through various interpretations of Vollmer's ideas, something was lost. Sir Robert Peel's basic principle that "the police are the public and that the public are the police" (Sewell 1985:17) became obscured in the effort to improve and modernize the law enforcement function.

This overreliance on technology, bureaucracy and criminal law distanced the police from the community, handicapped their efforts and led to roadblocks that impeded improvement. One of the predictable outcomes of this professionalization was a shifting of social control responsibility from the citizenry to the police. Not only did this make the job of the police a lot more difficult[2], but it also created a false sense of power, an imagery of total control that simply never existed. It was implicitly assumed that a properly trained police force with sufficient resources and the latest technology should be able to control any problem and solve any crime. By adopting this facade, police depart-

1. See Williams and Murphy (1990), however, for an alternative view on historical shifts in policing paradigms.

2. With an average ratio of one police officer for every 500 members of the public, simple arithmetic dictates the necessity of community involvement. Furthermore, studies have shown that most crimes are actually "solved" by the public and not by the police (Chaiken, Greenwood and Petersilia 1983: 168–170, 182).

ments set themselves up for failure and criticism—unjustly so, as such power or ability never existed and probably never could exist in any democratic society.

The main functions of the police and the criminal justice system are often seen as the reduction and control of criminal behavior. These efforts to reduce crime, however, are often less than successful and may have unintended consequences. Documented effects of control strategies include specific and general deterrence, incapacitation, rehabilitation, prevention, reduction, displacement, labeling, iatrogenic problems, and various combinations of such outcomes. While all of these results deserve detailed study, displacement is a particularly problematic consequence that, if more fully understood, could be controlled and positively employed for problem-oriented policing tactics.

PROBLEM-ORIENTED POLICING

The Concept

Problem-oriented policing is based on the premise that it is important to understand and address the underlying causes of crime-related community problems (Goldstein 1990; Spelman and Eck 1987). Traditional incident-driven policing only deals with symptoms, which often means that problems reappear, sometimes over and over again. A mid-level strategy appears to be more effective and efficient for solving problems than traditional responses. The police, in this age of diminishing resources and budgets, cannot keep responding to the ever-increasing call load. But if problem-oriented policing is to work, there must be cooperation from the community, other government agencies and private business.

Such an approach is distinct from deep-level crime reduction programs, which focus on such issues as unemployment, substance abuse, child upbringing, and socioeconomic inequalities. These approaches seek to address the very root of our social problems, and if successful, have the potential for significantly reducing crime. They are, however, beyond the means, mandate and resources of the police.

More and more police departments are adopting the problem-oriented approach as the "engineering" component of their community-based policing philosophies. This evolution has not occurred in a vacuum, and Goldstein (1991) identifies certain major forces that are creating the impetus for change in North American policing:

- The recent recession has necessitated government fiscal restraint, led to cutbacks in social and mental health services, and caused budget restrictions in most police departments.
- Increasing calls for service, especially in deteriorating inner urban areas, have placed demands and strains on many police departments. It has been suggested that these increases are partly the result of the reductions in social, educational and mental health services, mentioned above.
- There is an increasing lack of faith, by both the police and the community, in the criminal justice system. Part of this has been caused by courts and prisons' attempting to deal with a serious overload of their capacities. Historically, communities had informal social control mechanisms that addressed the majority of their problems, and criminal justice systems were never designed to deal with high volumes of crime.
- Police departments are periodically faced with such crises as internal scandals, violent crime sprees and urban riots. Even when the behavior of the police cannot be faulted, the media may still generate a "crisis," leading to outcomes just as real as if genuine malfeasance existed.

It is the need to do more work with fewer resources and with less dependence on the criminal justice system that has spurred the adoption of the problem-oriented policing concept.

Requirements

For problem-oriented policing to be successful, it is necessary for a police department to adopt certain critical elements (Eck and Spelman 1987; Goldstein 1990).

- A close, working relationship with the community, incorporating an effective and mutual exchange of information, must be established. The shift toward community-based policing seen in many American and Canadian police agencies can only assist the efforts to open up such lines of dialogue.
- Police agencies must expand their operational focus to include those social and community problems that create crimes and calls for service. A restrictive mandate only leads to a loss of control over the causes of crime.
- It is essential that police agencies move beyond the standardized and sometimes ineffective responses traditionally employed to "fight crime." Innovative and individualistic strategies for problem-solving must be developed.
- The expertise and creativity of line officers need to be tapped in the effort to develop such innovative strategies. The organizational structure should provide opportunities for its members to assume initiative and responsibility, and then reward such efforts accordingly.

The SARA Model

The problem-oriented policing approach is based on a four-stage model called SARA (Eck and Spelman 1987:42–51), containing the following components: scanning, analysis, response, and assessment.

Scanning

Problems must somehow come to the attention of the police before an effort can be made to solve them. This can be accomplished through open lines of communication with the community, the experiences of patrol officers, call-load and hot-spot examination, or sophisticated computer crime analysis. The problem may not fit into the usual police call or criminal law categories, but rather may be connected through such dimensions as geography, time or people. Consequently, alternative and innovative methods of looking at community issues will have to be adopted by those police departments wishing to identify problems in a timely manner.

Analysis

The exact nature of the problem and the characteristics of the incidents must be analyzed. Important factors to consider include where the incidents are occurring, at what times, who is involved, how and why the problem is occurring, and what solutions have been tried in the past. By determining the underlying causes of the problem through the gathering of detailed information, more effective policing strategies can be developed. Such information can come from the police, outside agencies and experts, the community itself, and even those offenders involved in the problem.

Response

With a thorough understanding of the problem, the police can develop specific strategies to help resolve it. Such tailored responses often involve creative policing approaches that incorporate community members, outside agencies and private business. For effective strategies to be identified and implemented, it is necessary for the police agency to have an organizational, command and reward structure that enables problem-oriented policing efforts at the line level.

Assessment

The outcome of the police response must be evaluated and honestly assessed. Unless an effort is made to determine which strategies and approaches are effective, police agencies will be seriously hindered in their efforts to improve their craft and assist their communities. Displacement is often an outcome of enforcement strategies, though a movement of the problem does not necessarily mean that the strategy was a failure.

Enforcement Outcomes

Since problem-oriented policing requires a shift in focus from the incident or offender to the problem and its underlying causes, different measures of success are required. John Eck has identified five possible objectives of problem-oriented policing (Sloan 1993): (1) elimination of the problem, (2) reduction in the number of incidents, (3) reduction of harm from each incident, (4) service improvement, and (5) interagency coordination. Objectives are not the same as outcomes, however, and any given strategy may be unsuccessful or may cause displacement of the problem. But displacement may still lead to reductions in incident numbers and impact, or conversely, if uncontrolled, it may lead to increases.

Consequently, displacement should be considered in the response as well as the assessment stage of problem-oriented policing. In other words, displacement can be more than an obstacle; it also can be a tool. Even when law enforcement efforts are unsuccessful at problem elimination, they still may lead to attenuation through strategic crime patterning.

DISPLACEMENT

Crime displacement can be defined as "the reappearance of criminality along some dimension(s) following the implementation of an ostensibly effective prevention program" (Gabor 1978:101), or as "movement [that] would not have occurred had some legal or criminal justice policy not been enacted (formally or informally)" (Lowman 1986:86). While displacement has been defined, categorized and researched at the scientific level, it almost has been ignored at the operational level of police and criminal justice functioning.

Displacement is a special case of crime spillover, a term used to describe all interjurisdictional criminal movement, whether attributable to destination (pull) factors involving increased attraction, or origin (push) factors involving increased risk (Hakim and Rengert 1981:14–15). Crime displacement is caused by such origin influences in a given area as target hardening (resulting, for example, from new crime prevention strategies) or increases in police patrols. Spillover is almost always seen as limited to neighboring zones, though some research has shown that the impacts may be nationwide (Rossmo 1987).

Types of Displacement

At least five possible forms of displacement have been recognized in the literature: (1) territorial, (2) temporal, (3) target, (4) tactical, and (5) functional (Reppetto 1976).[3] While criminal justice actions can create any of these forms of displacement, behavior is usually not the result of any single cause, but rather is the outcome of decisions influenced by a myriad of variables.

Geographic Displacement

Territorial, geographic or spatial displacement is perhaps the most common form of this phenomenon (Reppetto 1976:177). "In response to a reduction of opportunity or an increased risk of apprehension with respect to a particular offense, an offender may relocate his activity" (Gabor 1978:101). Since much of police work has a geographic component, spatial relocation is a frequent response by street criminals to official control efforts.

Bail and probation orders that include area restrictions as part of the conditions imposed on offenders often only result in the movement of their criminal activity to another area. This has been particularly noted in the cases of such "victimless" crimes as prostitution and drug trafficking, which seem to follow the same economic laws that influence the buying and selling of other, more legitimate commodities.

Temporal Displacement

Temporal displacement occurs when criminal activity shifts to a different time period in response to some change in enforcement, initiated either formally or informally, in an effort to prevent crime. This results when the change leads to a perceived alteration in the risk or target environment within which the offender operates. Criminal activity may then shift to a time when acceptable risk (low danger) levels exist in conjunction with the relative availability of feasible opportunities (easy targets).

Such a change in the risk environment could result from police departments' increasing their patrol levels during certain time periods, but not during others. Criminals might then modify their activity times in an attempt to work around the heavy patrolling periods. As an example, it was found that prostitutes in Vancouver attempted to discover, and then work around, the shift times of the police prostitution task force (Rossmo and Fisher 1993). These changes in working times were found to be related to "the next best" opportunities for customer attraction (i.e., an increase in evening patrols led to more prostitutes working during commuter and lunchtime periods).

Temporal shifts can also result from "natural" changes in target availability, though such movement would not be considered displacement unless it were occasioned by a control agency activity. Criminal behavior varies all the time, for many reasons not associated with official police or court actions.

3. Some writers have suggested that "statutory displacement" is a sixth form of the phenomenon (Gabor 1978:103). It is actually a cause, however, not an effect. Typically, it involves geographic movement occasioned by changes in the certainty or severity of court sentencing practices. For example, in 1984 the attorney general of British Columbia was granted an interlocutory injunction to prohibit prostitution in the West End community of Vancouver. This resulted in the geographic displacement of hundreds of prostitutes to other areas of the city, as they attempted to avoid the penalties associated with the attorney general's civil process (Cassels 1985:766–786). Legal or statutory charges can create other forms of displacement, in addition to geographic displacement. Police in Canada have suggested that the introduction of the Young Offenders Act in 1984 may have caused an increase in the level of criminal behavior of juveniles, particularly those under 12 years old, the age of criminal responsibility.

Target Displacement

Target displacement occurs when offenders select different premises, objects or subjects as the targets for their criminal activities. This shift may result from target-hardening activities, which typically involve neighborhood watch programs, increased use of security devices or alarm systems, and operation identification programs. Stickers or signs warning of these precautions may deter offenders from attacking the protected property, but displace them to the next closest residence. Car alarm systems, with precautionary labels, accomplish the same outcome—the auto thief just moves down the street to the next, unprotected vehicle.

Tactical Displacement

Tactical displacement occurs when alternative strategies are developed by offenders in an effort to achieve the same criminal goals. The introduction of alarms to many commercial establishments has resulted in modifications in the methods of committing commercial burglaries. Most break-and-enters are now accomplished in the form of "smash and grab," where the offenders spend no more than a minute or two at the scene, fleeing before they think the police will respond to the alarm. While the booty achieved by this method is not nearly as voluminous as what could have been taken in the days before alarm systems, when burglars literally had hours to clear out the contents of a premise, the proceeds are not trivial, and the risk to the offender is substantially lower.

Functional Displacement

Functional or activity displacement is the engagement in a different form or type of criminal behavior by the offender. For example, the enhanced technology incorporated in the design of bank vault systems since World War II has made safecracking a very rare crime in most Canadian metropolitan areas, creating both a geographic displacement of such offenders to small towns where older vaults are still used, and a functional displacement to other types of criminal activity. Of course, as technology closes down some opportunities, it opens up others. The growth in the use of credit cards during the past 30 years has given criminal offenders the potential for a variety of credit card fraud schemes.

Displacement Issues

The various forms of displacement are most often unanticipated side effects of control strategies designed to accomplish other goals. From a community perspective, the results of displacement may be either positive or negative. Displacement must be recognized and more fully understood by the various components of the criminal justice system so that its negative effects can be mitigated and its positive aspects can be effectively used for the protection of society. Unfortunately, this may require an admittance of the limitations of the police and the courts, an organizational and political hurdle that is definitely nontrivial. Such attitudes are barriers to true community-based policing, however, and are inappropriate for the creative solutions required by the problem-oriented policing approach (see Goldstein 1990).

Displacement, however, is by no means a certain result of control strategies (Miethe 1991:421–422). In the first place, if the strategy is not perceived by the offender to be effective, then it will have little consequence. Functional displacement is not likely to occur if the crimes lack similar structural features (Cornish and Clarke 1986; Miethe 1991:421; Reppetto 1976:175–177). If the offender lacks strong motivation, if the crime in question is particularly opportunistic, or if alternative targets show little promise of adequate rewards or unsuitable high-risk levels, then displacement is unlikely to result from target hardening strategies (Miethe 1991:422; Reppetto 1976:175–177).

Beyond the political and organizational difficulties that exist, the issue of intra- and interjurisdictional relationships must also be considered. Spatial displacement, in particular, may have consequences for other cities and police forces. Such displacement may, in fact, be a covert aim that is unofficially sanctioned by the agency responsible. Certain types of policy may be conscious efforts to relocate undesirable activities (Lowman 1982:329).

In a study of fugitives wanted on criminal warrants that were not in effect, because of policy decisions outside of the area of court origin, it was found that a significant relationship existed between the extent of fugitive migration and the warrant radius of return policy—the more restrictive the radius of warrant return policy from a given jurisdiction, the greater the number of fugitives from that location (Rossmo 1987:chap. 5). The study collected a sample of 757 unique cases in a 30-day period in Vancouver during the latter half of 1984, from a population of perhaps twice that number (Rossmo and Routledge 1990). As these fugitives were highly involved in criminal activity and were characterized as serial offenders with an average of 15.0 prior charges, and a rearrest rate during the month study period of 30.4 percent (Rossmo 1987:107), their presence in Vancouver was less than welcome. Also, it was suspected that these warrant return policies were designed to accomplish just such geographic displacement.

The overall advantages of displacing crime to another police jurisdiction are highly questionable.

> The political-legal implications of crime spillovers from one jurisdiction to another may be profound. Nonreciprocal spillovers from one jurisdiction to another may produce antagonistic relations between the two areas (Gabor and Gottheil 1984:268).

Even more baffling from a systems perspective is the random reallocation of street criminal activity within the same police jurisdiction. If officers move people "off their beats" without any thought as to where they may go, totally haphazard and unplanned results are likely to occur. On the other hand, real benefits may result from informed, coordinated strategies designed to implement positive forms of displacement.

The increase in burglary smash-and-grabs, in the example discussed above, can be viewed as a relatively positive outcome in that there is a reduction in the total losses through stolen property. A movement from commercial to residential break-ins would be seen as negative. Any shift to crimes of violence from those targeting property is most undesirable. Those enforcement activities that have resulted in the reduction in the use of heroin and an attendant increase in the use of cocaine are hardly successful, in that cocaine and crack produce more problematic behavior.

Strategic factors that should be considered include whether or not crime displacement will occur; what displacement types or combinations are likely to result from the control strategy; whether there will be a reduction in the displaced activity; the possibility of residual deterrence; the characteristics of the status quo (the area, the targets, the time, the modus operandi, the activities); the likely characteristics of the displacement outcomes; and what degree of effort and level of resources will be required to produce any productive change.

The characteristics of the status quo are very important for determining the desirability of displacement outcomes. In cases of geographic displacement, communities unprepared for crime problems may suffer more than those that have had some experience with the phenomenon. Certain areas may be inherently more vulnerable and may provide better opportunities for criminal activities, resulting in an increase in the level of the displaced problem. On the other hand, the new area may be more "suitable" for the criminal activity. The movement of prostitutes from residential to industrial areas, for example, has proved to usually mitigate the problems of disturbances, offense visibility, fear levels, and traffic congestion.

Deterrence

Residual deterrence has been suggested as a possible outcome of intermittent police crackdowns, effected through proper enforcement timing (Sherman 1990). By introducing short crackdowns directed against such problems as drug trafficking, street prostitution or drunk driving, followed by a reduction of enforcement, a "free" deterrent period can result. Upon the residual deterrence's waning, it can be reinforced by another enforcement campaign. In the interim, the police resources can be used to implement crackdowns in other areas. Such an approach minimizes displacement by focusing on several areas "simultaneously." Naturally, all such efforts must be assessed in terms of their cost effectiveness, and points of diminishing returns should be identified.

Disruption

If displacement does occur, there could well be a reduction in the level of criminal activity resulting from disruption. Criminals are often conscious of territory and require knowledge of their turf for effective operation (Fattah 1991:235–237; McIver 1981:22–23; Reppetto 1976:173–174). Questions about the effect of relocation on criminal activity; the level of inconvenience resulting from unfamiliarity with suitable targets, escape routes and accomplices; and the impact on police effectiveness caused by the introduction of unknown offenders into a new zone, should all be addressed by future research.

Free-Rider Effects

Free-rider effects can occur when hardened targets generate a "difficult" reputation that becomes mentally associated by the offender with the entire surrounding neighborhood.

> Contrary to the adverse effects of displacement, it is possible that target-hardening activities provide crime-reduction benefits for both the individual and others in the community. In other words, the crime control activities of others in a geographic area may "spill over" and reduce the risks for neighbors (free riders) who do not themselves take precautionary measures. This free-rider effect is based on the assumption that signs of high guardianship in an area translate into cost for would-be offenders (e.g., higher risks of detection and apprehension) and may be sufficient to deter crime even against those who are least protected (Miethe 1991:422).

In looking for displacement of free-rider effects, it is critical to test for both target and geographic displacement. Gabor (1978:105) criticizes "the assumption in the geographic studies, that displacement is localized," and Lowman (1983:chap. 9) found displacement to nearby neighborhoods (as opposed to houses or blocks) in Vancouver and Burnaby as the result of "Neighborhood Watch" break-and-entry prevention programs.

Nearest-neighbor and bordering-block effects must be examined in addition to larger scale impacts. It is also important to understand the influence of offenders' mental maps (Gould and White 1974) and the existing research on victim/target selection (Brantingham and Brantingham 1981, 1984, 1993a), routine activities and criminal mobility patterns (Brantingham and Brantingham 1981:30–32, 1984).

Offenders who perceive an entire area as target-hardened may move on to another neighborhood that is more conducive to their hunting requirements. The level of social control in the wider area is an important consideration.

> There was a clear trend for residents of high-protection areas to benefit from the crime control efforts of their neighbors (supporting free riding), whereas displacement effects were consistently observed in areas with lower levels of safety precautions (Miethe 1991:436).

Dispersion

Dispersion occurs when geographic displacement results in a scattering of the problem or the offenders to various other contiguous areas. This can lead to both positive and negative consequences. If police activities indiscriminately move prostitutes, enlarging their working areas through dispersion and increasing the scope of customers' search areas, the resulting community impact will have been exacerbated (Lowman 1989:chap. 5; Rossmo 1987:23–24). Court-imposed area restrictions often accomplish only the same result.

Dispersion can also break up hot spots and potentiation effects (see below), however, leading to a reduction in both the numbers and the impact of problem incidents. Computerized crime analysis systems, such as the Illinois Criminal Justice Information Authority's Spatial and Temporal Analysis of Crime (STAC) software used by the Baltimore County and Chicago police departments, can assist in the timely identification and analysis of hot-spot areas (Block 1990, 1993).

Potentiation

A potentiation effect, where the whole is greater than the sum of the parts, may occur with some types of offenders and some forms of crime (Rossmo and Fisher 1993). Potentiation has been noted in apartment buildings or housing complexes when a significant portion of the tenants become involved in criminal activity, usually vice crimes such as drug dealing or prostitution. In effect, the criminal element "takes over" the territory, developing support networks and dramatically increasing fear levels. Informal social control breaks down, crimes can be committed with impunity, and the area becomes a rookery, serving as a magnet for a host of other problems.

Spatial or temporal displacement may, however, disrupt such group interaction, communication and support networks, destroying the potentiation effect and reducing the levels of certain types of crime. The desirability of displacement outcomes is influenced by the characteristics of the area, the offenders, the criminal activities, and the time periods involved, suggesting the importance (and sometimes painful experience) of proper analysis and evaluation in the design of control strategies.

Potentiation is an important consideration for both environmental design and situational crime prevention efforts. Bars and nightclubs in close proximity and with simultaneous closing times can create crowd effects that lead to disturbances, crime and violence (Engstad 1975; Roncek and Maier 1991; Roncek and Pravatiner 1989; Rossmo and Fisher 1993). Conversely, their locations may be spatially patterned and their closures so scheduled as to minimize such problems. Proper urban planning can play a key preventative role in these circumstances.

STRATEGIC CRIME PATTERNING

In the effort to manage community problems, many police departments are recognizing the limits of their abilities to eliminate certain types of criminal behavior. The police are restricted by statute and case law, limited by personnel and financial resources, and confined by the capacities of the other components of the criminal justice system. While crime prevention and reduction remain the ultimate goals, it may be appropriate to consider crime management as an intermediate objective.

Certain types of social problems have remained remarkably resistant to policing strategies, "clean-up campaigns" or urban renewal. Prostitution, drug use, drunkenness, and other vice crimes are resilient and omnipresent problems in almost every city. Combat zones, tenderloin areas, red-light districts, and skid rows are often associated with high rates of crime. Youth and gang hangouts generate disturbances and increase fear levels in certain neighborhoods. These and similar activities are more often displaced than resolved by policing efforts. If such problems cannot be eliminated, then perhaps their locations can be strategically patterned within our cities to mitigate their impacts on communities.

There is considerable research in the area of situational crime prevention (see, for example, Brantingham and Brantingham 1984, 1993b; Clarke 1992; Clarke and Felson 1993; Cornish and Clarke 1986; Evans, Fyfe and Herbert 1992; Felson 1987; Figlio, Hakim and Rengert 1986), and this work can serve as a basis for an intelligent assessment of the limits of policing and optimal forms of urban crime patterning. We know that prostitution in residential neighborhoods creates more problems than in industrial areas. No one would rather have a drug market next to a school ground than in an abandoned building. Many more people are affected when a gang congregates in a park than when they hang out in a pool hall. None of this is to suggest that criminal behavior should be ignored, but rather, it is to propose that policing strategies take into account the limitations of enforcement, criminal law and the justice system in an effort to make communities more liveable places.

CONCLUSION

Displacement, though most often viewed as an unwanted by-product of control strategies, can result in beneficial outcomes if properly structured and directed (Miethe 1991:437; Reppetto 1976:169). As economists and planners must contend with the positive and negative effects of externalities, the courts and the police must understand and address the total consequences of criminal law and enforcement practices. Gabor (1978:105) calls for research that will "provide further knowledge regarding the extent of offender flexibility, mobility and opportunism."

All criminal justice system agencies should be aware of, and effectively utilize, the results of such research and abandon the mythology that crime can be controlled through more laws and more policing.[4] Such an attitude actually diverts scarce police resources from areas where they can be most effective. There needs to be a reconciliation among public expectations, criminal law, statutory powers, and enforcement realities. This requires honest dialogue between the community, the police, the judiciary, and the politicians. Until that debate occurs, we will continue to be guilty of indulging in "magical thinking" rather than working on problem solving.

REFERENCES

Bates, S. (1987). *Spatial and temporal analysis of crime* (research bulletin). Chicago: Illinois Criminal Justice Information Authority.

Biderman, A.D., and A.J. Reiss, Jr. (1967). On exploring the "dark figure" of crime. *The Annals of the American Academy of Political and Social Science* 374:1–15.

Block, C.R. (December 1990). *Hot spots and isocrimes in law enforcement decision making.* Paper presented at the conference on Police and Community Responses to Drugs: Frontline Strategies in the Drug War.

——— (1993). Automated spatial analysis as a tool in violence reduction. *CJ the Americas* 6(1):7–8, 10.

Bottomley, A.K., and C.A. Coleman (1976). *Understanding crime rates: Police and public roles in the production of official statistics.* Westmead, Farnborough, Hants: Saxon House.

Bottoms, A.E., and P. Wiles (1992). Explanations of crime and place. Pp. 11–35 in D.J. Evans, N.R. Fyfe and D.T. Herbert (eds.), *Crime, Policing and Place: Essays in Environmental Criminology.* London: Routledge.

4. See Rossmo and Routledge (1990) for a statistical evaluation of the minimal impact of bill C-49 (Canada's 1985 prostitution law) on Vancouver's street prostitution population.

Brantingham, P.J., and P.L. Brantingham (eds.) (1981). *Environmental Criminology.* Beverly Hills: Sage.

Brantingham, P.J., and P.L. Brantingham (1984). *Patterns in Crime.* New York: Macmillan.

Brantingham, P.L., and P.J. Brantingham (1993a). Nodes, paths and edges: Considerations on the complexity of crime and the physical environment. *Journal of Environmental Psychology* 13:3–28.

——— (1993b). Environment, routine and situation: Toward a pattern theory of crime. Pp. 259–294 in R.V. Clarke and M. Felson (eds.), *Routine Activity and Rational Choice.* New Brunswick, N.J.: Transaction.

Cassels, J. (1985). Prostitution and public nuisance: Desperate measures and the limits of civil adjudication. *The Canadian Bar Review* 63:764–845.

Chaiken, J., P. Greenwood and J. Petersilia (1983). The Rand study of detectives. Pp. 167–184 in C.B. Klockars (ed.), *Thinking about Police: Contemporary Readings.* New York: McGraw-Hill.

Clarke, R.V. (ed.) (1992). *Situational Crime Prevention: Successful Case Studies.* New York: Harrow and Heston.

Clarke, R.V. (November 1992). *Subway slugs: Tracking displacement on the London Underground.* Paper presented at the meeting of the American Society of Criminology, New Orleans, La.

Clarke, R.V., and M. Felson (eds.) (1993). *Routine Activity and Rational Choice.* New Brunswick, N.J.: Transaction.

Cohen, L., and M. Felson (1979). Social change and crime rate trends: A routine activity approach. *American Sociological Review* 44:588–608.

Cornish, D.B., and R.V. Clarke (eds.) (1986). *The Reasoning Criminal: Rational Choice Perspectives on Offending.* New York: Springer-Verlag.

Damer, S. (1974). Wine Alley: The sociology of a dreadful enclosure. *Sociological Review* 22:221–248.

Douthit, N. (1983). August Vollmer. Pp. 100–113 in C.B. Klockars (ed.), *Thinking about Police: Contemporary Readings.* New York: McGraw-Hill.

Eck, J.E. (1984). *Using Research: A Primer for Law Enforcement Managers.* Washington, D.C.: Police Executive Research Forum.

——— (1992). *Helpful Hints for the Tradition-Bound Chief.* Washington, D.C.: Police Executive Research Forum.

Eck, J.E., and W.G. Spelman (1987). *Problem-Solving: Problem-Oriented Policing in Newport News.* Washington, D.C.: Police Executive Research Forum.

Eck, J.E., and D. Stern (1992). *Revisiting Community Policing: A New Typology.* Washington, D.C.: Police Executive Research Forum.

Engstad, P.A. (1975). Environmental opportunities and the ecology of crime. Pp. 193–211 in R.A. Silverman and J.J. Teevan Jr. (eds.), *Crime in Canadian Society.* Toronto: Butterworth.

Epperlein, T., and B.C. Nienstedt (1989). Reexamining the use of seriousness weights in an index of crime. *Journal of Criminal Justice* 17:343–360.

Evans, D.J., N.R. Fyfe and D.T. Herbert (eds.) (1992). *Crime, Policing and Place: Essays in Environmental Criminology.* London: Routledge.

Fattah, E.A. (ed.) (1986). *From Crime Policy to Victim Policy: Reorienting the Justice System.* Houndsmills, UK: Macmillan Press.

Fattah, E.A. (1991). *Understanding Criminal Victimization: An Introduction to Theoretical Victimology.* Scarborough, ON: Prentice-Hall Canada.

Felson, M. (1986). Linking criminal choices, routine activities, informal control, and criminal outcomes. Pp. 119–128 in D.B. Cornish and R.V. Clarke (eds.), *The Reasoning Criminal: Rational Choice Perspectives on Offending.* New York: Springer-Verlag.

——— (1987). Routine activities and crime prevention in the developing metropolis. *Criminology* 25:911–931.

Figlio, R.M., S. Hakim and G.F. Rengert (eds.) (1986). *Metropolitan Crime Patterns.* Monsey, N.Y.: Willow Tree Press.

Gabor, T. (1978). Crime displacement: The literature and strategies for its investigation. *Crime and Justice* 6:100–106.

Gabor, T., and E. Gottheil (1984). Offender characteristics and spatial mobility: An empirical study and some policy implications. *Canadian Journal of Criminology* 26:267–281.

Georges-Abeyie, D.E., and K.D. Harries (eds.) (1980). *Crime: A Spatial Perspective.* New York: Columbia University Press.

Gill, O. (1977). *Luke Street: Housing Policy, Conflict and the Creation of a Delinquent Area.* London: Macmillan.

Goldstein, H. (1977). *Policing a Free Society.* Cambridge, Mass.: Ballinger.

——— (1990). *Problem-Oriented Policing.* New York: McGraw-Hill.

——— (Fall 1991). The *sine qua non* of policing. *Problem-Solving Quarterly* 5(1, Fall):6, 10–16.

Gould, P., and R. White (1974). *Mental Maps.* New York: Penguin.

Greenberg, D.F. (1979). *Mathematical Criminology.* New Brunswick, N.J.: Rutgers.

Griffiths, C.T., and S.N. Verdun-Jones (1989). *Canadian Criminal Justice.* Toronto: Butterworths.

Hakim, S., and G.F. Rengert (eds.) (1981). *Crime Spillover.* Beverly Hills: Sage.

Jakle, J.A., S. Brunn and C.C. Roseman (1976). *Human Spatial Behavior: A Social Geography.* Prospect Heights, Ill.: Waveland Press.

Kelling, G.L., and M.H. Moore (1988). *The Evolving Strategy of Policing* (Perspectives on Policing, No. 4, BJS Publication No. NCJ-114213). Washington, D.C.: U.S. Government Printing Office.

Kennedy, D.M. (1991). *The Strategic Management of Police Resources.* Unpublished manuscript, Harvard University, John F. Kennedy School of Government, Cambridge, Mass.

Klockars, C.B. (ed.) (1983). *Thinking about Police: Contemporary Readings.* New York: McGraw-Hill.

Lea, J., and J. Young (1984). *What is to be Done about Law and Order?* Harmondsworth, Middlesex: Penguin.

Lowe, J.C., and S. Moryadas (1975). *The Geography of Movement.* Prospect Heights, Ill.: Waveland Press.

Lowman, J. (1982). Crime, criminal justice policy and the urban environment. Pp. 81–94 in D.T. Herbert and R.J. Johnston (eds.), *Geography and the Urban Environment* (vol. 5). Chichester: John Wiley and Sons.

——— (1983). *Geography, Crime and Social Control.* Unpublished doctoral dissertation, University of British Columbia, Vancouver.

——— (1984). *Vancouver Field Study of Prostitution.* Ottawa: Department of Justice.

——— (1986). Conceptual issues in the geography of crime: Toward a geography of social control. *Annals of the Association of American Geographers* 76(1):81–94.

——— (1989). *Street Prostitution: Assessing the Impact of the Law, Vancouver.* Ottawa: Department of Justice.

McIver, J.P. (1981). Criminal mobility: A review of empirical studies. Pp. 20–47 in S. Hakim and G.F. Rengert (eds.), *Crime Spillover.* Beverly Hills: Sage.

Miethe, T.D. (1991). Citizen-based crime control activity and victimization risks: An examination of displacement and free-rider effects. *Criminology* 29:419–439.

Nettler, G. (1974). *Explaining Crime.* New York: McGraw-Hill.

Reppetto, T.A. (1974). *Residential Crime.* Cambridge, Mass.: Ballinger.

——— (1976). Crime prevention and the displacement phenomenon. *Crime and Delinquency* 22:166–177.

Rhodes, W.M., and C. Conly (1981). Crime and mobility: An empirical study. Pp. 167–188 in P.J. Brantingham and P.L. Brantingham (eds.), *Environmental Criminology.* Beverly Hills: Sage.

Roncek, D.W., and P.A. Maier (1991). Bars, blocks and crimes revisited: Linking the theory of routine activities to the empiricism of "hot spots." *Criminology* 29:725–753.

Roncek, D.W., and M.A. Pravatiner (1989). Additional evidence that taverns enhance nearby crime. *Sociology and Social Research* 73:185–188.

Rossmo, D.K. (1987). *Fugitive Migration Patterns.* Unpublished master's thesis, Simon Fraser University, Burnaby, BC.

Rossmo, D.K., and D.K. Fisher (1993). Problem-Oriented policing: A cooperative approach in Mount Pleasant, Vancouver. *RCMP Gazette* 55(1):1–9.

Rossmo, D.K., and R. Routledge (1990). Estimating the size of criminal populations. *Journal of Quantitative Criminology* 6:293–314.

Sewell, J. (1985). *Police: Urban Policing in Canada.* Toronto: James Lorimer.

Sherman, L.W. (1990). Police crackdowns. *NIJ Reports* 219:2–6.

Sloan, R. (Spring 1993). Leading the change: A different yardstick. *Problem-Solving Quarterly* 6(2):3–5.

Smith, S.J. (1986). *Crime, Space and Society.* Cambridge: Cambridge University Press.

Solicitor General Canada (1983). *Victims of crime* (Canadian Urban Victimization Survey Bulletin 1). Ottawa: Ministry of the Solicitor General.

Spelman, W.G. (1987). *Beyond bean counting: New approaches for managing crime data.* Washington, D.C.: Police Executive Research Forum.

Spelman, W.G., and D.K. Brown (1983). Response time. Pp. 160–166 in C.B. Klockars (ed.), *Thinking about Police: Contemporary Readings.* New York: McGraw-Hill.

Spelman, W.G., and J.E. Eck (1987). *Problem-Oriented Policing* (National Institute of Justice publication). Washington, D.C.: U.S. Government Printing Office.

——— (1989). Sitting ducks, ravenous wolves and helping hands: New approaches to urban policing. *University of Texas Public Affairs Comment* 35(2).

Stark, R. (1987). Deviant places: A theory of the ecology of crime. *Criminology* 25:893–909.

Taylor, P.J. (1977). *Quantitative Methods in Geography.* Prospect Heights, Ill.: Waveland Press.

Taylor, R.B., S.D. Gottfredson and S. Brower (1980). The defensibility of defensible space: A critical review and a synthetic framework for future research. Pp. 53–71 in T. Hirschi and M. Gottfredson (eds.), *Understanding Crime: Current Theory and Research.* Beverly Hills: Sage.

Williams, H., and P.V. Murphy (1990). *The evolving strategy of policing: A minority view* (Perspectives on Policing, No. 13, BJS Publication No. NCJ-121019). Washington, D.C.: U.S. Government Printing Office.

Zipf, G. (1950). *The Principle of Least Effort.* Reading, Mass.: Addison Wesley.

Chapter 2

STAC Hot-Spot Areas: A Statistical Tool for Law Enforcement Decisions[1]

Carolyn Rebecca Block
Statistical Analysis Center
Illinois Criminal Justice Information Authority

INTRODUCTION

The last 10 or 15 years have seen a quiet revolution in criminology and criminal justice. There has been a vast improvement in the quality and quantity of data and in the availability of that data to decision makers. Sufficient information is now available so that basic indicators related to criminal justice issues can be measured with a degree of precision that was not only unknown a few years ago, but was also unanticipated. Contrary to conventional wisdom, we are not plagued by a dearth of information in criminal justice (Block 1989). The problem is just the opposite. There are often so many pieces of information that it is impossible for the human mind to assimilate them, to sort them out, and to use them for tactical or crime analysis decisions before the window of opportunity has passed.

Even more recently, another revolution has not only precipitated a surge in the *amount* of information available, but has also *enlarged the nature* of that information to include two-dimensional space. This technological revolution, computer mapping, has generated a need for analytical methods and techniques to make spatial information a foundation for answering practical and policy questions. One of the most common spatial analysis questions asked in law enforcement is, Where are the densest concentrations of incidents or events on the map? The hot-spot area (the densest cluster of incidents on a map) capability of the STAC (Spatial and Temporal Analysis of Crime) software program was developed to answer that question.

This essay is an overview of the STAC approach to finding and describing hot-spot areas. It begins with a review of cluster analysis techniques as they have been applied to law enforcement. It then describes hot-spot area analysis in STAC, and provides an example of a Chicago violence-reduction project that uses hot-spot area analysis to identify street gang-violence crisis areas.

---

1. An earlier version of this paper was presented at the May 1993 meetings on environmental criminology, in Miami, Fla., and published in the proceedings of those meetings.

COMPUTER MAPPING: A TECHNICAL REVOLUTION IN LAW ENFORCEMENT

Computer mapping technology, coupled with the technology necessary to store and organize vast amounts of geocoded data, has expanded extremely rapidly in recent years, and there is no end to the expansion in sight. Only a few years ago, the only mapped information available to most police departments was limited to cardboard pin maps and colored plastic pins. Digitizing was (and still is) so expensive that the development of their own computerized street map was beyond the reach of most departments.[2] Cities that did have mapping capability usually housed it centrally, outside the police department (in city planning, for example), because mapping software and hardware were complex, requiring experts to use them, and too expensive for scattered-site applications. In these cities, police access to mapping was indirect, often cumbersome and time-consuming. In addition, maps developed for other city uses did not always meet law enforcement needs. (For example, we do not send a squad car to a census tract to answer a call, but rather, to an address.)

With the advent of accessible mapping software, PCs that can handle it, and the census TIGER files, all this has changed. The technological revolution in computer mapping means that spatial crime analysis is now a possibility, even for small police departments and neighborhood-level police districts. Mapping entrepreneurs, people with the vision to see the potential worth of automated mapping and the spirit and initiative to overcome any obstacle that might be in the way of realizing that potential, have sprung up in departments across the continent and around the world.

By its very success, however, this technological revolution has generated a "data overload" of unprecedented proportions. Mapped databases can quickly grow to contain much more information than a police analyst can possibly assimilate and use for timely decisions. Computer mapping technology, no matter how sophisticated, is not enough by itself to organize the vast amounts of spatial and other information generated by the reality of daily interaction in city neighborhoods, and to summarize that information so that it can support tactical deployment, investigation, early identification of crisis situations, and development of successful intervention strategies.

As Roncek and Maier (1991) argue, and Maltz, Gordon and Friedman (1991) found in their pilot study of computer mapping in police departments, the successful analysis of spatial patterns of crime requires that empirical mapping tools be guided by theory that can link place to crime, can unravel the spatial characteristics of different types of crime, and can provide explanations for the high vulnerability of some neighborhoods or demographic groups. In other words, we must link computer mapping technology to an information-organizing framework that encompasses both law enforcement and community information. The appropriate tools for a job such as this are statistics. Statistical tools (figure 1) can summarize enormous amounts of information and organize that information to answer specific, practical questions. They can provide a way to link mapping technology and information-organizing hypotheses.

We need statistical tools to control and manage data overload, so that law enforcement and community information can become a foundation for tactical, crime analysis and policy decisions. However, as the next section will show, statistical methods for using and interpreting mapped data, especially methods applicable to practical criminal justice situations, are still in their infancy. The development of statistics for geographic analysis has been outpaced by the creation of geocoded datasets and the software to map them. Methods for identifying hot-spot areas have been particularly problematic.

---

2. Digitizing is the development of a map, such as a city street map, in which features (streets, rivers, expressways, and so on) have x-coordinates and y-coordinates for automated mapping.

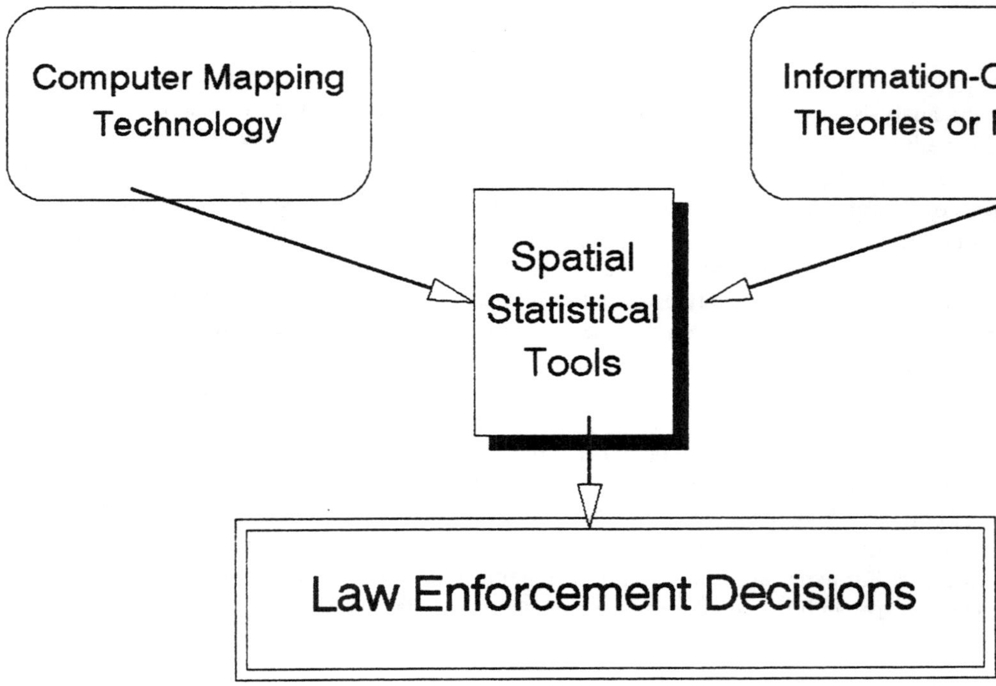

Fig. 1
Statistics: the vital link in an information foundation for law enforcement decisions

ATTEMPTS TO IDENTIFY HOT-SPOT AREAS

Maps, even a single map of one type of event in one time period, contain a huge amount of information, data that may be interpreted very differently by different observers with differing perceptions of spatial reality (cognitive maps).[3] The answer to a question such as whether or not the events within a certain area on the map are densely clustered, or are just one permutation of random distribution, depends on the eye of the observer. In such situations, when the amount of information is overwhelming, a quick, efficient and objective summary of reality—in other words, a statistical analysis—can provide a useful guide to interpretation. Unfortunately, however, spatial analysis statistics have lagged behind the revolutionary expansion of hardware and software technology.

What statistics are available for finding and defining a hot-spot area—the densest area on a map, an area that reflects the pattern of actual events, even if these natural clusters cross a boundary (police district or census tract boundaries, for example) or extend along a boundary (a street, for example)? Two approaches have been commonly used to find dense clusters, analysis of density within predetermined boundaries (areal analysis), and analysis of relative frequency of occurrence at specific places or addresses (pin-map frequency distributions).[4] Either may be useful

3. See Smith and Patterson (1980) for a discussion of cognitive maps.

4. In the nomenclature of cartography, maps based on areal units are referred to as *choropleth* maps. This presentation substitutes the less technical term *areal* where possible. It also uses *pin map* or *point* as synonyms for address-based information, because many of the events that must be mapped in a law enforcement application do not occur at addresses. For example, the location of the body of a homicide victim may be in

for answering certain other questions, but both suffer from serious limitations as methods for identifying and mapping a hot-spot area.

Areal Analysis

Statistical methods for the analysis of crime density within arbitrary areal units, such as police districts, political wards or census tracts, have been available in automated systems for some years, but they all suffer from serious problems in interpretation, such as aggregation bias. (See Brantingham and Brantingham 1984:15–18 for a review of these problems; examples of misinterpretation can be found in Pyle 1974, 1976; and Kohfeld and Sprague 1990.) Analysis within arbitrary boundaries cannot deal with a reality in which actual dense areas may cross boundary lines, occur along a boundary line, or occur in only a small but concentrated area within the arbitrary boundary. Aggregations to arbitrary areas are thus subject to what may be called an *area-unit fallacy,* which is analogous to the ecological fallacy. In the ecological fallacy, area-level characteristics are mistakenly applied to individuals. In the area-unit fallacy, the aggregate characteristics of an overall area are mistakenly applied to each section or neighborhood within that area.

Even though aggregate data within arbitrary boundaries are not an appropriate basis for an analysis of event clusters, sometimes the only data available may be area-level. To handle this situation, techniques have been developed to approximate clusters of points with aggregate area information. In *small-area* analysis, the areas analyzed are so small relative to the scale of the map that they begin to lose their two-dimensional aspect and seem to the observer to become points instead of areas. For example, Roncek and Montgomery (elsewhere in this volume) analyze block-level data across cities. However, even if the small areas are seen as points, there is still no systematic way to identify clusters of these "points."

Crime-gradient mapping (see Joelson and Fishbine 1980:251–255, and Rengert or LeBeau, elsewhere in this volume) is another technique to deal with area-unit data. Crime gradients are isopleths calculated by connecting the centroids of areas with similar rates.[5] Currently available software such as SYSTAT and Idrisi make it easy to produce topographical (three-dimensional) maps of crime gradients. However, because they are based on area data, these maps suffer from the limitations just discussed. They do not really represent clusters of points, but rather, the characteristics of the *aggregated* points within each area boundary.

Both the isopleth maps developed by Curtis (1974:119–158) and studies of "population potential" (Choldin and Roncek 1976; Felson 1986) use area rates to define central points (centroids) on the map, which are then linked. However, because the centroids are based on rates calculated within arbitrary spatial boundaries, not on specific address or pin distributions, such methods are subject to the same problems in misinterpretation and potential area-unit fallacy faced by all area-unit data.

In addition, topographical representations of clusters have a number of disadvantages from the point of view of reader perception. The peaks and valleys make it difficult for the audience to see multiple hot-spot areas, because a secondary peak may be hidden behind a larger primary peak. It is also difficult for a map reader to perceive the relationship between the topographical distribution and the position of other mapped objects (streets, buildings, parks). Topographical clusters of two separate variables (for example, abandoned buildings and drug offenses) are almost impossible to show clearly on the same map.

---

a river, underneath a viaduct, along railroad tracks, or in the middle of a large park or parking lot.

5. Isopleth maps define spatial similarities and enclose them with a boundary on the map. For example, weather maps often include isobars, lines connecting points having the same barometric pressure.

Pin-Map Analysis

Pin-map data, such as the locations of offenses, traffic accidents or known offender addresses, can provide a wealth of information, and statistical methods exist to organize that information into a useful form. It is possible to analyze flow from one point to another (such as the distance from an offender's address to the site of a burglary), to identify high-activity "nodes" that attract a certain type of activity (such as a tavern or a dangerous intersection), and to rank-order locations according to frequency of activity (such as addresses with extremely high calls for service). None of this can be done with area-unit data.

However, frequency distributions of pin-map or address data, by themselves, cannot define a particularly dense hot-spot *area*. A single address with more crimes than any other address may or may not be located within the highest-density crime area on the map. Although it is an increasingly common practice (Joelson and Fishbine 1980:256; Pierce 1987; Sherman et al. 1989; Uchida 1990; Linnell 1991) for crime analysts to define a single high-crime address as a "hot spot," and this designation may be useful for some applications, a hot-spot address is not necessarily a hot-spot area.

In general, though areal and pin-map analysis can provide answers to many other questions, neither can satisfy the basic requirement of hot-spot area analysis—to identify high-density areas without regard to artificial boundaries. The predefined, arbitrary boundaries of areal analysis are an obstacle to the identification of such real high-density areas. On the other hand, the unit of analysis in a pin map is so detailed that "area" takes on a qualitatively different meaning, and density could reflect some unique characteristic of the particular location. Just as the use of arbitrary area boundaries as the unit of analysis may hide spatial patterns that cross those boundaries, the use of addresses as a unit of analysis may hide patterns of density that occur across groups of contiguous addresses.

Building Nonarbitrary Areas From Pin-Map Data

As Joelson and Fishbine (1980:250) suggested over a decade ago, we need to overcome the limitations of arbitrary area boundaries by utilizing "address-level aggregations." In other words, we need to find a technique for building nonarbitrary summary areas from pin data. There have been some attempts to do this.

Methods based on pin-map information include the nearest-neighbor significance test for the clustering of events within a boundary (Brantingham and Brantingham 1984:222–223; Boots and Getis 1988), Selden's (1976) use of the PATTER program to define a point that is the shortest distance from all other points as a "hot spot," and, in general, centrographic analysis (Stephenson 1980:146–155; LeBeau 1987; Ebdon 1977), which can be used to find the imaginary point on the map that is closest to all events on the map (the mean center). These approaches begin with pin-map data, but they also end there. None of them yields a summary, bounded *area* that is calculated from individual points.

At least three research projects have explicitly confronted the problem of turning point data into area data. Joelson and Fishbine (1980:257–262) describe a project in which they drew isopleth maps based on assaults per square mile in concentric circles around a specific site in Minneapolis (Moby Dick's Bar). While this produced a bounded summary area from pin-map information, it did not necessarily target the densest area on the map. Linnell (1991), Weisburd, Maher and Sherman (1991), and Maltz, Gordon and Friedman (1991:41) examine the proximity of address-level "hot spots" (addresses where a relatively high number of events occur), but do not develop an objective rule for combining them into hot-spot areas.

Two of these studies, those of Weisburd, Maher and Sherman (1991), and Maltz, Gordon and Friedman (1991:41), rely on the judgment of experts to link together closely spaced hot-spot address locations. In the Weisburd study, the expert was a member of the research team who stood at the location of a hot address and recorded the physical characteristics of the area one block in every direction. In the Maltz study, people knowledgeable about the community were asked to draw freehand lines on a map around areas they considered to be high-crime or drug markets. Both methods defined hot-spot areas according to the given expert's cognitive map, not according to the actual clustering of events.[6] Cognitive maps can provide valuable information, but they are not tools for summarizing information about spatial clustering.

In summary, the available spatial statistics for finding and defining the densest area on a map—a hot-spot area—do not measure up to the need for an automatic, objective tool that turns points into areas. In general, analysis methods based on relative crime density within arbitrary areal units suffer from aggregation biases and serious problems in interpretation, and are subject to the area-unit fallacy, while available analysis methods based on pin-map data cannot identify particularly dense *areas*. The following section describes a spatial statistical tool that was developed in Illinois to answer the need to identify hot-spot areas.

STAC HOT-SPOT AREA ELLIPSES

When Illinois police jurisdictions first began to use computer mapping in the mid-1980s, they realized that they needed an objective and quick way to summarize mapped information. Several departments asked the Illinois Criminal Justice Information Authority for an automated, reliable method for identifying hot spots.[7] In response to these requests, the Authority developed the STAC (Spatial and Temporal Analysis of Crime) package, a spatial statistical toolbox for law enforcement.[8] The initial development of STAC was carried out by Samuel Bates, under the direction of Associate Director Ed Maier, and was supported by a grant from the Bureau of Justice Statistics (BJS) of the U. S. Department of Justice (Garry 1985).[9]

Although the current STAC package contains a number of statistical tools for spatial analysis, the hot-spot area was the original STAC capability, and is still the most used.[10] In one of the first public presentations of STAC hot-spot areas, to the board members of the Authority, Executive Director J. David Coldren showed examples of hot-spot area maps and commented (Coldren 1986),

> One of the more promising techniques is what we've been calling our hot-spot procedure. This is a procedure designed to look at all the crimes within a given area (such as a town) and search for the place of highest crime density, or where most of the crimes occurred. This is the so-called hot spot.

The initial STAC hot-spot area was not an ellipse, but rather, a circle. The STAC hot-spot program was an iterative search routine that identified one "hot circle," the densest circle on the map. Sam Bates's algorithm began by superimposing a grid over a study area, the boundaries of which were defined by the user. The grid could be rectangular or triangular. A circle, the radius of which was also defined by the user, was drawn around each node of the grid (figure 2). The nodes of the grid were spaced at one-half the radius, so that the circles overlapped, helping to ensure that no cluster would be overlooked. The number of events in each circle was counted, and the circles were ranked by this number.

---

6. For a study comparing cognitive hot spots to hot-spot areas of officially recorded crime, see the essay by George Rengert elsewhere in this volume.

7. The departments requesting hot-spot capability were users of the Authority's PIMS (Police Information Management System) who were using the computer-mapping software developed by PIMS and running on the HP 3000 minicomputer.

8. Responding to such requests is one of the functions of the Authority's Statistical Analysis Center (SAC). SAC staff help people use data. To do so, they search for, test, document, adapt, and, if necessary, develop statistical tools that are applicable to practical criminal justice situations.

9. Paul White, the Bureau of Justice Statistics grant monitor for the two STAC projects and for the Early Warning System project, had the vision to see the potential of STAC at its infancy. His enthusiasm about STAC and his moral support, encouragement and advice were invaluable. Without Paul White, STAC would not exist.

10. STAC currently has two modules, TIME and SPACE. SPACE currently includes nearest-neighbor analysis, mean center, radial searches around an address or other location, and another perspective on clustering, the isocrime. For more information about STAC, see the newsletter, *STACNews*.

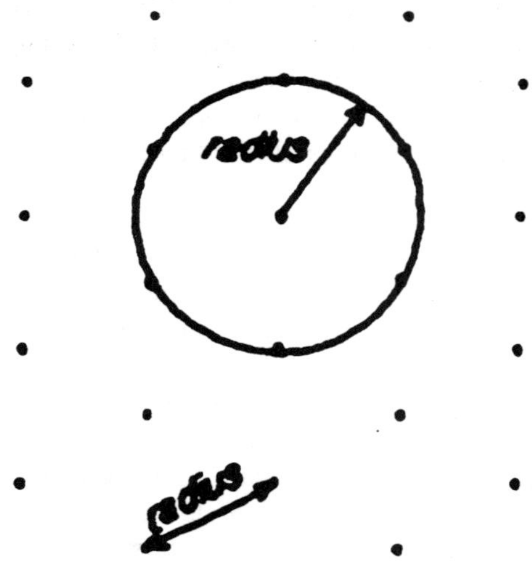

Fig. 2
Location of lattice points

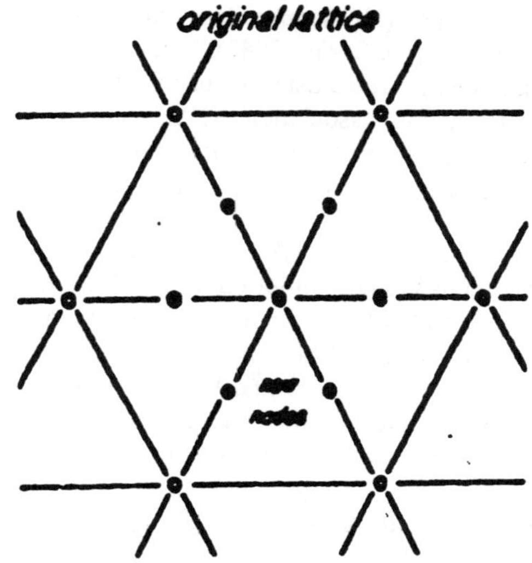

Fig. 3
Location of new nodes relative to the original lattice

Then a new grid was created, the nodes of which were a distance of half the radius from the initial nodes, and the process of drawing overlapping circles and counting events within the circles was repeated for this grid (figure 3). The second list of rank-ordered circles was added to the first, and the circle having the greatest number of events was chosen as the hot spot (hot circle). This initial hot-spot routine was tested with data on several types of offenses, over a number of months, from five Illinois police departments (Bates 1987).[11] The current STAC hot-spot area algorithm has been enhanced, but it is still based on this basic foundation developed by Sam Bates.

The potential of STAC seemed clear. However, there were two major drawbacks: it was a mainframe program, and it had never been tested in a police environment. Another grant from the Bureau of Justice Statistics (BJS) supported the translation of STAC from a mainframe to a PC program (written in C++), and testing in the Evanston, Ill., Police Department.[12]

In addition, extensive testing of STAC by Sam Bates and the current author with data from the five test departments raised additional questions about the interpretation of the hot circle as the "densest area on the map."[13] Empirically, this seemed to be true—STAC's hot circle always met the criterion of being denser (in incidents per square mile) than the rest of the map as a whole. However, every STAC hot-spot search would find a hot circle, even in maps that were purposely constructed so that there was no real clustering. To demonstrate this, we created two kinds of maps with no clustering: maps in which the incidents were uniformly dispersed throughout the study area, and maps in which the incidents were scattered randomly over the study area (using a program written by Sam Bates). In the random maps, the density of incidents in the hot-spot circle found by STAC was always greater than the density outside of the hot circle (see Bates 1987).

By definition, we knew that the higher density of hot circles in uniformly dispersed or randomly scattered maps represented only one permutation of random error. But this situation raised an important question: in general, when we do not know whether or not the incidents are really randomly distributed, how can we tell whether STAC's hot circle represents an area that is really more densely concentrated than other areas? Clearly, we needed a method to distinguish between "random" clustering and "real" clustering.

11. For testing, "flat files" were created by downloading data for a given month and offense type from the PIMS management system.

12. Sharyn Barrington-Carlson was the programmer who rewrote STAC in C++.

13. For a full discussion of this issue, with examples from the test departments, see Bates (1987).

James Spring, a geographer who worked on the STAC project under the second BJS grant, realized that nearest-neighbor analysis (NNA) provided exactly such a significance test for spatial clustering, and he added an NNA capability to STAC (see Spring 1987).[14] Our advice to STAC users is to first test a dataset for significant clustering using NNA, and then, given clustering, use STAC to locate and define where the clusters are.[15] This is analogous to statistical significance vs. association. STAC can describe where clustering occurs, assuming that it is occurring. However, NNA determines whether or not the clustering is significantly nonrandom. (For details of the "how hot is hot" question and the use of NNA in STAC, see Spring and Block 1987, 1988a, 1988b, 1989.)

Several problems in STAC interpretation still remained. First, the hot circle would commonly overlap and share the same incidents with other circles, and ties in the rank order of circles were not unusual, making the choice of a single circle as "hottest" somewhat arbitrary. Second, while a circle was sometimes an accurate description of the real shape of a dense cluster of events, often the actual shape was irregular or elongated and not well described by a circle. To solve both problems, James Spring elaborated the original hot spot circle to produce the hot-spot ellipse. Beginning with the iterative search routine described above for hot circles, the ellipse algorithm first determines whether or not any of these hot circles overlap each other. If they do, all the incidents occurring in a group of overlapping hot circles become a "hot cluster" (figure 4). All the incidents occurring in any hot circle that stands by itself are also a hot cluster. These clusters are ranked by the number of incidents (an incident that occurs in two or more overlapping circles is counted only once).[16] Then STAC calculates the best-fitting standard deviational ellipse (Lefever 1926; Furfey 1927; Hsu and Tiedemann 1968; Soot 1975; Stephenson 1980:151; LeBeau 1987) for each cluster (figure 5).

At this point in STAC development, we felt that we needed feedback not only from users in the field, but also from experts in statistics and computer science. We were concerned about whether we could really say that the area encompassed by a STAC hot-spot ellipse was denser than any other possible ellipse, whether the STAC hot circle was really "hotter" than any other circle that could possibly be drawn on a given map. Helmut Epp, chair of the computer science department at DePaul University and an expert in artificial intelligence, and two faculty members, volunteered to read through all the documentation on STAC and to tell us if the methodology was appropriate to answer the questions at hand. After evaluating the STAC package, this team of experts concluded that the hot-spot ellipse is, indeed, an appropriate method to locate and define the densest area(s) on the map. They pointed out that it is not a simple statistic, but more like an artificial intelligence, interactive procedure. STAC should be used to summarize and search for patterns, not as a parametric statistic. They also suggested that we continue to pursue the development of another tool for the STAC toolbox, the isocrime (Poethig 1989).

Compared to a circle, an ellipse can approximate much more closely the actual shape of a cluster of events. However, ellipses still cannot describe irregular clusters (L-shaped, for example). Another limitation of hot-spot ellipses is that they should not be compared across maps; each ellipse must be interpreted relative to a given hot-spot area search, with a certain configuration of incidents within a certain border.[17] This is because the hot-spot ellipse algorithm considers all the incidents within the study area border when it identifies each hot-spot area. High density is relative to the overall scatter of all these incidents. Therefore, the densest hot-spot area on a map in which most incidents are widely scattered may not be as dense as the densest hot-spot area on a map in which most incidents are clustered together.

14. James Spring's NNA program is written in FORTRAN. One of our priority STAC projects, given the resources, is to rewrite it in C++ and integrate it with the rest of STAC. For more information on NNA, see Boots and Getis (1988).

15. The NNA capability is currently limited in the STAC program to 400 cases. We hope to remedy this in the next version of STAC.

16. The current version of STAC ranks hot-spot areas by the number of incidents in the cluster. In the enhanced version now being developed, the user will have a choice of alternative ranking criteria, including density (incidents per area of the ellipse).

17. Although STAC identifies the densest areas on a map regardless of arbitrary boundaries within the study area, the outer border around the study area is still a factor. A cluster of events that crosses this outer boundary may not be identified as a hot spot area as readily as a cluster within the study area. This border problem has been generally recognized in spatial point-pattern analysis, but it is so far unsolved (see Boots and Getis 1988:45–49 for their discussion of "edge effects").

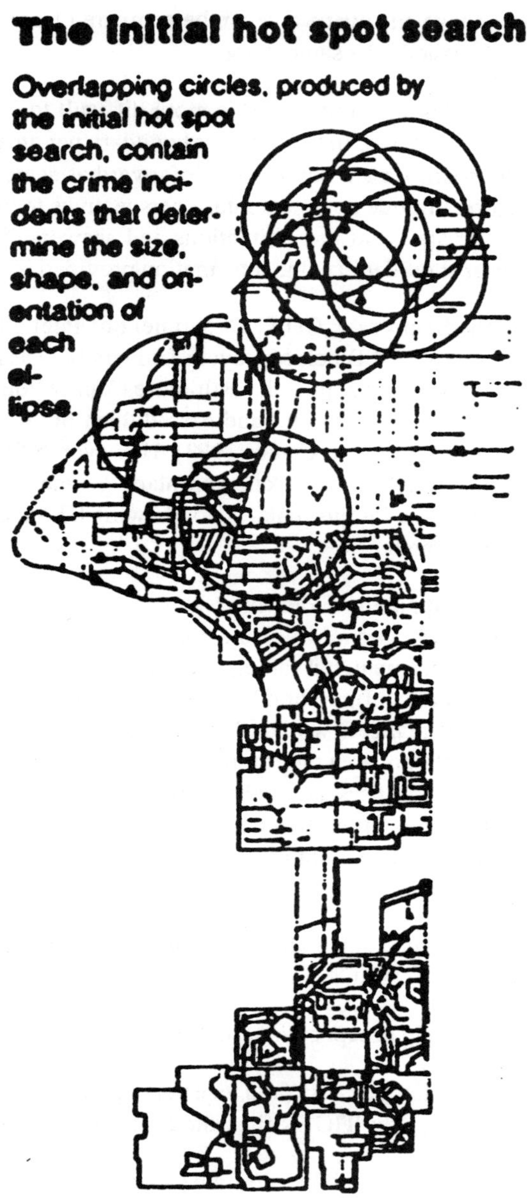

Fig. 4
Hot clusters

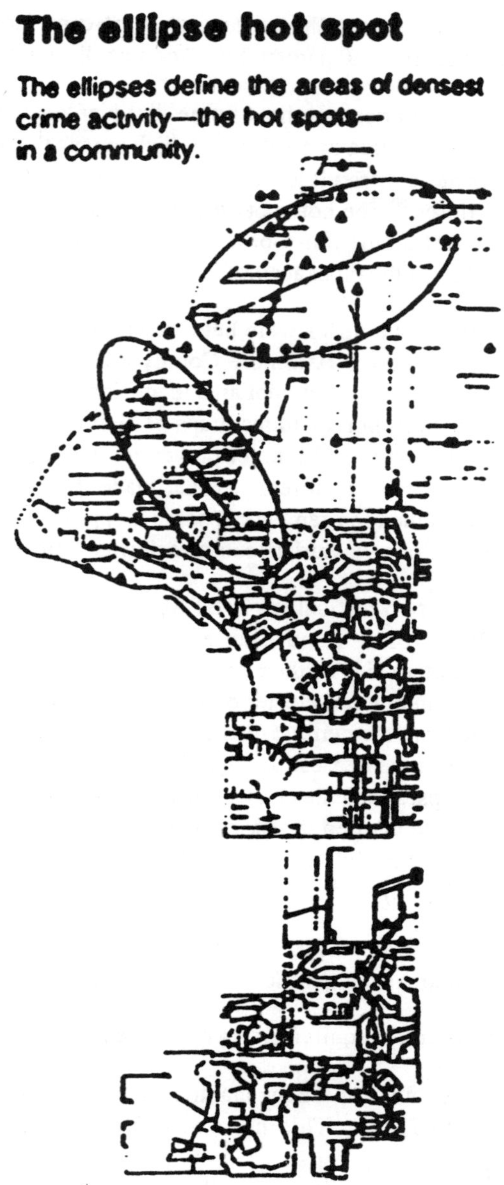

Fig. 5
Hot-spot ellipses

To handle both problems (irregular clusters and map-to-map comparisons), we added another tool to the STAC toolbox—the isocrime (see Bates 1987; Spring and Block 1988a, 1988b).[18] The isocrime describes a hot-spot area as a set of isopleth lines, each encompassing a given proportion of the total number of incidents on the map.[19] For example, an inner isopleth might enclose the densest 10 percent of incidents; a surrounding isopleth, the densest 20 per-

18. The process of drawing isocrimes is not yet fully automated in STAC. We expect to add it in the next version.

19. To identify isocrimes, we first find the most tightly clustered 30 percent of events within the study area (using nearest-neighbor analysis), and determine the mean center of these events (an imaginary point that is closer to all of these events than any other point). An enclosed irregular line is then drawn around the 10 percent that are closest to the mean center. Subsequent lines enclosing 20 and 30 percent may be drawn in other colors. Reader perception is improved if the inner (10%) isopleth is drawn in red, and the outer isopleths in cooler colors.

cent; and an outer isopleth, the densest 30 percent. Isocrimes can take any shape and can be compared from map to map. Two "isocrime 10 percent lines" on two different maps mean exactly the same thing.

Hot-spot isocrimes also have some disadvantages, compared to hot-spot ellipses. It is more difficult to compute their area than the area of an ellipse, which means that density (incidents within the hot-spot boundary per area of the hot spot) is more difficult to obtain. Also, searches for multiple isocrimes are not as straightforward as searches for multiple ellipses.[20] The hot-spot ellipse and the isocrime, therefore, provide complementary perspectives to help the user locate and define hot-spot areas. Each is particularly appropriate in different situations and answers different questions. To get the most accurate picture of a given map, the user should utilize the information provided by both.

STAC hot-spot ellipses were beta-tested by Wally Briefs in the Sunnyvale, Calif., Department of Public Safety, Philip R. Canter in the Baltimore County Police Department, and Richard Block of Loyola University. These tests showed the potential of hot-spot area identification for crime analysis. For example, the Baltimore County Police Department produced hot-spot area maps of Halloween vandalism in the previous year and passed them out to district officers, so that they could target prevention strategies in the current year (see Canter 1993). However, STAC still was limited by input requirements that made it awkward to use, and by its dependence on plane geometry, which conflicted with the requirements of some mapping software for longitude-latitude data. Also, drawing STAC ellipses on a map was still awkward, because each was defined by only four points.

In addition, two difficulties in STAC interpretation began to be apparent. Extensive testing by James Spring of hot-spot ellipses of the same offense and the same area over time found cases in which the hot-spot location suddenly moved to the other side of the map. These were not instances of displacement, but rather, occurred because there was really more than one hot cluster on the map. A slight change in spatial configuration had caused the second-densest cluster to become the densest cluster. A more realistic procedure, we realized, would identify and plot all of the hot clusters, not just the densest. Also, field tests of user perception of hot-spot area maps found that people tend to think that larger ellipses indicate denser clusters of incidents than do smaller ellipses. (Actually, empirical testing indicates that the opposite is often the case.) We realized that to avoid misinterpretation, two enhancements would be necessary for STAC: the ability to find and plot multiple hot spots, and the calculation of hot-spot area density (per area and per population).

In 1991, therefore, Graham Taylor, the STAC analyst who succeeded James Spring, worked with programmer Terese Brand to make the following modifications and enhancements to STAC:

- Data entry requirements were made friendlier. STAC now could accept comma-delimited data.
- They found a package that translates state-plane to longitude-latitude data (and vice versa), and incorporated it into STAC.[21] This meant that STAC could be used easily with the TIGER files and packages using them.
- The hot-spot ellipse module was revised so that more than one hot ellipse could be identified and mapped (the densest, second densest and so on). The program now told the user how many hot-spot areas it had found, and the user then could choose how many of these to map.

---

20. A secondary isocrime cluster can be identified by rerunning the isocrime routine on the remaining incidents after the first 30 percent have been eliminated from the dataset. To identify more than two isocrimes on the same map, the 30 percent criterion should be changed to 20 percent or less. However, be sure to document the criterion you use, because the centroid of the tightest 10 percent often differs from the centroid of the tightest 20 or 30 percent.

21. After a long but unproductive search by STAC staff, this package, a public-domain program published by the U.S. Bureau of Land Management (BLM), was finally found by STAC user Richard Block. Graham Taylor then wrote a "shell" program in C++, which took geocoded longitude-latitude data through the BLM translation to state-plane, ran STAC, then returned 64 points defining each ellipse boundary to the BLM translator to produce longitude-latitude coordinates for mapping. Richard Block further modified this program so that the dataset containing the points defining the ellipses is in the proper format for MapInfo boundary files. All of this is invisible to the user, who simply runs STAC and sees the results appear as ellipses on a map.

- The capability of drawing a complete standard deviational ellipse for every hot-spot area, instead of plotting only four points of the ellipse, was added to STAC.

Density by area unit became possible after Graham Taylor wrote a program to calculate the area of a hot-spot ellipse. It also can be calculated by using mapping software such as MapInfo to determine the area within a hot-spot boundary. A technique to calculate density per population or other census-block data was developed by Richard Block (see Block and Block 1993).

In 1992, STAC won a finalist award from the Ford Foundation/J. F. Kennedy School of Government, Harvard University, Innovations in State and Local Government Program. Part of that money was used to hold a computer-mapping workshop, and another part was used to publish *STACNews*, but about half of the grant award was used to enhance STAC. Under the Innovations grant, we were able to hire Yunus Mohammed, a student in computer science at the University of Illinois at Chicago, to improve the accessibility of STAC to the average user. We also were able to upgrade our computer-mapping software to support Mr. Mohammed in his efforts. The following are the changes made to STAC under the Innovations grant:

- Menus have been added on top of STAC. There are two menus, a main menu and a spatial analysis (SPACE) submenu.
- Coordinate conversions, which had been external to STAC, have now been incorporated into the STAC product. Before the enhancement, STAC required a user to run a separate "batch" program to prepare the data to run STAC. Now, this conversion process is "transparent" to the user. It is automatically done, without any thought or action on the user's part.
- A multiple-run facility has been added to STAC. Users now can bring in more than one input file at a time, without having to start STAC again from the beginning. However, all input files must be in the format: Identifier, x-coord, y-coord.
- Every STAC run now generates a log—a report of the files analyzed, statistical parameters requested and results (including number of incidents, number of hot-spot areas identified, location and density of each area). With these reports, it will be easy to document and reproduce hot-spot area maps.

There are many things that still could be done to make STAC more useful, more accurate and more accessible to users. As resources permit, we plan to make the following improvements to STAC:

- The STAC program should be modularized (in other words, each subroutine in the program should be individually documented and related to each other subroutine). This is necessary so that the Authority staff can support STAC and narrow down the search for bugs. In addition, we need more detailed documentation of the C++ code in STAC.
- We must correct bugs in Yunus Mohammed's beta version of STAC. For example, the beta version does multiple hot-spot searches, but writes over files when it does so.
- All STAC programs and functions should be accessible through menus. Now, only some of them are.
- More information is needed for the log report.
- The user should be able to specify the location of fields. File formats should allow for the reverse of x and y coordinates, to agree with geographic practice.
- The current beta version is user-friendly for a specific application, but not for others. The new version should include input and output options for users of all applications.

- The maximum number of cases for the hot-spot search is 15,000; the maximum number of cases for NNA is 400. It should be possible to override these defaults.
- NNA, which is now written in FORTRAN, should be integrated into the C++ program.
- The algorithm for isocrimes should be standardized and automated more completely.
- More ellipse print options are needed. The user should be able to specify thresholds or priorities for printing multiple hot-spot area results. The user should have the option, for example, to print ellipses according to density (incidents per area in each hot-spot ellipse) or according to the number of incidents in the hot cluster. Also, the user should be able to specify a minimum number of incidents in a hot-spot area or a hot cluster for printed results.
- Finally, we must address the border problem. That is, we should introduce a weight in the iterative search routine that gives more weight to circles in which part of the circle is across the outer border (and about which nothing is known). Boots and Getis (1988) describe such an algorithm.

These enhancements and improvements, completed and planned, will make STAC easier to use and easier to interpret, and therefore more accessible to officers, crime analysts and community problem-solvers. However, since STAC is more of an interactive artificial intelligence tool than a cut-and-dried statistic, its use and interpretation is more an art than a science. The quality of STAC analysis, particularly analysis in real-life tactical and problem-solving situations, therefore, depends to some extent on the quantity of analysis. That is, the more STAC (or any other spatial statistical tool) is used to solve a practical law enforcement problem, the more it will be used, and the more effectively it will be used. Users will support each other with hints, war stories and practical advice.

Most of the early users of STAC concentrated on the analysis of property crime, such as burglary, automobile theft or vandalism. To demonstrate the possibility of using STAC as an "information foundation for violence reduction," the Authority and the Chicago Police Department applied for and received a grant from the Bureau of Justice Statistics to develop such an information foundation for the identification of street gang-violence crisis areas in Chicago. In the following section, we outline how STAC and a geoarchive of law enforcement and community information have been combined to target an escalating high-risk situation, while there is still time to intervene and save lives.

AN EXAMPLE OF STAC AT WORK: THE EARLY WARNING SYSTEM PROJECT

The Early Warning System for Street Gang Violence, a joint project of the Chicago Police Department and the Illinois Criminal Justice Information Authority, is now under way in Chicago's Police Area Four, an area containing some of the riskiest neighborhoods for street gang violence in the city. The purpose of the project is to develop an automated early warning system for law enforcement, which will identify potential neighborhood crisis areas, areas that are at high risk for suffering a "spurt" of serious street gang-related violence and homicide. This early warning system will be based on a statistical model, which consolidates spatial information obtained from a variety of community and law enforcement sources and organized in a geoarchive, and then uses automated hot-spot area identification and other geographic statistics as tools to target crisis neighborhoods.[22]

The Early Warning System project is founded on the premise that, since street-gang violence is spatially anchored and occurs as the culmination of escalating incidents of revenge and retaliation, information compiled by community and neighborhood organizations, as well as by law enforcement, could be used to develop an "early warning system"

22. A geoarchive is a database containing address-based data from both law enforcement and community sources, linked to computer-mapping capability, and set up so that it can be updated, maintained, mapped, analyzed, and used by those who are developing and implementing strategies of crime reduction in the community. It is an "Information Foundation for Community Policing."

of neighborhoods in crisis (see Spergel and Curry 1990). Continuing escalation would then be prevented by crisis intervention and dispute mediation, using both internal community influences and external police support. Such a program has shown success in two pilot projects, in Chicago's Humboldt Park and in Philadelphia (Spergel et al. 1984; Spergel 1986), but requires the strong support of neighborhood agencies, churches, community groups, and the police department.

The Early Warning System project uses automated hot-spot area identification as a targeting tool. One of the most important defining characteristics of street-gang violence is territoriality. However, the territorial unit most likely to become the site of serious violence is not a large or predefined area like a police district, but rather, a smaller area defined by the gang (Suttles 1972:187–201). In addition, violence changes over time, following patterns of escalation, retaliation and revenge, often across a spatial border that may also change over time (see Weisburd, Maher and Sherman 1991:20). Therefore, a quick, objective statistical tool like the hot-spot area ellipses is vital to target specific neighborhood areas that are at high risk of becoming a violence crisis area, so that crisis intervention, heading off the cycle of retaliation and retribution, is possible.

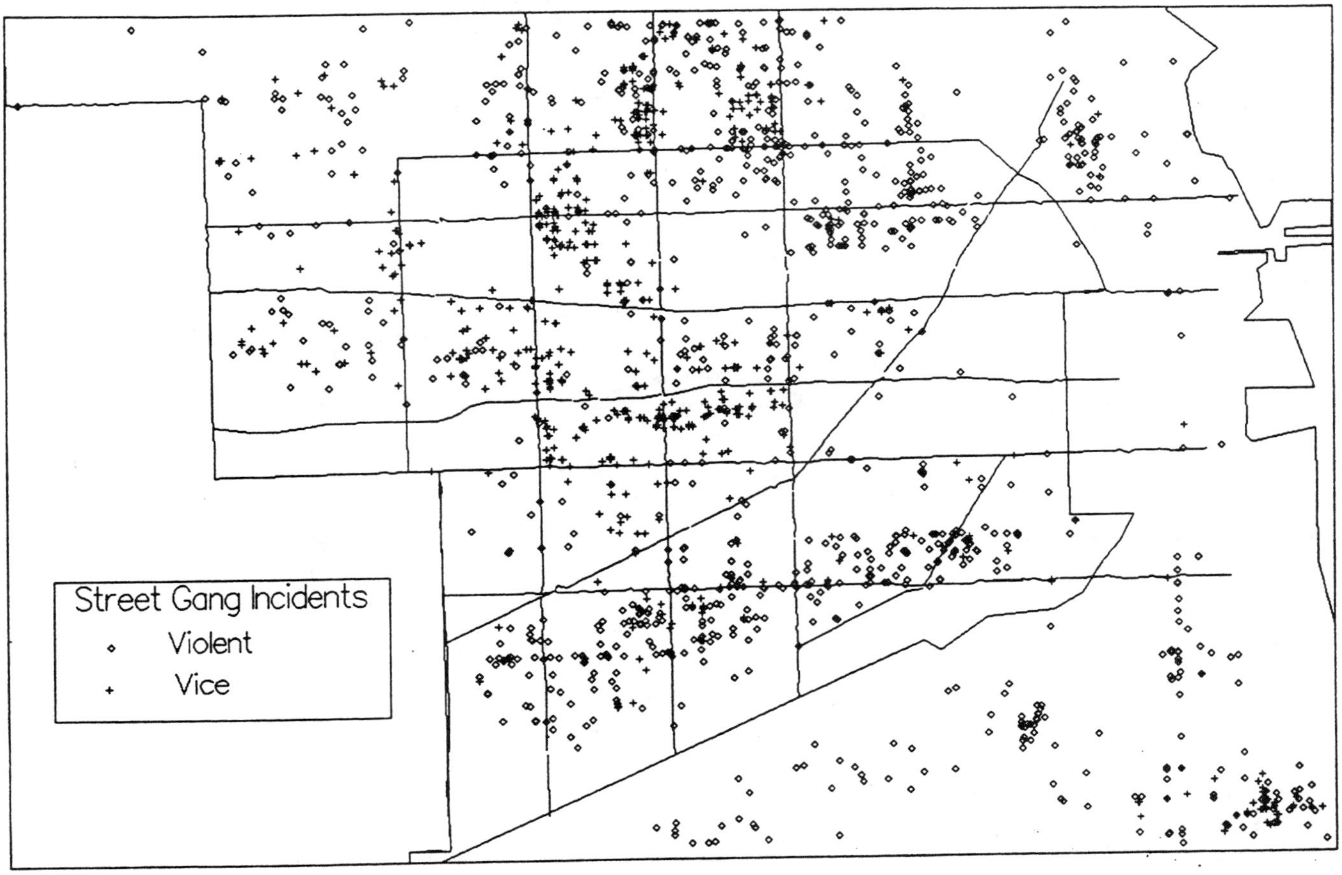

Fig. 6
Street gang-related incidents, by type: vice incidents and violent incidents

The datasets in the geoarchive provide the basis for analysis of patterns in the study area. For example, the map in figure 6 shows street gang-related criminal incidents in Area Four in 1992. Drug (vice) offenses are shown as "+" and violent offenses are shown as "o." The densest concentrations of street gang-related drug incidents are shown as light-line ellipses in figure 7, and the densest concentrations of street gang-related violent incidents are shown as heavy-line ellipses. This analysis shows that some neighborhoods have a hot-spot area of street gang-related drug offenses, others have a hot-spot area of street gang-related violent offenses, and still others have both. However, drug hot spots and "turf battle" hot spots are not necessarily in the same place (see Block and Block 1993). If we are to develop a successful intervention strategy for street gang activity, we first must find out what kind of activity exists in a specific neighborhood. A citywide program aimed at drug offending would have little impact in neighborhoods in which the preponderance of street gang-related incidents are not drug offenses, but violent offenses.

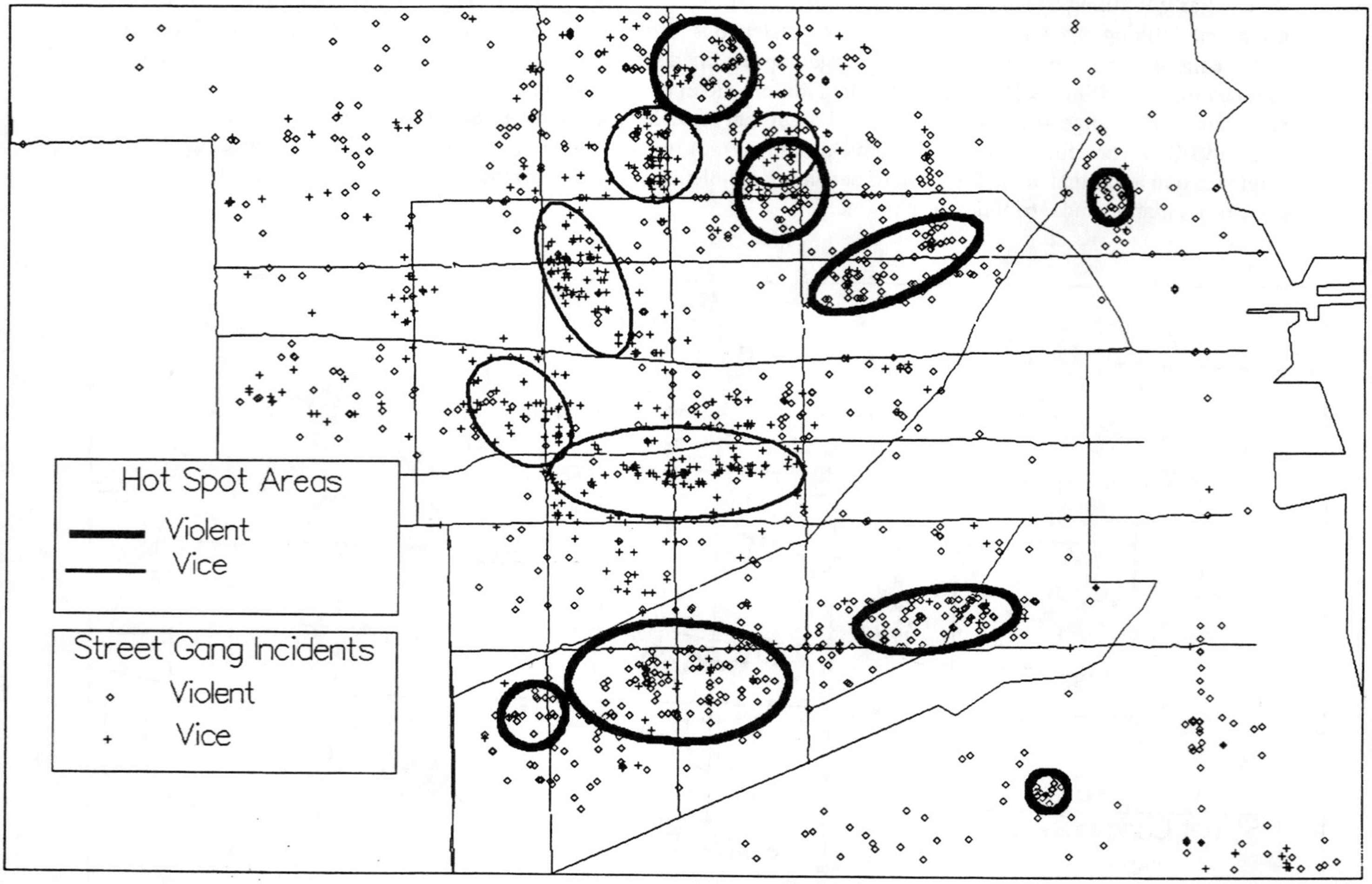

Fig. 7
Hot-spot areas

No matter how successfully we can develop an Early Warning System predictive model, however, it will not save lives unless there is a program that can use that information and intervene in a potential crisis situation to save lives. Fortunately, the Gang Violence Reduction Program has been established in District 10 of the Area Four study area, to do just that (CPD 1993). The goal of the program is to reduce street gang-related violence by a collaborative multiagency and community law enforcement approach. The geoarchive and STAC are being used as an information foundation for developing intervention strategies and responding to crisis situations.

The long-range goal of the Early Warning System project is to develop a computer-assisted Early Warning System for neighborhoods in crisis, which will be transferrable to other police departments and communities throughout the country. Because of the importance of transferability of this project, the geoarchive and computer-assisted Early Warning System are being set up so that they can be updated, maintained, mapped, and analyzed by police analysts within the area headquarters. We hope that the project will become a prototype for other neighborhoods and cities in developing similar automated systems for hot-spot area identification.

In summary, STAC is a database-driven, objective statistical tool that begins with individual pin-map data and builds areas. STAC hot-spot areas reflect the actual scatter of events on a map, not arbitrary boundaries or predefined areas. Such statistical tools are necessary to control the "data overload" of law enforcement and community information, so that this information can become a foundation for community problem-oriented policing and other neighborhood-based problem-solving strategies. With a geoarchive database of current, local-level law enforcement and community information, a theoretical framework and a statistical toolbox to organize this information, and cooperative community and law enforcement resources to intervene in a problem or crisis situation once identified, we can not only reduce levels of property crime, but we can also reduce the risk of injury and death from violence.

REFERENCES

Bates, Samuel (1987). *Spatial and Temporal Analysis of Crime.* Research bulletin, April 1987. Chicago: Illinois Criminal Justice Information Authority.

Block, Carolyn Rebecca (1989). The Application of Statistics to Criminal Justice Policy: A Populist Experiment. Invited paper, annual meeting of the American Association for the Advancement of Science, Jan. 18, 1989.

——— (1990). Hot spots and isocrimes in law enforcement decision making. Paper presented at conference on Police and Community Responses to Drugs, University of Illinois at Chicago.

Block, Carolyn Rebecca, and Richard Block (1993). *Street Gang Crime in Chicago.* Research in Brief, NCJ 144782, December 1993. Washington, D.C.: National Institute of Justice.

Block, Richard, and Carolyn Rebecca Block (1993). Spatial analysis to prevent gang violence: The Area 4 project. Paper presented at the American Society of Criminology meetings, Phoenix.

Boots, Barry N., and Arthur Getis (1988). *Point Pattern Analysis.* Vol. 8, Scientific Geography Series (Grantlan Thrall, ed.). Newbury Park: Sage Publications.

Brantingham, Paul J., and Patricia L. Brantingham (1984). *Patterns in Crime.* New York: Macmillan Publishing Co.

Canter, Philip (1993). Hot-Spot Area Analysis in Baltimore County. *STACNews,* vol. 1, no. 1 (Winter 1993).

Choldin, Harvey M., and Dennis W. Roncek (1976). Density, population potential and pathology: A block-level analysis. *Journal of Public Data Use* 4:19–29.

Coldren, J. David (1986). Application of Spatial and Temporal Analysis to Law Enforcement. Presentation to the Illinois Criminal Justice Information Authority, June 3, 1986.

CPD (Chicago Police Department) (1993). The gang violence reduction program. Pp. 3 and following. *CAPS News.* Chicago: Chicago Police Department. December 1993.

Curtis, Lynn A. (1974). *Criminal Violence: National Patterns and Behavior.* (chap. 7, "Spatial Distributions"). Lexington, Mass.: Lexington Books.

Ebdon, David (1977). *Statistics in Geography.* Great Britain: Basil Blackwell, Inc.

Felson, Marcus (1986). Predicting crime potential at any point on the city map. Pp. 127–136 in Robert M. Figlio, Simon Hakim and George F. Rengert (eds.), Metropolitan Crime Patterns. Monsey, N.Y.: Criminal Justice Press, Willow Tree.

Furfey, Paul Hanley (1927). A note on Lefever's "standard deviational ellipse." *The American Journal of Sociology* XXXIII(1):94–98.

Garry, Steve (1985). Development of practical applications for the use of spatial and temporal data in crime analysis. Proposal submitted to the Bureau of Justice Statistics, Jan. 29, 1985. Chicago: Illinois Criminal Justice Information Authority.

Georges-Abeyie, Daniel E. (1981). Studying black crime: A realistic approach. Pp. 97–109 in Brantingham and Brantingham (eds.), *Environmental Criminology.* Beverly Hills: Sage.

Hsu, Shin-yi, and Clifford E. Tiedemann (1968). A rational method of delimiting study areas for unevenly distributed point phenomena. *The Professional Geographer* XX (Nov. 6):376–381.

Joelson, Mitchell R., and Glenn M. Fishbine (1980). The display of geographic information in crime analysis. Pp. 247–263 in Georges-Abeyie and Harries (eds.), *Crime: A Spatial Perspective.* New York: Columbia University Press.

King, Leslie J. (1969). *Statistical Analysis in Geography.* New Jersey: Prentice-Hall.

Kohfeld, Carol W., and John Sprague (1990). The organization of homicide events in time and space. Paper presented at annual meeting, American Society of Criminology.

LeBeau, James L. (1987). The methods and measures of centrography and the spatial dynamics of rape. *Journal of Quantitative Criminology* 3 (June 2):125–141.

Lefever, D. Welty (1926). Measuring geographic concentration by means of the standard deviational ellipse. *The American Journal of Sociology* XXXII(1):88–94.

Linnell, Deborah Diane (1991). *The Geographic Distribution of Hot Spots of Rape, Robbery and Automobile Thefts in Minneapolis.* M.A. thesis, University of Maryland.

Lowe, John C., and S. Moryadas (1975). *The Geography of Movement.* Boston: Houghton Mifflin.

Maltz, Michael D., Andrew C. Gordon, Robert K. Lebailly, Warren Friedman, Marc Buslik, and Matthias Casey (1987). Crime Statistics in the Small: Mapping Individual Events. Presented at the annual meeting of the American Society of Criminology.

Maltz, Michael D., Andrew C. Gordon and Warren Friedman (1991). *Mapping Crime in Its Community Setting: Event Geography Analysis.* New York: Springer-Verlag.

Pierce, Glenn L. (1987). The Development of a Police Problem/Crime Analysis Work Station. Presented at conference on law enforcement computer mapping, Illinois Criminal Justice Information Authority, Sept. 9, 1987.

Poethig, Margaret (1988). Hot spots and Isocrimes. Pp. 11–13 in *The Compiler* 9 (2, Fall). Chicago: Illinois Criminal Justice Information Authority.

Pyle, Gerald F. (1974). *The Spatial Dynamics of Crime.* Chicago: University of Chicago, Department of Geography. With Edward W. Hanten, Patricia Garstang Williams, Allen L. Pearson II, J. Gary. Doyle, and Kwame Kwofie.

——— (1976). Spatial and temporal aspects of crime in Cleveland, Ohio. *American Behavioral Scientist* 20(2):175–197.

Roncek, Dennis W., and Richard L. Block (1983). The effect of neighborhood change on homicide in Chicago. Paper presented at the American Society of Criminology meetings.

Roncek, Dennis W., and Pamela A. Maier (1991). Bars, blocks and crimes revisited: Linking the theory of routine activities to the empiricism of "hot spots." *Criminology* 29(4):725–758.

Selden, Robert (1976). Recognizing the pattern of crime. *Energy and Technology Review*. Livermore, Calif.: Lawrence Livermore Laboratory (November 1976).

Sherman, Lawrence W., Patrick R. Gartin and Michael E. Buerger (1989). Hot spots of predatory crime: Routine activities and the criminology of place. *Criminology* 27(1):27–55.

Silk, John (1979). *Statistical Concepts in Geography*. Great Britain: George Allen & Unwin, LTD.

Smith, Christopher J., and Gene E. Patterson (1980). Cognitive mapping and the subjective geography of crime. Pp. 205–218 in Georges-Abeyie and Harries (eds.), *Crime: A Spatial Perspective*. New York: Columbia University Press.

Soot, Siim (1975). *Methods and Measures of Centrography: A Critical Study of Geographic Applications*. Occasional Publications of the Department of Geography, Luis E. Ortiz and Susan Gross (eds.). Urbana, Ill.: Geography Graduate Student Association, University of Illinois.

Spelman, William (1988). *Beyond Bean Counting: New Approaches for Managing Crime Data*. Washington, D.C.: Police Executive Research Forum.

Spergel, Irving A. (1984). Violent gangs in Chicago: In search of social policy. *Social Service Review* 58 (2, June):199–226.

——— (1986). The violent gang problem in Chicago: A local community approach. *Social Service Review* (March): 94-130.

Spergel, Irving A., Paul Colson, Francine Atwell, and Sherri Dinguss (1984). Reduction of gang violence: A community development approach. Presented at the Second Annual Symposium on Street Work, University of Tubingen, West Germany, September.

Spergel, Irving A., and G. David Curry (1990). Strategies and perceived agency effectiveness in dealing with the youth gang problem. Pp. 288–309 in C. Ronald Huff (ed.), *Gangs in America*. Newbury Park: Sage.

Spring, James Vincent (1987). Spatial and temporal analysis of crime. Paper presented at the annual meeting of the Illinois Sociological Association.

Spring, James Vincent, and Carolyn Rebecca Block (1987). Spatial and Temporal Analysis of Crime. Paper presented at annual meeting of American Society of Geographers.

——— (1988a). Finding crime hot spots: Experiments in the identification of high-crime areas. Paper presented at the Midwest Sociological Society, March 25.

——— (1988b). Hot spots and incident-level data in law enforcement. Paper presented at the American Society of Criminology meetings, Nov. 12.

——— (1989). *STAC Users Manual*. Chicago: Illinois Criminal Justice Information Authority.

Stephenson, Larry K. (1980). Centrographic analysis of crime. Pp. 247–63 in Daniel E. Georges-Abeyie and Keith D. Harries (eds.), *Crime: A Spatial Perspective*. New York: Columbia University Press.

Suttles, Gerald D. (1972). *The Social Construction of Communities*. Chicago: University of Chicago Press.

Uchida, Craig (1990). NIJ Sponsors System to Speed Information to Police on Drug Hot Spots. Pp. 8–9 in *NIJ Reports*, no. 221 (Summer).

Weisburd, David, Lisa Maher and Lawrence Sherman (1991). Contrasting crime general and crime specific theory: The case of hot spots of crime. (With Michael Buerger, Ellen Cohn and Anthony Petrosino.) *Forthcoming in Advances in Criminological Theory*. New Brunswick, N.J.: Transaction.

Chapter 3

Comparing Cognitive Hot Spots to Crime Hot Spots

George F. Rengert
Department of Criminal Justice
Temple University

INTRODUCTION

The location of points in a pattern may be analyzed with respect to the study area or with respect to each other. In the former case, we are examining the *dispersion* of points within a study area. Nearest-neighbor or quadrant analysis is the technique most often used. In the latter case, we are studying the *arrangement* of the points. Since the arrangement of points refers to properties of the relative locations of points, they can be analyzed when the real boundary of the study area is unknown or difficult to define (Boots and Getis 1988). Most crime patterns are of this nature. Criminals do not stop their search at arbitrary political or neighborhood boundaries. When analyzing these point patterns or arrangements, geographers often make use of a scheme that involves establishing a theoretical pattern with respect to which other patterns are compared statistically. Examples of these theoretical patterns are the "bull's eye," "bi-modal," "teardrop," and "windshield" patterns (see Reboussin *et al.*, elsewhere in this volume).

In the present analysis, we have an example of the analysis of the dispersion of points within an area and the perception of this same area. The analysis will have more of an applied than a technical focus. The genesis of this analysis came about in the early 1990s, when the business and civic organizations became concerned with the image and use of inner-city Philadelphia. They wanted a cleaner, friendlier and safer place that would attract customers, tourists and businesses to the center of Philadelphia. The question turned on how to improve the quality of life in this area for day- and nighttime users.

It was decided that one should not turn to the traditional source of community service, the already overburdened Philadelphia police, to reconstitute this area of the city. First, equity considerations argue against the powerful business and civic organizations consuming more than their fair share of scarce police resources needed in other parts of the city as well. Secondly, the police may not be the best vehicle for improving the overall quality of life in the inner city. Community policing concepts are just beginning to diffuse through the Philadelphia Police Department, and not all officers embrace these concepts wholeheartedly.

It was decided to supplement the already existing police detailed to the inner city with "community service representatives," who would have quasi-police powers and who would be trained from the beginning to embrace a "problem solving" approach to better the quality of life in inner-city Philadelphia. The business and civic community of inner-city Philadelphia decided to fund this project with private monies contributed by their constituents. The training of these community service recruits is the focus of this analysis.

At the outset, it became apparent that the preconceived notions of these community service recruits could affect their job performance, since effective community service entails an accurate, intimate knowledge of the community the officer is assigned to serve. The heart of modern community service is not only the effort, but is also the desire of a community service officer to become familiar with the special problems faced by the residents of their assigned community. This accumulation of knowledge is a continual process that requires persistent interaction of the officer with the community.

Also important is the baseline from which the prospective community service officer starts. As has been well documented in the psychology of dissonance and consonance, preformed opinions of new recruits are often difficult to erase (Festinger 1957). Once a person has made up his or her mind about the characteristics of an area, it is more difficult to correct faulty impressions than to teach correct opinions in the first place. Furthermore, the less well known an area is, the more likely it is that negative connotations are ascribed to it (Golledge and Stimson 1987). For example, subjects nearly always rate their own cities as safer than other cities, and their own residential neighborhoods as safer than less well-known surrounding neighborhoods. Therefore, the level of knowledge is believed to be an important determinate of the positive or negative perception of an area. The people assigned to train these community service recruits became concerned with their preexisting knowledge and perception of inner-city Philadelphia.

DATA

In the following analysis, recruits being trained to serve the inner city of Philadelphia are examined to determine whether their level of knowledge of this community is indeed related to their perception of the relative safety of this area. Data, collected during a training session conducted by one of the authors, consisted of two parts: 1) information on the knowledge the recruits possess of the location of important landmarks of inner-city Philadelphia, and 2) information on the perception the recruits have of the relative safety of the communities composing inner-city Philadelphia.

In order to record each community service recruit's knowledge of inner-city Philadelphia, each was handed a base map of this area with the major streets recorded on it. They also received a list of 33 major landmarks located within this area. Then they were asked to place a dot on the base map where they believed each landmark is located and to number this dot with the corresponding number of each landmark. This resulted in a map of 33 dots corresponding to where the recruits believed each landmark to be located.

The perception of inner-city Philadelphia was recorded for each community service recruit on a second base map. In this case, the inner city of Philadelphia was divided into 16 nearly equal areas. The recruits were asked to identify the area that is in the most dangerous neighborhood of inner-city Philadelphia and give it a score of zero. They were asked to locate the safest neighborhood in inner-city Philadelphia and record a 10 for the area contained within this community. Given these anchors, the recruits were then asked to scale all remaining areas between zero and 10 with regard to whether they were like the most dangerous or the safest neighborhoods in inner-city Philadelphia.

THE ANALYSIS

The above data allow the measurement of each community service recruit's knowledge and safety perception of inner-city Philadelphia. Knowledge of the area is assumed to be directly related to the ability of each recruit to accurately locate major landmarks on the base map. The level of knowledge is measured by determining how many inches on the map their plotted location is, in a straight line from the actual location of each landmark. This measurement of error is summed over the 33 landmarks and then divided by 33 to determine the average error per landmark for each recruit. This average error is our measure of the relative knowledge of each community service recruit of inner-city Philadelphia.

The perception of relative safety is measured in a slightly different manner. Since each community service recruit is compared with all others, the first task is to determine the norm with which to make this comparison. In this case, the perceived level of safety is summed over all community service recruits for each of the 16 areas and divided by 24 (the number of recruits) to obtain the average value for each location in inner-city Philadelphia. Then this average is subtracted from the score each recruit placed on an area, to obtain a measure of deviation from the mean for each neighborhood for each recruit. Finally, this deviation is summed over all 16 areas and divided by 16 to obtain the average deviation from the mean for each recruit. This average deviation is our measure of the relative perception of safety of inner-city Philadelphia. The higher the score, the safer the recruit perceives the overall inner city to be relative to his or her fellow recruits.

THE RESULTS

Table 1 lists the landmarks of inner-city Philadelphia, ranked in the order of how well-known their locations are to the community service recruits. Notice that City Hall is the best-known landmark in inner-city Philadelphia. Notice, also, that the two least-known locations of landmarks are religious centers. One might speculate that these community service recruits know government centers better than religious centers. However, it is surprising that the Police Administration Building ranked 21 out of 33 sites. In general, centrally located sites were more accurately located than those toward the edge of the map. Maps 1 to 4 are examples of the scatter of points plotted by all recruits as the location of a landmark around the actual locations of these landmarks.

Map 5 portrays the average perceived daylight walking safety of inner-city Philadelphia by these community service recruits. Contour lines have been drawn to highlight the relative perceived safety of each area. Table 2 lists the deviation of each recruit's safety perception from the average of the entire group, summed over all sections of inner-city Philadelphia. Table 2 also lists the average knowledge of the location of the landmarks for each recruit, as measured by a straight line from the plotted locations to the actual locations. The rank of each recruit on each measurement is also given in table 2.

Table 1
Major Landmarks and Error in Their Location

Landmarks	*Error in Knowledge of the Location*
City Hall	.23
Gallery Shopping Plaza	.50
Independence Hall	.54
Academy of Music	.73
Chinese Arch	.81
Hershey Hotel	.83
Franklin Institute	.87
Masonic Temple	.88
Main Branch of Free Library	.88
Penns Landing	.89
Rittenhouse Square	.95
Hahneman Hospital	.98
Logan's Circle	.98
Jefferson Medical College	.99
Reading Terminal Market	1.00
Betsy Ross House	1.05
Art Museum	1.13
Cathedral of St. Peter and Paul	1.14
Natural Science Museum	1.32
Philadelphia Community College	1.37
Police Administration Building	1.46
Society Hill Towers	1.53
Academy of Fine Arts	1.53
City Tavern	1.79
Ben Franklin Court	1.92
Roman Catholic High School	1.96
Graduate Hospital	2.03
TLA Cinema	2.19
Jefferson Hospital	2.20
Ben Franklin Bridge	2.30
Washington Square	2.48
Friends Meeting House	3.43
Christ Church	4.74

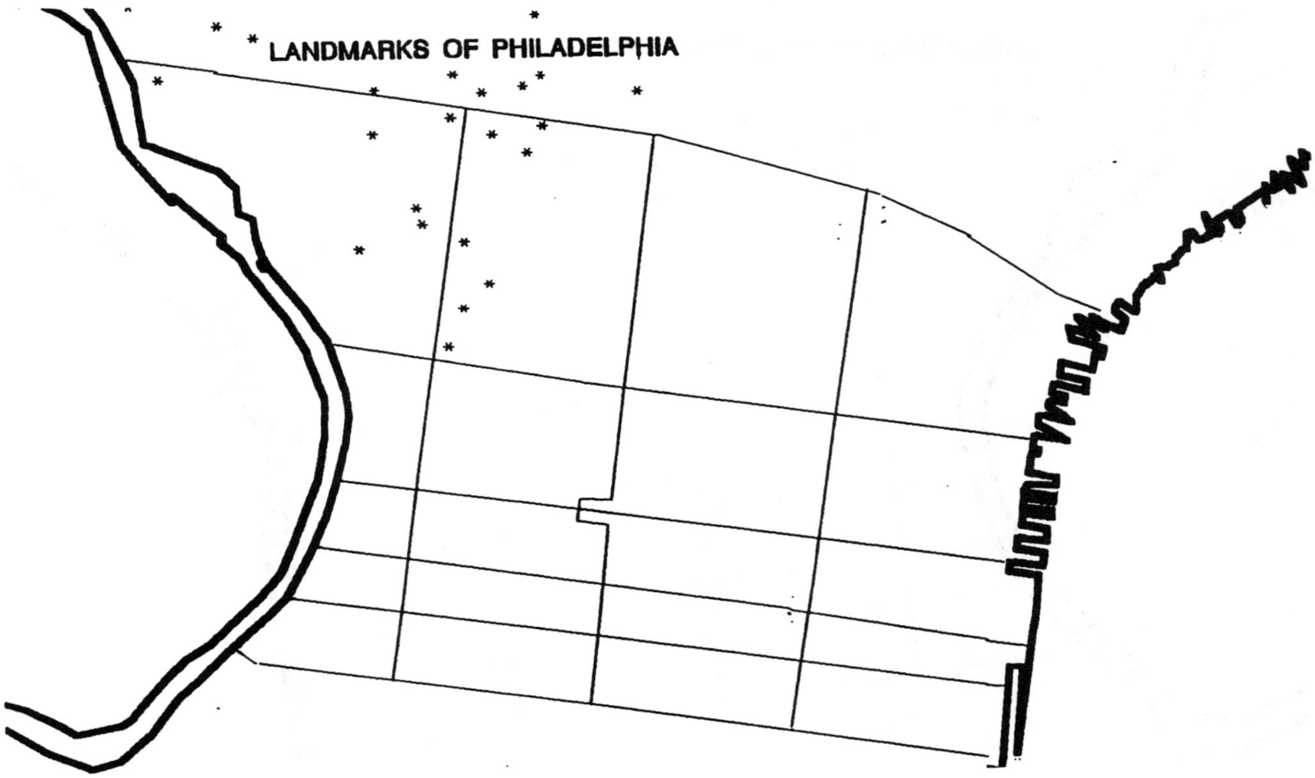

Map 1
Accuracy of cognitive maps: Free Library

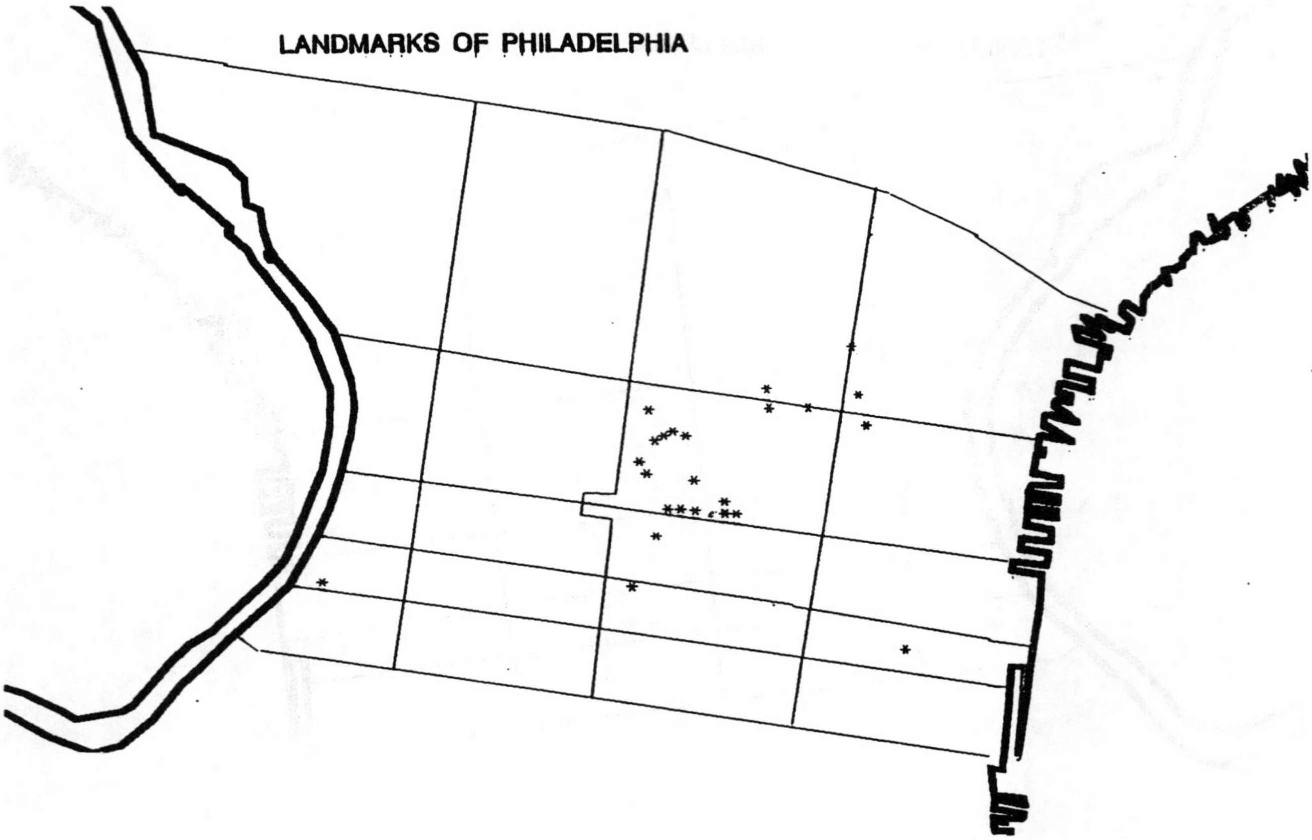

Map 2
Accuracy of cognitive maps: Reading Terminal Market

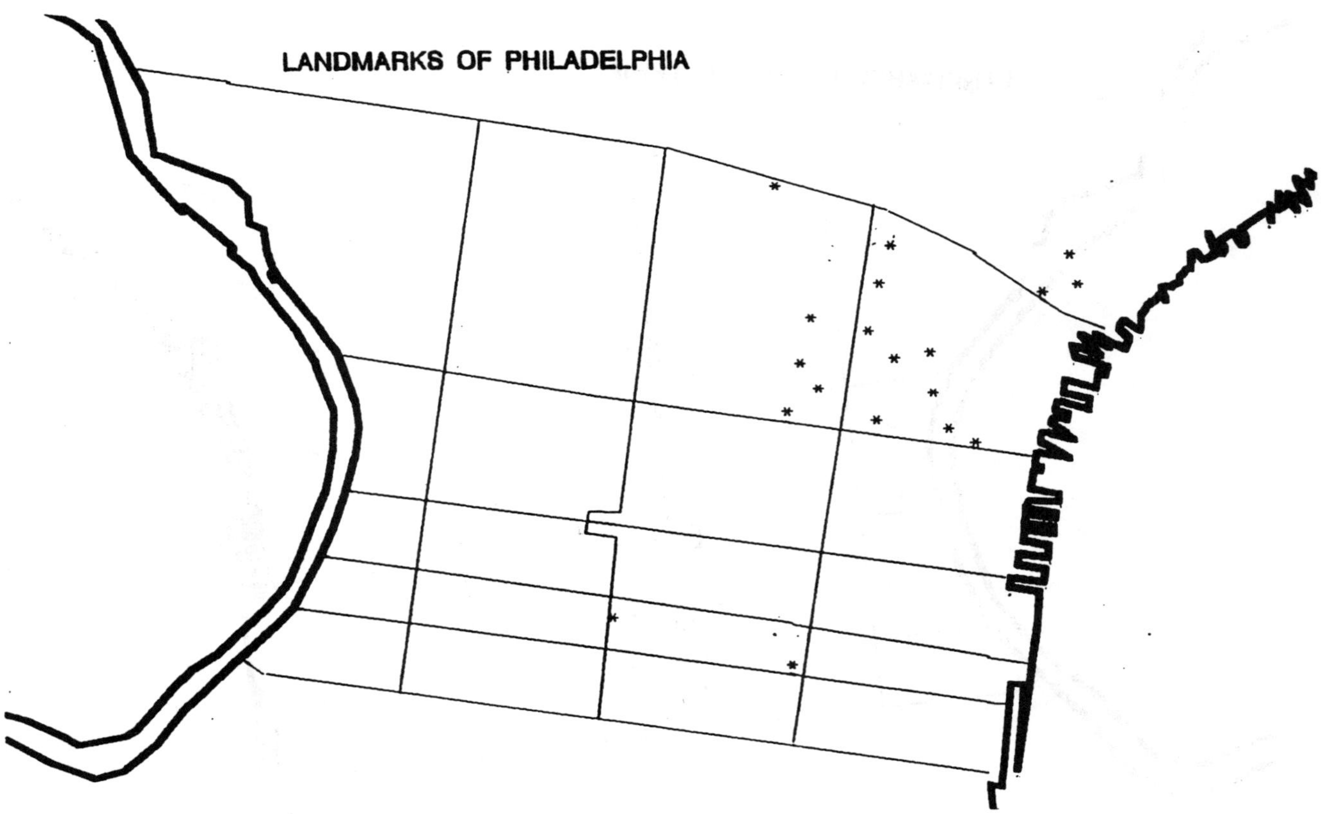

Map 3
Accuracy of cognitive maps: Police Administration Building

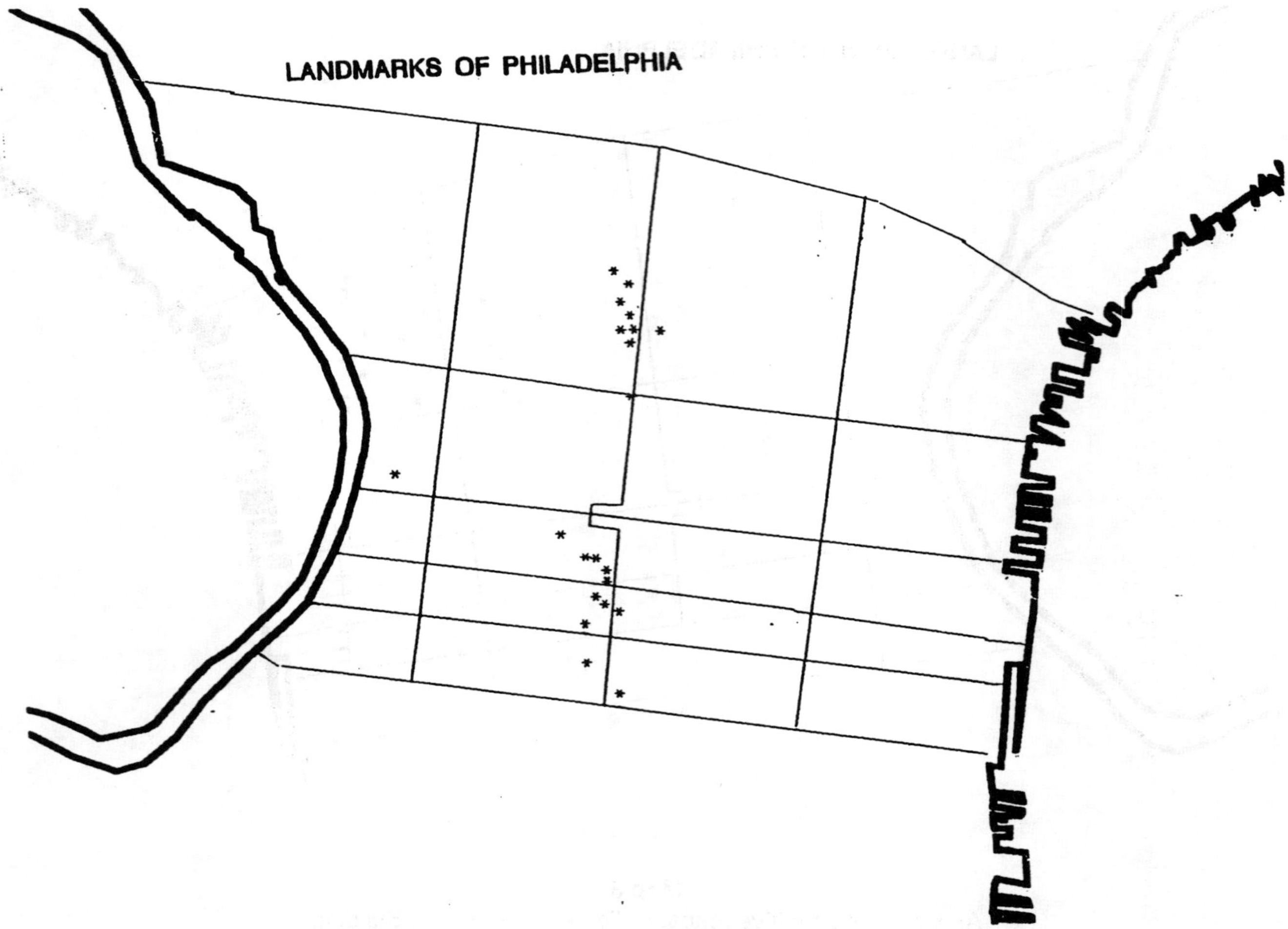

Map 4
Accuracy of cognitive maps: Academy of Fine Arts

Inner City Philadelphia

Map 5
Average perceived daylight walking safety

Table 2
Knowledge and Perceived Danger

Recruit	Perceived Safety	Rank	Knowledge of Landmarks	Rank
1	–.68	10	.4297	2
2	–24.68	24	1.0606	18
3	–12.68	21	.6506	3
4	4.32	9	.8952	12
5	20.32	3	1.7586	21
6	–6.68	15	1.9063	22
7	–8.68	16	2.1953	23
8	–11.68	20	.7976	9
9	–9.68	17	.3789	1
10	–13.68	22	.7887	8
11	–.68	11	.9815	15
12	26.32	1	1.1827	19
13	–3.68	12	1.0086	16
14	–14.68	23	.9436	13
15	14.32	4	.7833	7
16	–4.68	13	.6364	5
17	5.32	7	.6515	6
18	7.32	6	.7984	10
19	–10.68	19	3.1724	24
20	5.32	8	1.0577	17
21	23.32	2	.9516	14
22	–6.68	14	.8750	11
23	–9.68	18	.6212	4
24	13.32	5	1.4306	20

As can be seen at the outset, our initial proposition that the better known the inner city of Philadelphia is to a community service recruit, the safer he or she will perceive the area does not hold up. A simple regression model of the standardized variables of the form,

Perceived Safety = Constant + b*knowledge,

produces a coefficient of knowledge of .016 and a squared *r* value of 0.00. This is as close to no statistical relationship as one can get! In other words, for this group of recruits, relative knowledge of the inner city does not translate into perceived safety. Since this finding runs counter to previous research, we must ask why this is the case for this group of recruits. Could it be that the inner city is indeed dangerous, so that the better one knows it, the more accurately he or she perceives the danger? This could be tested by scaling the actual crime rates for the 16 inner-city areas between zero and 10, and testing whether those recruits who have the most accurate knowledge of the location of major landmarks also have the most accurate knowledge of the relative safety of different parts of the inner city.

In this analysis, we scaled only the violent crimes of robbery, assault, homicide, and rape—crimes that instill the most fear in users of the inner city. This was accomplished by dividing the inner city into 16 areas of nearly the same size and counting the number of these crimes (unweighted for severity) that occurred in each area in 1992. These values were divided by the largest value evident, so that the area with the highest number of violent crimes has a value of one, and all other areas are measured by the proportion they are of this value. These numbers are now subtracted from one so that the highest-crime area has the lowest value (zero), as was the case when the recruits scaled the areas. The result is multiplied by 10, so that the possible range is zero to 10. This resulted in a range of values from zero to 8.4, with five values above the midpoint of five and seven values below. In other words, it is nearly a normal distribution, with few areas clustering about any value. Inner-city Philadelphia is not a uniformly dangerous or safe area. There is considerable variation between regions.

A regression analysis is calculated using the following variables. The dependent variable is the deviation when the actual level of safety is subtracted from the perceived level of safety for each recruit, and the absolute values summed over the areas to provide a measure of how far from reality each recruit views the various areas in inner-city Philadelphia in either a positive or a negative direction. The independent variable is the deviation resulting when the actual locations are subtracted from the perceived locations for the 33 landmarks in inner-city Philadelphia. The result is a very weak positive coefficient of .003 and a squared r value of only .113. When the two variables were ranked across all recruits to control for some extreme values, the Spearman rank-order correlation coefficient is .336. In both cases, there is a very weak and insignificant positive relationship between knowledge of the inner city and perceived safety of the area.

Since the relationship between knowledge of the inner city and perceived safety of the area is so weak, we must ask if we can identify by personal characteristics who is most likely to accurately identify the location of landmarks, and who is most likely to rate inner-city Philadelphia as safe or unsafe. In other words, is there a type of recruit who does not know the inner city but rates it as a safe area, or vice versa?

Again, we will make use of previous research to guide our analysis. Past research has shown that women tend to have poorer spatial skills than men (Macoby 1966). Therefore, we expect the nine female community service recruits to have performed less well in locating major landmarks than their 14 male counterparts. When we sum the distance that each male recruit had plotted the location of major landmarks from their actual locations and divide by the number of male recruits, we obtain an average value of 1.48 inches on the scaled map used. When we compute the mean for the nine women recruits, it is a slightly larger 1.63 inches, on average. So the women are slightly less knowledgeable or accurate in locating major landmarks in inner-city Philadelphia than their male counterparts. This is as expected.

Next, we consider feelings of safety during the daytime in inner-city Philadelphia. Past research would lead us to believe that males will perceive the area to be safer than females, for two reasons. First, males are expected to explore space and to feel more secure in strange areas, while females are socialized to play it safe and to remain in more secure, known areas (Bardwick 1972). Secondly, since the males have more accurate knowledge of the inner city than the female police recruits, they are expected to feel safer in these more-known areas than their female counterparts.

However, when we sum their mean deviation from the average perceived safety level for inner-city Philadelphia, we find a big surprise! The average deviation from the mean for the 14 male recruits is –39.20. The average deviation for the nine female recruits is +19.88. In other words, the women recruits perceived inner-city Philadelphia to be much safer than their fellow male recruits. This is a surprising finding, and the one that caused our initial propositions to be rejected.

Since there is considerable variation in the violent offenses between sections of inner-city Philadelphia, the question turns on who can most accurately identify this variation—the men or the women community service recruits. The results do not demonstrate much difference between the men and women recruits. When the actual safety level is subtracted from the perceived safety level, the mean absolute deviation is 46.76 for the women recruits and 45.55 for the men recruits. The men are a bit more accurate in perceiving the safety level than the women, as we expected. But the difference is small. In other words, neither the men nor the women are very accurate in identifying the relative level of safety in inner-city Philadelphia. The question now turns on which areas are causing the errors in the recruits' perceptions of relative safety.

We have constructed two maps in which the contours of the perceived and the contours of the actual safety are portrayed (maps 5, above, and 6) to partially answer this question. Notice that there are extreme differences between these maps. The community service recruits perceived the center of the city to be the safest (especially the area around Rittenhouse Square), with a ridge of decline in either direction away from the center of Philadelphia. In actuality, violent crime in Philadelphia is spatially arranged as a "hot spot" centered just to the southeast of the center of the city. In other words, the community service recruits incorrectly perceived crime to increase toward the edge of the inner city, where low-income residential areas begin, while in reality, violent crime decreases in these directions. In fact, the safest area in inner-city Philadelphia is the Logan Circle area to the far northwest of the inner city, an area the community service recruits rated as one of the least safe in the inner city.

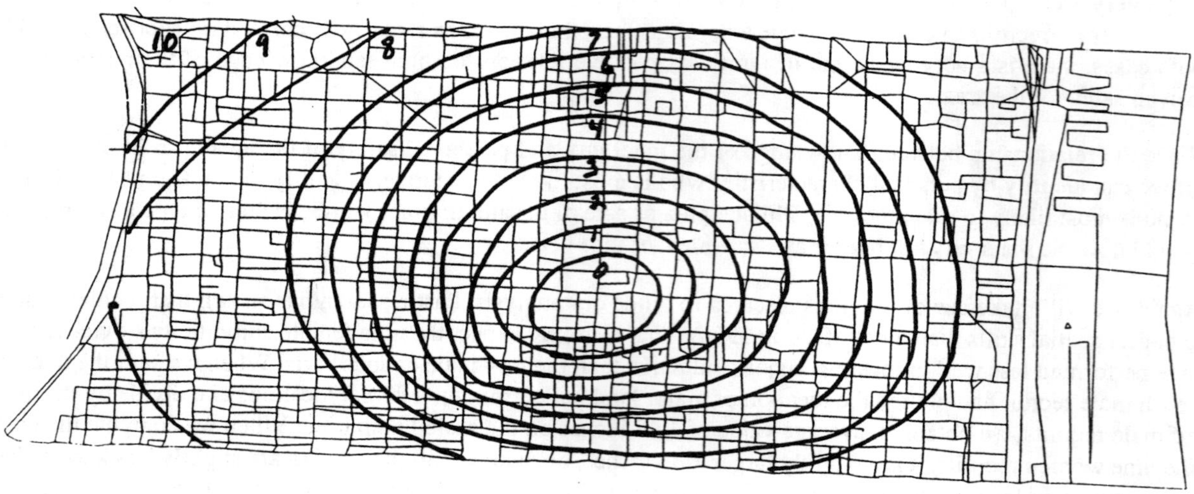

Map 6
Actual daytime safety: inner-city Philadelphia

A clearer picture of the violent crime pattern in inner-city Philadelphia develops when we allow multiple rather than a single hot spot to be identified. This analysis makes use of the STAC (Spatial and Temporal Analysis of Crime) program developed by the Illinois Criminal Justice Information Authority (Bates 1988). Maps 7 to 10 illustrate these multiple hot spots. Map 7 is the picture using a search radius of 300 feet. This results in 14 hot-spot ellipses. When the search radius is increased to 500 feet, these ellipses are aggregated to the six portrayed in map 8. A 600-foot radius search results in three ellipses (map 9), and map 10 is two ellipses resulting from an 800-foot search radius. Notice that when the search radius increases, the hot-spot ellipses are aggregated. In all cases, the hot-spot areas center around central Philadelphia just south of City Hall, as was the result in the previous analysis. This is very different from the perceived safety of the recruits.

Rectangular Search

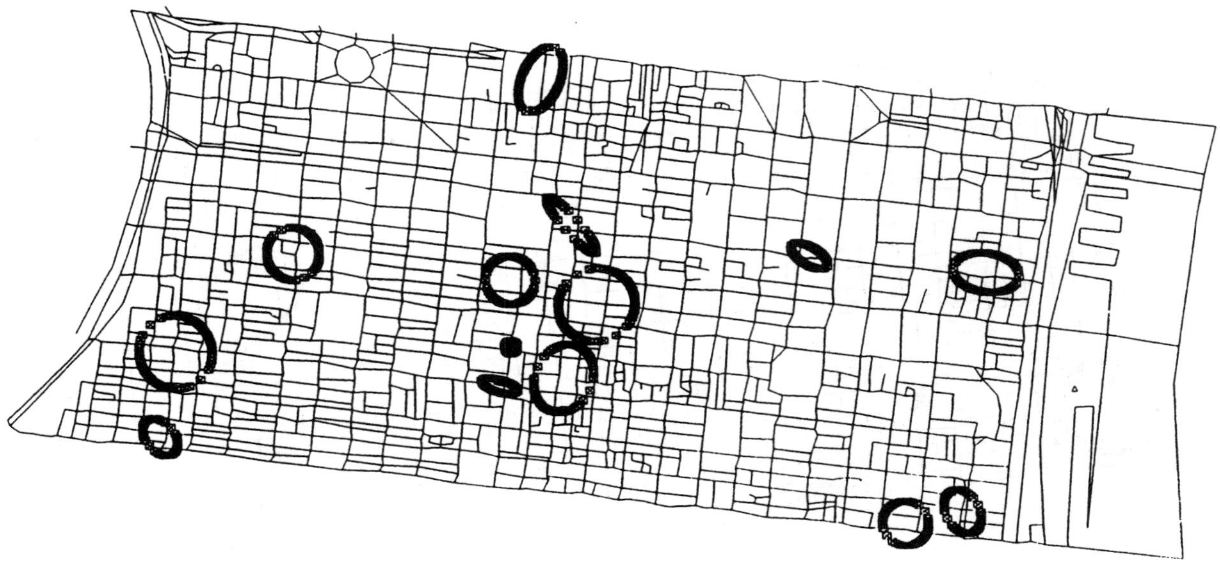

Map 7
STAC analysis: 300-foot search radius

Triangular Search

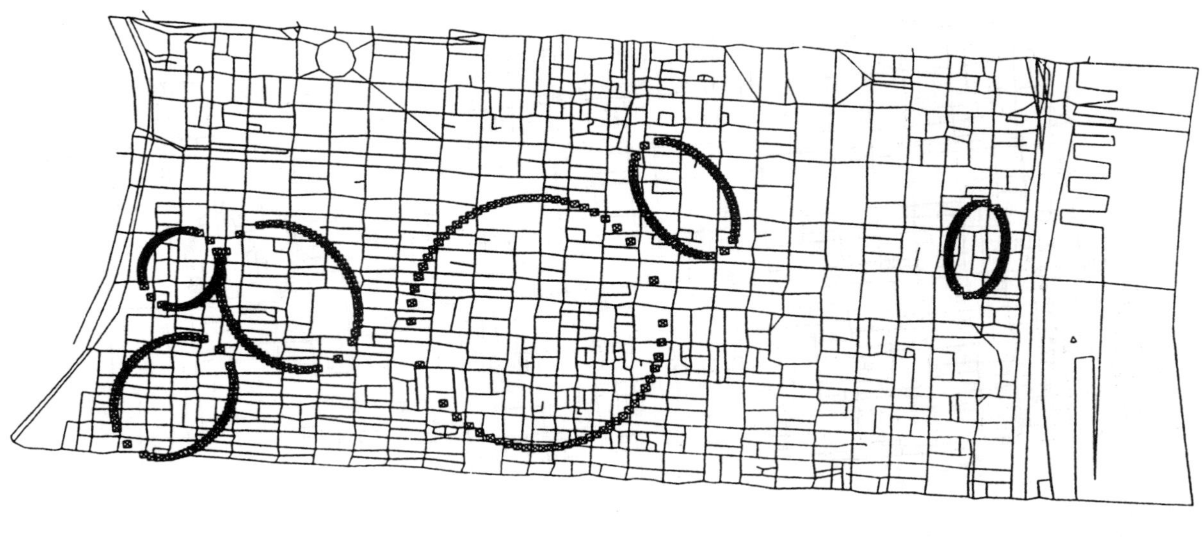

Map 8
STAC analysis: 500-foot search radius

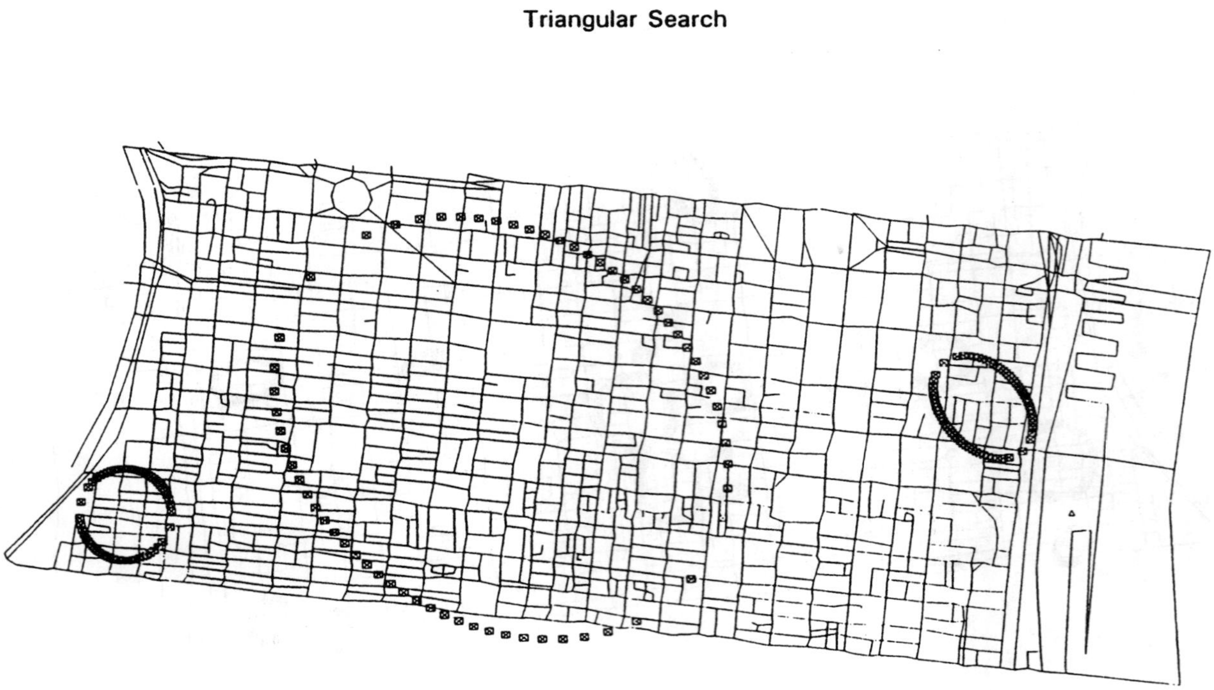

Map 9
STAC analysis: 600-foot search radius

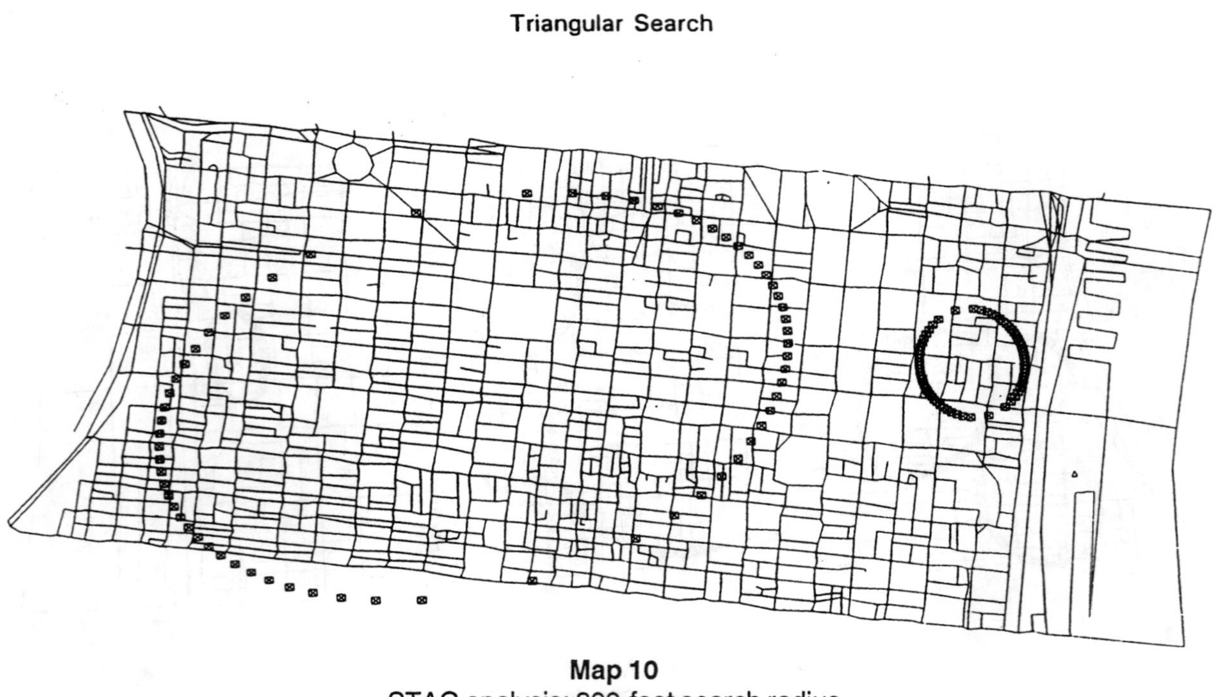

Map 10
STAC analysis: 800-foot search radius

The reason for the variation between the recruits' perceived safety and actual safety may revolve around a conceptual problem. What the recruits may have been scaling is "potential safety" rather than "actual safety." In other words, an area may be relatively safe because, in actuality, people avoid the area. Both routine-activity theory (Cohen and Felson 1979) and Jayne Jacob's (1965) critical-intensity theory of land use explain that a potential victim must be present for a crime to take place. We are left with the question of whether an area is unsafe if so many people avoid it that few, if any, crimes take place there. In actuality, it is not unsafe if people avoid the area, so that no crimes take place. But it is *potentially* unsafe if one were to wander into the area. Therefore, the actual safety level is lower in parts of the inner city that are heavily utilized. Actual safety is higher in areas less used. What we are missing is a measure of the "population at risk." Again, is it safe if few people go into an area?

A better approach may have been to ask each recruit where the most violent crime occurs, rather than where the safest areas in the inner city are located. As long as we have no statistics on how many people use each area of the inner city, so that we can measure the population at risk, we cannot compute an accurate measure of the actual safety level of each area. We are left with a measure of how much violent crime takes place and the recruits' perceptions of where it is the most and least safe to walk in the inner city. With regard to potential safety, they may be more accurate than the violent-crime statistics. But in reality, if they are to serve the communities of the inner city, they must have accurate knowledge of where the most violent crime takes place.

REFERENCES

Bardwick, Judith (1972). *Readings on the Psychology of Women.* New York: Harper and Row.

Bates, Samuel (1988). *Spatial and Temporal Analysis of Crime.* Research bulletin. Chicago: Illinois Criminal Justice Information Authority.

Boots, Barry, and Arthur Getis (1988). *Point Pattern Analysis.* Newbury Park: Sage Publications, Scientific Geography Series, vol. 8.

Cohen, Lorance, and Marcus Felson (1979). Social change and crime rate trends. *American Sociological Review* 44:588–605.

Davis, Ed, and Anthony Pinizzoto (1993). *Killed in the Line of Duty.* Washington, D.C.: Federal Bureau of Investigation, Uniform Crime Reporting Section.

Festinger, Leon (1957). *A Theory of Cognitive Dissonance.* New York: Harper and Row.

Golledge, Reginald, and Robert Stimson (1987). *Analytical Behavioral Geography.* New York: Croom Helm.

Jacobs, Jayne (1961). *The Death and Life of Great American Cities.* New York: Vintage Books.

Macoby, Eleanor (1966). *The Development of Sex Differences.* Stanford, Calif.: Stanford University Press.

Newman, Oscar (1972). *Defensible Space: Crime Prevention Through Urban Design.* New York: Collier Books.

Chapter 4

Spatial Autocorrelation Patterns With Regard to Suicide in the United States[1]

Ira M. Wasserman
Department of Sociology
Eastern Michigan University

Steve Stack
Department of Sociology
Wayne State University

ABSTRACT

Research on aggregated geographical data in such fields as genetics and epidemiology has produced biased findings caused by spatial autocorrelation. However, studies of suicide have neglected a systematic investigation of this potential cause of bias. It is unclear as to whether the wealth of research findings on suicide behavior across geographical space is flawed due to the presence of spatial autocorrelation. The present study employs Odland's test for spatial autocorrelation, which uses Moran's I as a means of ascertaining its presence. Data from the 50 states, as well as from 64 parishes in Louisiana, are examined. No evidence of spatial autocorrelation was found in these two studies, since the standard normal deviate was not significant at the .05 level. Spatial autocorrelation may not be a serious problem in geographic suicide research, because of the individual nature of the behavior.

INTRODUCTION

In geographical studies, the estimation of the parameters in the model may be biased by the presence of *spatial autocorrelation*, which is related to the effect of contiguous geographical units on each other (Cliff and Ord 1973, 1981; Haining 1987; Odland 1988).

> Spatial autocorrelation arises because of a possible diffusion effect in geographic data. Spatial autocorrelation statistics are numerical measurements of some basic properties of geographic phenomena—the extent and nature of their relations with phenomena at other locations ... This basic property of geographic phenomena means that geographical data will often fail to fulfill a basic condition for most of the statistical methods that are used to analyze relations among variables—that of independence among the observations (Odland 1988:15).

1. The authors would like to thank Professor John Odland of Indiana University for kindly supporting the Auto computer program used in the study, as well as sample data to check the validity of the program.

A number of disciplines have been concerned with the presence of spatial autocorrelation. In the area of epidemiology, Cliff and Ord (1981:1–7) examined its impact for studies of the cholera epidemic in London in 1848 and 1849; Kennedy (1988) considered its influence when she examined the distribution of lung cancer for men and women in the southeastern United States; Kemp (1987) found that accidents exhibited a spatial pattern. Cliff and Ord (1973:53–58) studied its impact in relation to the agricultural characteristics of counties in Ireland, while Epperson (1990) studied its influence in relation to the distribution of gene types. A number of studies in the genetic area (Sokol and Uytterschaut 1987; Sokol, Jacquez and Wooten 1989; Slotkin and Arter 1991) have also considered its potential effect. Finally, its presence was considered in a recent study of the linkage of economic concentration and corporate political contributions (Mizruchi and Koenig 1988). In all of the previously cited studies, there is an assumption that geographic concentration systematically influences social behavior and biases the estimated terms in the model. For example, Kennedy (1988) found that spatial autocorrelation was present for males who had lung cancer in southeastern counties in the United States, but was not present for women. She concluded that this gender difference was related to the workplace location of men, who traveled to sites where they were at higher risk of contracting lung cancer. Women tended to be located at home and did not exhibit this pattern.

In a recent study of suicide, Lester (1989) found that suicide studied at the state level exhibited spatial autocorrelation patterns, and concluded that all geographical studies of suicide must correct for its presence. In geography, there are maximum-likelihood estimation procedures (Ord 1975; Doreian 1980, 1981; Loflin and Ward 1983) that can be employed to correct the estimates. However, before making such corrections, it is necessary to adequately test for its presence by using such measures as Moran's I (Griffith 1988; Grunsky and Agterberg 1991). Spatial autocorrelation is usually caused by common social features of a geographic area (e.g., presence of certain industry or population characteristics), or the spread of various types of social behavior across geographical areas (Doreian 1981:363). In general, suicide involves individual behavior that is not influenced by the suicide behavior of others. Imitation effects (Wasserman 1984) and mass altruistic behavior (e.g., Japanese suicides at the end of World War II, and Jonestown in 1978) are exceptions to this general rule. This paper will study the possible presence of spatial autocorrelation in geographic suicide data by testing for its presence in a recent study of suicide at the national level that uses states as the unit of analysis, and will then perform a similar test for a state study (Louisiana) that employs parish data.

METHODOLOGY

In order to determine whether spatial autocorrelation is a serious problem in suicide studies that employ geographical data, this inquiry examines two recent studies at different levels of aggregation and determines whether spatial autocorrelation is present. The authors of both of these studies have kindly supplied the present authors with the statistical data necessary to ascertain whether spatial autocorrelation is a serious problem. The first study (Zimmerman 1987) involves an examination, at the state level, of the influence of state welfare payments on state suicide rates. For the 50 states, the dependent variable is the state suicide rate in 1982, and the independent variables are state welfare expenditures per capita, the state divorce rate in 1980, the population change between 1970 and 1980, and the percent of the population in the state with incomes between \$10,000 and \$19,999. Since two states (Alaska and Hawaii) are outside the continental United States and cannot be contiguous with any other state, they were eliminated from the study.

The second study (Wasserman and Stack 1993) examined suicide in Louisiana in relation to the religious culture of the state. The dependent variable was the average suicide rate in each of the 64 parishes in Louisiana between 1975 and 1980, while the independent variables were the percentage Catholic in 1974, the percentage urban in 1980, the percentage nonwhite in 1980, the SES in 1980, and the percentage living alone in 1980.

In order to determine whether spatial autocorrelation is present, it is necessary to compute Moran's I (Odland 1988). Moran's I is used for continuous data to assess whether there is spatial autocorrelation. Under conditions of randomization, its expected value (E[I]) for the dependent variable will be $-1/(n-1)$, where n is the number of aggregation units. For example, for the 48 contiguous states, $E(I)$ would be $-1/(48-1) = -1/47 = -.0213$. One uses the Auto computer program to compute the actual value of I, and then relates the computed to the expected value. For regression models, the expected value is slightly different, and one uses regression residuals to determine the computed value of I (Odland 1988:54–57).

In order to employ the Auto program, it is necessary to construct a contiguous state and county matrix. The state contiguous matrix was determined from an examination of a map of the 48 contiguous states. For example, in the matrix, Maine was contiguous with only one other state (New Hampshire), while Tennessee and Missouri were contiguous with eight other states. The remaining states varied in their contiguousness with other states. In order to construct a contiguous matrix for the parishes of Louisiana, government data that listed the contiguousness of all counties and parishes were used (Bureau of the Census 1991). In his study of spatial autocorrelation, Lester (1989) only determined whether the dependent variable (the suicide rate) exhibited spatial autocorrelation. However, in multivariate studies, it is more important to determine whether the residual terms exhibit spatial autocorrelation, since this is the model being examined. For this study, Moran's I will be computed with the Auto program for both the suicide rate and the residual terms.

DISCUSSION

Figure 1 indicates the distribution of the suicide rate in the United States in 1982. Suicide rates are higher in the American West, but the remainder of the nation exhibits no spatial pattern. The fact that the state study (Zimmerman 1987) controlled for population changes between 1970 and 1980 should remove spatial effects, since the West is the area of the nation that exhibited the greatest rate of population growth and also had the highest suicide rate.

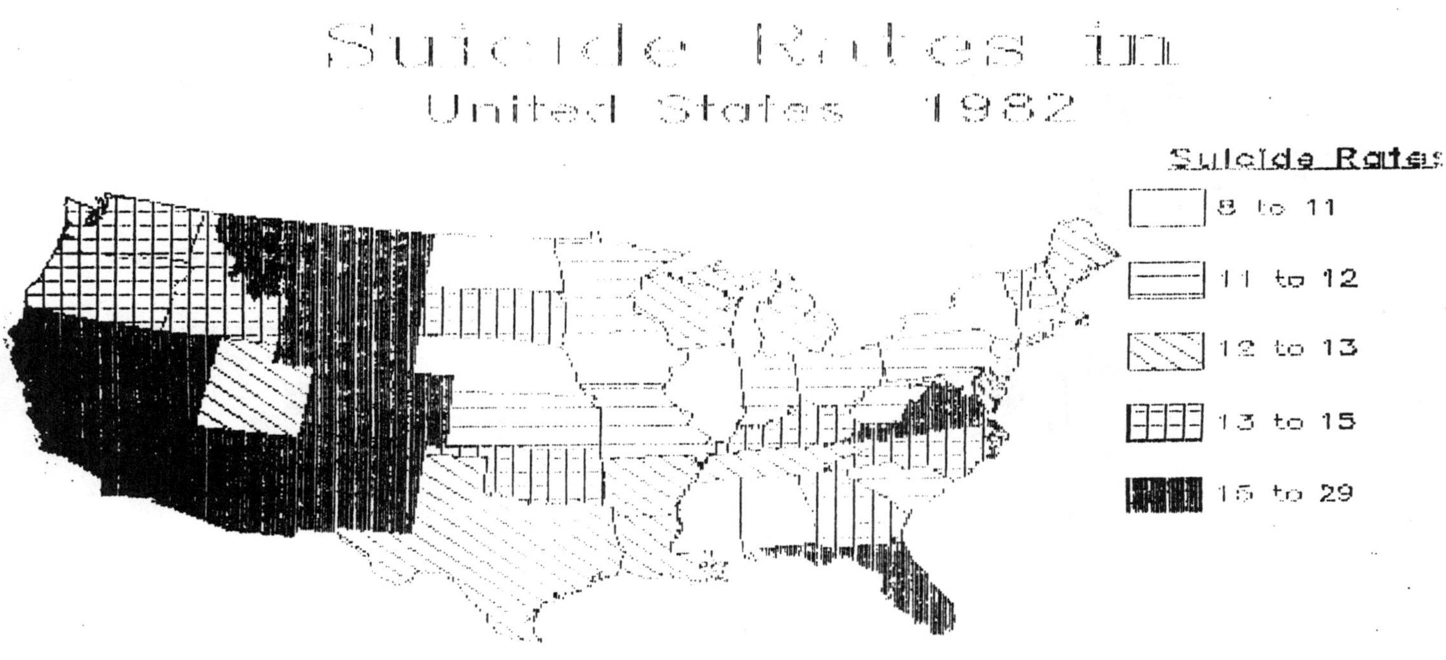

Fig. 1
Suicide patterns in the United States in 1982

Table 1 indicates the computation of Moran's I for the state data, and the probability that the computed value is significantly different from the expected value under conditions of randomization. For both the suicide rate and the residuals, there is no significant spatial effect, using the standard .05 level of significance as the cutoff point. The relatively high probabilities suggest that suicide rates in one state do not significantly influence suicide in other states.

Table 1
Test for Spatial Autocorrelation in State Study of Political Behavior and Suicide

	Moran's I	Expected Value	Variance	Standard Normal Deviate	Probability
Dependent Variable: Suicide Rate, 1982	.0298	–.0213	.0050	.7235	.2350
Residual Terms in Linear Model	.0369	–.0173	.0617	.8790	.1890

Figure 2 indicates the suicide patterns in the parishes of Louisiana between 1975 and 1980. Suicide is slightly higher in the Catholic southern portion of the state, but there is no clear spatial pattern. Table 2 presents the Moran I values and the probabilities for suicide and the residuals. Using the .05 level of significance, spatial autocorrelation is not present. The residual terms have less spatial effects than the suicide rate, probably because controls for percentage Catholic and urbanization were introduced into the model.

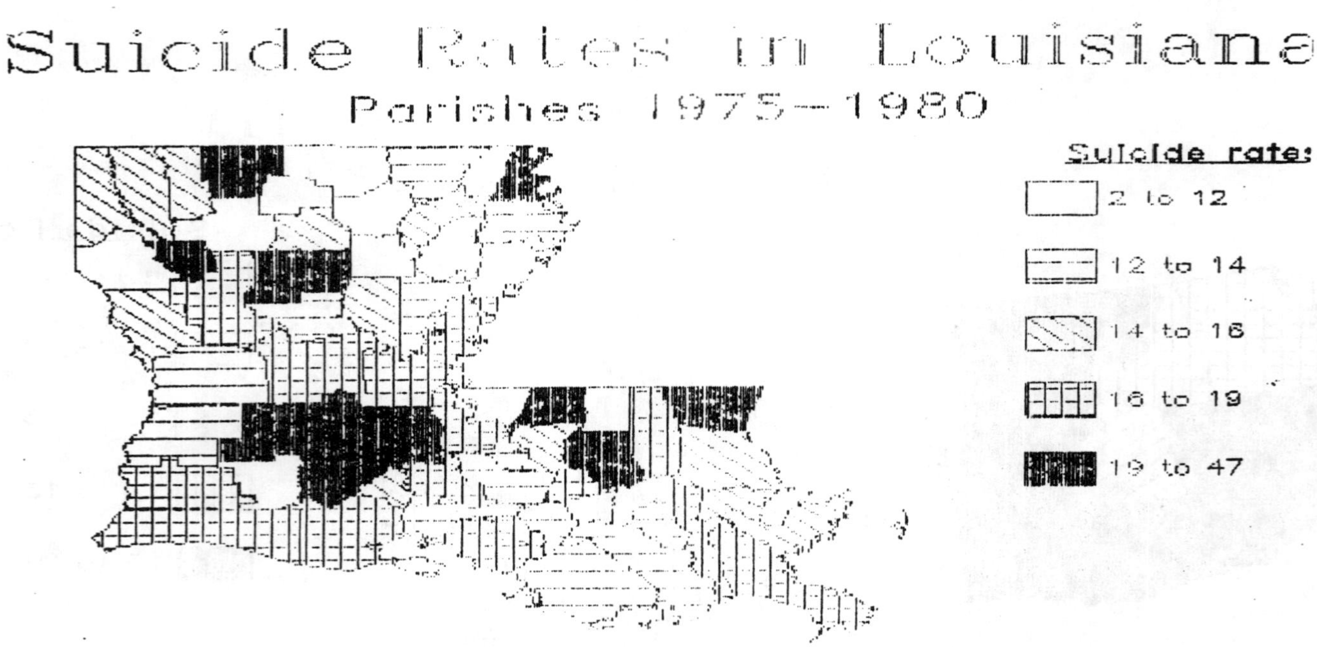

Fig. 2
Suicide patterns in Louisiana parishes: 1975 to 1980

Table 2
Test for Spatial Autocorrelation in Suicide Study of Political Behavior in Louisiana Parishes

	Moran's I	Expected Value	Variance	Standard Normal Deviate	Probability
Dependent Variable: Suicide Rate, 1975–1982	.0781	.0159	.0059	1.228	.1090
Residual Terms in Linear Model	–.0003	–.0102	.0617	.8790	.1890

CONCLUSION

The previous results imply that spatial effects are not a serious problem for suicide studies that employ geographical data. Suicide is usually an individual phenomenon, and the patterns in one geographical area will not usually influence patterns in other geographical areas. For other types of violent behavior, such as homicides and traffic accidents, it is possible that spatial effects may be present, and it will be necessary to test for its presence.

REFERENCES

Bureau of the Census (1991). *Contiguous County File 1991: United States.* Ann Arbor, Mich.: Inter-University Consortium for Political and Social Research.

Cliff, A.D., and J.K. Ord (1973). *Spatial Autocorrelation.* London: Pion Ltd.

——— (1981). *Spatial Processes: Models and Applications.* London: Pion Ltd.

Doreian, Patrick (1980). Linear models with spatially distributed data: Spatial disturbances or spatial effects? *Sociological Methods and Research* 9:29–60.

——— (1981). Estimating models with spatially distributed data. Pp. 359–388 in Samuel Leinhardt (ed.), *Sociological Methodology 1981*. San Francisco: Jossey-Bass.

Epperson, B.K. (1990). Spatial autocorrelation of genotypes under directional selection. *Genetics* 124:757–771.

Griffith, Daniel A. (1988). Estimating spatial autoregressive model parameters with commercial statistical packages. *Geographical Analysis* 20:176–186.

Grunsky, E.C., and F.P. Agterberg (1991). Funcorr: A Fortran-77 program for computing multivariate spatial autocorrelation. *Computers and Geosciences* 17:115–131.

Haining, Robert (1987). Spatial modelling and the statistical analysis of spatial data in human geography. *Mathematiques et Sciences Humaines* 25:5–25.

Kemp, C.D. (1987). On a contagious distribution suggested for accident data. *Biometrics* 23:241–255.

Kennedy, Susan (1988). A geographic regression model for medical statistics. *Social Science and Medicine* 26:119–129.

Lester, David (1989). Geophysical variables and behavior: LVI. The spatial autocorrelation of state's suicide and homicide rates. *Perceptual and Motor Skills* 68:218.

Loftin, Colin, and Sally K. Ward (1983). A spatial autocorrelation model of the effects of population density on fertility. *American Sociological Review* 48:121–128.

Mizruchi, Mark S., and Thomas Koenig (1988). Economic concentration and corporate political behavior: A cross-industry comparison. *Social Science Research* 17:287–305.

Odland, John (1988). *Spatial Autocorrelation*. Beverly Hills: Sage Publications.

Ord, Keith (1975). Estimation methods for models of spatial interaction. *Journal of the American Statistical Association* 70:120–126.

Slotkin, Montgomery, and Hubert E. Arter (1991). Spatial autocorrelation methods in population genetics. *The American Naturalist* 138:499–517.

Sokol, Robert R., and Hilde Uytterschaut (1987). Cranial variation in European populations: A spatial autocorrelation study of three time periods. *American Journal of Physical Anthropology* 74:21–38.

Sokol, Robert R., Geoffrey M. Jacquez and Michael C. Wooten (1989). Spatial autocorrelation analysis of migration and selection. *Genetics* 121:845–855.

Wasserman, Ira M. (1984). A reexamination of the Werther effect. *American Sociological Review* 49:427–436.

Wasserman, Ira M., and Steve Stack (1993). The effect of religion on suicide: An analysis of cultural context. *Omega* 27:295–305.

Zimmerman, Shirley L. (1987). States' public welfare expenditures as predictors of state suicide rates. *Suicide and Life-Threatening Behavior* 17:271–287.

Chapter 5

Tracking Critical-Incident Zones Over Time in Peoria[1]

Ron Moser
Ottumwa (Iowa) Police Department

PROBLEM STATEMENT

A research study of murder in Peoria revealed that the vast majority of these cases involved circumstances of lethal street violence (see Peoria Police Department 1992 for details). These murders frequently were associated with drugs, gangs and, to a lesser extent, robbery. Only one of the 12 cases was related to a domestic dispute. Firearms were the killing weapon used in 10 (83%) of the murders. The homicides were not dispersed throughout the city, but occurred primarily in the same geographic area.

DATA ANALYSIS

Information derived from the 1993 Peoria homicide study showed that murder was associated with lethal street violence and was geographically confined. Therefore, further research was developed to determine specifically where certain lethal incidents occur.

The smallest geographic areas available for study were found to be 495 zones that divide the city. Data was obtained weekly for each zone regarding the following lethal incidents:

I. Police Dispatch Calls for Service

- Person with a gun
- Shots fired
- Unlawful use of weapon

II. Actual Police Reports

- Murder
- All robberies and armed robberies
- All aggravated batteries with firearm
- All aggravated assaults with firearm

1. This is a revision of a paper presented at the 1993 workshop of the Homicide Research Working Group, at the FBI Academy in Quantico, Va. (Block and Block 1993).

The analysis of the above data for the first 4 months of 1993 revealed the following:

- Six hundred thirteen lethal incidents occurred during this time period.
- Three hundred eight zones (62%) had no incidents during the time period.
- Six zones recorded 10 or more incidents (these zones are labeled *critical-incident zones*).
- The total number of incidents that occurred in those six zones was 145 (24% of the city). However, these six zones comprise only 1 percent of the geographic area of the city.
- Twenty-five zones were found to have from five to nine incidents (these zones are labeled *medium-incident zones*).
- The total number of incidents that occurred in these 25 zones was 166 (27% of the city). However, these 25 zones comprise only 5 percent of the geographic area of the city.
- The 31 zones that recorded at least five incidents account for 311 total lethal incidents (51% of the city). These 31 zones comprise only 6 percent of the geographic area of the city.

In addition to the data from the 1992 homicide study, the six murders that have occurred in Peoria in 1993 have been examined as to location. From the 18 total murders for 1992 and 1993 to date, the following information was determined:

- Seven of the 18 murders (39%) were committed in critical-incident zones.
- Four of the 18 murders (27%) occurred in medium-incident zones.
- In total, 11 of all 18 homicides (61%) occurred in a critical- or medium-incident zone.
- Of the remaining seven homicides, six occurred within 1,500 feet of a critical- or medium-incident zone.
- Four murders were committed in Harrison Homes (a critical-incident zone where 31 total incidents occurred), all within 1,500 feet of each other.
- Three murders were committed in Warner Homes (a critical-incident zone where 34 total incidents occurred), all within 1,000 feet of each other.

PROGRAM GOAL AND HYPOTHESIS

The program goal is to reduce lethal street violence and homicide. The program hypothesis is as follows: Increased police presence in areas of lethal street violence is associated with a decrease in lethal street violence.

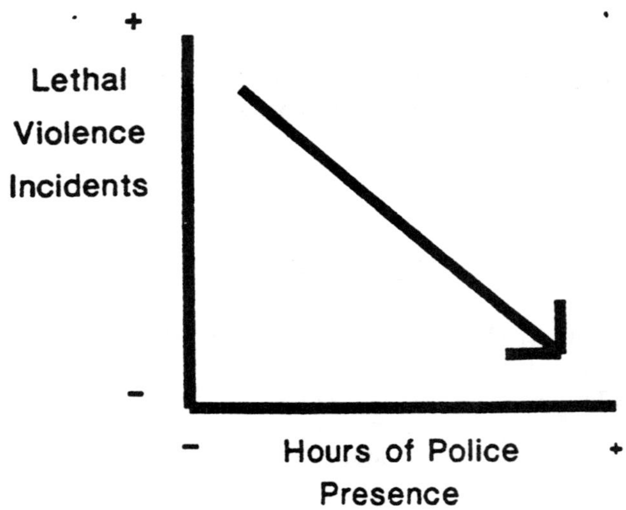

Fig. 1
Police presence and lethal violence

ACTION PLAN

Designated patrols in the critical-incident zones will be conducted by uniformed police officers. Officers will be encouraged to spend discretionary time in these zones. The mobile command post (a large camper/recreational vehicle with police markings) will be assigned to stationary deployment in the critical-incident zones.

The strategic planning office will receive weekly reports on hours of designated patrol and hours of command post deployment per critical-incident zone. Associations will be computed, and geographic shifts in lethal violence will be tracked.

Information will be relayed to operation bureau command for monthly redeployment of patrol personnel and mobile command post.

TRADITIONAL PATROL MODEL VS. REVISED MODEL

The traditional model of preventive patrol involves cruising while waiting for calls for service. Directed patrol, however, allocates patrol service in a directed manner based on crime analysis (see Thibault, Lynch and McBride 1990:198–206). The usefulness of traditional preventive patrol was refuted by the 1970 Kansas City study (Wilson 1975:89–91).

In three cases of directed patrol projects, problems emerged due to methodology of implementation (see Thibault, Lynch and McBride 1990:207–208 for details of each study). In New Haven, Conn., officers were assigned deterrent runs. These "D-runs" lasted 45 minutes to an hour, with directions on how to patrol a specific area. Officers felt that it was a waste of time and that they were turned into robots. A "split force" concept was used in Wilmington, Del. Some officers were assigned to fixed posts in high-crime areas as a deterrent. A rebellion occurred over movement restrictions. In Kansas City, the patrol supervisor would split a squad into normal or directed patrol, based on crime analysis. Complaints of boredom were frequent.

CONCLUSION

This plan attempts to reduce lethal street violence through directed patrol. The pitfalls of previous directed patrol operations are avoided. Officers are not assigned boring, detailed plans to follow, but are encouraged to use directed patrol as a tool to reduce violence.

REFERENCES

Block, Carolyn Rebecca, and Richard Block (eds.) (1993). *Questions and Answers in Lethal and Nonlethal Homicide: 1993.* Proceedings of the Homicide Research Working Group workshop, Quantico, Va.: Washington, D.C.: National Institute of Justice.

Thibault, Edward, Lawrence M. Lynch and Bruce McBride (1990). *Proactive Police Management.* Englewood Cliffs, N.J.: Prentice-Hall, Inc.

Wilson, James Q. (1975). *Thinking About Crime.* New York: Basic Books, Inc.

Peoria Police Department (1992). Homicide study.

Chapter 6

Mapless Mapping in Analyzing the Spatial Distribution of Serial Rapes[1]

Roland Reboussin
FBI Academy

Janet Warren
University of Virginia

Robert R. Hazelwood
FBI Academy

Brantingham and Brantingham (1981) have observed that, while observations of spatial crime patterns have been diverse, explanations of the patternings have been "simplistic" and based primarily on area correlations between crime patterns and other social phenomena.

Based on the assumption that most offenders commit their crimes close to home, Brantingham and Brantingham suggest that the most simple search pattern would be characterized by a uniform circle, with the offender's residence at the center and the probability of any potential target becoming an actual target decreasing as the distance from the offender's home increases. Integrating concepts of mobility and perception into the cognitive "template" of criminals, they in turn posit that "criminals engage in search behavior that may vary in intensity," that "criminals use previous knowledge to evaluate and select targets," and that additional patterns can be deduced based on varying spatial distributions of victims or targets within hypothetical urban forms. Based upon these hypothetical templates, Brantingham and Brantingham (1981:50) assert,

> criminals are not random in their behavior and . . . by exploring urban structures and how people interact with urban spatial structure, it should be possible to predict the spatial distribution of crime and explain some of the variation in volume of crime between urban areas and between cities.

In a report submitted to the U.S. Department of Justice, Rengert and Wasilchick (1990) apply principles of cognitive mapping deriving in part from the work of Coucelis, Golledge, Gale, and Tobler (1987) and Huff (1984). Rengert and Wasilchick (1990:50) comment on the ubiquitousness of criminal opportunities, a "distance bias" that motivates a burglar to stay close to important "anchor points," and a "directional preference" wherein a burglar tends to operate in "more familiar rather than less familiar areas." They propose a series of six models for the patterning of burglaries describing the distribution of crimes around the home and a second "focus."

1. This research was conducted under Interagency Reimbursable Agreement No. 91-IJ-R-027, awarded to the authors by the National Institute of Justice. The authors would like to express their appreciation for the invaluable work of Susan Trumbetta and Natalie Gibbs in coding and analysis of the data, and Andrea Cummings in her work with MapInfo. An earlier version of this paper was presented at the June 1993 conference of the Homicide Research Working Group, and published with the proceedings of that conference (*Questions and Answers in Lethal and Nonlethal Violence: 1993*, National Institute of Justice, 1994).

Recently, Canter and Larkin (1993), studying the spatial patterns of 45 serial rapists, have discussed models of the relationships that exist between an individual's range of criminal activity and the location of the home base. Hypothesizing a "marauder" and a "commuter" model, they found evidence primarily of the former, in which the offender moved out from his home base in order to commit crimes. Canter and Larkin further found that offenders tended to offend in a distinct offense region and that the distance they travel to offend correlates highly with the distances between their offenses. Based upon these findings, the authors conclude that the principle of "domocentricity" is relevant to the patterning of sexual crime, and that this determination may prove useful in solving these crimes.

The present study falls within the same tradition and thus examines the spatial distribution of crime not only in its geographical context, but also as an expression of human cognition and perception.

The data for this project were derived from two sets of serial rape cases. The data discussed in this paper are from a set of 112 cases, which collectively total 898 rapes and other incidents. The cases, which all involve apprehended offenders, have been collected from police departments across the country. They were acquired through the course "Violence in America," taught at the FBI Academy. As part of their participation in the course, students were given the option of either writing a term paper or submitting a complete solved serial rape case from the files of their own department or another department. The case was to include detailed victim statements, police reports and a map showing the location of each rape, as well as the location of the home and place of employment of the offender. Criminal history summaries were also obtained for each offender.

At the time of this writing, this research is in progress. At this point, the victim statements for every rape have been coded using a 28-page protocol that summarizes the nature of the relationship between the offender and the victim, the nature of the approach used by the rapist in procuring a victim, the site of the contact, the victim's characteristics, the characteristics of the release site, and the factual components of the rape itself (e.g., sexual acts committed, use of weapon), as well as 56 scales that quantify the behavioral, verbal and sexual interactions of the rapist with the victim. Each of the case maps has now been geocoded[2] with latitude and longitude shown to six decimal places. This level of measurement is accurate to a few inches. Before continuing with the geographic part of this study, though, its three theoretical components should be mentioned.

A significant theoretical thrust of the study has to do with the quantitative analysis of rape. Warren, Reboussin, Hazelwood, and Wright (1991) originally developed a set of 33 five-point scales, which were used in discriminant analyses of an earlier set of rapes. For the present study, we developed a new and seemingly improved set of scales in which many of the previous scales were revised or expanded. In the 1991 study, we were able to "predict" which rapists would eventually become more violent, based on their first rapes. At the moment, we are able to replicate this finding in the present study, but only using the old scales. In the 1991 study, we also tried to discriminate rapist types, based on the scales, and while the results looked promising, the discriminant functions were not significant. In the present study, we do get significant results with both old and new scales. This has interesting implications; not only does it facilitate the derivation of replicable rape type based on crime information only, but it also raises the possibility of conceptualizing rapist types not as categories *per se*, but as points in a multivariate space.

A second analytical focus involves the empirical derivation of conceptual factors that underlie the rape incident. Currently, the principal factors are rapist force and victim resistance, rapist involvement with the victim, rapist verbalization, scripting of the victim, rapist preparation and planning, rapist masculine stereotypes, narcissism, and seduction.

I think it is fair to say that this is the first time anyone has looked at a large sample of serial rapes in this quantitative way. We see these scales as tools for the quantitative analysis of rapes, which will open all kinds of new doors. For example, they should make it possible to sort out objectively, as opposed to clinically, the rapes of an individual rapist from among a larger set of rapes, using cluster analysis. This would also facilitate the "profiling" of offenders by investigators who are not highly trained criminal investigative analysts.

2. The extensive geocoding work was done for us by Mr. Ruben Rodriguez of the National Center for Missing and Exploited Children (NCMEC). We are very grateful for the time and effort he put into this project.

Very briefly, the third component of the study involves the question of taxonomy of serial rape. The behavioral science unit presently uses a four-part taxonomy developed by Groth (Groth, Burgess and Holstrom 1977) and modified by Hazelwood and Burgess to classify rapes. However, we are interested in seeing whether the more differentiated and sophisticated taxonomy being developed by Prentky and his colleagues (Prentky, Knight and Rosenberg 1988) can be transposed into a crime scene framework and hence made more useful to law enforcement officers.

Despite these theoretical interests, there is no doubt that the nature of the rape as it pertains to the pattern of offending manifest by the rapist lies at the core of our inquiry. It is our hope that the behavior of the rapist demonstrated during the rape will relate to the pattern of offenses, and through the pattern of offending, to the rapist's residential and employment fields of activity. It is this analysis that we currently seek to develop.

Our geographical data are being analyzed using MapInfo. We are, however, using MapInfo in ways that are generally not traditional in mapping. We are not intensively studying one city, as the Blocks are doing with Chicago, as Harries is doing with Baltimore, and as Rengert is doing with Philadelphia, but rather, we are creating geographical patterns that are without reference to the surface features of the geographical area being analyzed. We have begun to call this process "mapless mapping." In approaching geographical patterns from this cognitive perspective, we are able to analyze cases from all over the country without the accompanying street maps for each area. Rather, we work with the pattern, displaying latitudes and longitudes accurate to within inches, for every rape and every rapist residence and workplace.

We have created a matrix that allows for the calculation and display for each pattern of the distance of any given rape from the centroid of the pattern, from the first rape and from the rapist's residence. This matrix is a "mapless map": the map it represents exists on a grid of latitude and longitude, but in a space that is otherwise completely blank, with no representation of the earth's surface. The characteristics of the map, including the area and shape of the polygon formed by the rapes and the distances involved, have been transferred to SPSS and are being used in analyses that link the patterns to the data that describe the offender's behavior during the rape.

A number of interesting questions present themselves in light of this data that pertain solely to the geographical data, without regard to the issue of how it may relate to the taxonomic data or to the scales. First is the question that started the whole thing, directionality. As stated earlier, a number of people have discussed (LeBeau 1993) or proposed models for the spatial distribution patterns of the crimes of individual criminals, among them the Brantinghams (1981, 1984), Rengert and Wasilchick (1985, 1990) and, most recently, Canter and Larkin (1993). The most basic of these models is what Rengert refers to as the "uniform model"—Canter calls rapists who behave as per this model "marauders"—in which crimes are more or less uniformly distributed in a circle around the criminal's base of operations. This model is, in fact, used at the National Center for the Analysis of Violent Crime in the investigation of arson cases.

However, when the maps of serial rapes were examined, it became apparent that they were also characterized by a distinct sense of directionality. Over and over, a distinct pattern emerged that might be described as a "windshield wiper" or "pie slice" pattern. It appeared to represent a pattern of interest both practically, because of the implications it has for locating the rapist's residence given a group of rapes, and theoretically, because of the implications for cognitive mapping. Based on these observations, MapInfo was used to ascertain for each case whether or not the residence lay inside the pattern of offenses (the polygon formed by connecting the rapes). Interestingly, it appears that in over 75 percent of cases, the residence is not inside the pattern, and this is true whether just rapes or all known offender crimes are considered. While this represents a crude measure of directionality, efforts are under way to develop more expressive measures, and it is clear that this finding rejects the uniform model, at least for this set of offenses. It probably represents a pattern very different from Canter and Larkin's finding that 87 percent of their offenders operated in accordance with the circle hypothesis, but we cannot be sure until we apply the same measures used by Canter and Larkin to our data.

Another finding reported by Canter and Larkin suggests that the distance between offenses is correlated with the distance from the rapist's home—the farther he goes from home, the farther it is between offenses. We will be looking to see whether this finding can be replicated with our data.

Based on these preliminary observations, a number of other interesting possibilities have presented themselves. For instance, we can use the geodata to examine the distance from the residence to the closest rape, and see the size of the "safety zone" described by the Brantinghams. In our data, the mean distance from the residence to the closest rape is 2.7 miles, and it is not different by rapist type, increaser status (whether the rapist becomes increasingly violent), indoor or outdoor location of the rape, or whether the residence is inside or outside the rape polygon.

The mean distance from the residence to the first rape was 5.4 miles, so we can see that, on the average at least, the first rape is not the closest rape. As with closest distance, we have not so far been able to relate this distance to other variables of interest, such as rapist type.

However, one geographic variable is providing some possibly interesting results. The area of the polygon differs by increaser status, and so, not surprisingly, do the distance to the farthest rape and the distance to the average of all rapes; increasers (rapists who get more violent over time) cover larger areas. But distance to the closest rape does not differ by increaser status or any variable we have found so far.

Similarly, the area of the polygon is larger when the residence is inside it, but the distance to the closest rape and to the first rape are not different when the residence is inside vs. when it is outside. One would think this means that when the residence is inside the polygon, it tends to be near the edge, not in the middle, and a very preliminary look at our maps seems to indicate that this is true.

Based on these preliminary findings, we could take as a working hypothesis that how widely the rapist ranges may be a function of a number of variables, but his closest approach to home, the safety zone, is relatively constant.

One last geographic analysis may be worth mentioning. We were interested in whether a discriminant analysis could classify rapes as to whether they occurred indoors or outdoors, as there is some reason to believe that indoor vs. outdoor rapes may reflect fundamentally different rapist motivation. It will not surprise you to hear that the one group of scales that can classify rapes in this way is the one concerned with protection of rapist identity, with amount of rapist planning, and with opportunistic, spur-of-the-moment execution. The analysis accounts for 43 percent of the variance and classifies 83 percent of cases correctly. Finding nothing major on this front, we tried a more cognitive approach, looking at "his turf" vs. "her turf," but while this is an interesting thought, the variable seems unrelated to our scales.

As we undertake these different types of analyses, we are also trying to determine the potential relevance of our "mapless map" approach. Clearly, "mapless mapping" produces generalities that are true across geographical locations, and hence are not tied to the topography of any particular location. This is both the central strength and weakness of the approach. It is our perception, at this point anyway, that this approach creates generalizations about how people tend to move about in space and how their cognitive maps of the space around them influence their patterns of movement. Thus, it appears that we are then addressing the principles of cognitive mapping reflected in the tradition of Coucelis, Golledge and Rengert, not to mention E.C. Tolman. Perhaps Rengert's work on the spatial movements of burglars in Philadelphia has influenced us the most. Rengert holds that individuals, including criminals, probably tend to follow familiar routes, to move about in areas where they feel comfortable, and to move about in relation to "anchor points" or "foci" such as residence, workplace or criminal markets that are important to them.

Despite this apparent usefulness, it is also clear to us that "mapless mapping" can only take one so far. The cognitive schema is obviously influenced by local terrain. Once our results have been more developed, our plan, therefore, is to apply them to a single geographical area. We are currently in the process of acquiring the Baltimore base map, a very complete and accurate digitized map of Baltimore and surrounding counties. We will then apply our results to patterns of serial rape in this area. We hope this will allow us to relate our very abstract generalities to the local topography of this one particular area, and assess the significance of these two geographical components in the decision making of the serial rapist.

In closing, we should mention some of the analyses yet to be done. Still within the geographical data, there is the question of temporal sequencing, looking for regularities in the ways rapists space their rapes out over time. Obviously, all types of rapists may not do this in the same way. This analysis of autocorrelated data is being conducted by Dick McCleary, at the University of California in Irvine. Aside from predicting when and where the rapist might strike next, every police officer's dream, we would obviously also like to be able to say something about the probable location of the rapist's base of operations.

Finally, there will be the analyses of the other parts of our data and their relationship to the geographic variables. Will we be able to relate our taxonomy of rapist motivation (type) to differences in geographical pattern? Our first few passes at this have not been promising, except for increaser status. Will the taxonomy developed by Prentky and Knight prove workable, and even if it is workable, will it be more effective than our current system in relating to the geographic variables? We are looking forward to a comparison of empirical groupings of rapes created by cluster analysis with groupings based on existing taxonomies. In the fullness of time, we hope to have answers to some of these questions, but for now, this is how things stand.

REFERENCES

Brantingham, P.J., and P.L. Brantingham (1981). Notes on the geometry of crime. Pp. 27–54 in Brantingham, P.J., and P.L. Brantingham, *Environmental Criminology*. Beverly Hills: Sage.

——— (1984). *Patterns in Crime*. New York: Macmillan.

Canter, D., and P. Larkin (1993). The environmental range of serial rapists. *Journal of Environmental Psychology* 13:63–69.

Coucelis, H., R. Golledge, N. Gale, and W. Tobler (1987). Exploring the anchor point hypothesis of spatial cognition. *Journal of Environmental Psychology* 7:99–122.

Groth, N., A. Burgess and L. Holstrom (1977). Rape, power, anger, and sexuality. *American Journal of Psychiatry* 134:1239–1243.

Huff, J.O. (1984). Spatial aspects of residential search. Pp. 169–199 in W. Clark (ed.), *Modelling Housing Market Search*. New York: St. Martin's Press.

LeBeau, J.L. (1993). Four case studies illustrating the spatial-temporal analysis of serial rapists. *Police Studies* 15:124–145.

Prentky, R., R. Knight and R. Rosenberg (1988). Validation analyses on a taxonomic system for rapists: Disconfirmation and reconceptualization. Pp. 21–40 in R. Prentky and V. Quinsey (eds.), *Human Sexual Aggression: Current Perspectives*. (Annals, 528). New York: New York Academy of Sciences.

Rengert, G., and J. Wasilchick (1985). *Suburban Burglary: A Time and Place for Everything*. Springfield, Ill.: Charles C. Thomas.

Rengert, G., and J. Wasilchick (1990). *Space, time and crime: Ethnographic insights into residential burglary*. Report submitted to the U.S. Department of Justice, National Institute of Justice, Office of Justice Programs.

Warren, J.I., R. Reboussin, R. Hazelwood, and J. Wright (1991). Prediction of rapist type and violence from verbal, physical and sexual scales. *Journal of Interpersonal Violence* 6:55–67.

Chapter 7

Overview:
Multivariate Spatial Profiles as a Tool in Crime Investigation[1]

D. Kim Rossmo
School of Criminology
Simon Fraser University
Vancouver Police Department

INTRODUCTION

"Interview the subjects, what they'll tell you is, is the thing that was really appealing to them was the hunt, the hunt and trying to look for the vulnerable victim" (Nova 1992).

Clues derived from the locations of violent serial crimes, including serial murder, rape and arson, can be of significant assistance to law enforcement. Such locations include encounter or apprehension sites, murder scenes and body or property dump sites. This information allows police departments to focus their investigative activities, geographically prioritize suspects and concentrate saturation or directed patrolling efforts in those zones where the criminal predator is most likely to be active.

The process whereby the probable spatial behavior of the offender is derived from the information and context of the locations of the crime sites is termed *geographic profiling*. This form of analysis has both subjective and qualitative dimensions and is related to the broader investigative strategy of criminal or psychological profiling.

Geographic profiling is concerned with the analysis of spatial behavioral patterns. A variety of techniques exist for such an analysis, including distance to crime research, demographical analysis, centrographic analysis, point-pattern analysis, point-spread analysis, crime-site residual analysis, spatial-temporal ordering, directional analysis, and criminal geographic targeting (Rossmo 1994).

Criminal geographic targeting (CGT) appears to be a particularly useful technique for the needs of police investigators attempting to solve complex serial crimes. By examining the spatial data connected to a series of crime sites, the criminal-geographic-targeting methodological model generates a three-dimensional probability surface, represented as an isopleth map, that indicates those areas most likely to be associated to the offender—home, work site, social venue, or travel routes.

Based on the Brantingham and Brantingham (1981:chap. 1) model for crime site selection, and the routine activities approach (Felson 1986), criminal geographic targeting was developed from a perspective informed by the theory

1. An earlier version of this paper was presented at the seminar on Environmental Criminology and Crime Analysis, Miami, Fla., on May 28, 1993.

and practice of environmental criminology. In this sense, it goes beyond centrographic analysis, though the formulation of the model owes much to earlier studies in the geography of crime. Parameters are empirically derived from specific serial-crime geographic research, and the methodology is sensitive to the target/victim opportunity backcloth, landscape issues, anisotropic spaces, and problems of spatial "outliers."

SERIAL MURDER INVESTIGATION

Investigative Difficulties

The nature of serial murder creates unique problems for law enforcement, requiring special police responses and investigative strategies. It has been suggested that there are only three ways to solve a crime: (1) via a confession, (2) through a witness, and (3) by using physical evidence (Klockars 1983:134–135). Traditionally, the search for witnesses, suspects and evidence has followed a path, originating from the victim and the crime scene, outward. Most homicides are cleared for the simple reason that they involve people who know each other, and the process of offender identification is often only one of suspect elimination.[2]

Such obvious connections rarely exist in cases of serial murder. The lack of any relationship between the victim and the offender makes these crimes difficult to solve. Working outward from the victim during the investigation of stranger homicides is a difficult task. The alternative, then, is to work inward, trying to establish some type of link between potential suspects and the victim or the crime scene.

Such a process requires the determination and delineation of a likely group of potential suspects. This effort typically involves the inspection of those parties with relevant criminal records, the accumulation of intelligence, and the collection of suspect tips from members of the public. Because these efforts can produce a large number of potential suspects, often numbering into the hundreds and even thousands, problems with information overload usually develop.

In the still unsolved Green River Killer case, for example, 18,000 suspect names have been collected, but as of February 1992, the police have had the time and resources to check out only some 6,000 of these. The police have collected 8,000 tangible items of evidence from the crime scenes, and a single television special on the case generated 3,500 tips (Montgomery 1992). The Yorkshire Ripper case had, by the time it was solved, 268,000 names in the nominal index. The police had initiated 115,000 actions and taken 31,000 statements. Up to 1,000 letters were received daily from the public, and a total of 5.4 million vehicle registration numbers were recorded by investigators (Doney 1990:101–102).

Corollaries to this problem include the strains placed on police resources by too many suspects and too much information, and the high costs involved in such extensive, long-term investigations. Green River task force costs were, up to early 1992, approximately $20 million (Montgomery 1992), while the Yorkshire Ripper investigation involved over 5 million hours of police time, at a cost of 4 million pounds (1981 figures) (Doney 1990:102).

It is also important for police detectives to know which murders are connected and which ones are not, so that information between related cases can be collated and compared.[3] In some cases, particularly those involving high-risk victims, the authorities may not even be aware that a serial murderer is operating within their jurisdiction.

With mobile killers who do not commit their crimes in a single area, the problem can become much worse. When a criminal investigation has to cross jurisdictional boundaries, issues of coordination, cooperation and competition

2. Boyd (1988) found that 80 percent of convicted murderers in Canada had killed either family members or acquaintances. It should be realized, however, that the arrest of the offender, a prerequisite for conviction, is more likely to occur in those cases where a close relationship exists between the killer and the victim.

3. See Egger (1990:156–158) for a discussion of this problem in the Henry Lee Lucas investigation.

arise. This "lack of sharing or coordination of investigative information relating to unsolved murders and to the lack of adequate networking among law enforcement agencies" has been termed *linkage blindness* (Egger 1984:348). This problem can even occur within a single police organization, if it is large enough. Such an oversight occurred in the early part of the Son of Sam case, when David Berkowitz killed his first victims in different police precincts within New York City (Bufton 1993:8–9; Leyton 1986:chap. 5).

Several other investigative difficulties exist that complicate efforts to link and solve serial murders and to identify and apprehend the killer(s) (Egger 1990:177–179; Holmes and De Burger 1988:112–121, 148–154; James 1991:1–4). These problems include the following: (1) the intense public, media and political pressure surrounding such cases; (2) the learning process experienced by organized offenders as they become "practiced" at killing; (3) the false confessions from unbalanced people attracted by the publicity; (4) the possibility of copycat murders occurring; and (5) the personnel and coordination issues (especially when multiple agencies are involved).

Investigative Responses

In efforts to overcome the investigative obstacles faced during serial murder cases, a variety of law enforcement strategies have been developed over the past few years (Egger 1990:180–198). One of the most important responses has been the effort to create systems of information management, methods of prioritizing potential suspects so that the investigation can proceed in the most effective and efficient manner possible. Proper scrutiny of suspects, in the effort to work backward to the victim, is a difficult and time-consuming process. Comprehensive interrogations of suspects, detailed interviews of suspect associates (who may be witnesses, whether they know it or not), and thorough searches for and analyses of physical evidence consume valuable and limited resources. By using a prioritization methodology, the comprehensiveness of the investigative approach can be tailored to the priority rating of the individual suspect. By focusing on the most probable suspects, the identification of the offender, all else being equal, is more likely to occur sooner.

Criminal or psychological profiling is one of the primary investigative tools used to prioritize suspects in serial murder cases. Profiling seeks to develop a behavioral composite—a social and psychological assessment—of the perpetrator of certain types of crimes. This process is based on the premise that the proper interpretation of crime scene evidence can indicate the personality type of the individual(s) who committed the offense. Certain personality types exhibit similar behavioral patterns, and knowledge of these patterns can assist in the investigation of the crime and of potential suspects. Criminal profiling is also used to perform linkage analysis. In the United States, investigative support, research and training in this area is provided by the Behavioral Science Unit at the FBI Academy. The Royal Canadian Mounted Police's Violent Crime Analysis Section provides a similar service in Canada.

The major response to the problem of linkage blindness has been the establishment of centralized investigative networks such as the Violent Criminal Apprehension Program, developed at the National Center for the Analysis of Violent Crime, in Quantico, Va. Some states have their own computerized investigative systems, including the Homicide Assessment and Lead Tracking system in New York, the Homicide Investigation Tracking System in Washington, and the Indiana Criminal Apprehension Assistance Program. Canada has, through the RCMP, the Violent Crime Linkage Analysis System. In Britain, Scotland Yard uses the Home Office Large Major Inquiry System for managing large volumes of investigative case data (Doney 1990).

Geographic Analysis in the Investigation of Serial Murder

In addition to psychological profiling and computerized linkage analysis systems, other creative investigative methodologies have been advanced in recent years to assist in efforts to solve cases of serial murder. Still others are currently being developed and experimented with by police agencies and universities. One of the more promising research directions is in the area of geographical pattern analysis (Egger 1990:197). This enterprise involves the examination of spatial information, derived from the geographic locations of the crime sites, as a basis for efforts to find or track the repetitive killer.[4]

There have been only a few documented cases where a geographical analysis was applied to a serial murder investigation. During 1977, in an effort to focus the Hillside Strangler investigation, the Los Angeles Police Department (LAPD) attempted to determine the most likely location of the scene of the homicides. It was correctly suspected that the actual murders had occurred in the residence of one of the serial killers. The police knew where the victims had been apprehended and where their bodies had been dumped, and the distances between those two points (Gates and Shah 1992:163–167). Computer experts Bill Herrman and Carl Holt, both retired LAPD officers, viewed the problem in terms of Venn diagrams. The center of each circle represented victim availability, the circumference represented capacity, and the radius represented ability (Holt, personal communication, Feb. 22, 1993).

From this perspective, they developed a technique using vectors drawn from the point where the victims were abducted to the location where their bodies were found. The vectors were then resolved down to a common radius, the circle of which encompassed an area they called the "sphere of concern." The resulting circle, however, with a radius of approximately one mile and an area of over three square miles, was large.

The LAPD saturated this zone with 200 police officers in an attempt to find the murderers (Gates and Shah 1992:166). While they were not successful, it is possible that the heavy police presence inhibited the killers and prompted murderer Kenneth Bianchi's move from Los Angeles to Bellingham, Wash. (Holt, personal communication, Feb. 22, 1993). The location of the center of the "sphere of concern," the LAPD later found out, was not far from co-murderer Angelo Buono's automobile upholstery shop-cum-residence (Gates and Shah 1992:166).

Geographic techniques were also applied in the Yorkshire Ripper investigation. With the murders still unsolved after five-and-a-half years, Her Majesty's Inspector of Constabulary Lawrence Byford implemented a case review process (Kind 1987a). An advisory group composed of senior police officers and a home office forensic scientist met in December 1980 to examine the investigation (Doney 1990:103; Kind 1987a:385–386). Detectives had become divided over the issue of the killer's residence. One school of thought, led by the chief investigating officer, proposed that the Ripper was from the Sunderland area, while other investigators thought he was a local man. After an intensive investigative review, the Byford advisory team came to the latter conclusion.

To help test this deduction, they applied two "navigational metrical tests" to the spatial and temporal data associated to the crimes (Kind 1987a:388–390). The first test involved the calculation of the center of gravity (spatial mean) for the 17 crimes (13 murders and four assaults) believed to be linked to the Yorkshire Ripper. The second test consisted of plotting time of offense against length of day (approximated by month of year). The rationale behind this approach had its basis in the theory that the killer would not be willing to attack late at night if his return journey to home was too far.

The first navigational test resulted in the finding that the center of gravity for the Ripper attacks lay near Bradford. The second test determined that the later attacks were those located in the West Yorkshire cities of Leeds and Bradford. Both tests therefore supported the team's original hypothesis that the killer was a local man. The advisory group's interim report recommended that "a special team of high-grade detectives be dedicated to enquiries in the Bradford area" (Kind 1987a:390).

Three weeks later, in January 1981, Peter William Sutcliffe was arrested by two patrol officers in Sheffield. Sutcliffe resided in the district of Heaton in the city of Bradford. While the resolution of the case occurred independent of the advisory group's interim report, the recommendation to focus on the Bradford area was valid and might have, if made sooner, led to an earlier case closure, resulting in fewer deaths (Kind 1987a:392).

4. Research has also been conducted on the geography of other types of serial violent criminals, including serial rapists (Canter and Larkin 1993; LeBeau 1987a, 1987b, 1992), and serial arsonists (Icove and Crisman 1975).

Newton and Newton (1985) applied what they termed *geoforensic analysis* to a series of unsolved female homicides that occurred in Fort Worth, Texas, from 1983 to 1985. They found that localized serial murder or rape tends to form place-time patterns different from those seen in "normal" criminal violence. The unsolved Fort Worth murders were analyzed by employing both quantitative (areal associations, crime-site connections, centrographic analysis) and qualitative (landscape analysis) techniques.

Newton and Swoope (1987) also applied geoforensic techniques in a retrospective analysis of the Hillside Strangler case. Different geographic centers (see below) were calculated from the coordinates of the locations of various types of crime sites. They discriminated between points of fatal encounter, body or car dump sites, and victim's residences, and found that the geographic center of the body dump sites most accurately predicted the location of the residence of murderer Angelo Buono. A search radius (circumscribing an area around the geographic center in which the killers were most likely to be found) was also calculated, the range of which decreased with the addition of the spatial information provided by each new murder.

When they plotted these locations on a map of Los Angeles, Newton and Swoope detected what they termed a *coal-sack effect*—the presence of an area surrounding the home of Buono in which no crimes were known to have occurred. This appeared as a conspicuous void in the pattern of points that represented the crime sites of the Hillside Strangler. They suggest that the discovery of such a phenomenon, presumably resulting from a desire on the part of the killer to avoid drawing attention too close to home, should alert police to the investigative significance of the area.

Rogers, Craig and Anderson (1991) discuss the potential application of geographic information systems (GIS's) to the investigation of serial murder. Since a GIS can store geographic attributes and integrate spatial and other data for analytic purposes, it could assist in the reduction of linkage blindness and help identify crime series. They quote from a 1975 International Association of Chiefs of Police (IACP 1975:17) report:

> Geographically coded information from police records can be used to detect crime trends and patterns, confirm the presence of [people] within geographic areas, and identify areas for patrol unit concentration.

They also suggest that it might be possible to identify serial murder solvability factors, using GIS, through retrospective analysis of known cases. Such knowledge might then assist investigators in their efforts to apprehend criminal offenders in unsolved murders.

Geographic Profiling

For any violent crime to occur, there must have been an intersection in both time and place between the victim and the offender (Felson 1987:912). How did this happen? What were the antecedents? What do the spatial elements of the crime tell us about the offender and his or her actions? What are the hunting patterns of such killers? Efforts can be made to understand the spatial behavior of such offenders through information derived from known crime site locations, their geographic connections and the surrounding areas. This approach is known as geographic profiling and has both quantitative and qualitative dimensions (Rossmo 1993).

Geographic profiling examines the target location patterns of serial violent criminals in an effort to determine spatial information about the offender—in particular, residential location. This process is done from a perspective informed by theoretical principles and practical ideas developed in studies within the areas of environmental criminology[5] and the geography of crime. Such an approach suggests the need to be aware, at a microspatial level, of the dimensions of the offender, the victim, the crime, and the environment.

5. "Environmental criminologists set out to use the geographic imagination in concert with the sociological imagination to describe, understand and control criminal events" (Brantingham and Brantingham 1981:21). The concern with the geographic environment, and a change in focus from

Since a criminal profile provides insight into the probable motivation, behavior and lifestyle of the offender, the two profiling processes act in tandem to help investigators develop a "picture" of the person responsible for the crimes in question. The geographic profile will therefore be optimized if a psychological profile has first been completed.

Also, since geographic profiling is based on an analysis of crime site locations, a linkage analysis is a necessary prerequisite to determine which crimes are part of the same series and should be included in the development of the profile.[6] While the inclusion of an unrelated crime or the exclusion of a connected crime is not necessarily debilitating, the product of the profile is dependent on the quality of the initial information used for the analysis.

It should be noted that not all types of offenders or categories of crime can be geographically profiled. In appropriate cases, however, such a spatial analysis can produce very practical results from the police perspective. There are a variety of ways that geographic information about the offender can assist the investigation, including the prioritization of suspects by address or area, the direction of patrol saturation efforts, and the establishment of computerized database search parameters.

HUNTING PATTERNS

The Brantingham and Brantingham Model

The locations where crimes occur are not completely random, but instead often have a degree of underlying spatial structure. As chaotic as some crimes may appear to be, there is often a rationality influencing the geography of their occurrence. Using an environmental criminology perspective, Brantingham and Brantingham (1981:chap. 1) have developed a model to assist in the understanding of the processes affecting the geography of crime.

Crimes tend to occur in space at those locations where suitable (in terms of profit and risk) victims or targets are found by offenders as they move throughout their activity spaces. As an offender travels between his home, workplace and social activity sites, his or her activity space (composed of these locations and their connecting paths) describes an awareness space that forms part of a larger mental map—an "image of the city" built upon experience and knowledge.

Brantingham and Brantingham (1981:chap. 1) suggest that the process of criminal target selection is a dynamic one. Crimes occur in those locations where suitable targets are overlapped by the offender's awareness space (figure 1). Offenders may then move outward, following a distance decay function, in their search for more targets. Search pattern probabilities can be modeled by a Pareto function, originating from the locations and routes that compose the activity space, and then decreasing with distance away from the activity space. There may also be a "buffer zone," centered around the criminal's home, within which the offender sees targets as being too risky to victimize because of their proximity to his or her residence (cf. the "coal-sack effect," Newton and Swoope 1987).

An awareness of certain geographic concepts and terms can help in the analysis of criminal target patterns and in understanding the model of crime site selection proposed by Brantingham and Brantingham (1981:chap. 1, 1984:chap. 12). Perhaps one of the most basic of these heuristics is the nearness principle, known in psychology as the least-effort principle (Zipf 1950). All else being equal, a person who is "given various possibilities for action... will select the one requiring the least expenditure of effort" (Reber 1985:400). This maxim describes a great deal

---

the offender to the criminal event, distinguish environmental criminology from the earlier ecological work of the Chicago School (Brantingham and Brantingham 1981:18). This also represented a shift to a uniquely criminological perspective.

6. In certain cases, where the crimes are unusual or the modus operandi distinct, a formal linkage analysis is not necessary. The Dallas Eyeball Murderer, operating during the period from late 1990 to 1991, surgically removed his prostitute victims' eyeballs before he dumped them on residential streets (Hollandsworth 1993). Authorities immediately made the obvious connection between the bizarre killings.

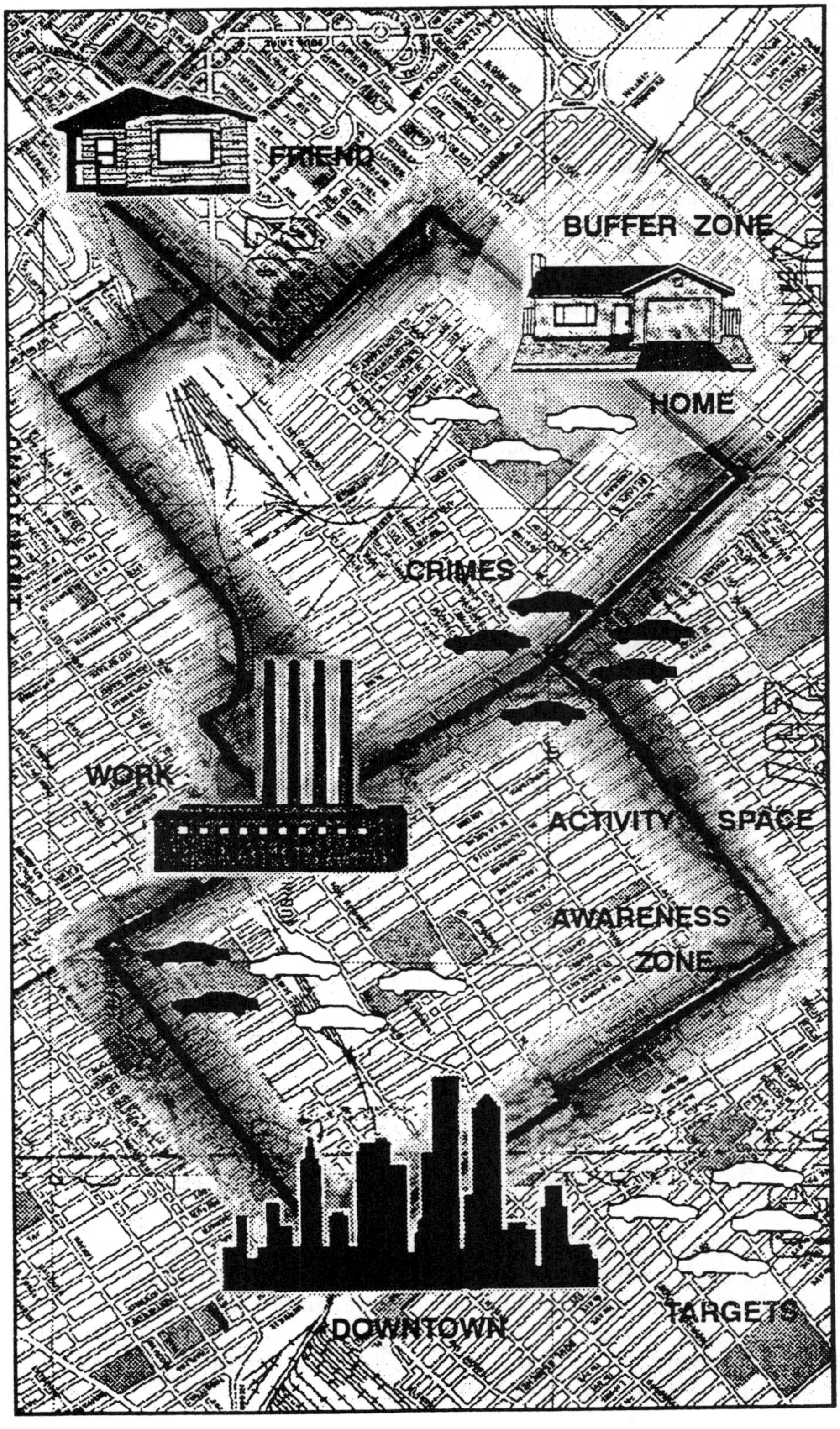

Fig. 1
Crimes occur where suitable targets overlap the offender's awareness space

about human spatial action, but it is important to remember that many factors come into play in decision making and choice behavior (Cornish and Clarke 1986; Luce 1959; Tversky and Kahneman 1981).

The least-effort principle, as applied to geography, means that when multiple destinations of equal desirability are available, all else being equal, the closest one will be chosen. The determination of "closest," however, can be somewhat problematic. Isotropic spaces, exhibiting equal physical properties in all directions, are rarely found within the human geographical experience. Instead, people are usually confronted with anisotropic surfaces where movement is easier in some directions or along certain routes, and harder along others. People travel through networks of roads and highways by "wheel distance" (Rhodes and Conly 1981), rather than by euclidean distance.

Other factors are just as important as physical space. Macrolevel travel choices are usually based on minimizing time and money expenditures. Air flight bookings are made by considering connections, time and cost—not actual distances covered. Income and socioeconomic status thus have an important influence on spatial behavior, as a shortage or lack of financial resources will constrain choices and determine which options are seen as being viable.

Microlevel movement within cities is similarly affected; urban areas are primarily anisotropic, often conforming to some variation of a grid or Manhattan layout (Lowe and Moryadas 1975:15–17), with dissimilar traffic flows along different routes. As it is not just a question of minimizing distance, but of reducing time, effort and costs, the geographic layout of the city, the offender's modes of transportation, and any significant mental or physical barrier must be considered in the spatial analysis of crime patterns.

The subjective psychological perception of distance is just as critical as the objective physical space involved. An individual's perception of distance is influenced by several factors, including the following (Stea 1969): (1) the relative attractiveness of origins and destinations, (2) the number and types of barriers separating points, (3) the familiarity with routes, (4) the actual physical distance, and (5) the attractiveness of routes. Cognitive images may vary in relation to a person's biography, social class, geographical location, and environment; however, most people's mental maps have much in common. Humans tend to perceive things in a like fashion. Lynch (1960:47–48), for example, states that image composition is based on five elements: (1) paths (routes of travel that tend to dominate most people's images of cities, such as highways or railways); (2) edges (boundaries of lines that help to organize cognitive maps, such as rivers or railroads); (3) districts (subareas with recognizable unifying characteristics, possessing well-established cores but fuzzy borders, such as financial districts or skid rows); (4) nodes (intense foci of activity, such as major intersections, railroad stations or corner stores); and (5) landmarks (symbols that may not be entered but are still used for orientation, such as signs, buildings or trees).

Criminal or psychological profiling can assist in determining the relationships between a suspect's personality, lifestyle and activities, and target patterns. Disorganized offenders, for example, will tend to strike closer to the nodes and routes that compose their activity spaces, while organized offenders will be more likely to expand the boundaries of their awareness space and hunt in areas located farther away from home. Additionally, the size and complexity of their awareness space will probably be greater than that found for more disorganized offenders.

Studies of the Journey to Crime

The journey-to-crime literature contains numerous studies of crime trips and has examined a variety of offense types for several North American and European cities. The influence of additional variables, usually grouped into offender and offense characteristics, is also often explored. Offender characteristics have included sex, race, age, prior criminal experience, and nature of home area; offense variables have covered crime type, target area attributes, and perceived level of potential criminal gain (Baldwin and Bottoms 1976; Capone and Nichols 1975; LeBeau 1987a; Nichols 1980; Reppetto 1974; Rhodes and Conly 1981).

Journey-to-crime research results are usually reported in one of three manners: mean crime trip distances, medial circles or mobility triangles. Studies of the first type compute the arithmetic average for the distance traveled by offenders from home to offense location. Some researchers have used the geometric mean to avoid the distortion of extreme values (LeBeau 1987a:133). Others have provided additional descriptive statistics, such as the mode (Rhodes and Conly 1981:179), maximum crime-trip distance (Canter and Larkin 1993:67), range (Turner 1969), and directional information (Rengert and Wasilchick 1985:68–74).

The major problem with the use of the mean or mode is caused by the limited information a single descriptive measure provides. The mean is also susceptible to the influence of outliers and may say very little about the typical crime trip. And since an average crime-trip distance is produced from an aggregation or series of trips, typically involving several offenders, it might not actually describe any one type of criminal very well.

Studies of the second sort provide their results in the form of a given radial distance, which defines a circle, within which a certain percentage of the offenses were found to have occurred. For example, in a study of robbery within Boston, Reppetto (1976) found that 90 percent of the offenses occurred within 1.5 miles of the offender's residence. Such results are equivalent to the median for the specific case of 50 percent. Like the first approach, this method supplies only a single measure of the nature of crime journeys, says little of the typical crime trip, and says almost nothing about the cases that fall outside the artificially established radius.

Studies of the third type employ some form of mobility triangle to examine the question of crime location. Mobility triangles were first used by Burgess (1925) to describe those situations where offense location and offender residence were in different neighborhoods; this was in contrast to neighborhood triangles, in which the crime took place in the offender's home area.

Subsequent developments of the mobility triangle concept used various possible combinations of crime scene, offender residence and victim residence spatial conjunction (Amir 1971; Normandeau 1968). Crime-journey research findings are often presented in the form of the percentage of offenses that could be described by the neighborhood triangle designation (Amir 1971; Normandeau 1968; Ploughman and Ould 1990; Rand 1986).

One difficulty with the mobility/neighborhood triangle approach centers on the question of how the research defines the concept of "neighborhood." Most studies have used census tract delineations, a highly problematic assumption (see Brantingham and Brantingham 1984:215–219). Census tracts are only rough approximations of neighborhoods, and more sophisticated concepts of mobility, routine activities and target selection are available (for example, Brantingham and Brantingham 1981; Felson 1986).

The most useful presentation of crime-trip data has been the graphical curve approach that shows the number of trips for several different radii (for example, half-mile increments) from the offender's residence (see, for example, Capone and Nichols 1976:206–207; Rhodes and Conly 1981:179; also Baldwin and Bottoms 1976:chap. 3). Such graphs or tables allow for an inspection of the distance-decay function and a fuller understanding of the nature of crime journeys, and provide a greater level of information for further analysis.

Several common findings exist in the journey-to-crime literature. These are reviewed in table 1, and include the following:

- Most crimes occur in relatively close proximity to the home of the offender (McIver 1981:24–25). "While criminals are mobile, they don't seem to go very far in committing a crime. A majority of crimes appear to take place within a mile of the criminal's residence" (McIver 1981:22). Time is seen as a commodity, and almost all people act in a manner to conserve its use (Brantingham and Brantingham 1984:344; LeBeau 1992:125–126; Rengert and Wasilchick 1985:20; Rhodes and Conly 1981:172). Such a pattern is consistent with the nearness and least-effort principles.

- Crime trips follow a distance-decay function, with the number of crime occurrences decreasing with distance from the offender's residence (Brantingham and Brantingham 1984:344–346; Capone and Nichols

1975; Rhodes and Conly 1981:178). This is a pattern very similar to that seen exhibited by other forms of human movement (Jakle, Brunn and Roseman 1976:105–109).

- Juvenile offenders are most likely to commit their crimes within their home areas, and adult offenders possess a greater degree of mobility than do juvenile offenders (Baldwin and Bottoms 1976:79–80; Gabor and Gottheil 1984:270).

- Differences in crime-trip distances have been found consistently between offense types. Violent offenses, for example, usually occur closer to the offender's residence than do property offenses (Baldwin and Bottoms 1976:79–80; Gabor and Gottheil 1984:270; LeBeau 1987a; Rhodes and Conly 1981:169–179).

- Most cities contain high-crime-rate neighborhoods, and the existence and arrangement of these areas influence the patterning of journeys to crime (Gabor and Gottheil 1984:270; Rhodes and Conly 1981:171, 183–188).

In addition, there is a possibility that as an offender's criminal career matures, journey-to-crime distances lengthen and hunting-area size increases (Brantingham and Brantingham 1981:45–46; Canter and Larkin 1993:68). The FBI believes that the first murder in a serial killer series is the one most likely to be closest to the offender's home. This suggests the importance of a temporal dimension in the analysis of spatial crime patterns (see Kind 1987a; LeBeau 1992; Newton and Newton 1985; Newton and Swoope 1987).

Table 1
Common Findings in Journey-to-Crime Research

SOURCE	CRIME	LOCATION	YEAR	CRIME TRIP DISTANCE	COMMENTS
Amir (1971)	rape	Philadelphia	1958-1960	72% within home area (5 blocks)	mobility triangles
Baldwin & Bottoms (1976)	property crime	Sheffield	1966	47% < 1 mi; 69% < 2 mi	
Baldwin & Bottoms (1976)	breaking offence	Sheffield	1966	54.4% < 1 mi; 74.8% < 2 mi	
Baldwin & Bottoms (1976)	larceny offence	Sheffield	1966	51.9% < 1 mi; 74.3% < 2 mi	
Baldwin & Bottoms (1976)	taking & driving offence	Sheffield	1966	45% < 1 mi; 63.3% < 2 mi	
Boggs (1965)	homicide & assault	St. Louis		most likely within residential area	
Boggs (1965)	rape & robbery	St. Louis		most likely within nonresidential area	
Bullock (1955)	homicide	Houston	1945-1949	40% < 1 block; 57% < 0.4 mi; 74% < 2 mi	
Canter & Larkin (1993)	serial rape	London area	1980s	1.53 mi (minimum crime trip distance)	87% noncommuters
Capone & Nichols (1975)	armed robbery	Miami	1971	23% < 1 mi; 59% < 3mi	
Capone & Nichols (1975)	unarmed robbery	Miami	1971	36% < 1 mi; 75% < 3mi	
Chappell (1965)	burglary	England	1965	50%/85% < 1 mi (under 21/14 yrs)	
Erlanson (1946)	rape	Chicago		87% within home neighbourhood	home neighbourhood = police precinct
Gabor & Gottheil (1984)	total of 10 crimes	Ottawa	1981	1.22 mi (70.5% in-towners)	out-of-towners, NFAs, & n/k excluded
Gabor & Gottheil (1984)	homicide	Ottawa	1981	0.54 mi (71% in-towners)	out-of-towners, NFAs, & n/k excluded
Gabor & Gottheil (1984)	rape & indecent assault	Ottawa	1981	1.43 mi (90% in-towners)	out-of-towners, NFAs, & n/k excluded
Gabor & Gottheil (1984)	armed robbery	Ottawa	1981	1.22 mi (80% in-towners)	out-of-towners, NFAs, & n/k excluded
Gabor & Gottheil (1984)	unarmed robbery	Ottawa	1981	0.62 mi (55% in-towners)	out-of-towners, NFAs, & n/k excluded
Gabor & Gottheil (1984)	assault	Ottawa	1981	1.33 mi (90% in-towners)	out-of-towners, NFAs, & n/k excluded
Gabor & Gottheil (1984)	break & enter	Ottawa	1981	0.35 mi (65% in-towners)	out-of-towners, NFAs, & n/k excluded
Gabor & Gottheil (1984)	auto theft	Ottawa	1981	1.24 mi (70% in-towners)	out-of-towners, NFAs, & n/k excluded
Gabor & Gottheil (1984)	theft over $200	Ottawa	1981	1.74 mi (90% in-towners)	out-of-towners, NFAs, & n/k excluded
Gabor & Gottheil (1984)	theft under $200	Ottawa	1981	1.19 mi (60% in-towners)	out-of-towners, NFAs, & n/k excluded
Gabor & Gottheil (1984)	cheque fraud	Ottawa	1981	1.74 mi (35% in-towners)	out-of-towners, NFAs, & n/k excluded
LeBeau (1987a)	rape	San Diego	1971-1975	2.5 mi	geometric mean; Manhattan geometry
LeBeau (1987a)	serial rape	San Diego	1971-1975	1.77 mi	geometric mean; Manhattan geometry
LeBeau (1987a)	nonserial rape	San Diego	1971-1975	3.5 mi	geometric mean
LeBeau (1992)	serial rape & related crime	San Diego	1971-1975	25.88/1.89/0.52/3.33 km (4 serial rapists)	attempts, sex-related crimes, & burglaries
Normandeau (1968)	robbery	Philadelphia		1.57 mi; 33% within home census tract	mobility triangles
Pope (1980)	burglary	6 CA urban areas		52% < 1 mi	
Pyle (1974)	rape	Akron	1972	1.34 mi	
Pyle (1976)	crime against the person	Cleveland		61% within home census tract	
Pyle (1976)	property crime	Cleveland		48% within home census tract	
Rand (1986)	total of 8 crimes	Philadelphia	1968-1975	30.77% within home census tract	juvenile offenders; mobility triangles
Rand (1986)	criminal homicide	Philadelphia	1968-1975	53.13% within home census tract	juvenile offenders; mobility triangles
Rand (1986)	rape	Philadelphia	1968-1975	53.13% within home census tract	juvenile offenders; mobility triangles

Table 1
Continued

Rand (1986)	robbery	Philadelphia	1968-1975	31.87% within home census tract	juvenile offenders; mobility triangles
Rand (1986)	aggravated assault	Philadelphia	1968-1975	38.60% within home census tract	juvenile offenders; mobility triangles
Rand (1986)	burglary	Philadelphia	1968-1975	42.02% within home census tract	juvenile offenders; mobility triangles
Rand (1986)	larceny	Philadelphia	1968-1975	14.77% within home census tract	juvenile offenders; mobility triangles
Rand (1986)	vehicle theft	Philadelphia	1968-1975	23.05% within home census tract	juvenile offenders; mobility triangles
Rand (1986)	simple assault	Philadelphia	1968-1975	39.41% within home census tract	juvenile offenders; mobility triangles
Reiss (1967)	Part I & Part II Offences	Seattle	1965	not likely to be in home census tract	
Rengert & Wasilchick (1985)	suburban burglary	Delaware Co.		52% < 5 mi; 71%/40% un/employed	work & recreation site directional biases
Reppetto (1974)	burglary	Boston		0.5 mi	
Reppetto (1976)	robbery	Boston		0.6 mi; 90% < 1.5 mi	
Reppetto (1976)	residential burglary	Boston		0.5 mi; 93% < 1.5 mi	
Rhodes & Conly (1981)	rape	Washington, DC	1974	1.15 mi; 0.73 mi median; 62% < 1 mi	wheel distance
Rhodes & Conly (1981)	robbery	Washington, DC	1974	2.10 mi; 1.62 mi median; 37% < 1 mi	wheel distance
Rhodes & Conly (1981)	burglary	Washington, DC	1974	1.62 mi; 1.20 mi median; 47% < 1 mi	wheel distance
Suttles (1968)		Chicago		65% within home area	juvenile offenders
Topalin (1992)	serial rape	London area	1980s	2.81 mi; 20% in or close to home	0-27 mi range; first convicted offence
Turner (1969)	assault & vandalism	Philadelphia	1960	0.4 mi; 75% < 1 mi; 87% < 2 mi	0-23 mi range; juvenile offenders
Waller & Okihiro (1978)	burglary	Toronto		50% < 0.5 mi	
White (1932)	violent crime	Indianapolis	1930	0.85 mi	
White (1932)	property crime	Indianapolis	1930	1.72 mi	
White (1932)	manslaughter	Indianapolis	1930	0.11 mi	
White (1932)	rape	Indianapolis	1930	1.52 mi	
White (1932)	robbery	Indianapolis	1930	2.14 mi	
White (1932)	assault	Indianapolis	1930	0.91 mi	
White (1932)	burglary	Indianapolis	1930	1.76 mi	
White (1932)	embezzlement	Indianapolis	1930	2.79 mi	
White (1932)	auto theft	Indianapolis	1930	3.43 mi	
White (1932)	grand larceny	Indianapolis	1930	1.53 mi	
White (1932)	petty larceny	Indianapolis	1930	1.42 mi	
Wolfgang (1958)	homicide	Philadelphia		50%+ within home of offender or victim	

Note: Unless otherwise specified, the figures in the Crime Trip Distance column refer to mean journey to crime distance.

Hunting and Target Pattern Types

Most commentaries on geographic categorizations of serial murder have been descriptive (Egger 1990:26–27; Hickey 1991:17, 78–81, 132–138; Holmes and De Burger 1988:49, 54, 73). A serial murder spatial taxonomy that moves from empirical to theoretical description must incorporate at least the following three elements: (1) the activity space of the offender, (2) the changes over time in that activity space, and (3) the hunting style (in relation to the activity space) of the offender. These, in conjunction with each other, define the target pattern types.

The first step in the process of constructing such a taxonomy is the development of relevant categories for both activity spaces and hunting styles. One of the purposes of this exercise is the identification of those situations where an analysis of the relationship between the offender activity space and the crime location is appropriate. This allows those cases where such an analysis is impossible or redundant to be eliminated.

For example, the peripatetic movements of Henry Lee Lucas produce such a random pattern that little can be derived from his target sites. In effect, he did not have a residence to relate to the locations of his crimes. John Wayne Gacy Jr. buried most of his victims under his own house, making the form of examination proposed here redundant. And commuting offenders, who live in one area and commit their crimes in another, may not be amenable to this type of analysis.[7] It is important to determine the limits of geographic profiling, so as to prevent inappropriate application.

Target Backcloth

The locations of suitable victims may not be uniformly distributed within the killer's hunting areas. The Brantingham and Brantingham model implies that the structure of this distribution is important for an understanding of the geographic arrangement of crime sites. The target backcloth is the spatial and temporal distribution of "suitable" (as seen from the offender's perspective) crime targets or victims across the physical landscape. The availability of such targets might vary significantly according to neighborhood, area or even city, and victim selection opportunities may also be influenced by time, weekday and seasonality (Brantingham and Brantingham 1984:104–106, 158, 361–363).

The availability and locations of suitable targets play a key role in the determination of where and when offenses will occur. Victim selections that are nonrandom or based on specific and rare traits will require more searching on the part of the offender than those that are random, nonspecific and common (Holmes and De Burger 1988:51–52). For example, if an arsonist prefers to select warehouses as targets, their availability and distribution, geographically determined by city zoning bylaws, will have a strong influence on where the crimes occur. If the arsonist has no preference as to structure, then the target backcloth will probably be more uniform, as houses and buildings abound, at least in urban areas. The target sites of a predator who seeks out prostitutes will be determined primarily by the locations of the various "hooker strolls" in the area, while the attack sites of an offender who is willing to prey on any woman found on the street could be located almost anywhere in the city.

In the latter cases, the more or less uniform victim backcloth means that target patterns are influenced to a large extent by the offender's activity space, while in the former cases, crime geography is closely related to the victim backcloth. In the extreme cases of an arsonist for hire or a contract killer, victim location totally determines crime site. Victimology thus has an important role to play in the development of an accurate geographic profile.

7. In a study of 45 serial rapists, responsible for a total of 251 offenses committed during the 1980s in Greater London and Southeast England, Canter and Larkin (1993:67–68) found little support for the commuter hypothesis. Only 13 percent of the rapists had their home base situated outside of what was termed the *circle hypothesis prediction area* (the diameter of which was defined by a line connecting the two crimes farthest away from each other—comparable to the concept of offender hunting area as defined below). There appear to be strong similarities between the hunting patterns of serial murderers and those of serial rapists.

Crime Location Types

There may be several spatial points involved in a case of serial murder, each with a slightly different geographic meaning (cf. Newton and Swoope 1987), including the following:

- victim's last known location,
- victim-offender encounter site (stalking site),
- attack location (contact location),
- holding location,
- murder scene,
- body dump site,
- vehicle and property disposal site, and
- travel route.

In many cases, some of these locations could be the same (e.g., the body dump site may also be the murder scene). While all of these sites are important in the construction of a geographic profile of the offender, their locations are not always known to the investigating police officers. Prior to the apprehension of the killer, the only way these places can be determined is through evidence recovery or by witness statements. Typically, the police only know the body dump site (which may or may not be the murder scene) and the place where the victim was last seen. In some circumstances, they may only know the latter location.

Additionally, not every type of site has the same degree of relevance for all cases. If target selection is specific, as in a series of prostitute murders, then the encounter locations will be restricted, influenced more by the victim backcloth (i.e., where the red-light district is located) than by the offender's activity space. Actual murder scenes may not be known to the police, but dump sites will be, at least in those cases where the victims have been discovered. Since bodies can be disposed of in a multitude of locations, dump sites are relatively unrestricted and might well be the most significant location type for an understanding of the offender's geographic profile (see Newton and Swoope 1987; Rossmo 1993).

Cases with minimal spatial information can hinder efforts to spatially analyze a series of crimes. The victims' last known location may not be close to the sites of victim-offender encounters, and thus would not provide much information about the murderer. Nonuniform target backcloths can control the offender's selection of victim encounter sites. Multiple bodies may be dumped in a single location, providing only one geographic point for analysis. Thus, the numbers of locations, their types and the victim backcloth are all relevant variables in the construction of a geographic profile.

It is important to be aware of both internal and external influences on the offender's hunting process. Serial offenders can gain knowledge with each new crime, and they often learn from their experiences. Media disclosures and certain investigative strategies, particularly patrol saturation tactics, can create spatial displacement (Gabor 1978:101; Reppetto 1976:177), altering the geographic behavior of the offender to the point that apprehension can be hindered or delayed. Such influences, while often unavoidable, can change or alter spatial target patterns.

CRIMINAL GEOGRAPHIC TARGETING

The Brantingham and Brantingham model of crime site selection can be used as a heuristic for constructing a model designed to locate offender residence. As Brantingham and Brantingham seek to describe where crimes are most likely to occur on the basis of the offender's activity space, the current effort is, in effect, an attempt to invert their model, using crime locations as the means for predicting the most probable areas in which the murderer's residence or workplace might be found. So while the two models have different purposes, the underlying concepts and ideas are similar.

The Brantingham and Brantingham model predicts, for the simplest case, that offender residence would lie at the center of the crime pattern and therefore could be approximated by the spatial mean. The intricacy of most activity spaces, however, suggests that more complex patterns may be appropriate. Rengert (1990, 1991) proposes four hypothetical spatial patterns that could be used to describe the geography of crime sites: (1) a uniform pattern with no distance-decay influence; (2) a bull's-eye pattern with spatial clustering, exhibiting distance decay, centered around the offender's primary anchor point; (3) a bimodal pattern with crime clusters centered around two anchor points; and (4) a teardrop pattern with a directional bias oriented toward a secondary anchor point.[8]

Situations also can be distorted by a variety of other real-world factors: movement often follows a Manhattan metric, traffic flows can distort mobility patterns, variations exist in zoning and land use, and crime location clustering may depend upon the nature of the target backcloth. The spatial mean is therefore limited in its ability to pinpoint criminal residence. Can centrographic principles and journey-to-crime research be combined, in a manner informed by environmental criminological theory, to produce a viable method for predicting the location of offender residence from crime site coordinates?

Figure 2 shows a Venn diagram for three hypothetical crimes, all committed by the same offender and part of the same series. The medial circles surrounding each crime site location are defined by a radius equal to journey-to-crime-distance d, within the range of which percentage p (> 0.5) of the offender's crimes occur. The probability of the offender's residence lying within the area circumscribed by a single circle is therefore also p. Because the crimes are connected, one of the lune overlap areas (shown in light gray) is more likely to contain the offender's residence. And in the region where all three of the circles intersect (shown in dark gray), there is an even greater probability.

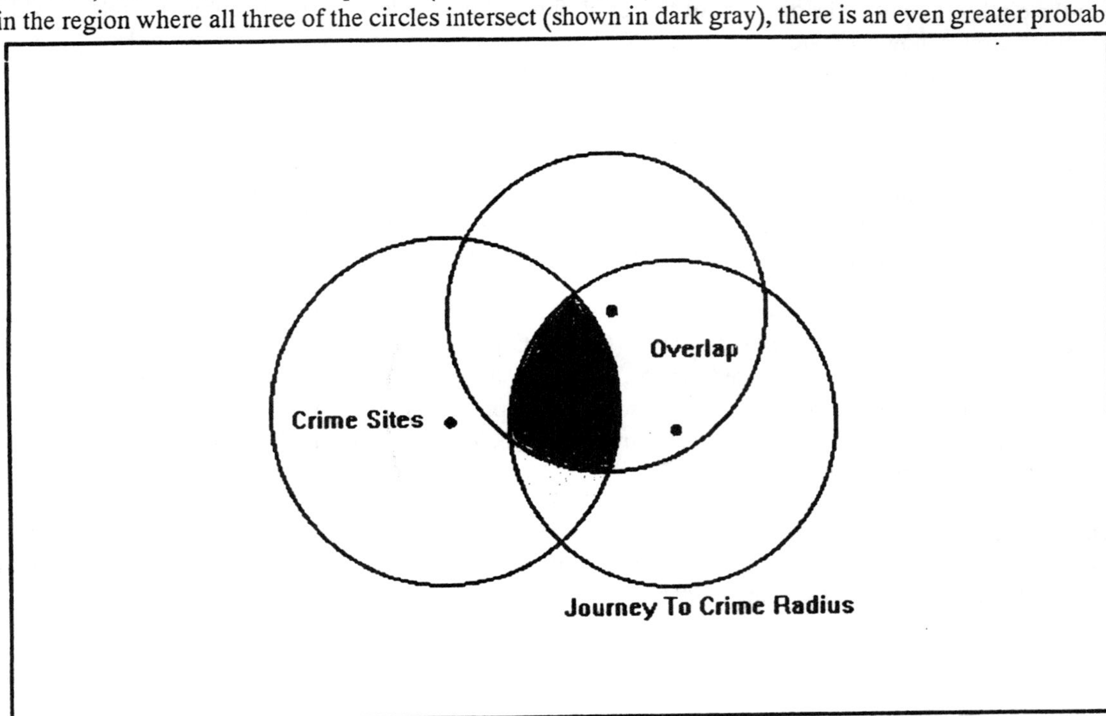

Fig. 2
Journey to crime: Venn diagram

8. Many researchers have noted the importance of direction as well as distance in the analysis of spatial patterns of criminal behavior. Rengert and Wasilchick (1985:68–74) found directional biases of burglaries toward offender workplaces and recreation sites. Costanzo, Halperin and Gale (1986:90–93), who conducted a nonparametric assessment of the level of spatial autocorrelation present in the orientation of criminal travel, suggest that such directional information could assist in police investigations of certain types of crimes.

Therefore, the points most likely to mark the residence of the offender are in the dark gray intersection, those next most likely in the light gray lunes, those third most likely in the white circles, and those least likely in the background area. The areal probabilities for figure 2 are the following:

$$P(C_i) = p(1-p)^2$$

$$P(C_i \cap C_i) = p^2(1-p)$$

$$P(C_i \cap C_j \cap C_k) = p^3$$

$$P(C_i \cup C_j \cup C_k) = (1-p)^3$$

where

P(A) is the probability that the offender's residence lies within area *A*,

C_x is the area around crime site *x* circumscribed by radius *d*, and

p is the probability that the offender's crime journeys will be $\leq d$.

Relative probabilities for the points within the various areas can be obtained by dividing the areal probabilities by area size (or number of "points").

This process can be viewed as a simple dichotomous function, dependent only on whether or not a point lies inside one of the circles. Points in the overlaps of two or all three of the circles are given double or triple the value, respectively. Such circles, however, are an oversimplified representation of journey-to-crime travel. Both research and theory suggest that crime trip behavior is better modeled by some form of Pareto function, which incorporates the concept of a buffer zone.

A more sophisticated response to the problem of locating offender residence could be obtained by replacing the circles in figure 2 with a distance-decay function, $f(d)$, that simulated actual journey-to-crime behavior. The value assigned to point (x, y), located at distance *d* from crime site *i*, would then be equal to $f(d_i)$. The final value for point (x, y) would be determined by adding together the *n* values derived at that point from the *n* different crime sites.

Preliminary work in the area of developing such a model has led to the creation of a computerized geographic profiling model called *criminal geographic targeting* (CGT).[9] Criminal geographic targeting, by analyzing the spatial information associated to a series of linked crimes, attempts to determine the most probable areas in which the offender's residence might be located. It addresses some of the problems associated with centrography and uses the information and insights provided by journey-to-crime research. The process can also handle the effects of anisotropic travel and nonuniform target backcloths.

The use of CGT in actual police investigations of serial murder and serial arson, and tests of the model on solved cases of serial murder and serial rape, have produced promising results, usually locating the offender's residence in the top 5 percent or less of the total hunting area.

9. Due to the large number of calculations involved (up to 100,000), the model has been computerized by writing the process in the QuickBasic language. By creating a software program that automates the mathematical procedures, the required computations can be done in just a few minutes.

The CGT model is based on the following four-step process:

1. Map boundaries delineating the offender's hunting area are first calculated from the crime locations.[10] The borders are determined by adding to the northernmost point one-half of the average y interpoint distance, subtracting from the southernmost point one-half of the average y interpoint distance, adding to the western-most point one-half of the average x interpoint distance, and subtracting from the easternmost point one-half of the average x interpoint distance (assuming a Manhattan grid oriented along north-south and east-west axes).[11]

2. The Manhattan distances from every point on the map to each crime location are then determined. While there are an infinite number of mathematical points in any area, the model uses a limited number of "points" (on the order of 10,000), based on the measurement resolution of the x and y scales.

3. Next, this Manhattan distance is used as an independent variable in a function that produces a value that meets either of the following criteria: (a) if the point lies outside the buffer zone, the value becomes smaller the longer the distance, following some form of distance decay; or (b) if the point lies inside the buffer zone, the value becomes larger the longer the distance. A value is computed from this function for each of the crime locations. For example, if there are 12 crime locations, each point on the map will have 12 values associated with it.

4. Finally, these multiple values are added together to produce a single score for each map point. The higher the resultant score, the greater the probability that the point contains the offender's home or workplace. The function is of the form

$$P_{ij} = \prod_{c=1}^{T} k \left[\phi/(|x_i - x_c| + |y_j - y_c|)^f + (1 - \phi)(B^{g-f})/(2B - |x_i - x_c| - |y_j - y_c|)^g \right]$$

where

$$|x_i - x_c| + |y_j - y_c| > B \supset \phi = 1$$

$$|x_i - x_c| + |y_j - y_c| \leq B \supset \phi = 0$$

and

P_{ij}	is the resultant probability for point ij,
k	is an empirically determined constant,
B	is the radius of the buffer zone,
T	is the total number of crime sites,
f	is an empirically determined exponent,
g	is an empirically determined exponent,
x_i, y_j	are the coordinates of point ij, and
x_c, y_c	are the coordinates of the *cth* crime site location.

When the probabilities are calculated for every point on the map, the end result is a three-dimensional probability surface that can be represented by an isopleth map (figures 3 to 5). Alternatively, if viewed from above, the probabil-

10. These crime locations could be victim encounter points, murder scenes, body dump sites, or some combination of these. The term *hunting area* is therefore used broadly in the sense of the geographic area within which the offender chose (after, presumably, some form of search or hunting process) a series of locations in which to engage in one of the above offense-related actions. There may be other crime locations not known to the authorities and therefore not included in the analysis. Also, this approach does not contain those locations in which the offender searched for victim/dump sites/etc., but was unsuccessful or chose not to act.

11. For example, the northernmost point (y_{high}) is calculated as follows: $y_{high} = y_{max} + (y_{max} - y_{min})/2(T - 1)$. See Boots and Getis (1988:39–45) for a discussion of alternative techniques for dealing with edge effects.

ity surface can be depicted by a two-dimensional choropleth map (Harries 1990:31–37). Figure 6, for example, is a choropleth map derived from figure 3. In the latter case, the result can be overlaid on a city map of the involved area, and specific streets or blocks prioritized according to the associated values shown on the CGT choropleth probability map.

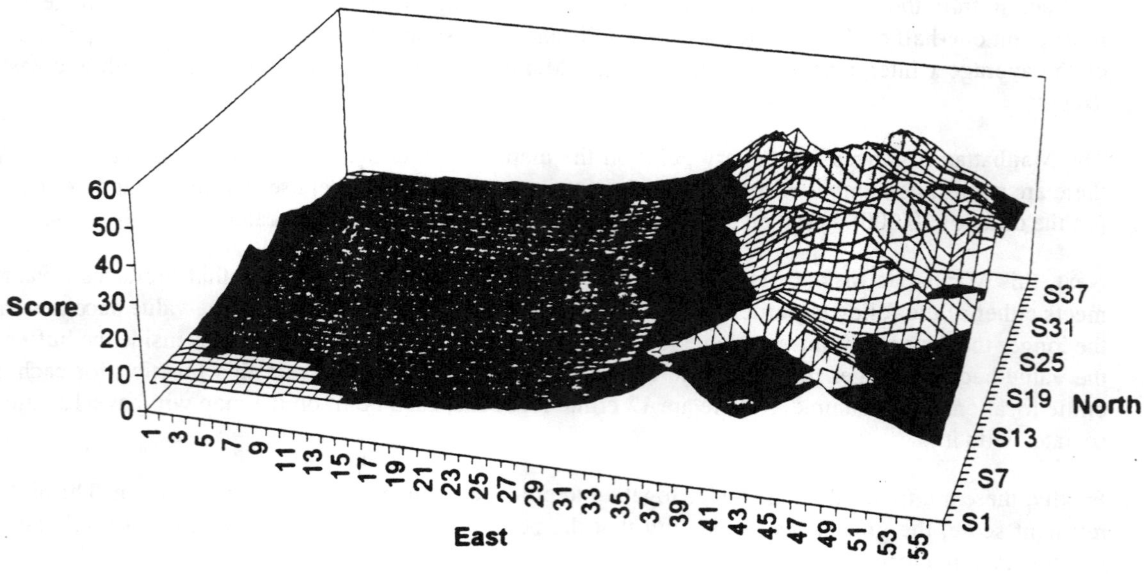

Fig. 3
Three-dimensional isopleth map (serial arsonist)

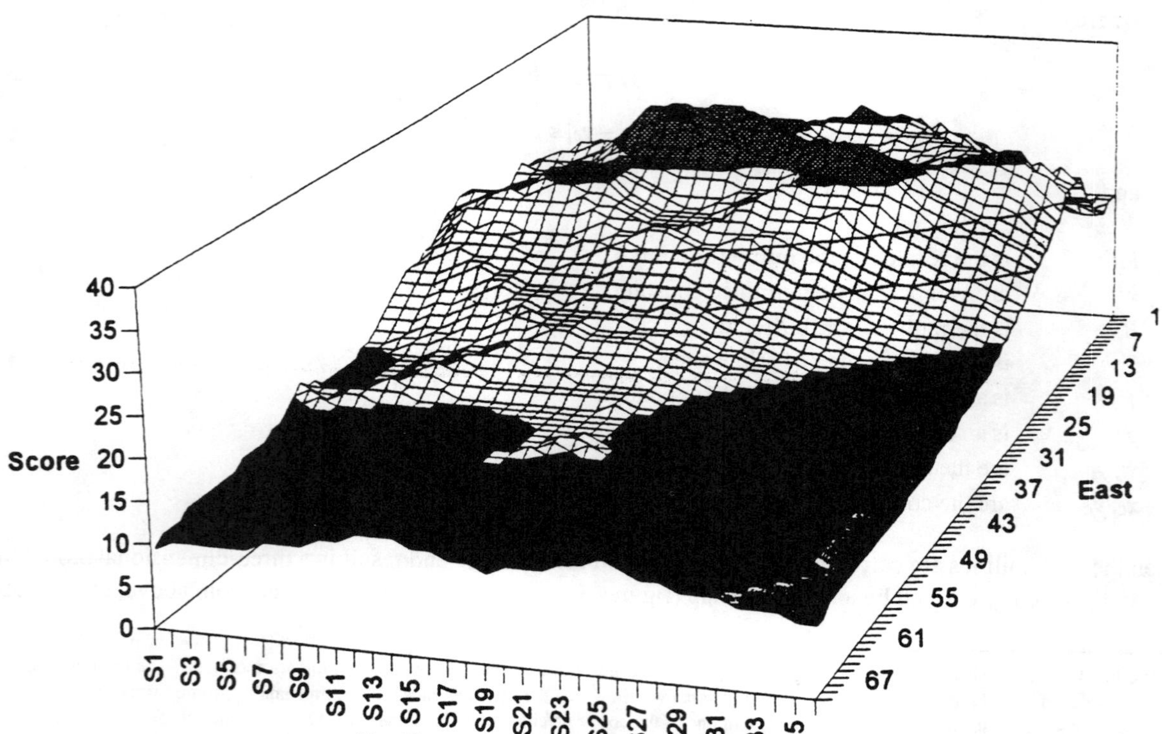

Fig. 4
Three-dimensional isopleth map (serial rapist)

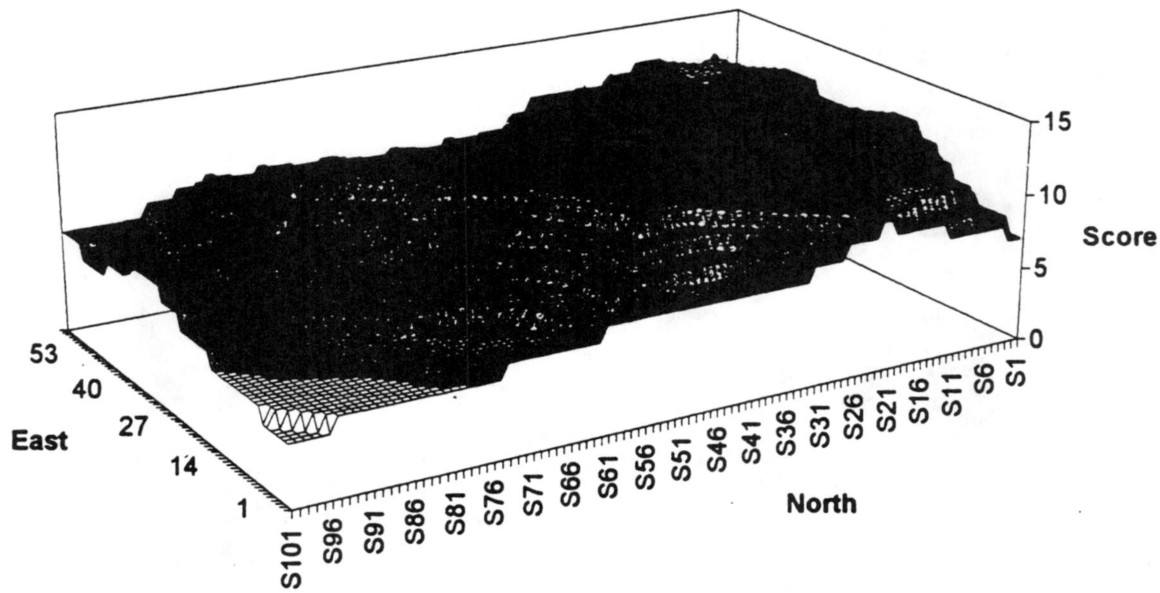

Fig. 5
Three-dimensional isopleth map (serial murderer)

Key to this process is the above function, which assigns probability values based on the distances between map points and crime locations. While the Brantingham and Brantingham model suggests that the criminal search process can be modeled by a form of Pareto function involving distance decay, the presence of a buffer zone in which no or few crimes are likely to be committed, centered around the residence of the criminal, has also been proposed. Developing and optimizing the specific parameters of this function, the size and nature of the buffer zone, and examining the influence, if any, of other variables on the model (such as spatial-temporal ordering influences, directional effects, land use and area characteristics,[12] size of hunting area, offender mobility, organized vs. disorganized behavior, etc.) are the goal of ongoing research.

Any methodology, whether investigative or scientific, should meet three important criteria—validity, reliability and utility. The CGT model works on the assumption that a relationship, modeled on some form of distance-decay function, exists between crime location and offender residence. The process can be thought of as a mathematical method for assigning a series of scores to the various points on a map that represents the killer's hunting area. Since the use of an appropriate typology excludes all commuting murderers from the analysis, by definition the offender's residence must lie somewhere on the hunting-area map.

For the CGT model to be valid, the score it assigns to the point containing the offender's residence should be relatively high; that is, there should be few points on the hunting-area map with equal or higher scores. This can be shown as a distribution curve indicating the number of points with various scores (see figure 7). The "success" of the CGT model in a given case can be measured by determining the ratio of the total number of points with equal or higher scores to the total number of points in the hunting area. In other words, in what percentage of the total area would the offender's residence be found by a process that started in the locations with the highest scores and then worked down? The smaller that percentage (referred to as the "hit percentage"), the more successful the model.

12. It may be possible, for example, to predict whether an offender's anchor point is the residence or workplace from the zoning classification of the hunting area.

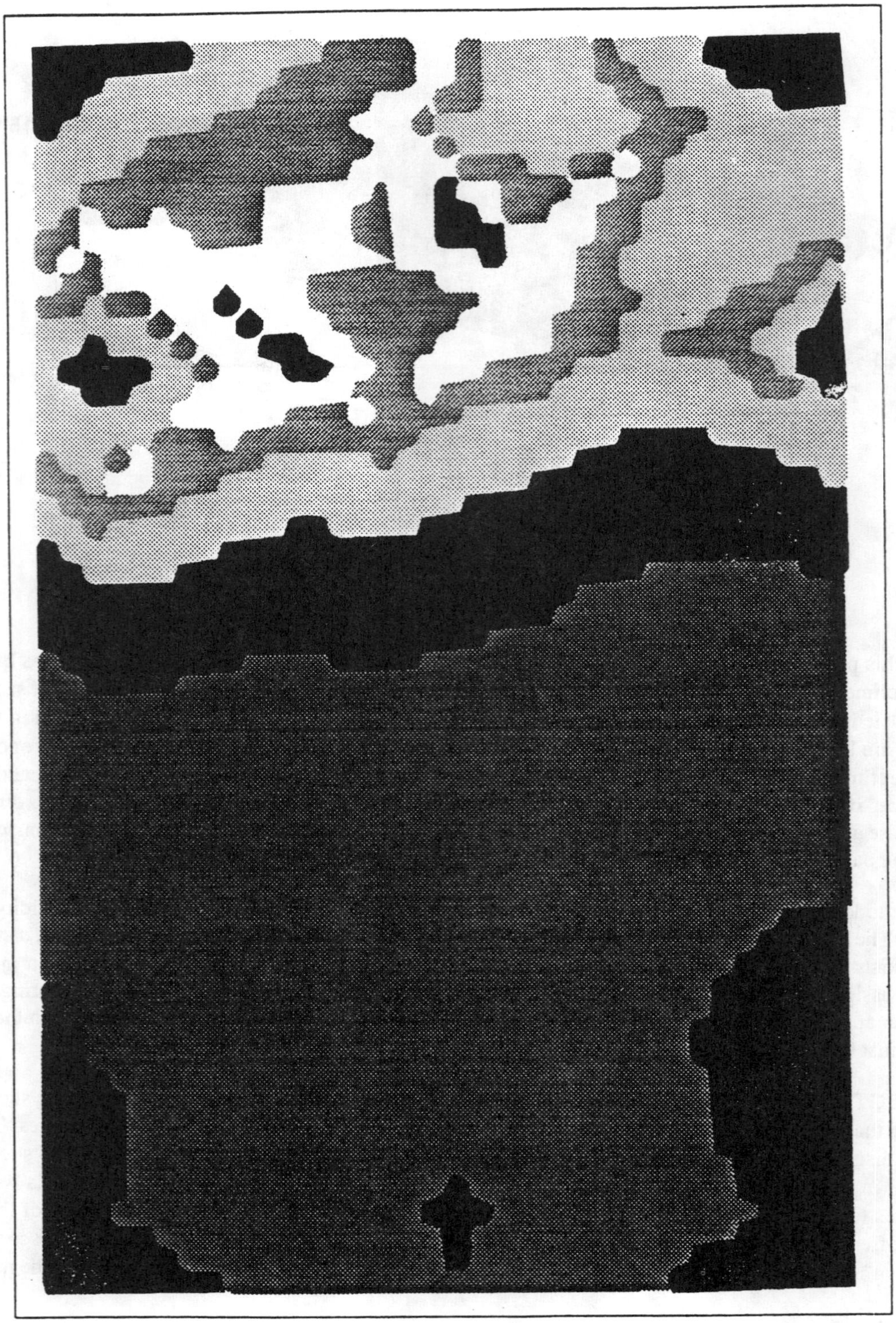

Fig. 6
Choropleth map derived from figure 3 data

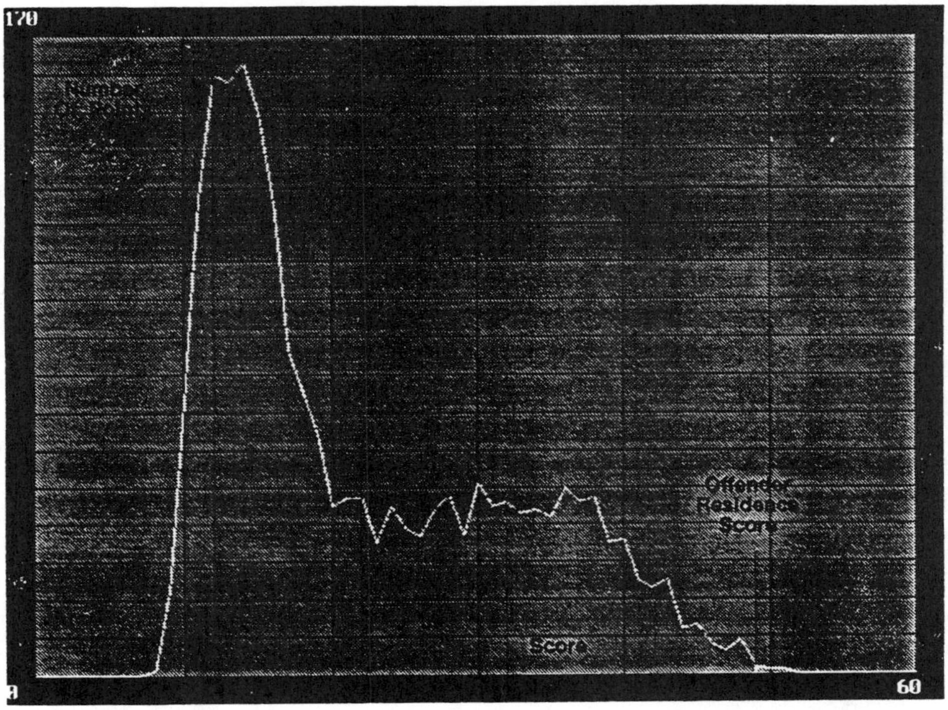

Fig. 7
CGT score distribution

While the geographic pattern for a crime series may yield several forms of information (coordinates, crime location type, area characteristics, nearest-neighbor distances, point pattern, clustering, temporal ordering, and so on), the randomness inherent in most human behavior limits the conclusions that can be derived from a small number of crime sites. More locations reduce the impact of chance. The performance of the CGT model is thus related to the number of points available for analysis—the more crime locations, the more information, and therefore the more precision. Validity of the CGT model is therefore a function of number of locations.

Monte Carlo testing, accomplished through a computer program that creates random crime site coordinates based on a buffered distance-decay function, was conducted to estimate the theoretical maximum efficiency of the model.[13] The testing produced the "learning curve" shown in figure 8, which displays the relationship between the number of crime sites available for analysis and the hit percentage produced by the CGT model. This process established that at least six crime locations are necessary to produce hit percentages under 10 percent (though some test variations of the model are able to accomplish this level of prediction ability with only five crime sites).

13. When applied to other forms of hypothetical crime site geography, such as Rengert's (1990, 1991) teardrop, bimodal or uniform spatial patterns, the CGT model is slightly less efficient.

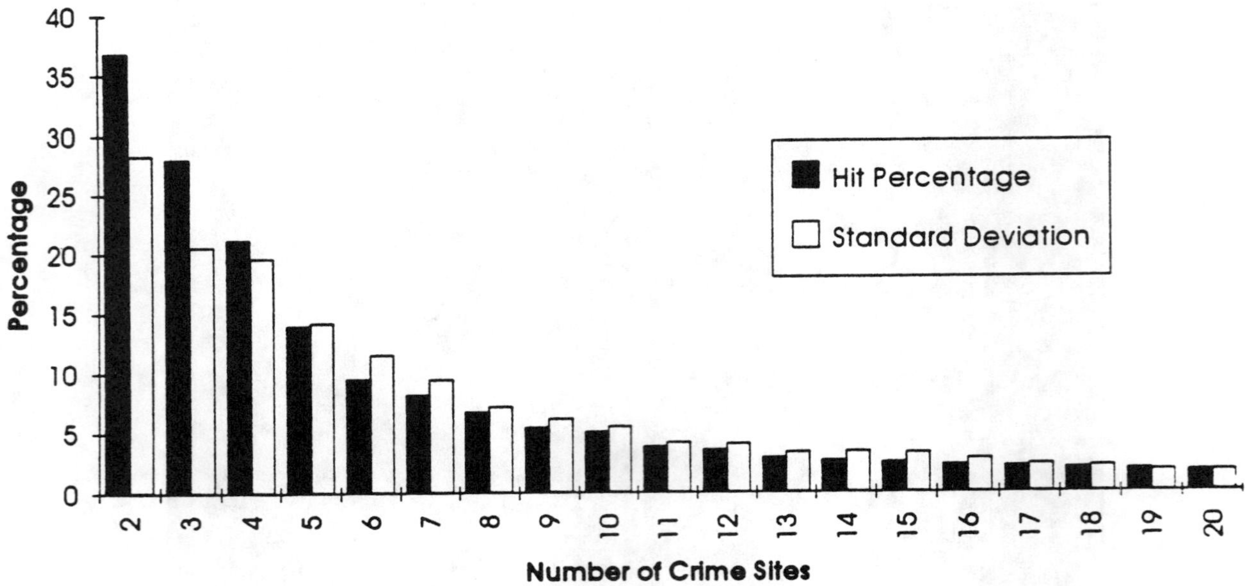

Fig. 8
Monte Carlo testing results

The reliability of the CGT model is high, as the calculations are mathematically straightforward and the procedure has been computerized. The determination of exactly which crime locations in a given case are relevant to the analysis (see above), however, is a subjective process dependent on the knowledge, experience and interpretation of the profiler. The qualitative dimensions of geographic profiling are also subject to personal biases.

No matter how valid or reliable a particular investigative technique is, it will have little practical value if it cannot be effectively used by police detectives in the real world of murder investigation. The utility of the CGT model is best demonstrated by the various geographically based investigative strategies that such a process makes possible. Some examples of these are described in the following section.

INVESTIGATIVE STRATEGIES

Once a geographic profile has been constructed, a variety of criminal investigative strategies can be employed in a more effective and efficient manner. While the specific approaches are best determined by the police investigators familiar with the case in question, some examples of tactics used or suggested in the past are presented below. The development of further spatially based applications and innovative investigative techniques is an interactive process that involves the police officers responsible for the case in question.

Suspect Prioritization

If a lengthy list of suspects has been developed, the geographic profile in conjunction with the criminal offender profile can help prioritize individuals for follow-up investigative work. The problem in many serial violent crime investigations is one of too many suspects rather than one of too few. Profiling can help prioritize lists of sometimes hundreds if not thousands of suspects, leads and tips.

Patrol Saturation

Areas that have been determined to most probably be associated with the offender can be used as a basis for directed or saturation police patrolling efforts. This strategy is particularly effective if the offender appears to be operating during certain time periods. Prioritized areas can also be employed for neighborhood canvassing efforts, area searches, information sign posting, and community cooperation and media campaigns. Police departments have used this approach to target areas for leaflet distribution, employing prioritized letter carrier (LC) walks for strategic household mail delivery. For example, LeBeau (1992:136) mentions the case of a serial rapist in San Diego who was arrested through canvassing efforts in an area determined from the locations of his crimes.

Police Information Systems

Additional investigative leads may be obtained from the information contained in various computerized police dispatch and record systems (e.g., a computer-aided dispatch [CAD] system, records management system [RMS], RCMP Police Information Retrieval System [PIRS], and the like). Offender profile details and case specifics can help focus the search at this point. For example, if the police are searching for an anger-retaliatory rapist, it might be worthwhile to examine CAD data for domestic disturbance calls from the dates of the rapes to see which ones are located near the areas most probably associated with the offender, as determined from the geographic profile.[14]

Those police agencies that contain computerized records detailing the descriptions, addresses and modus operandi of local offenders can also use profiling information, including probable area of residence, as the basis for developing search criteria. Many departments have such files for specific types of criminals, such as parolees or sex offenders.

Outside Agency Database

Data banks are often geographically based, and information from parole and probation offices, mental health outpatient clinics, social services offices, and similar agencies located in the most probable areas can also prove to be of value. For example, LeBeau (1992:133) discusses the case of a serial rapist who emerged as a suspect after the police checked parolee records for sex offenders.

Postal Code Prioritization

The geographic profile can also prioritize postal codes in a city. If suspect offender description or vehicle information exists, prioritized postal codes (representing the most probable 1 or 2 percent of a city's area) can be used to conduct effective off-line computer searches of registered vehicle or driver's license files contained in provincial or state motor vehicle department records. These parameters act as a form of linear program to produce a surprisingly small set of records containing fields with all the appropriate data responses. Such a strategy can, therefore, produce significant results by focusing on limited areas that are of a manageable size for most serious criminal police investigations.

14. Such a process is particularly powerful with police record systems founded on geographical information systems. The Chicago Police Department, for example, has the capability, with the Illinois Criminal Justice Information Authority's Spatial and Temporal Analysis of Crime (STAC) software, to search for crimes or calls for service by area and by time (Block 1990, 1993a).

The following is one example of the use of this approach. The postal codes for a city neighborhood within which a violent sexual offender was attacking children were prioritized by using the criminal geographic targeting model. First, the relevant forward sorting areas (FSAs)—the first three digits of the postal code—were identified. The criminal geographic targeting probability map was then superimposed over the letter carrier walks (LC), which could then be prioritized by probability.

Planning and zoning maps were used to eliminate industrial, commercial and other nonresidential areas. Socioeconomic and demographic census data were also consulted to reevaluate the priority of those neighborhoods that were inconsistent with the socioeconomic level of the offender as suggested by the psychological profile. Finally, the local distribution units (LDUs)—the last three digits of the postal code—associated with the letter carrier walks were determined.

The complete postal codes, ranked by priority of probability, were then used to conduct an off-line computer search of the provincial motor vehicle department records, which contain postal codes within the addresses connected to the vehicle registered owner and driver's license files. Suspect vehicle information and an offender description had been developed by the detectives working on the case, and this was combined with the geographic data to effectively focus the off-line search.

For example, a new red station wagon driven by a tall white middle-aged male with dark hair may seem to be somewhat vague information. The description actually contains several parameters, however: (1) vehicle style, (2) vehicle color, (3) vehicle year range, (4) driver height range, (5) driver race, (6) driver hair color, and (7) driver age range. When combined with a prioritized list of postal codes, representing the most probable 1 or 2 percent of a city's area, these parameters can narrow down hundreds of thousands of records to a few dozen vehicles or drivers. This is sufficient discrimination to allow a focused follow-up by police investigators.

Task Force Computer Systems

Task force operations that have been formed to investigate a specific series of major crimes usually collect and collate their information in some form of computerized system. Often, these operations suffer from information overload and can benefit by the prioritization of data and by the application of correlation analysis. Geographic profiling can assist in these tasks through the prioritization of street addresses, postal codes (FSAs, LCs, LDUs) and telephone number (NNX) areas. The details of the specific computer database software used by the task force, including information fields, search time, number of records, and correlational abilities, determine the most appropriate form that the geographic profile should take to maximize its usefulness to the police investigation.

CONCLUSION

> We were just hunting humans. I guess because we thought they were the hardest things to hunt, but humans are the easiest things to hunt . . . . Sad to say, but it's true (convicted Canadian murderer, interviewed in Boyd 1988:2–58).

All violent offenses have crime scenes. The offender and the victim have to encounter each other at some point in time and space, and these points form spatial and temporal patterns (LeBeau 1992:124–126). Whether these patterns have meaning and whether that meaning is significant for law enforcement depend on a variety of factors. Offender type, activity space, hunting style, target backcloth, area characteristics, physical and psychological barriers, land use, and neighborhood demographics are all relevant variables in an analysis of criminal target patterns.

Geographic profiling infers spatial characteristics of the offender from these target patterns. This method has qualitative and quantitative approaches that attempt to understand the pattern from both subjective and objective perspectives. Criminal geographic targeting is a specific statistical method that enhances the efforts of geographic profiling by delineating the most probable areas to which the offender might be associated.

This prioritization, which can be at the postal code, block or letter carrier walk level, allows for the focusing of police investigative efforts. Suspects can be prioritized and patrol saturation efforts directed. In cases of serial murder and other serial violent crimes, there are usually heavy pressures, both external and internal, to apprehend the offender(s). When traditional law enforcement strategies have not been successful, or when the number of suspects or volume of information is high, geographic profiling can help prioritize areas and focus investigative strategies. This can lead to a quicker case resolution, thereby reducing police costs and increasing community safety.

Geographic profiling, therefore, appears to have significant investigative value in certain types of criminal cases. It is also a practical example of the application of criminological theory to a criminal justice problem. Environmental criminology, because of its rich context and diverse roots, has been particularly fruitful in this area and holds the promise of many future practical applications.

Geographic Profiling Requirements

The following is a standard list of geographic profiling information requirements. Any particular case may require additional details. The majority of the information will likely have already been collected during the course of the investigation, and the remainder is readily obtainable from most city or regional planning departments. The absence of some of the requirements should not be seen as a barrier or reason to delay the analysis, as alternative sources of information may be available. In such cases, consult with the geographic profiler.

Crime Data

- Case summaries for all the crimes believed to be part of the series, including any details regarding locations, directions, movements, and other spatial data.
- Information should include crime type, modus operandi, weapon type, date, day of week, time, weather.

Geographic Data

- For all relevant sites (i.e., where victims last seen, first contact sites, crime sites, victim/body/property/vehicle dump sites, evidence recovered sites, etc.):

  a. exact location (address and cross streets);

  b. location type (residential, commercial, industrial, including relevant buildings);

  c. neighborhood demographics and general area description (census demographic details, including age and sex ratios, socioeconomic character, overall crime rate, relevant specific-area crime problems, and transiency levels);

d. maps (city or region, arterial routes, bus routes, crime scenes, land use, zoning); and

e. photos (crime scenes, general area, aerial).

Victimology

- For all victims: sex, race, age, risk level assessment, residence, business, social, transportation methods and routes.

Criminal/Psychological Profile

- The criminal profile plays a very important role in determining the probable life and mind-set of the offender and consequently is of great value when constructing a geographic profile, particularly in those cases where there is a minimum amount of spatial information (i.e., only a few relevant crime locations).

Suspect Data

- If available: sex; age; race; criminal record; previous police contacts; psychological/psychiatric history; location of present/past residences, present/past schools and present/past occupations; social activities; transportation methods and routes; addresses of family members and friends.

REFERENCES

Amir, A. (1971). *Patterns in Forcible Rape*. Chicago: University of Chicago Press.

Baldwin, J., and A.E. Bottoms (1976). *The Urban Criminal: A Study in Sheffield*. London: Tavistock Publications.

Barker, M. (1989). *Criminal activity and home range: A study of the spatial offence patterns of burglars*. Unpublished master's thesis, University of Surrey, England.

Bates, S. (1987). *Spatial and Temporal Analysis of Crime* (research bulletin). Chicago: Illinois Criminal Justice Information Authority.

Block, C.R. (December 1990). *Hot spots and isocrimes in law enforcement decision making*. Paper presented at the conference on Police and Community Responses to Drugs: Frontline Strategies in the Drug War.

——— (1993a). Automated spatial analysis as a tool in violence reduction. *CJ the Americas* 6(1):7–8, 10.

——— (1993b). Lethal violence in the Chicago Latino community. Chap. 15 in A.V. Wilson (ed.), *Homicide: The Victim/Offender Connection*. Cincinnati: Anderson.

Block, C.R., R.L. Block, M. Wilson, and M. Daly (November 1990). *Chicago homicide from the sixties to the nineties: Have patterns of lethal violence changed?* Paper presented at the meeting of the American Society of Criminology, Reno, Nev.

Boggs, S. (1965). Urban crime patterns. *American Sociological Review* 30:899–908.

Boots, B.N., and A. Getis (1988). *Point Pattern Analysis*. Sage university paper series on scientific geography, no. 8. Beverly Hills: Sage.

Boyd, N. (1988). *The Last Dance: Murder in Canada*. Scarborough, ON: Prentice-Hall.

Brantingham, P.J., and P.L. Brantingham (eds.) (1981). *Environmental Criminology*. Beverly Hills: Sage.

Brantingham, P.J., and P.L. Brantingham (1984). *Patterns in Crime*. New York: Macmillan.

——— (1993). Nodes, paths and edges: Considerations on the complexity of crime and the physical environment. *Journal of Environmental Psychology* 13:28–33.

Brooks, P.R., M.J. Devine, T.J. Green, B.L. Hart, and M.D. Moore (1987). Serial murder: A criminal justice response. *The Police Chief* (June):40–44.

Bufton, K. (1993). *"Son of Sam": The serial murders of David Berkowitz*. Unpublished manuscript, Simon Fraser University, School of Criminology, Burnaby, BC.

Bullock, H.A. (1955). Urban homicide in theory and fact. *Journal of Criminal Law, Criminology and Police Science* 45:565–575.

Burgess, E.W. (1925). The growth of the city. Pp. 47–62 in R.E. Park, E.W. Burgess and R.D. McKenzie (eds.), *The City*. Chicago: University of Chicago Press.

Canter, D. (1989). Offender profiles. *The Psychologist* 2(1):12–16.

Canter, D., and R. Heritage (1990). A multivariate model of sexual offence behaviour: Developments in "offender profiling." *Journal of Forensic Psychiatry* 1:185–212.

Canter, D., and P. Larkin (1993). The environmental range of serial rapists. *Journal of Environmental Psychology* 13:63–69.

Canter, D., and S. Tagg (1975). Distance estimation in cities. *Environment and Behaviour* 7:59–80.

Capone, D.L., and W.W. Nichols Jr. (1975). Crime and distance: An analysis of offender behaviour in space. *Proceedings, Association of American Geographers*:45–49.

——— (1976). Urban structure and criminal mobility. *American Behavioral Scientist* 20:199–213.

Chappell, D. (1965). *The development and administration of the English law relating to breaking and entering*. Unpublished doctoral dissertation, University of Cambridge, Cambridge.

Clark, W.A.V. (1986). *Human Migration*. Sage university paper series on scientific geography, no. 7. Beverly Hills: Sage.

Clarke, K.C. (1990). *Analytical and Computer Cartography*. Englewood Cliffs, N.J.: Prentis Hall.

Cohen, L., and M. Felson (1979). Social change and crime rate trends: A routine activity approach. *American Sociological Review* 44:588–608.

Cornish, D.B., and R.V. Clarke (eds.) (1986). *The Reasoning Criminal: Rational Choice Perspectives on Offending*. New York: Springer-Verlag.

Costanzo, C.M., W.C. Halperin and N. Gale (1986). Criminal mobility and the directional component in journeys to crime. Pp. 73–95 in R.M. Figlio, S. Hakim and G.F. Rengert (eds.), *Metropolitan Crime Patterns*. Monsey, N.Y.: Willow Tree Press.

Cryan, M.P. (1988). Halt program joins VICAP in hunting serial criminals. *Trooper Magazine* (May/June):8–9.

Dietz, P.E. (1985). Sex offender profiling by the FBI: A preliminary concept model. Pp. 207–219 in M.H. Ben-Aron, S.J. Hucker and C.D. Webster (eds.), *Clinical Criminology: The Assessment and Treatment of Criminal Behaviour*. Toronto: M and M Graphics.

Doney, R.H. (1990). The aftermath of the Yorkshire Ripper: The response of the United Kingdom police service. Pp. 95–112 in S.A. Egger (ed.), *Serial Murder: An Elusive Phenomenon*. New York: Praeger.

Douglas, J.E., A.W. Burgess, A.G. Burgess, and R.K. Ressler (1992). *Crime Classification Manual*. New York: Lexington Books.

Douglas, J.E., R.K. Ressler, A.W. Burgess, and C.R. Hartman (1986). Criminal profiling from crime scene analysis. *Behavioral Sciences and the Law* 4:401–421.

Egger, S.A. (1984). A working definition of serial murder and the reduction of linkage blindness. *Journal of Police Science and Administration* 12:348–357.

——— (1985). *Serial murder and the law enforcement response*. Unpublished doctoral dissertation, Sam Houston State University, Huntsville, Texas.

——— (1990). *Serial Murder: An Elusive Phenomenon*. New York: Praeger.

Erlanson, O.A. (1946). The scene of sex offences. *Journal of Criminal Law and Criminology* 31:339–342.

Felson, M. (1986). Linking criminal choices, routine activities, informal control, and criminal outcomes. Pp. 119–128 in D.B. Cornish and R.V. Clarke (eds.), *The Reasoning Criminal: Rational Choice Perspectives on Offending*. New York: Springer-Verlag.

——— (1987). Routine activities and crime prevention in the developing metropolis. *Criminology* 25:911–931.

Figlio, R.M., S. Hakim and G.F. Rengert (eds.) (1986). *Metropolitan Crime Patterns*. Monsey, N.Y.: Willow Tree Press.

Gabor, T. (1978). Crime displacement: The literature and strategies for its investigation. *Crime and Justice* 6:100–106.

Gabor, T., and E. Gottheil (1984). Offender characteristics and spatial mobility: An empirical study and some policy implications. *Canadian Journal of Criminology* 26:267–281.

Gates, D.F., and D.K. Shah (1992). *Chief*. New York: Bantam Books.

Geberth, V.J. (1990). *Practical Homicide Investigation: Tactics, Procedures and Forensic Techniques* (2nd ed.). New York: Elsevier.

Georges-Abeyie, D.E., and K.D. Harries (eds.) (1980). *Crime: A Spatial Perspective*. New York: Columbia University Press.

Goodchild, M.F., K.K. Kemp and T. Poiker (1990). *Introduction to GIS* (NCGIA Core Curriculum). National Center for Geographic Information and Analysis.

Gould, P. (1975). Acquiring spatial information. *Economic Geography* 51:87–99.

Gould, P., and R. White (1974). *Mental Maps*. New York: Penguin.

Greenberg, D.F. (1979). *Mathematical Criminology*. New Brunswick, N.J.: Rutgers.

Hakim, S., and G.F. Rengert (eds.) (1981). *Crime Spillover*. Beverly Hills: Sage.

Harries, K. (1990). *Geographic Factors in Policing*. Washington, D.C.: Police Executive Research Forum.

Haynes, K.E., and A.S. Fotheringham (1984). *Gravity and Spatial Interaction Models*. Sage university paper series on scientific geography, no. 2. Beverly Hills: Sage.

Hazelwood, R.R., and A.W. Burgess (eds.). (1987). *Practical Aspects of Rape Investigation: A Multidisciplinary Approach*. New York: Elsevier.

Hazelwood, R.R., and J.E. Douglas (1980). The lust murderer. *FBI Law Enforcement Bulletin* 49(4):18–22.

Hazelwood, R.R., and J. Warren (1990). The criminal behavior of the serial rapist. *FBI Law Enforcement Bulletin* 59(2):11–16.

Hickey, E.W. (1991). *Serial Murderers and Their Victims*. Pacific Grove, Calif.: Brooks/Cole Publishing.

Hollandsworth, S. (1993). See no evil. *Texas Monthly* (May):92–97, 128–140.

Holmes, R.M. (1989). *Profiling Violent Crimes*. Beverly Hills: Sage.

Holmes, R.M., and J.E. De Burger (1988). *Serial Murder*. Newbury Park, Calif.: Sage.

Icove, D.J., and J.J. Crisman (1975). Application of pattern recognition in arson investigation. *Fire Technology* 11(1):35–41.

Icove, D.J., and P.R. Horbert (1990). Serial arsonists: An introduction. *The Police Chief* (December):46–48.

International Association of Chiefs of Police (1975). *Geographic Base Files for Law Enforcement*. Gaithersburg, Md.: Author.

Jakle, J.A., S. Brunn and C.C. Roseman (1976). *Human Spatial Behavior: A Social Geography*. Prospect Heights, Ill.: Waveland Press.

James, E. (1991). *Catching Serial Killers*. Lansing, Mich.: International Forensic Services.

Jenkins, P. (1988a). Myth and murder: The serial killer panic of 1983–5. *Sam Houston State University Criminal Justice Research Bulletin* 3(11).

——— (1988b). Serial murder in England, 1940–1985. *Journal of Criminal Justice* 16:1–15.

——— (1989). Serial murder in the United States, 1900–1940: a historical perspective. *Journal of Criminal Justice* 17:377–392.

Johnston, R.J. (1975). Map pattern and friction of distance parameters: A comment. *Regional Studies* 9:281–283.

Keppel, R.D. (1989). *Serial Murder: Future Implications for Police Investigations*. Cincinnati: Anderson.

Kind, S.S. (1987a). Navigational ideas and the Yorkshire Ripper investigation. *Journal of Navigation* 40:385–393.

——— (1987b). *The Scientific Investigation of Crime*. Harrogate: Forensic Science Services.

Klockars, C.B. (ed.) (1983). *Thinking about Police: Contemporary Readings*. New York: McGraw-Hill.

Knoke, D., and J.H. Kuklinski (1982). *Network Analysis*. Sage university paper series on quantitative applications in the social sciences, no. 28. Beverly Hills: Sage.

LeBeau, J.L. (1985). Some problems with measuring and describing rape presented by the serial offender. *Justice Quarterly* 2:385–398.

——— (1987a). The journey to rape: Geographic distance and the rapist's method of approaching the victim. *Journal of Police Science and Administration* 15:129–136.

——— (1987b). The methods and measures of centrography and the spatial dynamics of rape. *Journal of Quantitative Criminology* 3:125–141.

——— (1987c). Patterns of stranger and serial rape offending: Factors distinguishing apprehended and at-large offenders. *Journal of Criminal Law and Criminology* 78:309–326.

——— (1992). Four case studies illustrating the spatial-temporal analysis of serial rapists. *Police Studies* 15:124–145.

LeBeau, J.L., and R.H. Langworthy (November 1992). *The journey to get stung*. Paper presented at the meeting of the American Society of Criminology, New Orleans, La.

Levin, J., and J.A. Fox (1985). *Mass Murder*. New York: Plenum.

Leyton, E. (1986). *Hunting Humans*. Toronto: McClelland-Bantam.

Lowe, J.C., and S. Moryadas (1975). *The Geography of Movement*. Boston: Houghton Mifflin.

Luce, R.D. (1959). *Individual Choice Behavior*. New York: John Wiley and Sons.

Lynch, K. (1960). *The Image of the City*. Cambridge, Mass.: MIT Press.

Maltz, M.D., A.C. Gordon and W. Friedman (1991). *Mapping Crime in Its Community Setting: Event Geography Analysis*. New York: Springer-Verlag.

McIver, J.P. (1981). Criminal mobility: A review of empirical studies. Pp. 20–47 in S. Hakim and G.F. Rengert (eds.), *Crime Spillover*. Beverly Hills: Sage.

Montgomery, J.E. (February 1992). *Organizational survival: Continuity or crisis?* Paper presented at the Police Studies Series, Simon Fraser University, Vancouver, BC.

Morrill, R., G.L. Gaile and G.L. Thrall (1988). *Spatial Diffusion*. Sage university paper series on scientific geography, no. 10. Beverly Hills: Sage.

Newton, M.B., Jr., and D.C. Newton (October 1985). *Geoforensic identification of localized serial crime: Unsolved female homicides, Fort Worth, Texas, 1983–85*. Paper presented at the meeting of the Southwest Division, Association of American Geographers, Denton, Texas.

Newton, M.B., Jr., and E.A. Swoope (1987). *Geoforensic analysis of localized serial murder: The Hillside Stranglers located*. Unpublished manuscript.

Nichols, W.W., Jr. (1980). Mental maps, social characteristics and criminal mobility. Pp. 156–166 in D.E. Georges-Abeyie and K.D. Harries (eds.), *Crime: A Spatial Perspective.* New York: Columbia University Press.

Normandeau, A. (1968). *Trends and Patterns in the Crime of Robbery.* Unpublished doctoral dissertation, University of Pennsylvania, Philadelphia.

Norris, J. (1988). *Serial Killers.* New York: Doubleday.

Nova (1992). Mind of a Serial Killer. Transcript, show no. 1912, Supervisory Special Agent John Douglas, Federal Bureau of Investigation. Denver: Journal Graphics.

Olson, C.R. (1992). *The Phenomena of Serial Murder—Ten Questions.* Unpublished manuscript.

Pinto, S., and P.R. Wilson (1990). *Serial Murder* (Trends and Issues in Crime and Criminal Justice No. 25). Canberra: Australian Institute of Criminology.

Ploughman, P.D., and P.J. Ould (November 1990). *Toward a self-protective, rational calculus: The nexus of routine activities and rape victimization risk.* Paper presented at the meeting of the American Society of Criminology, Baltimore, Md.

Pope, C.E. (1980). Patterns in burglary: An empirical examination of offense and offender characteristics. *Journal of Criminal Justice* 8(1):39–51.

Pyle, G.F. (1974). *The spatial dynamics of crime* (research paper no. 159). Chicago: Department of Geography, University of Chicago.

——— (1976). Spatial aspects of crime in Cleveland, Ohio. *American Behavioral Scientist* 20:175-198.

Rand, A. (1986). Mobility triangles. Pp. 117–126 in R.M. Figlio, S. Hakim and G.F. Rengert (eds.), *Metropolitan Crime Patterns.* Monsey, N.Y.: Willow Tree Press.

Reber, A.S. (1985). *The Penguin Dictionary of Psychology.* Harmondsworth, Middlesex: Penguin.

Reboussin, R., and J. Cameron (1989). Expert systems for law enforcement. *FBI Law Enforcement Bulletin* 58(8):12–16.

Reiss, A.J., Jr. (1967). *Place of residence of arrested persons compared with the place where the offence charged in arrest occurred for Part I and II offences.* A report to the President's Commission on Law Enforcement and Administration of Justice, Washington, D.C.: U.S. Government Printing Office.

Rengert, G.F. (1975). Some effects of being female on criminal spatial behavior. *The Pennsylvania Geographer* 13(2):10–18.

——— (November 1990). *Drug purchasing as a routine activity of drug dependent property criminals and the spatial concentration of crime.* Paper presented at the meeting of the American Society of Criminology, Baltimore, Md.

——— (November 1991). *The spatial clustering of residential burglaries about anchor points of routine activities.* Paper presented at the meeting of the American Society of Criminology, San Francisco.

Rengert, G.F., and J. Wasilchick (1985). *Suburban Burglary.* Springfield, Ill.: Charles C. Thomas.

Reppetto, T.A. (1974). *Residential Crime.* Cambridge, Mass.: Ballinger Publishing.

——— (1976). Crime prevention and the displacement phenomenon. *Crime and Delinquency* 22:168–169.

Ressler, R.K., A.W. Burgess and J.E. Douglas (1988). *Sexual Homicide: Patterns and Motives.* Lexington, Mass.: Lexington Books.

Ressler, R.K., A.W. Burgess, J.E. Douglas, C.R. Hartman, and R.B. D'Agostino (1986). Sexual killers and their victims: Identifying patterns through crime scene analysis. *Journal of Interpersonal Violence* 1:288–308.

Ressler, R.K., and T. Shachtman (1992). *Whoever Fights Monsters.* New York: St. Martin's Press.

Rhodes, W.M., and C. Conly (1981). Crime and mobility: An empirical study. Pp. 167–188 in P.J. Brantingham and P.L. Brantingham (eds.), *Environmental Criminology.* Beverly Hills: Sage.

Rogers, R., D. Craig and D. Anderson (March 1991). *Serial murder investigations and geographic information systems.* Paper presented at the conference of the Academy of Criminal Justice Sciences, Nashville, Tenn.

Rossmo, D.K. (1987). *Fugitive migration patterns.* Unpublished master's thesis, Simon Fraser University, Burnaby, BC.

——— (1993). Target patterns of serial murderers: A methodological model. *American Journal of Criminal Justice* 17(2):1–21.

——— (1994). Targeting victims: Serial killers and the urban environment. In T. O'Reilly-Fleming and S. Egger (eds.), *Serial and Mass Murder: Theory, Research and Policy.* Toronto: University of Toronto Press.

Shaw, C.R., and H.D. McKay (1972). *Juvenile Delinquency and Urban Areas* (rev. ed.). Chicago: University of Chicago Press.

Simonetti, C. (1984). *Serial murders: 1970–1983.* Unpublished master's thesis, State University of New York at Albany, Albany, N.Y.

Stea, D. (1969). The measurement of mental maps: An experimental model for studying conceptual spaces. Pp. 228–253 in K.R. Cox and R.G. Golledge (eds.), *Behavioral Problems in Geography.* Evanston, Ill.: Northwestern University Press.

Stephenson, L.K. (1974). Spatial dispersion of intra-urban juvenile delinquency. *Journal of Geography* 73(3):20–26.

——— (1980). Centrographic analysis of crime. Pp. 146–155 in D.E. Georges-Abeyie and K.D. Harries (eds.), *Crime: A Spatial Perspective.* New York: Columbia University Press.

Stoufer, A. (1960). Intervening opportunities and competing migrants. *Journal of Regional Science* 1:1–20.

Suttles, G.C. (1968). *The Social Order of the Slum.* Chicago: University of Chicago Press.

Taylor, P.J. (1977). *Quantitative Methods in Geography.* Prospect Heights, Ill.: Waveland Press.

Tomlin, C.D. (1990). *Geographic Information Systems and Cartographic Modeling.* Englewood Cliffs, N.J.: Prentice-Hall.

Topalin, J. (1992). *The journey to rape.* Unpublished master's thesis, University of Surrey, England.

Turner, S. (1969). Delinquency and distance. Pp. 11–26 in M.E. Wolfgang and T. Sellin (eds.), *Delinquency: Selected Studies.* New York: John C. Wiley.

Tversky, A., and D. Kahneman (1981). The framing of decisions and the psychology of choice. *Science* 211:453–458.

Unwin, D. (1981). *Introductory Spatial Analysis.* London: Methuen.

Upton, G.J.G., and B. Fingleton (1989). *Spatial Data Analysis by Example: Vol. 2. Categorical and Directional Data.* Chichester, N.Y.: Wiley.

U.S. Department of Justice (1990). *Annual report 1990* (National Center for the Analysis of Violent Crime). Washington, D.C.: U.S. Government Printing Office.

——— (1991). *Serial/Mass Murder* (National Institute of Justice topical search TS 011664). Washington, D.C.: U.S. Government Printing Office.

Waller, I., and N. Okihiro (1978). *Burglary: The Victim and the Public.* Toronto: University of Toronto Press.

Walmsley, D.J., and G.J. Lewis (1984). *Human Geography: Behavioural Approaches.* London: Longman.

Werner, C. (1985). *Spatial Transportation Modeling.* Sage university paper series on scientific geography, no. 5. Beverly Hills: Sage.

White, R.C. (1932). The relation of felonies to environmental factors in Indianapolis. *Social Forces* 10:498–509.

Wilson, C., and D. Seaman (1990). *The Serial Killers: A Study in the Psychology of Violence.* London: W.H. Allen Publishing.

Wolfgang, M.E. (1958). *Patterns of Criminal Homicide.* Philadelphia: University of Pennsylvania Press.

Zipf, G. (1950). *The Principle of Least Effort.* Reading, Mass.: Addison Wesley.

Chapter 8

Spatial Autocorrelation Revisited: Conceptual Underpinnings and Practical Guidelines for the Use of the Generalized Potential as a Remedy for Spatial Autocorrelation in Large Samples[1]

Dennis W. Roncek
Department of Criminal Justice
University of Nebraska at Omaha

Andrew Montgomery
Survey Research Laboratory
University of Illinois at Chicago

ABSTRACT

We revisit the initial work of Roncek and Montgomery on spatial autocorrelation and the use of the generalized potential as a strategy for coping with this issue in research analyses of large samples. We present the conceptual development of the generalized potential and explain in nonmathematical terms how its use provides the essential key for handling spatial autocorrelation effects. Practical concerns about the construction of the generalized potential so that it more accurately reflects social processes are discussed. Also incorporated in conceptual terms are the recommendations of Land and Deane, on which we expand for the special case of analyzing crime data. Finally, additional strategies for using the generalized potential in special cases are discussed, and the general procedure for its use is summarized in four simple steps.

Spatial autocorrelation must become as standard a concern among criminologists and other analysts of ecological or spatial data as is temporal autocorrelation among time-series analysts. Failing to recognize that the results of any ecological analyses of crime across states, metropolitan areas, counties, cities, suburbs, census tracts, or city blocks can be distorted by the effects of spatial autocorrelation can only lead to a misunderstanding of the social processes underlying crime and, consequently, to ineffective prevention strategies.

Despite these severe dangers, crime researchers using aggregate crime data for spatial or ecological areas such as states (Huff-Corzine et al. 1989) completely ignore these issues. At times, such omissions may have occurred through ignorance, because simple and easy-to-compute tests and remedies for spatial autocorrelation for small data

1. We are grateful to Kenneth Conrow, associate director of the Kansas State University Computer Center, whose revisions to our original computer program greatly increased its efficiency. We also appreciate the time that Patrick Doreian, Kenneth C. Land and Colin Loftin gave to the senior author (Roncek) for discussions of the issues presented in this article and its predecessor drafts. Yet the views stated in this paper are solely those of the authors, and any remaining faults are solely their responsibility.

sets have been available for years (Cliff and Ord 1973). Over a decade ago, Doreian (1980,1981) presented further refinements and simplifications for research problems with up to 100 cases.

Because of technical difficulties, at least part of which still exist today, none of the small-sample solutions of Cliff and Ord (1973), Ord (1975) or Doreian (1980,1981) is applicable to research problems involving several hundred or thousands of cases (e.g., analyzing crime across all the city blocks of a major city) (Roncek and Maier 1991). For such problems, the conceptualization necessary for the solution, its operationalization into a calculable variable, as well as the computer program necessary to create the needed variable, were developed only a few years later in the first version of this article (Roncek and Montgomery 1984), which was followed by a pilot study by Roncek and Robinson (1984). The final mathematical proof and other details for the large sample solution for which Roncek and Montgomery (1984) provided the basis were made by Land and Deane (1992) and published before its predecessors.

The highly mathematical treatment of the issue by Land and Deane (1992) and the lack of wide availability of Roncek and Montgomery (1984) or Roncek and Robinson (1984) make a revisiting and updating of the original work by Roncek and his colleagues necessary to provide a useful guide for researchers who use ecological or spatial data in any substantive specialty and, particularly, for crime analysts. Prior to Roncek and Montgomery's development of the generalized potential, which was first operationalized for urban crime research as "crime potential," neither the small-sample tests nor Doreian's extension could be used for large data sets. These earlier tests and procedures all required inverting and multiplying with an $N \times N$ adjacency matrix that identifies how close each block in a city was to every other block. The size of this matrix greatly exceeds the capability of mainframes to even store the matrix, let alone manipulate it. For a large city such as Chicago, with 15,000 city blocks, the adjacency matrix would contain 225 million elements.

In making this revised presentation of our earlier work more accessible, we begin with a simple, conceptual approach focused on urban crime (the substantive focus of the senior author). Researchers in other substantive areas can freely substitute their choice of dependent variable whenever the word *crime* is mentioned without any change in the implementation of the strategies presented.

A CONCEPTUAL EXAMPLE OF SPATIAL AUTOCORRELATION

Consider two conventional city blocks that are identical in the social composition of their residents, the physical structure of their housing stocks, and the amounts and character of the nonresidential land uses on them. Indeed, let these blocks or cases be identical for every characteristic that can be used as an independent variable pertaining to anything on the blocks themselves in a statistical analysis such as multiple regression (OLS). Because these two city blocks have identical values of all the independent variables, each will and must have the same predicted value of crime. In a "statistically" ideal world, their actual levels of crime and their residuals from a regression-type equation will be only random fluctuations from these predicted values. This state of affairs is typically found in survey research that uses probability samples of individuals. Few or none of most surveys' respondents are likely to know each other or have any other interconnection, so that the answers to a questionnaire given by one respondent will not affect the answers given by another identical respondent.

Unfortunately, this "ideal" situation is not encountered when analyzing spatial or ecological data. Regardless of whether the areas being analyzed are large, such as nations or states, or small, such as city blocks, they are not unconnected with each other, as are survey respondents. Quite the contrary, each has neighbors that are literally "next door to each other." And, in most cases, each area and all its neighbors are in the analysis. Worse yet, the number of crime incidents in one area can be expected to affect the amount of crimes in neighboring areas through diffusion-type processes. Such interconnection is very likely for phenomena like crime that are produced by individuals. Offenders living on, walking on, committing offenses on, or driving by one block can easily cross from one side of the street at the corner, in the middle or catercorner to commit a crime on the other side of the street, which could be in a different block, a different census tract, a different city or suburb, a different metropolitan area, or a different state, as in the case of consolidated statistical areas such as the Chicago-Gary, Ind., CSA. In some extreme cases, simply walking over a bridge can produce a crime in a different country. In short, the amount of crime in the surroundings of a place can affect the amount of crime in that specific area.[2]

Five easily understood and deleterious consequences follow from crime (or any other dependent variable) in one area being affected by crime in its surroundings. First, identical city blocks or other areas are no longer identical in every way if the amounts of crime in their surroundings differ. This situation is illustrated in figure 1 for two identical blocks, marked with the letter *I* in the diagram. Clearly, the block in the high-crime surroundings (block I2) will typically have more crime than the one in the low-crime surroundings (block I1).

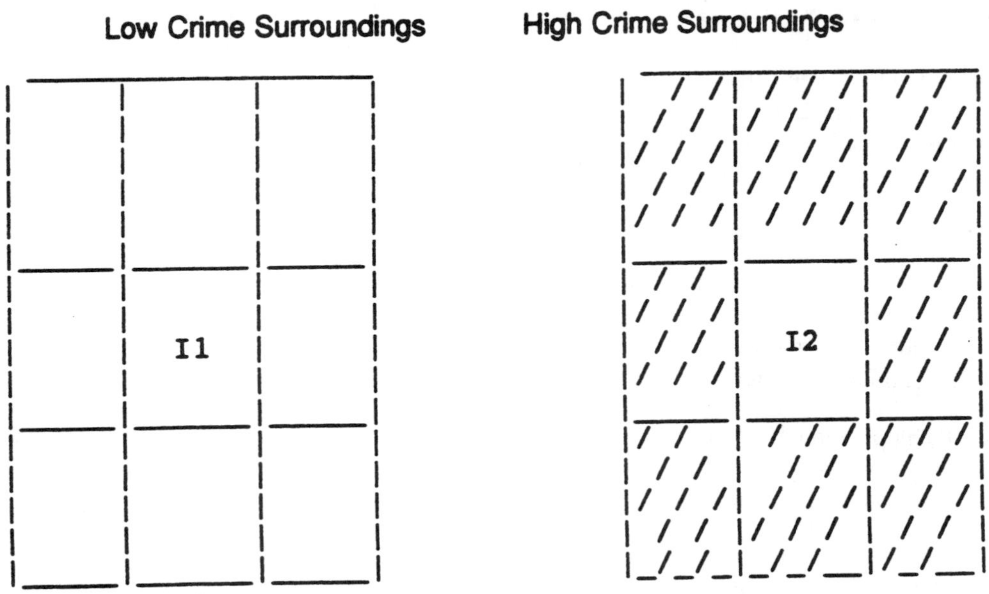

Fig. 1
Two identical blocks in different surroundings

As a consequence of the difference in the actual levels of crime, the sizes of their residuals from a regression-type analysis will not be merely random fluctuations around their identical predicted values. Thus, the second problem is that tests of statistical significance cannot be validly conducted because of the lack of random deviation of the residuals from the predicted values. Third, if crime or some other characteristics of the surroundings are causes of crime in a surrounded area, then any analysis that fails to include measures of these causes is misspecified. Thus, the third problem is that a critical assumption for the use of most analysis techniques such as regression is violated. Fourth, as a result of misspecification, the effects of other independent variables can be wrong and are likely to be overestimated, because the effects of the surroundings will be at least partially incorrectly attributed to the independent variables in the analysis. Fifth, any efforts at crime prevention based on analyses not taking the effects of the surroundings (i.e., spatial autocorrelative effects) into account can be less effective than expected because of the overestimation of the effects of the included variables.

Finally, the sixth and quite technical consequence or problem that arises is that the errors of statistical prediction for the blocks (or other spatial units of analysis) that are near each other in either of the two surroundings will be correlated with each other. This correlation among errors for areas that are physically proximate to each other violates one of the assumptions of regression-type techniques because it is a form of autocorrelation (Greene 1990:144), spa-

2. Several studies by Roncek and his students find statistically significant and substantively important effects from being located next to high-crime areas, such as those with housing projects (Roncek et al. 1981; Roncek 1992) and high schools (Roncek and Lobosco 1983; Roncek and Faggiani 1985).

tial autocorrelation.[3] Just as temporal autocorrelation is a critical issue in time-series analyses, so also is spatial autocorrelation in spatial or ecological analyses.

With this overview of the importance of spatial autocorrelation, attention can now turn to resolving these problems. The concept that is now called the generalized potential, originally developed by Roncek and Montgomery (1984), is the key to the solution. Before explaining this concept and how it is to be used, briefly reviewing its development from the older measure of population potential is useful.

POPULATION POTENTIAL: THE BASIS OF THE GENERALIZED POTENTIAL

The generalized potential developed by Roncek and Montgomery (1984) is an extension of the measure called population potential that Duncan, Cuzzort and Duncan (1963) brought into wider academic view, although not generally used apart from the work of the senior author. Population potential is a measure of population distribution that can be understood as a measure of population congestion. Equation 1 defines population potential in its simplest form.

$$\text{Equation (1)} \quad PP_i = P_1/D_1 + P_2/D_2 + \dots + P_n/D_n$$

where

PP_i is the population potential for a particular place or location, such as each of the blocks labeled *I* in figure 1, for which a value of population potential is being computed in a particular iteration;

$P_{1 \text{ through } n}$ is the population of every other place, the blocks in each part of figure 1 that are not marked with an *I*, or the blocks in the surroundings of the specific place, the blocks in each part of figure 1 that are marked with an *I*, for which population potential is being computed; and

$D_{1 \text{ through } n}$ is the distance of each other place in the surroundings from the one specific place for which the value of population potential is being computed in an iteration. The distances are based on the distances between the centroids of the places.

The calculation of population potential for all subareas of the larger area to which they belong (e.g., all blocks or census tracts in a city or all states of the U.S.) requires calculating the right-hand side of equation 1 for every subarea in turn. If each part of figure 1 were a small city, then equation 1 would have to be calculated nine times for each part, that is, once for each of the nine blocks in each city. Care, however, must be taken in using equation 1 to calculate the value of population potential. In calculating this potential for a specific subarea or city block such as I1, the right-hand side of equation 1 must not include a term for I1, because the distance of I1 from itself (or the distance of any other subarea from itself) is zero, and division by zero is not permissible mathematically. Finally, in Duncan, Cuzzort and Duncan's presentation of population potential, the distance measure in the denominator of each term on the right-hand side is euclidean (linear or "crow-flight") distance, although other distance measures could be used and are frequently preferable to euclidean distance.

Population potential is a measure of congestion in the surroundings; it is distinct from any measure of population concentration on the blocks themselves. To help understand this, briefly reinterpret figure 1 as portraying the number of residents on each block. Because both the blocks labeled *I* in figure 1 are identical in all their characteristics, including the number of residents and their physical areas, they have the same density. Whatever this density is, it is

3. Autocorrelation with spatial data for large units of analysis such as states is particularly pernicious because of the tendency of researchers to construct their data files by putting the states of the U.S. in alphabetical order. Such ordering completely ignores how far or close the states are from or to each other. In reality, Alabama is not the nearest neighbor of Alaska, or even of Arizona. Alphabetizing states is analogous to randomizing the order of years in a time-series analysis, which would make tests for temporal autocorrelation (e.g., the Durbin-Watson) useless. The error in predicting Alabama's crime is unlikely to be correlated with the error for Alaska or Arizona, although Alabama's error may very well be related to that for Mississippi and Georgia.

clearly inadequate as a measure of the amount of population congestion to which the residents of the two blocks are exposed. The density of these two blocks does not reflect the concentration of people around them in nearby areas. Clearly, people on the second block, I2, which is surrounded by the hatched and heavily populated blocks, will encounter more people in the course of their routine activities than those living on block I1 in the more sparsely settled environment. Such differences will occur regardless of the density of each of these blocks being identical. Thus, density is clearly inadequate as a measure of the congestion that the residents of the two identical blocks experience.

The same problem occurs when studying crime across areas within a city. Just as people can come from other areas to increase congestion, offenders can wander from or diffuse from nearby areas to commit crimes in other areas. Thus, the amount of crime on a block or the value of any other dependent variable for areas within a city can also frequently depend not only on the characteristics of those areas themselves, but also on the characteristics of the places to which they are near. This problem and the inherent concept of diffusion reflected in population potential led to the development of the generalized potential by Roncek and Montgomery (1984).

THE GENERALIZED POTENTIAL

The generalized potential is also computed from the formula in equation 1, but with one very major difference. The value of the dependent variable (e.g., crime in each subarea in the surroundings) is in the numerator of each term on the right-hand side of equation 1. For intrametropolitan analyses, we also recommend against using euclidean distance for the denominators of the right-hand side and will explain why in a later section of the article. After adjustment to handle other statistical issues, using the adjusted generalized potential in regression-type analyses as an independent variable simultaneously provides (1) a test for spatial autocorrelation, (2) a measure of the effects of spatial autocorrelation on a dependent variable, and (3) adjustments to the effects of all other independent variables. Understanding how the use of an adjusted generalized potential accomplishes all these tasks requires discussing several aspects of this measure.

First, the generalized potential is what can be called an absorbing variable. Its values, by definition, reflect the influences of all possible causes of crime (or other dependent variables), because it is computed from the amount of crime on each of the blocks in the surroundings.[4] This is both a great blessing and a minor curse.

The great blessing is that having the values of crime for places in the surroundings of each area in the numerator of equation 1 obviates the need to compute any other potentials based on the original independent variables, unless a researcher is interested in specific effects of the distribution of a particular variable in the surroundings of the areas being analyzed.[5] Logically, the generalized potential includes all the effects of all causes of crime, because it is computed from the amount of crime that occurs. Understanding this idea is facilitated by examining briefly an example of how the effects of a particular characteristic of subareas of the city that affects crime are automatically included in the generalized potential.

If some characteristic such as a high concentration of apartment buildings facilitates crime, then it must do so on each and every block in a city. This means it must facilitate crime on the blocks marked *I* in each part of figure 1, as well as on those in the surroundings of each of the I blocks. It is not sensible to argue that having a particular charac-

4. Researchers must be careful not to ignore the likelihood that subareas on the borders of their study site that are adjacent to other places outside the study area will still have their levels of the dependent variable affected by diffusion from these other places. For example, those city blocks or census tracts that border the suburbs rather than a lakefront can have crime diffusing from the suburbs to these border areas. Terms reflecting the amount of crime in these suburbs and their distance from places within the city should also be included in the computation of the generalized potential for each of the city areas. In general, approximating these influences by assigning all the crimes in a suburb to the suburb's centroid and then calculating the distances to each of the city's areas from this centroid for each suburb should be sufficient.

5. Despite its not being necessary to compute other potentials, the senior author has always computed and included the original population potential in his analyses. The amount of potential contact to which urban residents are exposed has been a central concern in urban sociology since Wirth (1938).

teristic can facilitate crime on only the I blocks, but not on the blocks in the surroundings. Thus, using the generalized potential, after adjustment, as an independent variable takes into account all the effects of all the independent variables or characteristics of areas in the surroundings, because it is computed using the final effect of these characteristics (i.e., crime). Clearly, the effects of these other characteristics, such as apartment buildings in the surroundings, on the amount of crime that can diffuse to nearby areas are already measured by simply using the amount of crime in each surrounding area as the numerator for the terms on the right-hand side of equation 1.

An additional advantage of the generalized potential is that its use eliminates the need to specify the range or distance over which diffusion effects operate, and therefore avoids another risk of specification error. The results of analyses based on distances that are not the ones over which diffusion effects operate can be misinterpreted to mean that no diffusion effects whatsoever exist. If, however, diffusion effects do exist but are not detected because incorrect distances are chosen, then a cause of crime has been omitted from the analyses, and the effects of other independent variables are also incorrect. Typically, no basis exists for choosing one distance or range rather than others prior to analyses. Because the generalized potential is computed for all areas in the surroundings, it measures all possible diffusion effects and avoids the possibility of selecting a distance or range that is not the one over which diffusion effects operate. Furthermore, much tedious labor is also avoided by not having to search successively for diffusion effects on areas that are one, two, three, or more areas away from each area in the analysis, unless there is a specific need to determine the exact range of diffusion effects.[6] Thus, the only remaining specification issues concern whether the correct independent variables are used for the subareas being analyzed.

After adjustment, the generalized potential measures how the error in statistical prediction for each block is affected by nearby cases (i.e., spatial autocorrelation). As simply another independent variable, regression-type analyses will produce a coefficient and a standard error for the adjusted generalized potential. With these, the test for statistically significant spatial autocorrelation effects becomes a simple test of the statistical significance of the coefficient of the adjusted generalized potential. The numerical effect and relative importance of spatial autocorrelation are directly identified by the sizes of the unstandardized and standardized coefficients for this potential. Finally, its direct inclusion in the analysis model as an independent variable explicitly adjusts the sizes of the coefficients of all other independent variables.[7]

THE EMPIRICAL USE OF THE GENERALIZED POTENTIAL

The two curses associated with the generalized potential both stem from its being based on the values of the dependent variable for other cases in the analyses and not being due to a characteristic of each particular case. Fortunately, both problems can be remedied. The first and most serious problem is that the generalized potential as computed by equation 1 must be correlated with the error term for the dependent variable in regression-type analyses.[8] The raw value of the potential for any specific area is merely the sum of the values of the dependent variable for all other areas in the analyses, except the specific one for which it is being computed, weighted by their distances from the specific area. (In intracity analyses, such as those for a city's residential blocks, terms for crime in the suburbs would

6. At other times, the range of diffusion effects can be important. One of Roncek et al.'s (1981) concerns was with identifying how close ordinary residential blocks had to be to public housing projects for families and for the elderly to experience significant crime diffusion effects. Roncek and Lobosco (1983) and Roncek and Faggiani (1985) examine the range of crime diffusion from high schools.

7. The amount of distortion introduced into the effects of other independent variables can be measured by comparing models with and without the generalized potential. Changes in the variance explained and the sizes of the coefficients are useful to examine across these two statistical models.

8. Unfortunately, one cannot simply compute the residual of a regression and then compute a correlation between the calculated residual and the generalized potential for the cases in the analysis, that, at the very least, are a sample in time, even if all the subareas in a larger area such as a city are used. The assumption of noncorrelation of the independent variables with the error term refers to noncorrelation in an unobserved and unobservable population. The generalized potential is analogous to a lagged endogenous dependent variable in time-series analyses, in that the potential is the level of crime for an observation that is physically near another observation, in much the same way that the values of a lagged endogenous dependent variable are the values of the dependent variable that are near other observations in time.

be included on the right-hand side of equation 1 to reflect diffusion from the suburbs to blocks in the city, but the suburbs themselves would not be included in the analyses). Because the generalized potential represents an influence on crime that is not directly due to the characteristics of a block itself, it must be related to the error term for the statistical model for each case or unit of analysis.[9] However, regression-type models all assume that the independent variables are not correlated with the error term for the model (Greene 1990:144).

As Land and Deane (1993:231–232) demonstrate, the problem of correlation with the error term can be resolved by creating and using an adjusted generalized potential. Two basic tasks are involved in the adjustment process. The first is to remove from the generalized potential any component that is part of the error term for the statistical model. The second is to avoid the adjusted potential's becoming a complete linear function of the other independent variables that pertain to blocks themselves.

These two tasks are accomplished by substituting the predicted values of the generalized potential on two groups of variables for its original values from equation 1. The first group of independent variables to be used as predictors of the original potential is the characteristics of the blocks themselves, that is, the independent variables of theoretical concern with regard to the dependent variable. Including the important block characteristics in this regression purges the predicted values of the potential of any correlation with the error or residual from the regression predicting crime. Unfortunately, using only the major independent variable to create predicted values of the generalized potential is not sufficient, because predicted values based on only these variables could not be used in a regression on crime along with the independent variables from which it is created. Attempting to do so would create perfect multicollinearity.

To avoid this trap, additional variables that will not be used as predictors of crime need to be included in the regression predicting the generalized potential (Land and Deane 1992). In econometrics, such variables are called instrumental variables. Although no procedure exists for readily determining which additional variables to select for this role, Land and Deane's (1992) choice of dummy variables representing larger regions than the counties that they analyzed provides a useful example to follow, since such variables are often available for other types of areas both larger and smaller than counties.

Cities themselves are typically divided into traditional regions for planning purposes and are also divided by residents into regions in their cognitive mapping of the city. Such intracity regional distinctions often come from and are related to the historical physical and social development of the city. Thus, these regional distinctions reflect aspects of a city that may not be easily quantified themselves, but nevertheless can be related to the values of the generalized potential that also reflect these same structural aspects. Thus, subcity regions are worth investigating as instrumental variables when other alternatives are not immediately apparent.

After selecting the instrumental variables to use in the regression predicting the generalized potential, this regression is computed and its predicted values are treated as a new independent variable for predicting crime on the blocks themselves. In this final regression, all the benefits mentioned above can be obtained from examining the coefficients of this adjusted potential.[10]

9. We are grateful to Kenneth C. Land for clarifying this point for us in discussions with the senior author about Roncek and Montgomery (1984) over the last five years.

10. In a later section of the paper, we also explain an additional strategy that can help ensure the lack of correlation between the error term for regressions involving specific types of crime as a dependent variable.

PRACTICAL CONSIDERATIONS FOR USING THE GENERALIZED POTENTIAL

Choosing a Measure of Distance for the Generalized Potential

Population potential, the precursor of the generalized potential, is based on euclidean (straight line or linear) distance between two points and is always the shortest distance between two points. However, moving in a straight line between two points or places in a city as required by euclidean distance may not always be possible. At times, such movement requires that people be able to walk or drive on a diagonal line passing through the walls of houses to go from one block to another. Thus, euclidean distance can often be a poor representation of the way in which individuals move through a city and the way in which crime or another dependent variable diffuses. When the units of analysis are the subareas of metropolitan statistical areas, counties or cities, what is called rectilinear distance can be a much better distance measure to use for computing the generalized potential (Roncek and Montgomery 1984). Rectilinear distance, the formula for which is in equation 2, is the sum of the distances traveled on both the *x* and *y* axes in a Cartesian plane.

$$\text{Equation (2)} \quad D_R = |X_i - X_d| + |Y_i - Y_d|$$

where

D_R is rectilinear distance,

X_i and Y_i are the X and Y coordinates of the starting or initial point,

X_d and Y_d are the X and Y coordinates of the destination point, and

the "|" operator indicates the absolute value of the result of the subtraction. Figure 2 shows the difference between these distance measures for a small group of areas (e.g., city blocks).

In panel A, euclidean distance between the centroids of two city blocks, each of which is marked with an *x*, is represented by the length of line *a* and rectilinear distance by the sum of the lengths of lines *b* and *c*. Panel B shows how rearranging parts of lines *b* and *c* produces a very realistic approximation to the way people would walk or drive from one block to another in a rectangular street grid.[11] In panel B, the sum of the lengths of lines *d* and *e* equals the length of the vertical line *b* in panel A, and the sum of the lengths of lines *f* and *g* equals the length of the horizontal line *c* in panel A. Rectilinear distance will be too long when travel involves diagonal streets, but works well when the entire grid is rotated.[12] The generalized potential based on rectilinear distance is the default potential calculated by Roncek and Montgomery's computer program.

We prefer using simple rectilinear distance over its square or the square of euclidean distance, either of which can be computed using the Roncek and Montgomery program. The rationales for this preference are that (1) the square of either distance does not represent any type of movement pattern, (2) no impediment to traveling longer distances other than linear time appears to be important in affecting longer rather than shorter movement, and (3) in empirical tests using generalized potentials based on the squares of rectilinear distance and euclidean distances, neither of the squared distances is as effective a predictor of crime as the potential using simple rectilinear distance (Roncek 1981).

---

11. For the most part, a rectangular grid is the predominant street layout in older cities and in the older and usually more crime-ridden parts of newer cities.

12. Although computer programs are available to compute the shortest travel route between two points over a street network, and these could be used as the denominator for the generalized potential, attempting to do so has severe costs. Even assuming that travel is always symmetric (i.e., the path from one place to another is always the same in the reverse direction), the number of unique distances to be calculated, stored and then matrix-multiplied to create the generalized potential is approximately $(N^2 - N)/2$, where N is the number of subareas for which potentials are calculated. For a city of only 1,000 blocks, 499,500 distances would have to be calculated and manipulated to compute a generalized potential. For Chicago's approximately 15,000 residential blocks, over 11 million distances would have to be used. Manipulating the distances to create potentials would be either extremely difficult or, in some cases, impossible. Since a large proportion of travel distances are likely to be rectilinear, little justification exists for using this alternative.

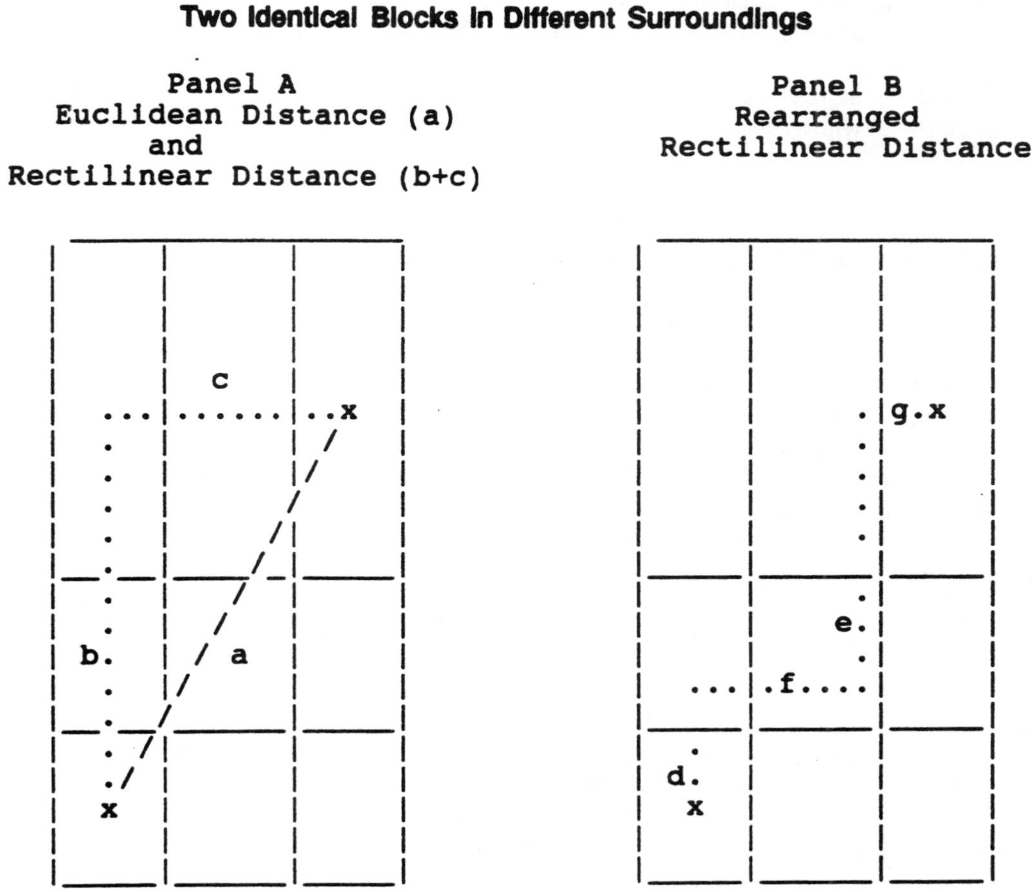

Fig. 2
Comparison of euclidean and rectilinear distances

Analyses Including More Than One Potential

The use of the adjusted generalized potential, based on crime or another dependent variable, as an independent variable empirically resolves the problem of spatial autocorrelation or diffusion effects. Its use does not, however, identify the type of diffusion that affects crime. As mentioned earlier, the senior author always uses ordinary population potential as a predictor in his analysis of urban crime patterns. Other researchers may want to use other types of substantive potentials, such as those based on the presence of young males (see Felson 1986) or nonintact families. Indeed, any alternative form of the generalized potential can be used to measure the effects of the overall or cumulative proximity to important crime generators (e.g., the project potential used by Roncek et al. [1981] to examine the diffusion of crime from housing for families). Such uses of variants of the generalized potential have much to recommend them. However, using both a variant of the generalized potential based on an independent variable and the adjusted generalized potential based on the dependent variable could produce severe multicollinearity, if the instrumental variables used to create the adjusted generalized potential are not reasonably powerful.

To remedy this problem, the best strategy is to locate additional instrumental variables so that the two potentials will not be highly correlated. This immediately eliminates any problem. Should this not be sufficient, the revised adjusted generalized potential should then be adjusted one more time before it is used in an analysis. Substituting the regression residual of the revised adjusted generalized potential from a regression on the substantive potential for the adjusted generalized potential will remove the collinearity. This recommendation follows from the principle of parsimony. A substantive potential based on only one explicit independent variable is simpler conceptually than a crime potential, because the former measures a single type of diffusion rather than the diffusion of a phenomenon that is a complex product of many influences. Because of its simplicity, the single-characteristic substantive potential should be given causal priority by allowing it to absorb any overlapping explanatory power in predicting the dependent variable that is shared with the more complex generalized potential. Removing from the adjusted generalized potential any of the variance it shares with a substantive potential accomplishes this task.

A Special Note on Creating Crime Potentials

When some form of criminal behavior (e.g., arrests or incidents) is the dependent variable, an additional strategy can facilitate avoiding the problem of a crime potential's being correlated with the error term for a statistical model. This strategy emerges from the complexity of crime as a phenomenon and the variability in what the final classification of a particular incident will be. The type of crime used to describe a particular criminal incident can depend on relatively fortuitous circumstances. A shooting of a victim can become a murder or an aggravated assault, depending on how fast an ambulance arrives. In addition, a high incidence of assaults on a block due to the presence of taverns could affect the number of rapes on nearby blocks, as former combatants leave the scene of the last conflict and encounter women in nearby areas. In short, the possibility exists that whatever draws offenders to or facilitates crime of any type in a specific area's surroundings could result in producing crimes of a different type in that specific area, depending on the opportunities for criminal activity in that area. Given this fortuitousness and differences in the structure of criminal opportunities, computing crime potentials (adjusted generalized potentials) on only the one specific type of crime being used as the dependent variable is very restrictive.

Crime potentials can be computed for specific crimes and categories of crimes such as violent crimes, property crimes, the traditional Part I crimes, and so on, and the effectiveness of the different potentials in an analytic model can be examined.[13] However, the inherent flexibility of criminal activity recommends following the strategy of Roncek and Maier (1991). They compute and use an adjusted crime potential for an aggregate of crimes, the total of the seven traditional Part I crimes, as an independent variable for each of the separate Part I crimes and the totals of violent, property and all Part I crimes.[14] Using such an aggregate potential allows taking into account the flexibility of crime, while at the same time necessarily decreasing the correlation with the model's error term, because the aggregate potential is not defined solely in terms of the dependent variable, except when the dependent variable is the same aggregate for which the potential is computed. This strategy extends in a practical fashion the aphorism that "violence begets violence" to crime begetting crime, but not necessarily of only one specific type.

DISCUSSION

In this updating of Roncek and Montgomery (1984), we reemphasize the importance of spatial autocorrelation for ecological analyses and present the issues underlying it in conceptual terms that can be easily followed by researchers without extensive mathematical or statistical backgrounds. Our presentation incorporates developments by Land and Deane (1992) for using the generalized potential developed by Roncek and Montgomery (1984) to test and correct for spatial autocorrelation in ecological analyses. We also address several specific issues in the computation of and use of the generalized potential and other variants of its precursor, population potential, for further explicating the extent and nature of diffusion effects.

13. Our crime potential program can compute several potentials simultaneously so that making such comparisons is not difficult. Original population potential can also be calculated at the same time.

14. The aggregate crime potentials can be obtained by merely summing the specific potentials for each of the separate crimes. For example, the value of a violent crime potential for any case is equal to the sum of the values of the murder potential, the rape potential, the robbery potential, and the assault potential. This additive property follows from the linear additive definition for the generalized potential.

We pay special attention to the effects of spatial autocorrelation for large-sample, ecological crime analyses. Our motivation stems from several sources. First, this is the substantive problem that drew our attention to spatial autocorrelation after its emergence into broad sociological view by Loftin and Ward (1983), and for which we found the inapplicability of earlier small-sample approaches. Second, the neglect of spatial autocorrelation in the ecological analyses of crime is particularly glaring, and this issue needs special attention in this substantive area because of the important deleterious consequences from neglecting it. Third, because crime is a topic of general interest, focusing on it helps attract and maintain a relatively broad readership and facilitates explaining this issue in terms that can be readily understood. We note repeatedly that our general strategies apply to other substantive areas, as Land et al. (1991) and Land and Deane (1992) clearly demonstrate. Finally, the nature of crime as a dependent variable in ecological crime analyses permits additional flexibility in resolving the most difficult technical problem in the use of the generalized potential to cope with spatial autocorrelation.

The strategies that we recommend are relatively simple and feasible and encompass only a few steps. First, create a generalized potential using either the dependent variable itself or a measure of the broader phenomenon from which it derives as the numerator in the potential formula and an appropriate measure of distance in the denominator. Second, choose instrumental variables that affect the value of the generalized potential but have no direct conceptual relationship to the major dependent variable. Third, compute the predicted values of the generalized potential from the major theoretically important independent variables for the areas being analyzed and the instrumental variables. Fourth, use the predicted values of the generalized potential from the preceding regression as an additional independent variable along with the major independent variables in a final regression to identify correctly the effects of these major variables. Doing so will, at the same time, assess and specify the effect of spatial autocorrelation.

In closing, we note that the focus of our recommendations and strategies is for large-sample problems for which the earlier small-sample solutions are not feasible for technical reasons. Our intent is not to replace these procedures for small-sample analyses such as those of crime patterns across the states of the U.S., but rather to provide a means of properly conducting large-sample analyses. For small samples, the rigor and directness of the procedures of Cliff and Ord (1973), Ord (1975), Doreian (1980,1981), and Anselin (1988) still remain the methods of choice. Unfortunately, the problem of spatial autocorrelation does not disappear for large samples. Thus, correctly estimating its effects and the effects of other independent variables becomes critically important as academic research begins to use units of analysis that are precise enough to allow the possibility of undertaking meaningful and potentially effective efforts at change. The success of such efforts, however, depends on obtaining accurate estimates of the associations of independent variables with crime or other phenomena. We hope that our work will provide some of the necessary guides to researchers of widely varying backgrounds to accomplish this task.

REFERENCES

Anselin, Luc (1988). *Spatial Econometrics: Methods and Models.* Dordrecht, The Netherlands: Kluwer Academic Publishers.

Cliff, Andrew D., and J. Keith Ord (1973). *Spatial Autocorrelation.* London: Pion.

Doreian, Patrick (1980). Linear models with spatially distributed data: Spatial disturbances or spatial effects? *Sociological Methods and Research* 9:29–60.

——— (1981). Estimating models with spatially distributed data. Pp. 359–388 in S.K. Leinhardt (ed.), *Sociological Methodology.* San Francisco: Jossey-Bass.

Duncan, Otis D., Ray P. Cuzzort and Beverly A. Duncan (1963). *Statistical Geography.* New York: Free Press.

Felson, Marcus (1986). Predicting crime potential at any point on the city map. Pp. 127–36 in R.M. Figlio, S. Hakim and G.F. Rengert (eds.), *Metropolitan Crime Patterns*. Monsey, N.Y.: Willow Tree Press.

Greene, William H. (1990). *Econometric Analysis*. New York: MacMillan.

Huff-Corzine, Lin, Jay Corzine and David C. Moore (1986). Southern exposure: Deciphering the South's influence on homicide rates. *Social Forces* 64:906–24.

Land, Kenneth C., and Glenn Deane (1992). On the large-sample estimation of regression models with spatial- or network-effects terms: A two-stage least squares approach. Pp. 221–48 in P.V. Marsden (ed.), *Sociological Methodology*. Washington, D.C.: American Sociological Association.

Land, Kenneth C., Glenn Deane and Judith R. Blau (1991). Religious pluralism and church membership: A spatial diffusion model. *American Sociological Review* 56:237–49.

Loftin, Colin and Sally Kent Ward (1983). Population density and fertility. *American Sociological Review* 48:121–38.

Ord, J. Keith (1975). Estimation methods for models of social interaction. *Journal of the American Statistical Association* 70:120–126.

Roncek, Dennis W. (1981). Dangerous places. *Social Forces 60*:74–96.

——— (1992). Housing projects and crimes revisited. Paper presented at the 1992 annual meetings of the American Society of Criminology, New Orleans.

Roncek, Dennis W., Ralph Bell and Jeffrey M.A. Francik (1981). Housing projects and crime: Testing a proximity hypothesis. *Social Problems* 29:151–66.

Roncek, Dennis W., and Donald A. Faggiani (1985). High schools and crime. *The Sociological Quarterly* 26:491–505.

Roncek, Dennis W., and Antoinette Lobosco (1983). The effect of high schools on crime in their neighborhoods. *Social Science Quarterly* 64:598–613.

Roncek, Dennis W., and Pamela A. Maier (1991). Bars, blocks and crimes revisited: Linking the theory of routine activities to the empiricism of "hot spots." *Criminology* 29:725–53.

Roncek, Dennis W., and Andrew Montgomery (1984). Spatial autocorrelation: Diagnoses and remedies for large samples. Paper presented at the 1984 annual meetings of the Midwest Sociological Society, Des Moines.

Roncek, Dennis W., and James Robinson (1984). The effects of crime in the surroundings of residential areas. Paper presented at the 1984 annual meetings of the American Society of Criminology, Cincinnati.

Wirth, Louis (1938). Urbanism as a way of life. *American Journal of Sociology* 44:1–25.

Chapter 9

The Temporal Ecology of Calls for Police Service

James L. LeBeau
Administration of Justice and Geography Departments
Southern Illinois University at Carbondale

INTRODUCTION

In its original format, this presentation involved 50 color slides, most of which were images emanating from a raster-based geographic information system (GIS) known as IDRISI. Because of the prohibitive costs of reproducing and printing color images and the technical problem of losing important information and effect from converting color images into gray scale images, this summary is a drastically modified and reduced version of the original.

The original presentation demonstrated how raster-based GIS, three-dimensional diagrams and spectral analysis are combined to illustrate how different types of calls for police service vary geographically and temporally across a city, and how different types of calls for service occurring in specific ecological areas exhibit distinctive temporal rhythms. The data for this presentation emanated from the computer-aided dispatch records of the Charlotte, N.C., Police Department.

The data for this presentation are calls for service involving domestic disputes during the years 1986 and 1990. The geographic unit of analysis is the police response area, which is smaller than a census tract and larger census block groups. The number of response areas is 499. The temporal unit of analysis used in the spectral analysis is the number of individual three-hour periods for a year; there are 2,920 three-hour periods.

RASTER GIS, GRIDDED DATA AND SPECTRAL ANALYSIS

A geographic information system is any manual or computer-based set of procedures used to store and manipulate geographically referenced data (Aronoff 1989:39). Computer-based geographic information systems represent digital data in either vector or raster formats. In the vector format, geographic features or boundaries are represented by a series of coordinate points and lines referenced by some form of grid system (such as *x-y* Cartesian coordinates or longitude-latitude). In the raster format, the geographic surface to be mapped is divided into a row-column matrix or grid lattice. Therefore, identifying a feature or boundary involves allocating a particular value or color shading to the cells containing the feature or boundary (Eastman 1992:22).

Both systems have their advantages and limitations. The raster format is very data-intensive and presents storage problems. The vector format is very good for database management, storage and production of attractive maps. The main advantage of the raster format is that it has much more analytical power than the vector system (Eastman 1992:22). Thus, vector systems produce pretty maps, while raster systems are more amenable to geostatistical analysis.

Related to the raster format is gridded data, or grids that describe a surface taken at regular intervals. Gridded data are location-based and describe what exists at a location, given a specific map scale (Langran 1992:45). A major drawback of gridded information, like raster, is that it is difficult to determine the perimeters, shapes and contiguities of different features (Langran 1992:45).

Spectral analysis is the appropriate technique for isolating significant temporal rhythms. The technique is used to break down a stationary and detrended time-series into uncorrelated cycles (Brantingham and Brantingham 1984). In other words, spectral analysis is an analysis of a time-series in the frequency domain. A cycle is basically when a phenomenon goes from its highest point to its lowest, and then back to its highest point.

> Each cycle is a sinusoidal function of time, and its frequency represents the fraction of the cycle completed in a given time unit. The period is the reciprocal of frequency and represents the number of time units required for the completion of the cycle (McPheters and Stronge 1974).

High- or fast-frequency phenomena have a higher proportion of the cycle completed per unit time, while low- or slow-frequency phenomena have a lower portion of the cycle completed per unit of time. The essential part of spectral analysis is the calculation of the spectral density estimate, which is the relative importance of each frequency in terms of its relative contribution to the variance of the entire time-series (Parkes and Thrift 1980). The highest spectral densities for particular frequencies are what constitute the rhythm.

In the IDRISI raster format, the 165.68-square-mile area of Charlotte, N.C., was represented by a 300-by-300 matrix, or 90,000 cells. The three-dimensional diagrams of Charlotte shown in this presentation utilized gridded data of a 21-by-21 matrix, or 441 cells. Therefore, the area covered by each cell in the latter data set encompasses more area than the raster format. This means that the number of domestic disputes in a specific cell or grid is an average of several contiguous response areas.

DOMESTIC DISPUTES: 1986 AND 1990

During 1986, the Charlotte Police Department responded to over 20,875 calls for service pertaining to domestic disputes. Figure 1 is a block diagram depicting the grid locations and the frequencies of domestic disputes. The southern portions of the city are relatively inactive compared to the central, northern and western sections. Some of the grids recording the higher frequencies of domestic disputes have large public housing projects located in them. If we examine the point on the "Frequency of Domestic Disputes" axis where the grids appear level or uniformly equal, we can see that the average number of disputes was approximately 30 during 1986.

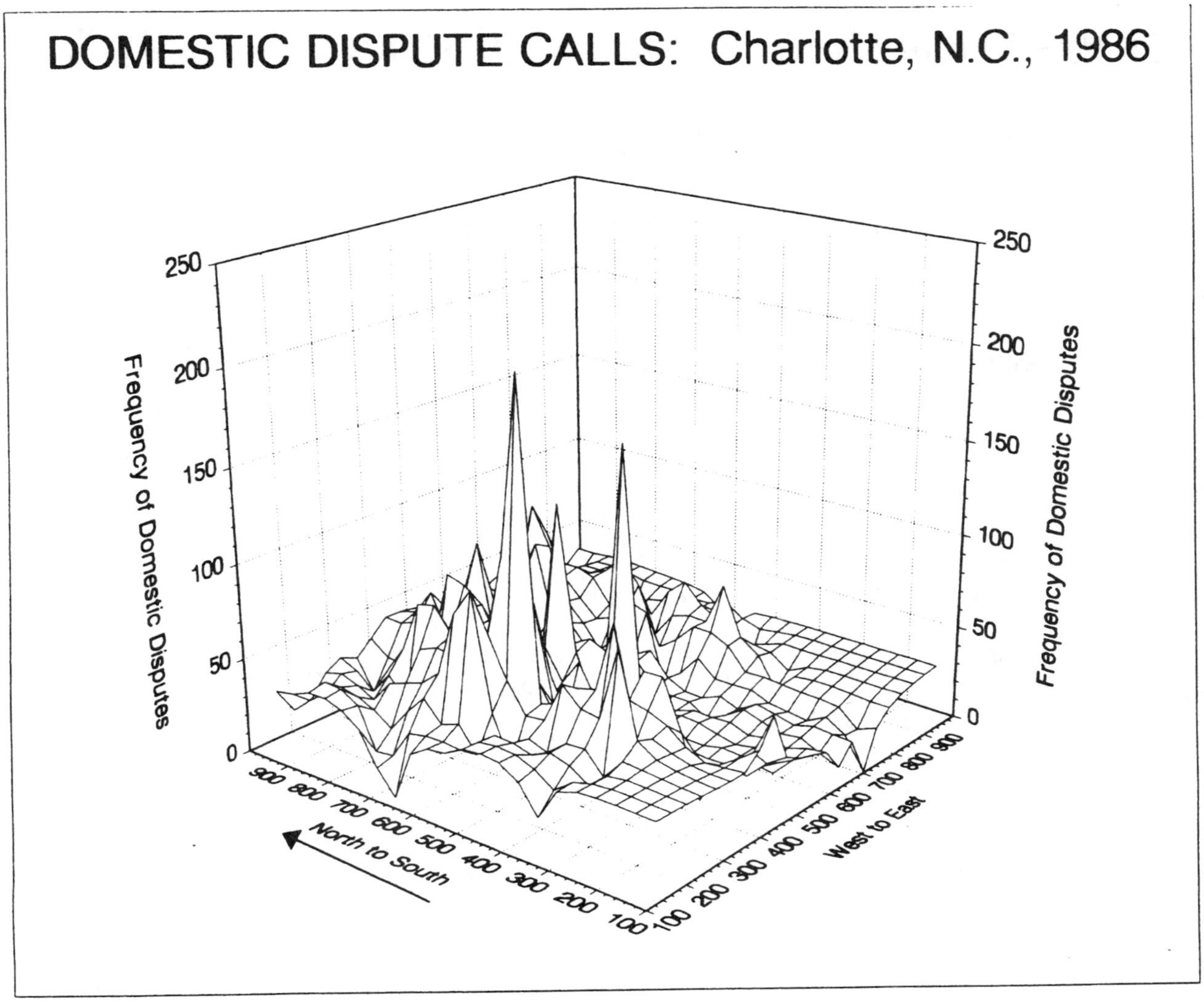

Fig. 1
Domestic dispute calls: Charlotte, N.C., 1986

During 1990, over 30,000 domestic dispute calls were received by the police (figure 2). The average level of calls rose to almost 50 for each cell. The same areas that were high during 1986 were high during 1990 (compare figures 1 and 2). Moreover, calls in the central eastern section of the city appear to increase dramatically (figure 2). As previously mentioned, one of the advantages of using raster or grid data is enhanced analytical capabilities. Thus, if one wants to examine the changes in the distribution and quantity of a phenomenon over time, all that is required is the mathematical manipulation of identical rasters or grids.

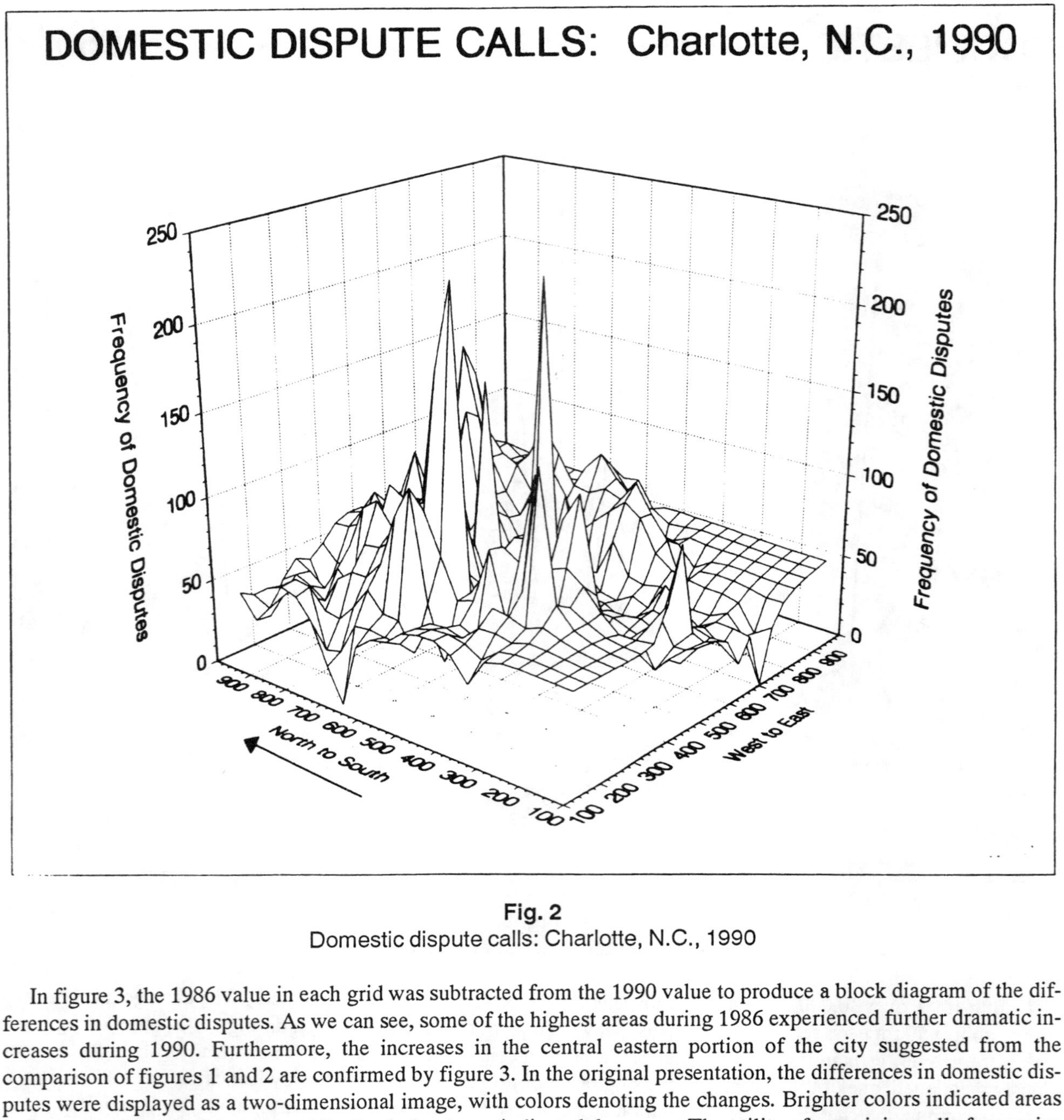

Fig. 2
Domestic dispute calls: Charlotte, N.C., 1990

In figure 3, the 1986 value in each grid was subtracted from the 1990 value to produce a block diagram of the differences in domestic disputes. As we can see, some of the highest areas during 1986 experienced further dramatic increases during 1990. Furthermore, the increases in the central eastern portion of the city suggested from the comparison of figures 1 and 2 are confirmed by figure 3. In the original presentation, the differences in domestic disputes were displayed as a two-dimensional image, with colors denoting the changes. Brighter colors indicated areas experiencing increases in calls, while the darker tones indicated decreases. The utility of examining calls for service in this matter is that it is an aid for strategic decision making, especially in regard to matters pertaining to workload analysis.

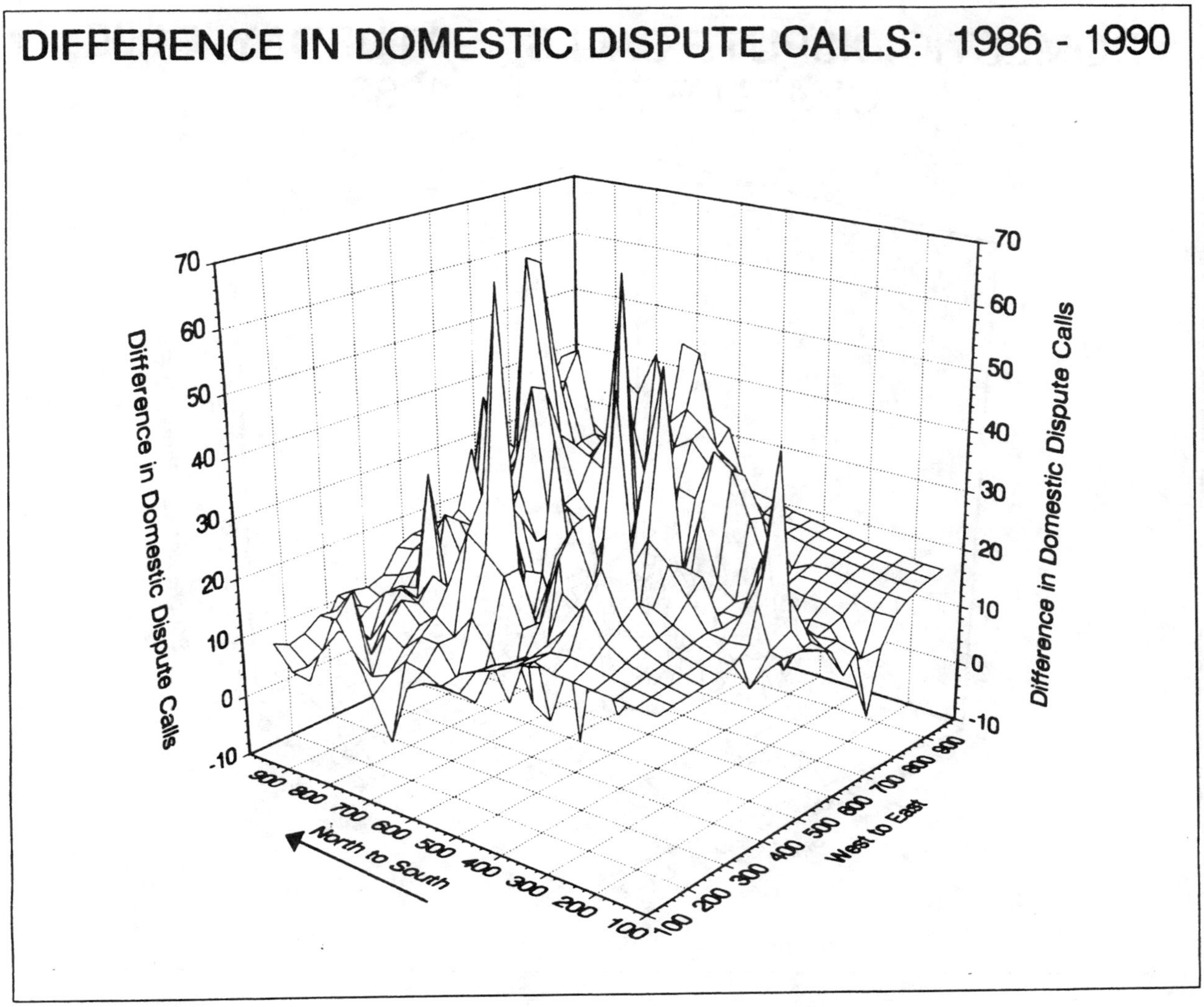

Fig. 3
Difference in domestic dispute calls: 1986 to 1990

DOMESTIC DISPUTE CALLS ON SATURDAYS

During 1986, 19.97 percent of the 20,835 domestic dispute calls occurred on Saturdays. The following eight figures depict the square root of the frequency of domestic dispute calls for every three-hour period on Saturdays during 1986. The three-hour periods emanate from another study, which examined domestic dispute calls with the oscillation of the temperature-humidity index. The three-hour periods correspond to the temporal unit used for recording weather data (LeBeau 1994). The three-hour period on each figure represents the midpoint of the interval. For example, the period 01:00 represents events occurring between 23:31 p.m. and 02:30 a.m.

The 01:00 period was the second highest period recording domestic dispute calls, with 782. The distribution of calls is depicted in figure 4. The highest areas at 01:00 during Saturday reflect the highest areas for the whole year. The southern and eastern sides of the city are relatively inactive compared to the western, central and northern sections of the city. The highest areas or grids are those containing large tracts of public housing.

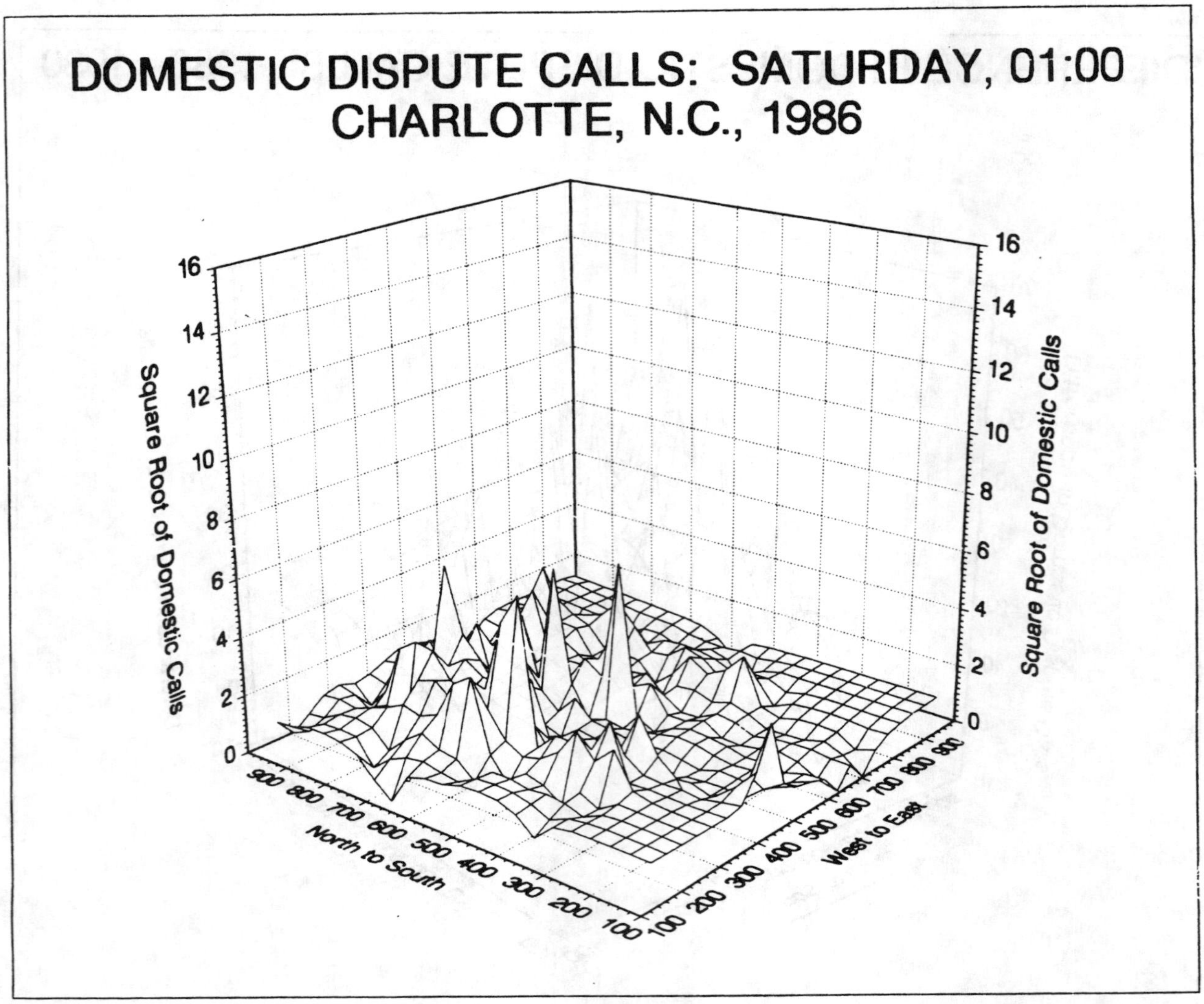

Fig. 4
Domestic dispute calls: Saturday, 01:00, Charlotte, N.C., 1986

During the 04:00 time period, 351 domestic disputes were reported in Charlotte (figure 5). While a majority of the grids or areas are inactive, many in the center of the graph, which is also near the center of the city, are relatively active. Furthermore, the same areas active during 04:00 are active during 07:00 (figure 6). The 07:00 period is the least active, with 236 calls. As a matter of fact, this hour is pivotal, or the trough of a cycle. In other words, the number of domestic disputes decreases from 01:00, bottoms out at 07:00 and increases during subsequent hours, achieving a zenith at 22:00.

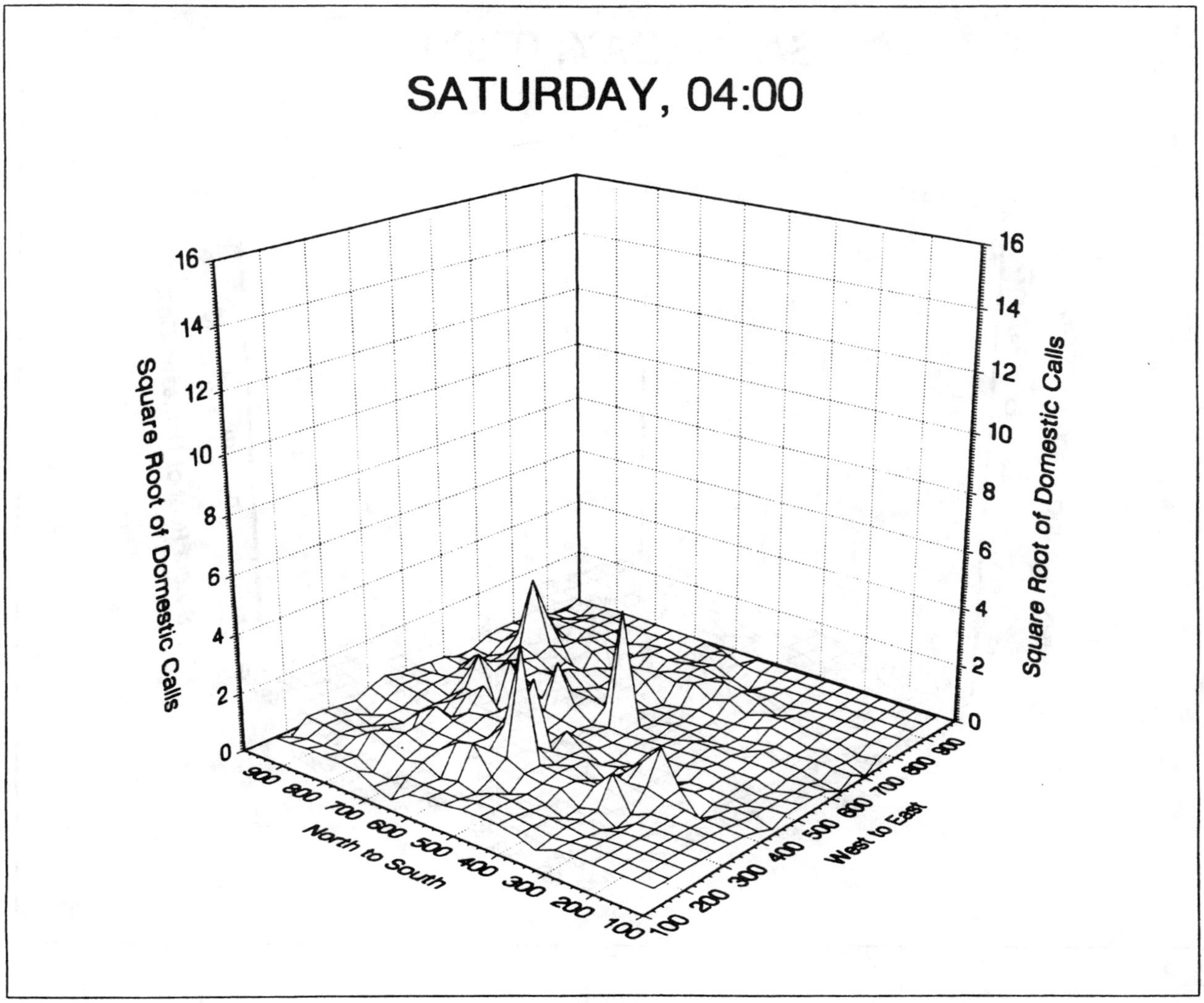

Fig. 5
Domestic dispute calls: Saturday, 04:00, Charlotte, N.C., 1986

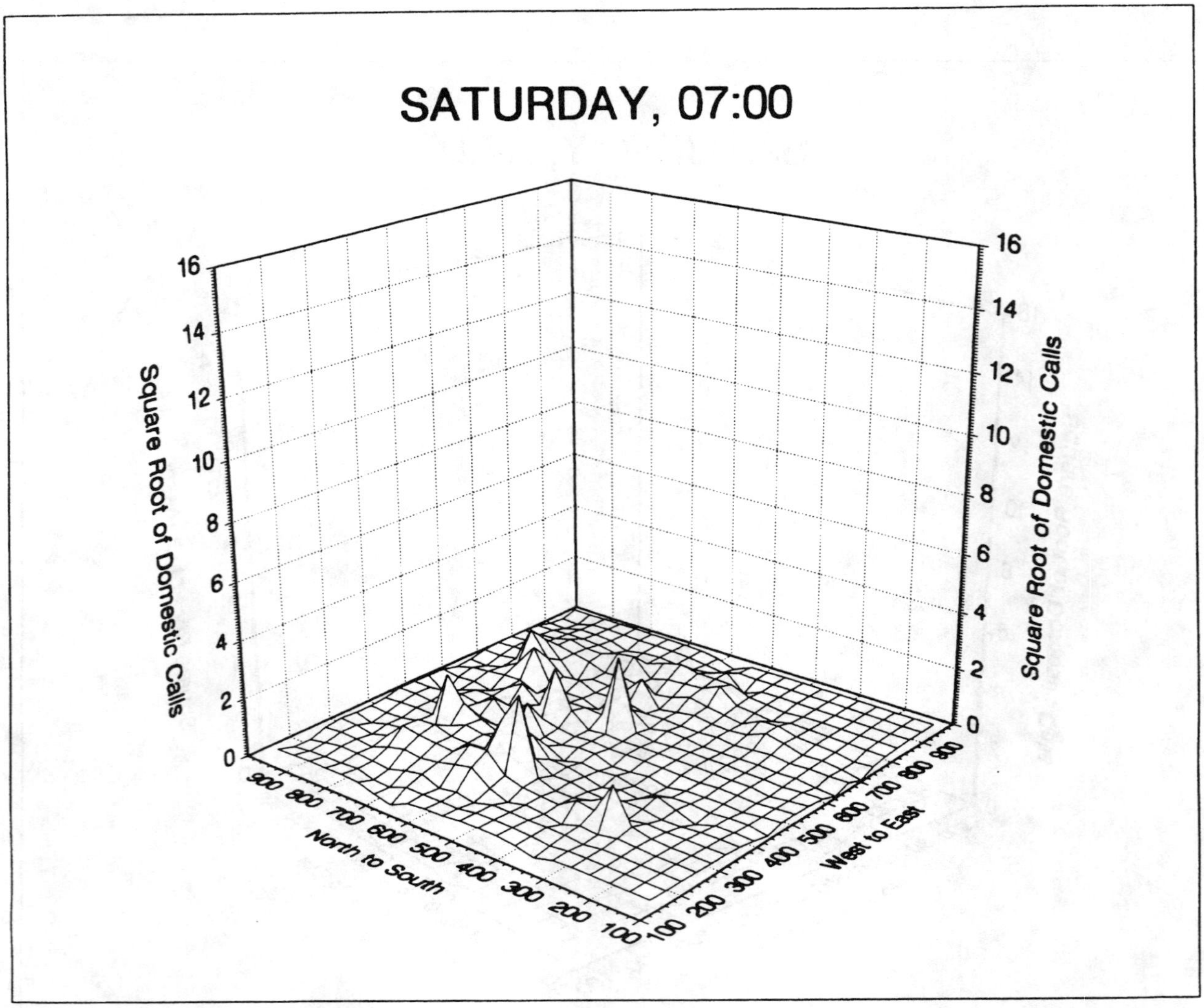

Fig. 6
Domestic dispute calls: Saturday, 07:00, Charlotte, N.C., 1986

The disputes recorded during 10:00, numbering 358, indicate more activity on the west side of the city, but still many of the areas that were active during 04:00 and 07:00 are active during this time (figure 7). The early afternoons (13:00) on Saturday produce 419 calls (figure 8). The distribution shows an increase in calls in the areas that are active during the morning hours (04:00, 07:00, 10:00). The 16:00 period during Saturday yields 483 calls (figure 9). Still, the distribution mirrors those occurring after 01:00.

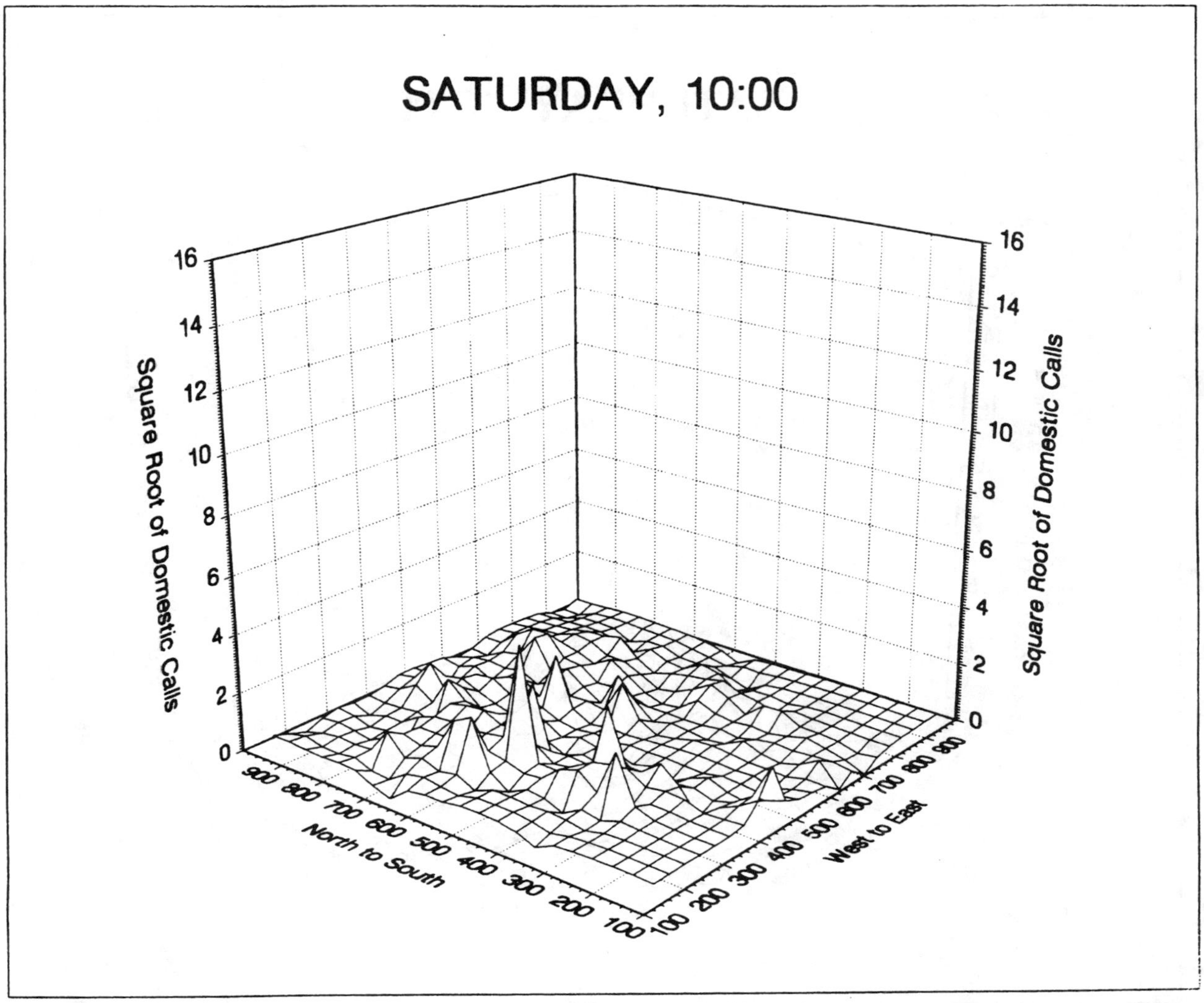

Fig. 7
Domestic dispute calls: Saturday, 10:00, Charlotte, N.C., 1986

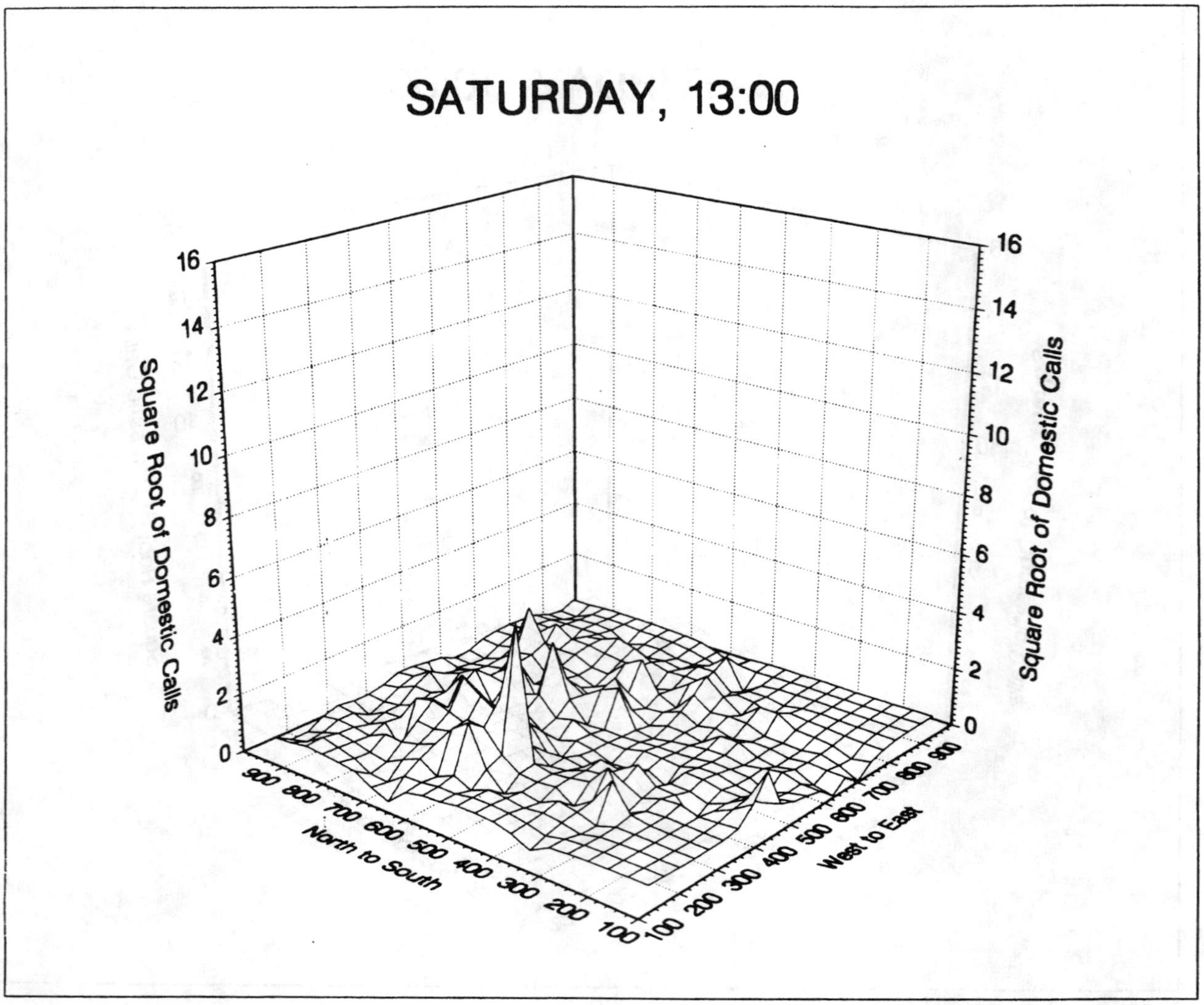

Fig. 8
Domestic dispute calls: Saturday, 13:00, Charlotte, N.C., 1986

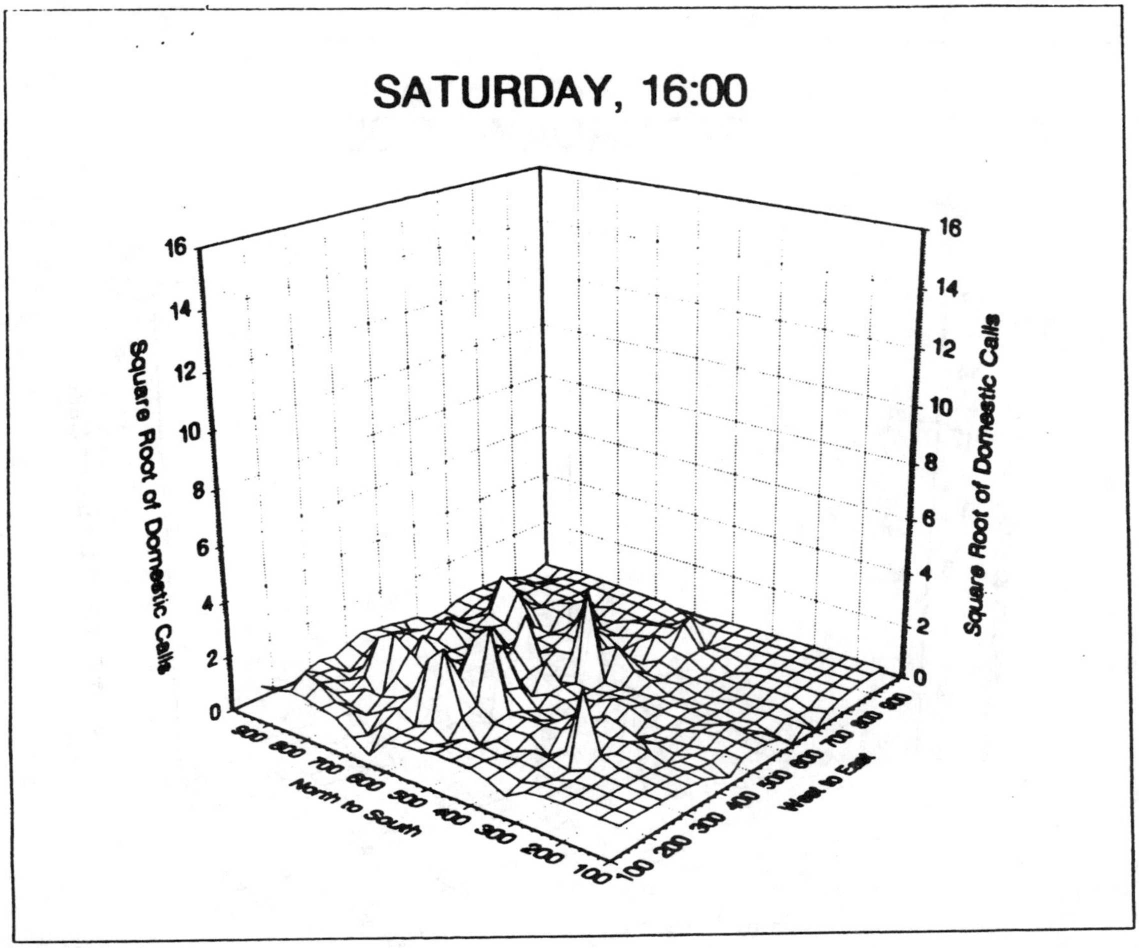

Fig. 9
Domestic dispute calls: Saturday, 16:00, Charlotte, N.C., 1986

The 19:00 period produces the third highest number of calls, with 732. Still, this distribution mirrors the other periods (figure 10). There is, however, a major difference in the distribution, in that the frequencies in some areas are becoming radically different from others and more pronounced. The differences between areas are intensified during 22:00 (figure 11). During this period, 800 calls were received. The majority of the high domestic dispute areas are located in the central, western and northern portions of the city. The highest area during 22:00, with almost 144 calls, is census tract 39, which is contiguous to the airport, with a majority of the residential land use in the tract public housing.

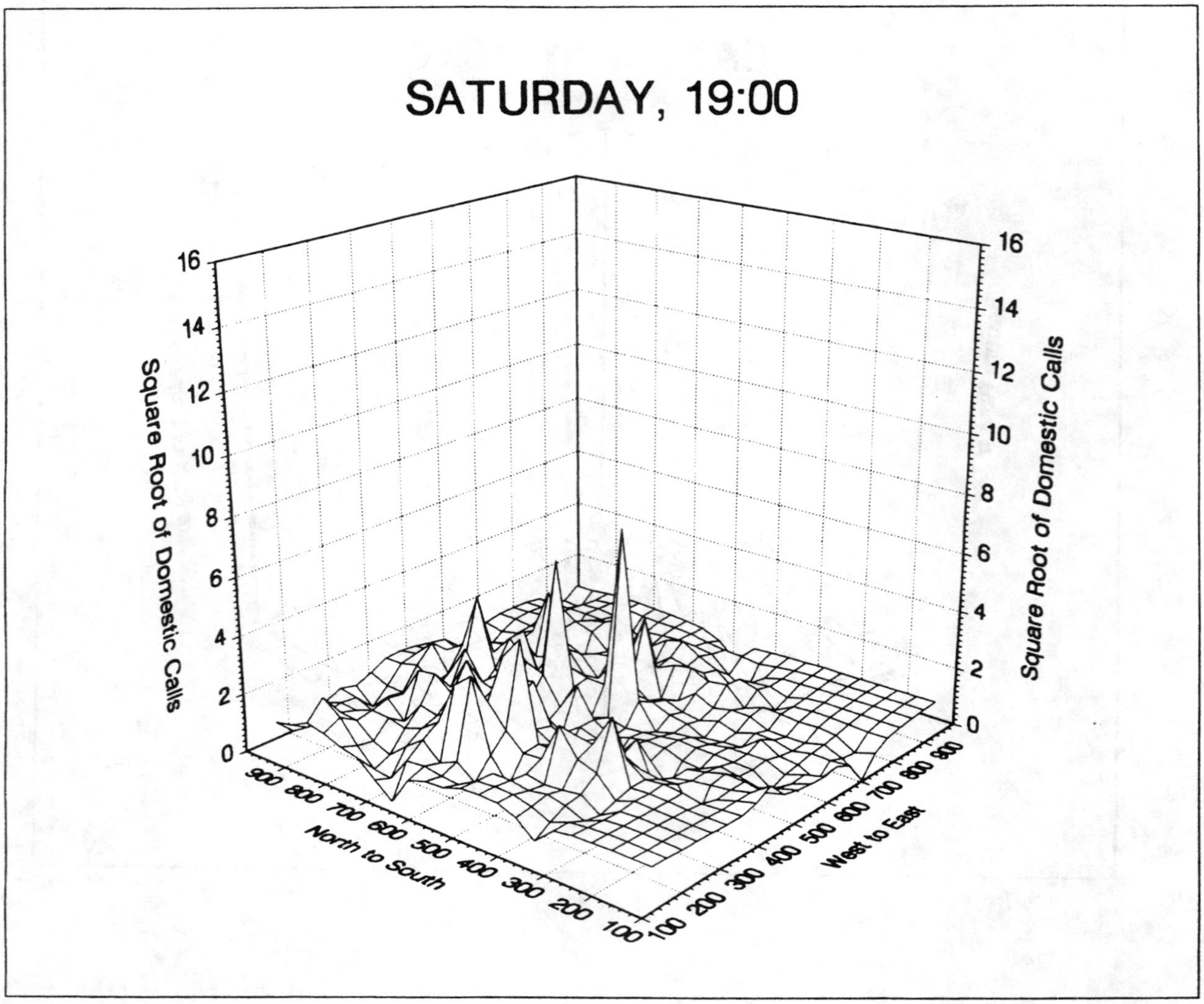

Fig. 10
Domestic dispute calls: Saturday, 19:00, Charlotte, N.C., 1986

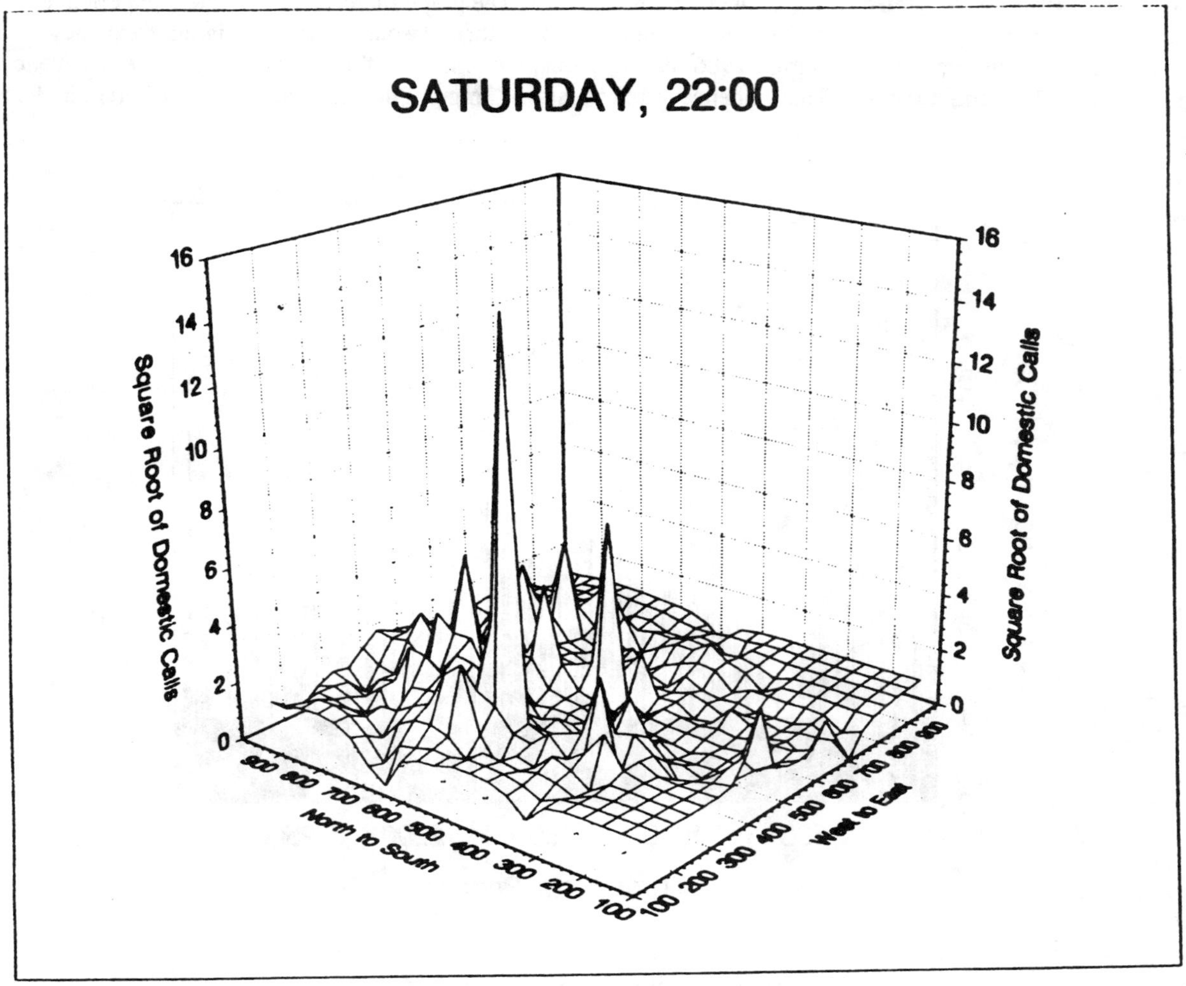

Fig. 11
Domestic dispute calls: Saturday, 22:00, Charlotte, N.C., 1986

This exercise and the associated graphics have illustrated how a particular type of call for service oscillates or varies throughout a day. This methodology would be useful for monitoring the spatial and temporal distribution of particular calls or types of problems, thus providing the baseline for measuring the effects of any intervention strategy.

THE TEMPORAL RHYTHMS OF DOMESTIC DISPUTES

The previous discussion has demonstrated how domestic dispute calls for service vary across space and time. This discussion focuses solely on the time, or temporal dimension, of the domestic disputes occurring in two census tracts. Both tracts are predominantly public housing projects. In terms of demographic, racial and socioeconomic status, the tracts are similar. One is more populated, possibly explaining a greater number of disputes. Yet the temporal rhythms of the two tracts are different.

Figure 12 shows the number of calls occurring every three hours in tract 39 during 1986. There were 1,408 domestic disputes during 1986, an average of .48 every three hours. The graph indicates that tract 39 experiences more domestic disputes during the spring and summer than during the other seasons.[1] Figure 13 is the frequency of disputes in tract 50, which totaled 968 during 1986. Conspicuously absent from this graph is any higher frequency of disputes during the warmer months. This evidence implies that the timing of domestic disputes is different in the two tracts.

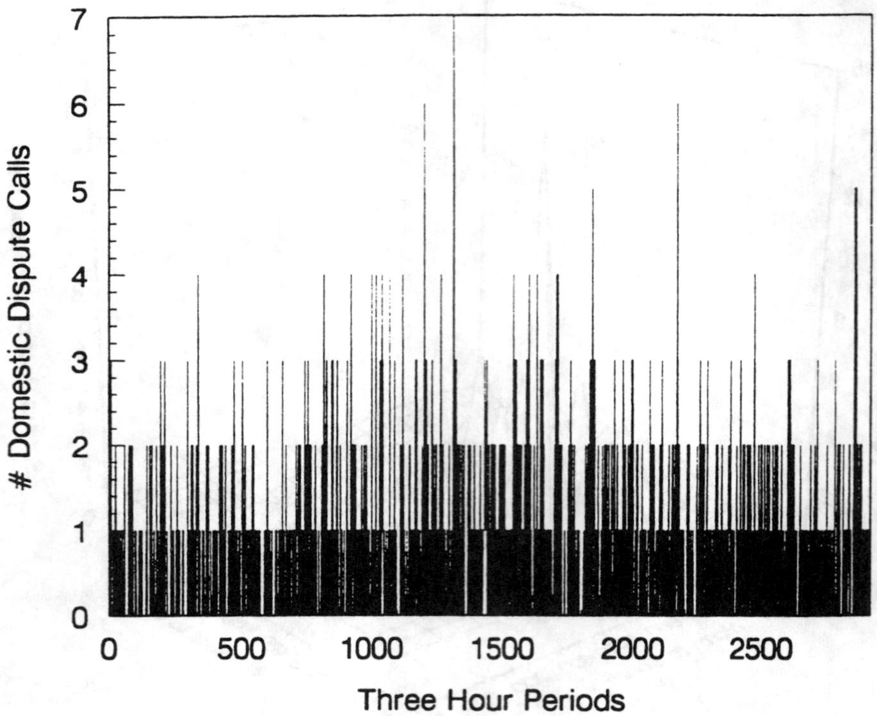

Fig. 12
Domestic dispute calls: 1986, tract 39

1. For reference, time period 1000 in figures 12 and 13 corresponds to 22:00, May 5; time period 1500 corresponds to 10:00, July 7; time period 2000 corresponds to 22:00, Sept. 7.

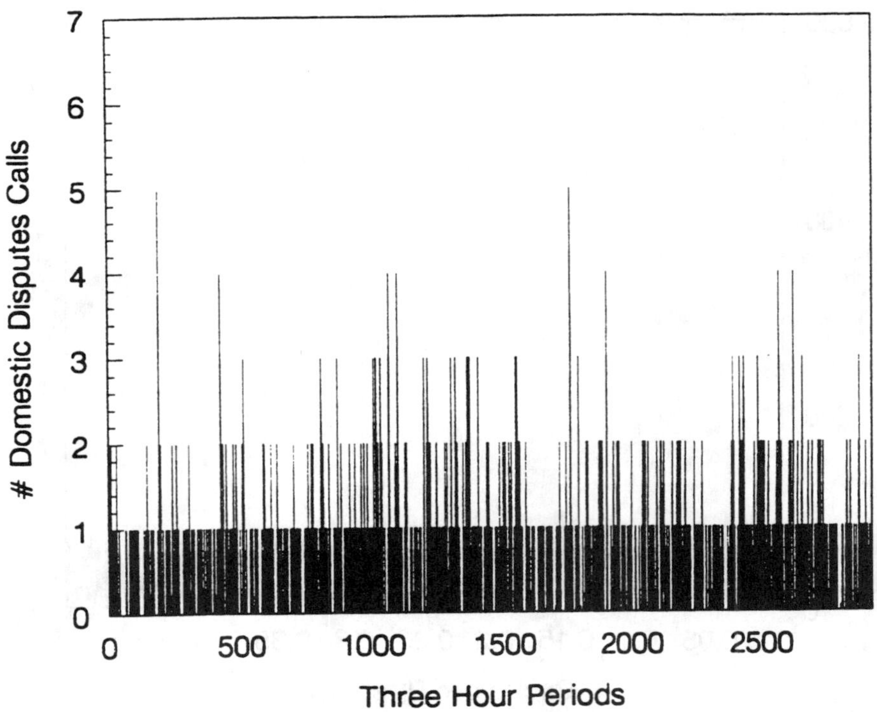

Fig. 13
Domestic dispute calls: 1986, tract 50

The time-series of domestic disputes for both tracts were submitted to a spectral analysis, in order to extract the significant cycles or rhythms. Figure 14 shows the spectral analysis for tract 39. The *x* axis is the number of cycles per three hours. Thus, the far-right figure on the *x* axis is interpreted as .5 cycle per three hours. This position on the scale indicates a six-hour rhythm, since in order to complete a full cycle, there must be two three-hour periods. Moving toward the left on the *x* axis, .25 cycle per three hours represents a 12-hour rhythm, since there must be four three-hour periods to achieve one full cycle. The large spike on the *x* axis at .125 cycle per three hours is the daily cycle, since it takes eight three-hour periods, or 24 hours, to obtain one cycle. As one moves to the right on the *x* axis, the faster the rhythms become; to the left, the slower the rhythms become. The *y* axis indicates the spectral density, or the strength of the rhythm at a particular frequency of cycles per three hours.

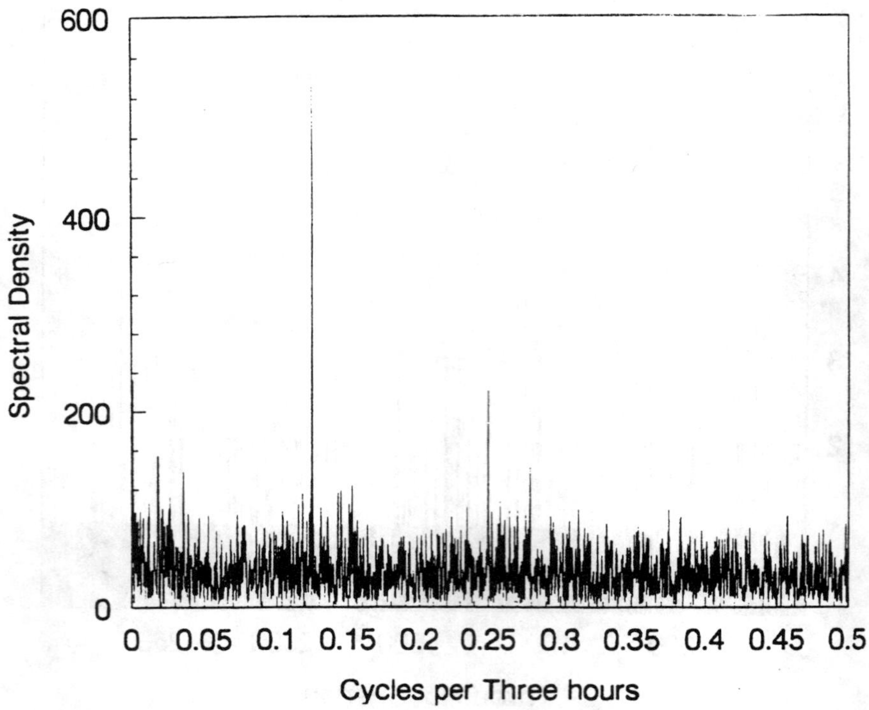

Fig. 14
Spectral analysis domestic disputes: tract 39

The 24-hour (.125 cycle) and the 12-hour (.25 cycle) rhythms are the strongest in tract 39. Moreover, there are many other significant faster rhythms to the right of 24 and 12 hours. The distinguishing characteristic that separates this tract from the other lies in the lower or slower frequencies to the left of the 24-hour rhythm and the 2.5-day rhythm at .05 cycle per three hours. Tract 39 has significant slower rhythms corresponding to the week and month, and at .00138 cycle per three hours (not visible on the graph), which is 90.57 days. The latter rhythm corresponds roughly to a seasonal cycle.

The spectral densities for tract 50 are presented in figure 15. Like tract 39, this one has significant 24-hour (.125 cycle per three hours) and 12-hour (.25 cycle per three hours) cycles, as well as many other faster cycles. However, the difference between the two tracts lies in the rhythms to the left of 24 hours (compare figures 14 and 15). Tract 50 does not have the longer cycles of tract 39, with very pronounced spectral densities at around 90 days or a month. Tract 50's longer cycles are between 2.5 days (.05 cycle per three hours) and 24 hours (.125 cycle per three hours). Thus, it appears from the graphs that tract 39 has a seasonal rhythm, but tract 50 does not.[2]

2. There are many other tests that can be used to determine if rhythms are significantly different. See Brillinger (1975).

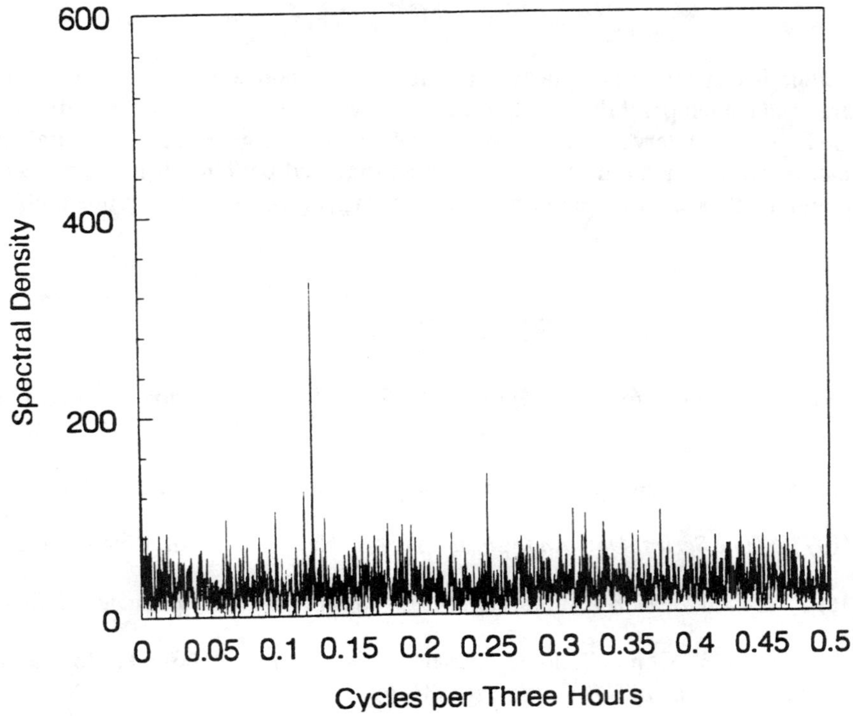

Fig. 15
Spectral analysis domestic disputes: tract 50

There are several reasons for the temporal differences between the tracts. The fact that one had more disputes than the other is a possible explanation. Significant differences may exist between the populations of the two tracts. However, difference in the locations of the tracts may explain the different rhythms. Tract 50 is situated in the northern portion of the city. The boundaries of the tract consist of major highways and interstates. Tract 39 lies on the west side of the city and was by far the most active single area during Saturdays at 22:00 (figure 11). Adjacent to the housing projects in tract 39 is the airport. The activities of this land use may have an influence on the rhythms of domestic disputes in the tract.

Research on temporal cycles and rhythms reveals that rhythms of one phenomenon may influence the rhythms of another. A *zeitgeber*, which is cyclic, is the rhythm-forcing agent that entrains or adjusts the cycles of another rhythm (Parks and Thrift 1980:18–19; Halberg and Katinas 1973). This situation may be occurring in tract 39, with the rhythm of airport activity influencing the seasonal or longer cycles of domestic dispute calls for service. As we all know, during the spring and summer the days become longer and the weather is warmer. Many public housing units lack air conditioning. Therefore, leaving the windows open is one of the few, yet marginally effective, measures for coping with heat discomfort. If airline traffic follows a seasonal cycle, with more business during the summer than in other months, this means more traffic and noise near the housing projects in tract 39. Seeking relief from the heat may involve increased consumption of alcohol, while increased exposure to the noise may induce sleep deprivation.[3] The presence of these factors presents opportunities for exacerbating existing disputatious relationships and for spawning new ones.

It will require additional research to assess the validity of the previous proposition. However, this exercise serves to illustrate how the interaction among space, time and the content of place produces distinct rhythms.

---

3. For a discussion of the interactions among the type of neighborhood, heat stress, alcohol consumption, and assault, see Harries, Stadler and Zdorkowski (1984).

CONCLUSIONS

Fine-tuning this methodology can have many practical implications for police planning. As previously stated, examining the spatial patterns and the temporal rhythms of different types of calls for service is useful for analyzing workload and estimating the impacts of interventions. However, isolating the zeitgebers that are entraining the rhythms of a particular type of call or crime has implications for problem-oriented policing. It may be possible to control or modify the entraining rhythm, thus exerting some control over the rhythm of the call or crime problem in question.

REFERENCES

Aronoff, Stanley (1989). *Geographic Information Systems: A Management Perspective.* Ottawa, Canada: WDL Publications.

Brantingham, Paul, and Patricia Brantingham (1984). *Patterns In Crime.* New York: Macmillan.

Brillinger, David R. (1975). *Time Series: Data Analysis and Theory.* New York: Holt, Rinehart and Winston, Inc.

Eastman, J. Ronald (1992). *IDRISI Version 4.* Worcester, Mass.: Clark University Graduate School of Geography.

Halberg, F., and G. Katinas (1973). Chronobiologic glossary of the International Society for the Study of Biologic Rhythms. *International Journal of Chronobiology* 1:31–63.

Harries, K.D., S.J. Stadler and R.T. Zdorkowski (1984). Seasonality and assault: Explorations in inter-neighborhood variation, Dallas 1980. *Annals of The Association of American Geographers* 74:590–604.

LeBeau, James L. (1994). The oscillation of domestic disputes with the temperature humidity index. *Journal of Crime and Justice* (forthcoming).

Langran, Gail (1992). *Time in Geographic Information Systems.* New York: Taylor & Francis.

McPheters, Lee R., and William B. Stronge (1974). Spectral analysis of reported crime data. *Journal of Criminal Justice* 2:329–344.

Parkes, David, and Nigel Thrift (1980). *Times, Spaces and Places.* New York: John Wiley & Sons.

Chapter 10

Location Quotients and Crime Hot Spots in the City

Patricia L. Brantingham
Paul J. Brantingham
School of Criminology
Simon Fraser University

OVERVIEW

Spatial analysis is not a simple type of analysis. Spatial processes are far removed from the types of events covered under classical statistical theory (Ripley 1988). They provide real challenges to researchers and trigger the development of new analytic tools.

This paper begins to explore an additional tool called location quotients of crime (LQC). We describe LQCs in detail, providing an example of their use and exploring how their use could add to other research. The use of LQCs is described within an approach that uses topological transformations of geographic space. Basically, location quotients of crime are used to look at what occurs in a specific area and to compare occurrences to what is happening in surrounding areas (Brantingham and Brantingham 1994; Barr and Pease 1990). Location quotients were developed in the field of regional science. Within regional science, location quotients were used to measure relative economic activity in an area and to provide a basis for measuring growth and change in economic activities.

LQCs are now being developed as a tool for the microanalysis of crime, in order to introduce a potential measure of subjective views of crime. That is, LQCs are being developed as a measure of crime occurrence that reflects the visual images of crime someone can have in a city she or he knows. These uses are distant from the uses to which location quotients are put in regional science.

BACKGROUND

Crime has never occurred randomly in time, in space or across sociodemographic groups. There are clear aggregate temporal patterns. Drunk driving does not occur very often at 10 a.m. on a Sunday; bar assaults are evening events, frequently peaking on Friday or Saturday night. Residential burglaries in many cities seem highest in the midmorning or midafternoon, when houses are empty. Murder is frequently a weekend event associated with weekend alcohol consumption.

Similarly, crime occurs in spatial patterns. Some parts of cities experience few crimes; others, many. Some crimes seem to cluster near certain types of locations. Obviously, to give an extreme example that is not open to debate, commercial shoplifting occurs in stores. As a less extreme example, assaults associated with alcohol occur in or near bars or residences. They occur near where people are drinking. Some crimes cluster near attractors. For example, Rengert (1992) has shown how some residential burglaries follow the location of crack houses.

For the most opportunistic types of crimes, the crime itself may just be a side product of the presence of a person in a location for another reason. The crime probably happens when there are ample suitable targets (Cohen and Felson 1979; Felson 1983, 1986, 1987, 1993) requiring no conscious searching. For less opportunistic crimes, there is normally a target search conducted in areas known to the intending offender (Brantingham and Brantingham 1991; Capone and Nichols 1976; Carroll and Weaver 1986; Canter and Larkin 1993; Feeney 1986). Most frequently, targets are plentiful in western societies and do not require that people search beyond known or easily knowable places (Felson 1993; Brantingham and Brantingham 1991). Offenders apparently feel a need for some anonymity where they offend, often producing a crime-free buffer area around home locations and other places where they might be known (Brantingham and Brantingham 1991; Canter and Larkin 1993; Rossmo 1993), but still take relatively short trips from known areas for many crimes (Costanzo et al. 1986; Lenz 1986; Rand 1986; Rhodes and Conly 1991). For some other types of crime, such as bank robbery, a person may travel farther to commit a crime, but probably still restrict his or her search to known or knowable areas (Capone and Nichols 1976; Feeney 1986; Costanzo et al. 1986; Lenz 1986; Rand 1986; Rengert 1992). The geometry of crime (Brantingham and Brantingham 1991) is understandable. Crime follows patterns that are conceptually reasonable.

Space/place and time are not unconstrained. There are both societal (Barker 1968) and geographic constraints imposed on potential offenders. This is not meant in a physically deterministic way. Crime is not stopped by walls or locks (Cromwell and Zahm 1991); but where a person looks for a victim or whether a person with low levels of motivation sees easily attractive targets is shaped by how urban areas are developed (Brantingham and Brantingham 1975; Beavon et al. 1994) and by a sociocultural urban mosaic (Timms 1965, 1971). This relationship is not normally a linear recursive relationship. The organization of a city helps shape movement patterns and residential choices. These, in turn, produce changes in the organization and form of that city.

This circular relationship may have a short cycle or a long one. For example, the creation of major highways produces a short cycle. Frequently, highways are designed to reduce some major traffic problem. They are designed for projected future traffic flow patterns. When first opened, they often have light traffic flows, but soon become busy and crowded. Traffic planners have learned that the presence of a good but not very crowded highway helps convince people to drive more or at least divert their usual driving path to the new highway. Good driving conditions encourage driving and frequently create poor driving conditions. But poor driving conditions do not discourage driving as much as good driving conditions encourage driving.

The circular relationship between planned development and behavior may pass through several lifetime iterations or may be shaped more deliberately through the development of municipal plans and regulations. Most western cities are shaped by zoning schemes and municipal plans for public space. These plans and zoning conditions shape development and redevelopment, which in turn help structure the environment in which many people who are not responsible for the plans and zoning decisions live. The past helps shape the present; changes in the present, in part reactions to changes in the past, help shape the future.

We live, work, travel, see friends, search for activities, and for some, commit crimes and engage in nuisance behaviors within an urban mosaic created by the past, the present and our expectations of the future. Since we pass our time within some specific part of the urban mosaic or move between similar parts of the urban mosaic, we frequently are not only unaware of how we influence our surrounds, but are also often unaware of what influences us.

ENVIRONMENTAL BACKCLOTH

In criminological research, we frequently try to be observers "at a distance" or "from close to or within" that which surrounds a criminal event. The *surrounds* are more than what some researchers call *context*. Conceptually, a context is treated as something fixed and stable during the time period researched. The surrounds are more the *environmental backcloth*, an ever-changing but comprehensible set of events, perceived sites, cognitive templates, and schemata (Brantingham and Brantingham 1993a, 1993b). This backcloth may be stable and regular, or it may be rapidly changing and irregular. The term *environmental backcloth* is used to attach a label to the infinite number of elements that may influence or be influenced by behavior. The elements within the backcloth are potentially interconnected at different levels. Actually, the level of interconnectedness is probably malleable, certainly changing as the time of day or day of week or month or season changes.

Crimes occur within or on this backcloth. What the crime pattern looks like depends on how the backcloth is seen. A pattern may be invisible when viewed from within the backcloth, but it may seem very clear when viewed from a distance.

Distance Effect

Geographical analysis has always been aware of the distance effect on our ability to see patterns. The observer's position in the cone of resolution and the shape and size of the measuring units employed help determine the patterns that can be seen (Brantingham et al. 1976). Figure 1 shows how distance away from or toward a simplified backcloth may create or eliminate what we see as patterns.

Stationarity Fallacy

Add to this the statistical difficulties in identifying clusters when the observations lack stationarity. We can fall into the trap of a stationarity fallacy, which is similar to the ecological fallacy. We can have a series of observations of criminal events that appear to cluster spatially, but only because different time periods are being combined.[1] For example, there may be a strong cluster of assaults and thefts from automobiles in a commercial/entertainment district of a city. It could be that the thefts are daytime activities and the assaults nighttime problems. When considered separately, the two types of crime might be rare enough that they form no discernible cluster. Alternatively, when considered separately, the two crimes, even when viewed at a level of resolution similar to figure 1c ("cluster even less pronounced"), may still only form a cluster if considered co-jointly and so may appear to the researcher more like the view depicted in figure 1b ("density, but less of a cluster").

Edge Problems

Research into crime patterns, particularly studies that look for clusters or hot spots (Block 1993, 1990; Sherman et al. 1989), needs to look at both some small area and some relevant broader area simultaneously so that there are areas for comparison. This need to be able to expand and contract the research view reflects one of the other classic problems in spatial pattern analysis: *border or boundary problems*, or, as they are sometimes called, *edge problems*. Edge problems develop when the researcher is looking at similarity between "neighbors," yet many of the "neighbors" fall outside the boundary for analysis. This is a substantial problem. The boundary effect can dominate the asymptotic

1. The definition of *cluster* and possible transformations will be discussed in more detail later in the paper.

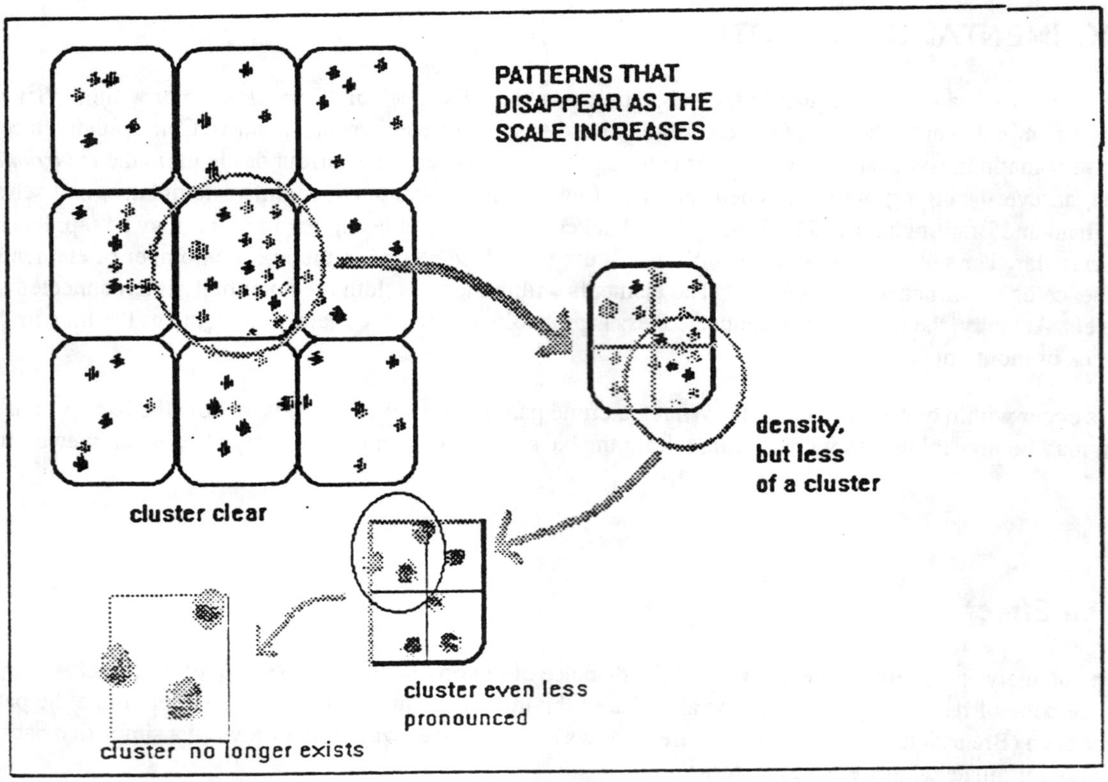

Fig. 1
Scale and the perception of clusters

distribution and restrict the meaning and measures of similarity. Boundary problems are addressed by transforming the area being studied into a torus, with obvious conceptual limitations; by considering a subspace for analysis; or by adjusting the distance measures to account for restrictions of boundaries, particularly by using an isotropic connection factor.

All edge or border problems are exacerbated when the number of cases is small. For practical purposes, this increases the likelihood of experiencing these problems in the spatial analysis of crime, where the number of cases under investigation in any particular jurisdiction or situation is typically small.

TOPOLOGY AS A METHOD FOR BACKCLOTH SIMULATION

Spatial analytic problems become less serious when the research uses techniques from the mathematical field of topology in creating some analytic working models of the environmental backcloth (Brantingham et. al. 1992; Brantingham and Brantingham 1978a). Most statistical techniques are based on a euclidean measure of distance. Euclidean distance (shown in figure 3, top left) is distance "as the crow flies." Such measures, however, are taught to people in school and probably do not measure how people perceive the environment that surrounds them (Piaget and Inhelder 1948; Heelan 1983; Brantingham and Brantingham 1993a, 1993b). Figure 2 provides a picture of how the space of an area may change for different viewers.

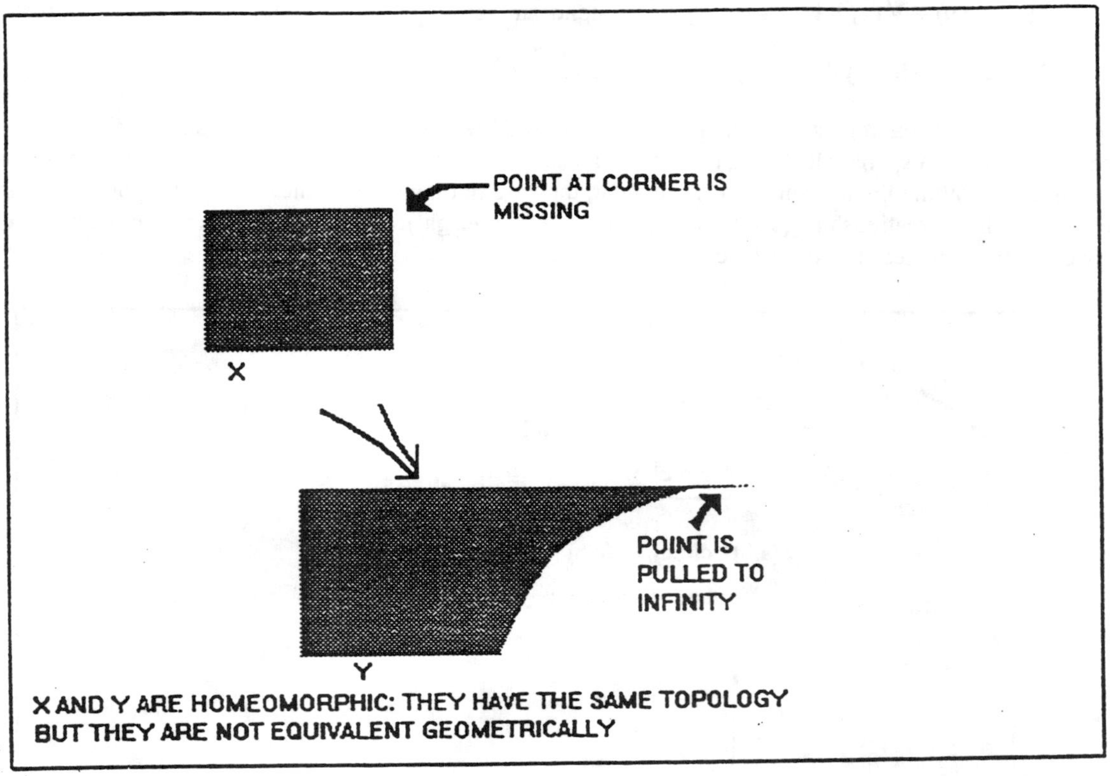

Fig. 2
Homeomorphic but not geometrically equivalent spaces

The two spaces (X and Y) shown in figure 2 are *homeomorphic.* That means that there is a function f: X_1 --> Y_1 from the metric space associated with the space X (X_1,d_1) onto the metric space associated with Y (Y_1,d_1), which is continuous and one to one. Each point in space X can be mapped onto a unique point in Y. When the distance between each pair of points in X can be transformed by a simple function to distances in Y, then the two spaces are *equivalent.* Figure 2 shows a situation where the spaces are homeomorphic but not equivalent, because there could be an infinite stretching of space.

For people within a city, their image of the city changes depending on which of the uncountable number of factors that could be considered are being considered. That is, depending on the situation, the foreground can become the background and the background can become the foreground. We all experience this continuous transformation. When you are late for work and cannot find your car keys or wallet, the micro aspects of a room become the foreground consideration. Memories and habits accentuate certain objects. When you are sitting down to eat, the objects central to the key or wallet search of the morning become part of the background, and other things come to the foreground of consideration.

These changes clearly occur for those who are looking for a criminal target (Macdonald and Gifford 1989; Cromwell et al. 1991) or can even be seen by the patterning of target locations (Rengert 1992; Canter and Larkin 1993; Block 1993; Felson 1986; LeBeau 1993).

Analyzing the patterns may become clear using a series of topological transformations of distance measures and consequently transforming statistical analysis away from euclidean distance measures. Probably the best known distance measure transformation is the Manhattan metric (equations 1, 2). Manhattan distance (figure 3, top right) is distance "around the corner."

Equation (1) $d(x,y) = \sqrt{(x_1 - y_1)^2 + (x_2 - y_2)^2}$ (euclidean metric)

Equation (2) $d(x,y) = |x_1 - y_1| + |x_2 - y_2|$ (Manhattan metric)

Figure 3 provides a visual representation of the euclidean and Manhattan metrics. Such a simple distance transformation could be used in a spatial clustering analysis to measure how far apart two points are in urban areas (Rossmo 1993; Turner 1969). While the measures are equivalent, they are not homeomorphic. Therefore, you would get different nearest-neighbor relationships (see figure 3, bottom left and right). Figure 4 shows how groups might cluster differently using the two measures of distance.

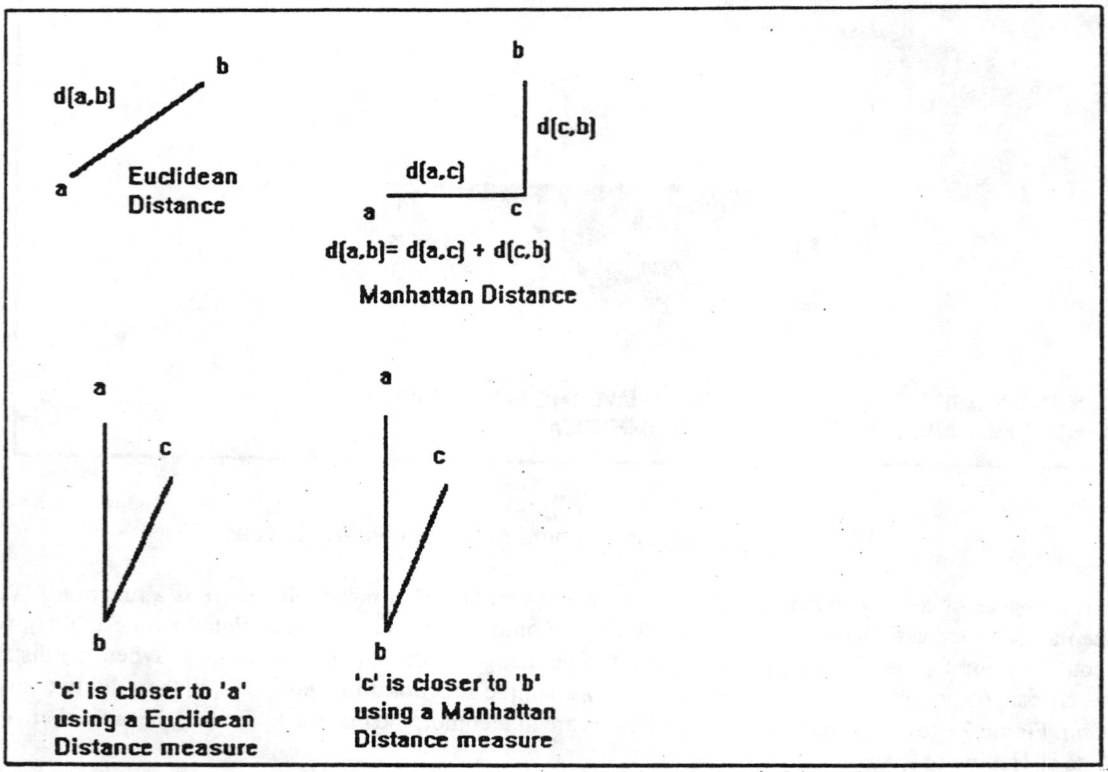

Fig. 3
Euclidean and Manhattan distance

Following the spatial transformations shown in figure 3, a euclidean distance measure can be used to measure, in miles or kilometers, the distance that must be traveled using existing roads instead of "crow flight" distances. Points *A* and *B* could be close in a euclidean sense, but separated by a river. To get from *A* to *B* you would then have to travel away from *B* until you come to a bridge, cross the river, then reverse directions until you come to *B*. (This is our own required travel path each morning as we commute to the university from home.) Figure 4 shows this type of transformation of the underlying space. Fortunately, within the United States, the census supplies TIGER files that make such transformations both possible and relatively easy.

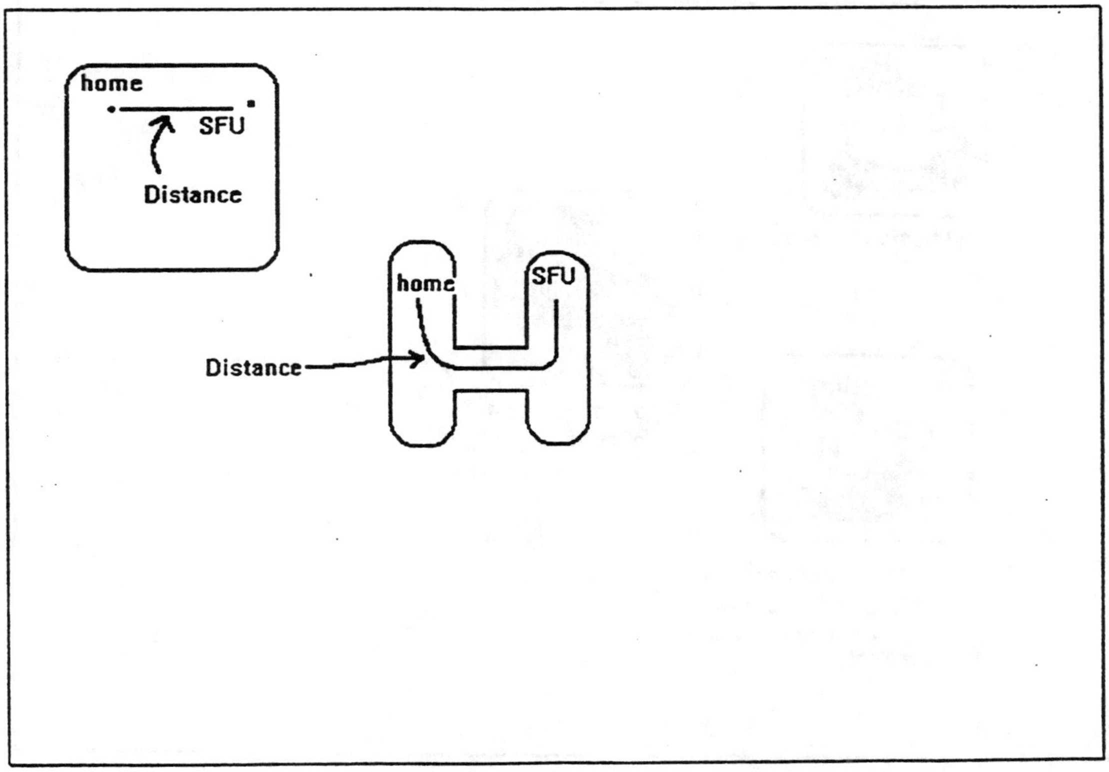

Fig. 4
Euclidean vs. Manhattan distance from home to Simon Fraser University

Figure 5 shows one of many possible types of topological transformation. We are limited in the transformations we utilize as researchers only by a requirement that we suggest transformations that can be reasonably supported. In a study of urban juvenile crime, for instance, the transformation might be from euclidean or Manhattan distances to travel-time distance. Travel-time distances could be transformed to fit what is known about perception of time based on familiarity. For example, looking back to the geometry of crime (Brantingham and Brantingham 1991), the basic model of likely awareness space could be transformed into a spatially variable distance model depending on the age of the potential offender. Younger people have much smaller awareness spaces.

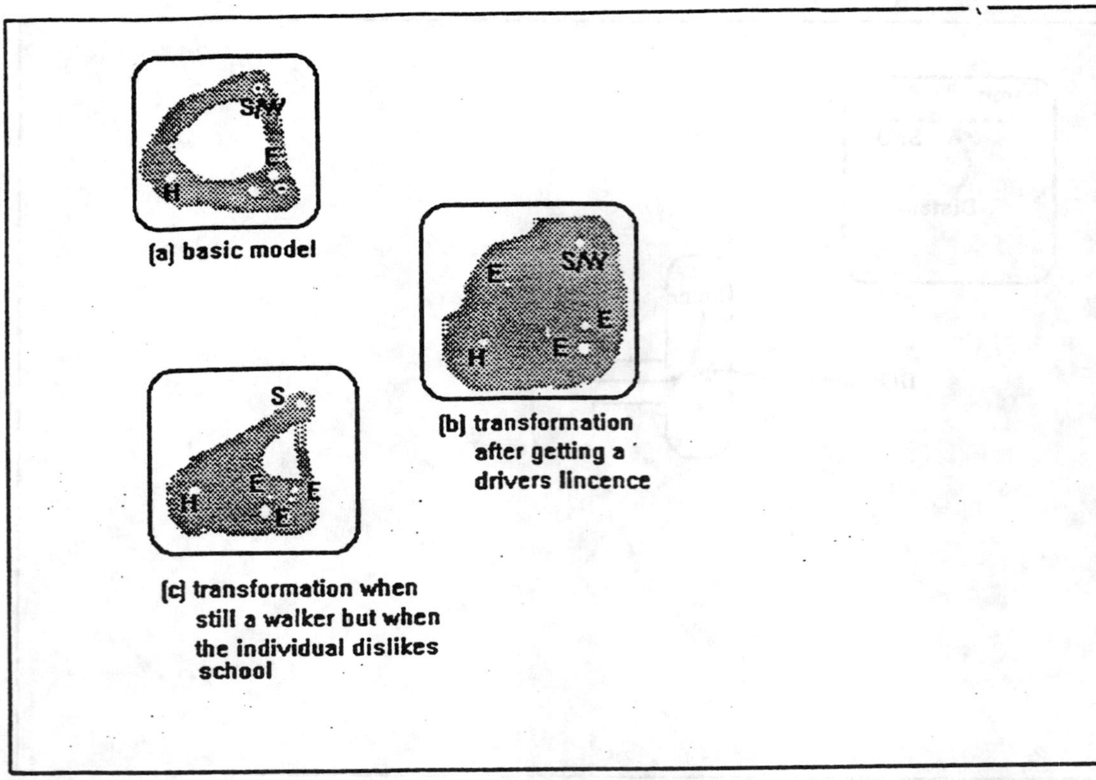

Fig. 5
Topological transformation with lifestyle transformation

These types of transformations could be done for individuals and utilized in the analysis of target choice patterns. This would mean that, for a teenager with a driver's license and car, the choice of a household burglary target or the search for a store to rob might fall in a search zone five kilometers from school. That euclidean-distance target search range for the driving juvenile might be equivalent to a one-kilometer search range for a younger person traveling and experiencing time on foot.

Since much spatial analysis of crime is done at some aggregate level, research might actually involve a topological transformation of the environmental backcloth as a first step, followed by an exploration of patterns laid out on that transformed space. Such topological transformations will have to be based on proper knowledge derived from environmental psychology and behavioral geography. This might best be illustrated using an example of location quotients of crime.

LOCATION QUOTIENTS OF CRIME

Location quotients are a measure developed in regional planning and economics to try to address questions about the relative importance of local economies, while conceptually avoiding some of the stationarity problems that bedevil spatial analysis.[2] Local areas are placed within some wider context for analysis. Regional science has always looked for ways to compare activity at metropolitan or regional levels of aggregation.

2. For a definition, see "Stationarity Fallacy," above.

From the planning perspective, the primary purpose of such analysis is to make predictions about future economic activity and to base those predictions on an understanding of how the area under study functions in relation to its surrounding area. What happens in one city is seen to depend not only on what happens in other cities, but also on what happens or what exists in locales surrounding particular cities. For example, what happens in Montreal or New York or Madrid depends on what happens in other large cities such as Paris or Los Angeles or Hong Kong, but also depends on what happens in the surrounding areas that encompass each of them. The interrelationships between different urban areas, between urban and rural areas, and between different sets of urban and rural areas are complex. Some linkages are strong; some are weak. But many linkages exist and all shape actual interrelationships.

In particular, regional sciences look at the relative importance of centers. Consider, for example, a study of consumer centers. Clearly, the researcher would look at what happens in large cities attracting huge numbers of consumers, but the researcher might also want to look at consumer centers in less densely settled areas. A town or small city in a farming or extraction area might be the local consumer center. It might not seem like a consumer center in comparison with the Loop in Chicago, but it would be the consumer center when compared with its own surrounding areas. While it will be covered in more detail later in the article, this example should bring criminological analogies to mind. A small town in the northern part of a Canadian province could be the center of drinking establishments for a large surrounding area. This town is likely to have, relatively, a large number of assaults. The total number could be small compared to a suburb of a large city, but great in comparison to the number of assaults in the areas around the small town. Small or large and great or small are relative relationships.

The relative activity of an area can be measured using a *location quotient.* Equation 3 contains the basic formula as used with respect to economic activity in regional science. While many economic activity indicators might be used, LQs are frequently calculated using employment data. Employment categories can be defined in many ways, but a frequently used scheme divides employment into service, manufacturing, and secondary and primary extraction groups. Each of these groups may be subdivided repeatedly, working down to detailed categories of activity.

$$\text{Equation (3)} \quad LQi_n = \frac{Ei_n}{Et_n} \Bigg/ \frac{\sum_{n=1}^{N} Ei_n}{\sum_{n+1}^{N} Et_n}$$

where

n = small area under study

N = total number of areas

E_i = employment in industry i

E_t = total employment in all industries

Location quotients are anchored by the basic notion that there is some "normal" distribution in a "standard" area; that is, a typical proportion of jobs will be found in each employment category in a typical "standard" area. Regional scientists use this "normal" number as a measure of the amount of activity needed to satisfy regional demand, that is, as a measure of local self-sustainability. When the local amount of activity falls below the normal amount, it is assumed that goods (or services) are imported; when local activity exceeds the normal level, it is assumed that goods (or services) are exported to other areas. Equation 3 shows the ratio for importing or exporting. The *numerator* counts the number of people employed in a particular type of job in a specific area divided by the total employed in that area. The *denominator* is a similar ratio for the larger surrounding comparison area that is being used as the "normal" distribution for the "standard" area.

The equation can be formulated for different study areas and for different categories of employment. Analysis can involve comparison of the numerator value with denominators produced by using different standard areas. While there are obvious problems with this measure, it does provide the potential for a relative crime measure in criminological studies.[3]

USE OF LOCATION QUOTIENTS IN CRIMINOLOGY

Location quotients in criminology would not use employment as the basic unit being counted, of course, but rather, would use crime occurrences. Equation 4 provides a criminological version of a location quotient (LQC).

$$\text{Equation (4)} \quad LQC_{i_n} = \frac{C_{i_n}}{C_{t_n}} \Bigg/ \frac{\sum_{n=1}^{N} C_{i_n}}{\sum_{n+1}^{N} C_{t_n}}$$

where

n = small area under study

N = total number of area

C_i = count of crime i

C_t = total count of all crimes

Using an LQC, some towns and cities would be identified as centers for violent crimes; some, for property crimes. Some are centers for robbery, some for burglary and some for automobile theft. The center in one region might not appear to be a center if compared to centers in other regions, just as a small town might be a center of commerce for a rural area, but not in comparison with the downtown in a metropolis. It is perhaps more important to note that, since this is a relative measure, a center cannot have high location quotients in all crimes. The LQC is a measure that identifies an area's *relative specialty* in crimes.

The advantage of an LQC in crime analysis is that there is no need to obtain the additional count of the number of targets at risk that is necessary for calculating a crime rate. The LQC for robbery is based on counts of robberies and total crimes, not on counts of population or number of target businesses.[4] The LQC for motor vehicle theft is based on crime counts, not on counts of the number of people or the number of motor vehicles. The problems highlighted by Boggs (1965) and Harries (1991) are minimized. Stationarity is still a problem, but it can be addressed by recalculations for different time periods.

Statistical models using LQCs are different from the models most commonly constructed by criminologists. LQCs are relative measures and are potentially helpful when analyzing fear or concern about crime. A widespread fear of murder by strangers can be triggered in a small community by a single local crime. In a large urban center, a similar level of fear might require clear evidence that a serial killer is active before it is triggered. Similarly, one or two bank robberies may seem like very little in New York City, but one or two may be a large number in Yellowknife or

3. Clearly, the location quotient approach has limitations in regional science. With major cities being linked economically, it is not possible to actually identify what activity in a "standard" area would be. This is similar to identifying what a "standard" crime pattern would be. In actual practice, LQs mean more for their relativity and defined context, which is taken as the "standard" for logical purposes.

4. Because LQC is a relative measure, the denominator can be flexible. For instance, with robbery in the numerator, the LQC might be calculated using the count of all violent crimes, or the count of all criminal code offenses, or the count of all offenses known as the denominator, depending on the context in which the analyst wished to comprehend robbery centers.

Prince Rupert, small cities in northern parts of Canada. LQCs may also prove good predictors of local media response to specific reported crimes or to variations in sentences in different places at different times.

LQCs also have a statistical model-building strength. In many models using crime rates, both the independent and the dependent variables are rates based on population. In such instances, the overall strength of the model may be the result of the same numbers being used as the denominators on both sides of the equation. With LQCs, the independent variables should not have the same base unless one crime's LQC is used to predict another crime's LQC.

LQCs are relative measures and are potentially useful when looking at crime on an ever-changing backcloth. LQCs can be looked at over a temporally and spatially varying cone of resolution. The focus area may be tuned in a way to be similar to the focus you use in a room when searching for your wallet or keys. The background becomes the surrounds where the wallet or keys are unlikely to be. When looking at the work done by a house painter, your focus becomes the walls of the house; the details within (such as furniture where a wallet or keys might be kept) recede into the background. For LQCs, the focus could be one shopping center, one strip commercial street, one park, or one apartment building. Alternatively, the focus might be all shopping malls, all strip commercial areas, all parks, or all apartments. At a broader level of resolution, the focus might be all residential areas of a particular type (e.g., Barr and Pease 1990). At a narrower level of resolution, the focus might be a serial rape suspect's known activity areas.

While the focus can change conceptually, computer programs need to be written to create "what if?" simulations of the environmental backcloth. Fortunately, such programs are technically feasible with relational databases. We even created an early version of this type of program in the 1970s for use in our burglary distribution studies (Brantingham and Brantingham 1975, 1978a).

We would like to present one example to illustrate how such a program might work. For this illustration, we analyzed all motor vehicle thefts reported to the Burnaby, British Columbia, RCMP for the year 1991 at the address level.[5] When mapped in a standard dot map, especially in conjunction with other parts of the Greater Vancouver Regional District, there was a clear, heavy concentration of this crime in Burnaby. Motor vehicle theft was a dominant offense in some high-crime areas of the city, but a relatively less important offense in some other high-crime areas. In some low-crime areas, motor vehicle theft was the relatively dominant type of crime and constituted a policing problem, even though crime levels were not substantial overall.

While this states things fairly simply, it is the case that crimes frequently occur where they do because potential offenders are attracted to general areas they know. Once in a familiar area, potential offenders conduct fine-grained searches for targets (Brantingham and Brantingham 1978b, 1991). While the process may not be overtly conscious, it does appear to conform to Clarke's (1980, 1992; Clarke and Cornish 1985) idea of the rationality or reasonableness of offenders' cognitive decisions. This means that some areas that are attractive or at least known to outsiders will suffer many crimes committed by people who live outside of them. This also means that when a particular area is not attractive to offenders living outside it, then the crimes that occur within it will, primarily, be committed by people living there. Whether the overall volume of crime in an unattractive area is high or low, some mix of crimes will dominate the area pattern. The dominant crimes within the area could be interpreted as the crimes of choice among local offenders. The victimized targets could be interpreted as indicating what the local offenders consider to be suitable targets.

Areas of a city that are highly attractive to many people for many reasons have different offender and offense profiles. Crimes in such areas are committed by people from many places: those living in the area, those working in the area, and those visiting the area. Depending on the overall use of the area, most offenses may be committed by outsiders, that is, people not living in the area. Major commercial centers are a principal example of such areas. When shopping, housing and businesses are concentrated in a highly accessible node, the possibility of that node being an

5. Burnaby is a city of 200,000, immediately to the east of the city of Vancouver, and is one of the larger constituent municipalities of the Greater Vancouver Regional District. The RCMP (Royal Canadian Mounted Police) police Burnaby on a contract basis. The Burnaby detachment is the second largest RCMP detachment in Canada.

attractor of potential criminals greatly increases (Brantingham, Brantingham and Wong 1990). Once outside offenders are in the area, they may distinguish suitable targets homogeneously, but considering the crime templates that offenders develop (Brantingham and Brantingham 1978b, 1991, 1992, 1993b; Canter and Larkin 1993; Macdonald and Gifford 1989; Cromwell et al. 1991), target choices are probably not stationary. (A house might be attractive to a burglar in the midafternoon generally, but not on a Sunday afternoon.) The movement pattern of potential offenders is of great importance in analyzing crime, but it is difficult to research. At a microlevel of analysis, location quotients add to what can be seen in the spatial point distribution of events and might be used to infer movements. The location quotients provide one measure of the relative attractiveness of areas for specific crimes and, when used with counts of criminal events, give some indication of whether offenders are area insiders or outsiders.

SHOPPING MALL CLUSTER

The example covers a cluster of *atoms*, that is, the lowest aggregate unit used by the RCMP in analyzing crime. This cluster of atoms includes and surrounds a major shopping center (actually three shopping centers linked together and joined to nonretail office space and a major public transit node by interconnecting walkways, passages, parking facilities, landscaping, and traffic routings). This major center represents an attempt by regional and municipal planners to create a nodal city center, a downtown, for a large bedroom suburb by designating an area for special development. There is a major road on the north side of the shopping center and a large metro transit station and bus loop (a node for buses and a transfer point between major bus lines and the metro). There is also a mixture of high-rise office space and residences. The residences include new high-rise condominiums, some older, lower-rise apartment buildings and single-family dwellings. The major road is a strip commercial road that predates the construction of the shopping center. Just as the shopping center attracts a broad range of customers and other people to the area, both inside and outside its structures, so the surrounding residential area is not homogeneous, having attracted a broad range of social and economic groups.

This area is a hot spot for crime, as might be expected from the theoretical literature in point (Brantingham, Brantingham and Wong 1990; Rengert 1988). Figure 6 shows the spatial patterning of motor vehicle thefts around this major shopping center, with each motor vehicle around the shopping center shown as a dot. The shopping center itself had 120 reported motor vehicle thefts and almost 1,500 reported criminal code offenses in 1991. (A problem with MapInfo geocoding limits the number of vehicle theft dots shown for shopping center addresses.)

As already described, police aggregate their crime data into small area units called "atoms" for administrative and analytic purposes. These units typically consist of one or two city blocks. Although we analyze data at the atom level, figure 6 omits atom boundaries at police request. The first ring of adjacent atoms surrounding this shopping center had, as a group, about 4,000 reported criminal offenses during the year. The impact of the shopping center greatly decreased in the next outward ring of atoms (table 1).

Auto theft provides an interesting example of micro, site-specific variations in attractiveness of criminal opportunities. The major shopping center, as already described, is right on a major strip shopping street with limited parking. Activity levels on this particular strip appear moderate, but with little parking except limited parallel parking.[6] Auto theft within this particular shopping center may also be more difficult. Most parking for this mall is underground, with limited entries and exits. The restricted entry and exit could make motor vehicles parked underground less attractive and unsuitable as targets (see Eck and Spelman 1992; Poyner 1992). Given the surrounding residential streets and cars parked by people using the public transit system, there were plenty of criminal opportunities in the area. The shopping center primarily attracts neighborhood outsiders such as shoppers and mall walkers out for a stroll in this suburban "downtown." The atoms in the first ring around the shopping center attract both outsiders (shoppers and commuters who park there) and neighborhood insiders (residents and workers). The second ring of

6. Obtaining detailed data on usage of this or other streets in Burnaby was beyond the scope of this study. It was possible to report only impressions gleaned from traveling along some of the more important streets in the municipality.

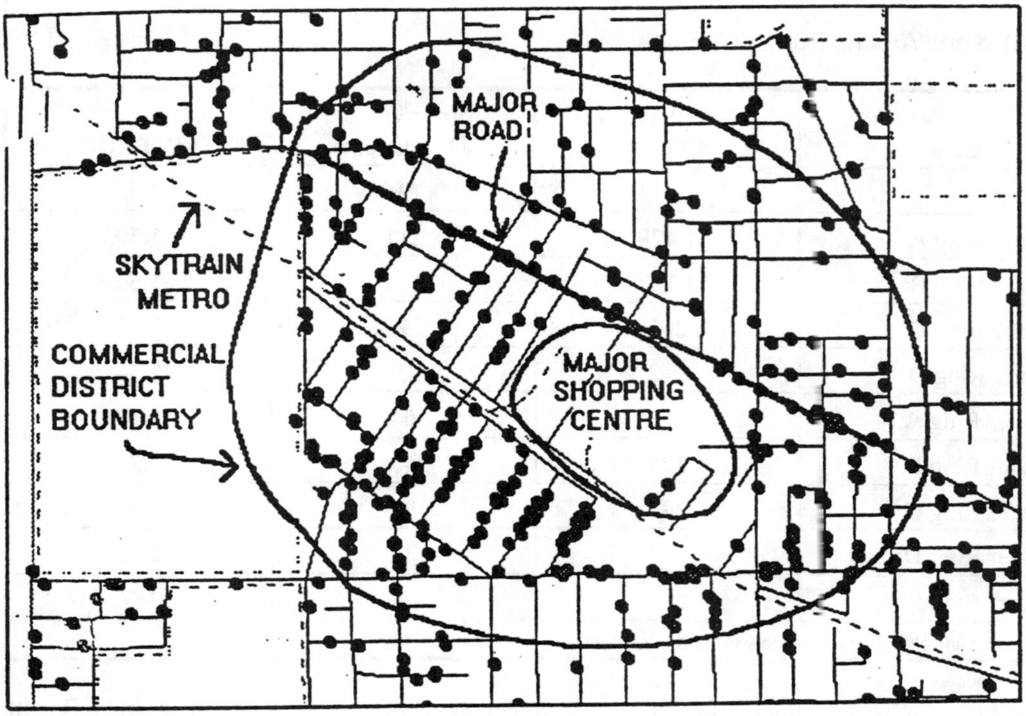

Fig. 6
Motor vehicle thefts around a major shopping center

atoms, surrounding this first ring, is used primarily by neighborhood insiders. It is filled with the cars of residents, workers and other neighborhood insiders.

Table 1 shows counts of total criminal code offenses, motor vehicle thefts and LQC values for auto theft for the shopping center and for both the inner (or first) and the outer (or second) rings of adjacent-edge atoms surrounding the shopping center. The amount of information in table 1 is too limited for any statistical analysis, but it does provide an indication of the value of LQCs in microanalysis using relative or context methods. The number of vehicles stolen from the shopping center is large, but vehicle theft is *relatively* less frequently reported in the shopping center itself than in the surrounding areas. The difference might even be greater if shoplifting were reported more frequently.[7] The motor vehicle thefts for the second, outer ring drop not only in number but also in the LQCs. Second ring LQCs fall from the peak levels observed in the first ring back toward the LQC level observed for the shopping center itself. The reduction in the LQC for the second, outer ring may reflect a movement back to the motor vehicle theft and general crime patterns of local insiders, that is, those living or working in the area, rather than the crime patterns attributable to the mix of insiders and outsiders who utilize the streets in the atoms composing the inner ring, immediately adjacent to the shopping center.

7. Shoplifting is frequently unknown as an actual event, only coming to light as an estimated component of stock "shrinkage" at inventory time. Even when an offender is caught shoplifting, store managers may not call the police.

Table 1
Vehicle Theft in and Around Burnaby's Super Mall

Area Atom	Criminal Code Counts	Motor Vehicle Theft Counts	MVT LQC
Shopping Center	1,453	126	0.85
Inner Ring A	1,479	211	1.39
Inner Ring B	1,127	184	1.66
Inner Ring C*	205	7	0.33
Inner Ring D	112	19	1.34
Outer Ring A	532	64	1.17
Outer Ring B	325	40	1.20
Outer Ring C	282	32	0.93
Outer Ring D	274	23	0.69
Outer Ring E	235	16	0.66

*Part of main shopping street—low value is expected.

Table 2 contains similar information for the strip commercial street the shopping center abuts. Reported crime counts are presented for just the first ring around the strip commercial street. The use of the word *ring* really comes from the idea of surrounding something. For a strip commercial street, the ring is two strip reporting areas on either side of the commercial street (Brantingham and Brantingham 1991:49–50). As suggested previously, it was expected that the number of motor vehicle thefts would be low on the commercial street and higher in the surrounding ring. Table 2 shows the lower LQC for the commercial street and the higher LQC for the adjacent ring. Car thieves in these areas are both insiders and outsiders, but given the limits on car theft sites and situations along the main road, the outsider thieves are ones who are adventurous enough to look for targets in areas adjacent to but not on the main road.

Table 2
Vehicle Theft for the Strip Commercial Street

Area Atom	Criminal Code Counts	Motor Vehicle Theft Counts	MVT LQC
Strip, Atom 1	235	16	0.66
Strip, Atom 2	205	7	0.33
Strip, Atom 3	168	10	0.49
Strip, Atom 4	267	19	0.59
Strip, Atom 5	198	21	0.87
Strip, Atom 6	295	21	0.59
Strip, Atom 7	90	16	1.54
Strip, Atom 8	121	7	0.50
Strip, Atom 9	250	17	0.59
Strip, Atom 10	71	6	0.73
Ring North, Atom 1	361	48	1.30
Ring North, Atom 2	95	13	1.30
Ring North, Atom 3	325	40	1.20
Ring North, Atom 4	282	32	0.93
Ring North, Atom 5	103	10	0.80
Ring North, Atom 6	245	19	0.64
Ring North, Atom 7	454	57	1.09
Ring North, Atom 8	138	9	0.57
Ring North, Atom 9	4	1	2.17
Ring North, Atom 10	313	31	0.86
Ring North, Atom 11	140	13	0.80
Ring South, Atom 1	1,479	211	1.39
Ring South, Atom 2	1,453	126	0.85
Ring South, Atom 3	112	19	1.66
Ring South, Atom 4	274	23	0.64
Ring South, Atom 5	280	42	1.23
Ring South, Atom 6	312	38	1.00
Ring South, Atom 7	73	11	1.24
Ring South, Atom 8	257	36	1.21
Ring South, Atom 9	271	40	0.53
Ring South, Atom 10	2	13	0.85

This microanalysis makes the most sense if viewed while considering crimes as occurrence points on a malleable backcloth. Since this is a simple example of the use of LQCs and backcloths, it is best to let your image of a major suburban shopping area be stretched and compressed, as shown in figure 5. Tables 1 and 2 list the LQCs for areas clustered by a distance measure based on connectivity (see Brantingham and Brantingham 1981, or Beavon et al. 1994, for other connectivity crime studies.) All the atoms connected to the strip commercial and shopping mall were identified as a ring. For the shopping mall, all the atoms connected to or touching the first ring were also identified.

The use of a center area and surrounding rings of atoms described so far is based on actual physical geographic connections, that is, atom *A* shares a common border with atom *B*, so they are judged to be connected. It does, however, rely on connections or connectivity between areas, not the euclidean or "crow flies" distance measures. In essence, the street network shown in figure 6 is transformed into a conceptual connections model shown in figure 7. When routine activities and likely associated awareness spaces are added to the topological backcloth shown, figure 7 would be transformed into a cognitive connections model, as shown in figure 8. That is, a euclidean awareness space would be transformed into a perceptual awareness space.

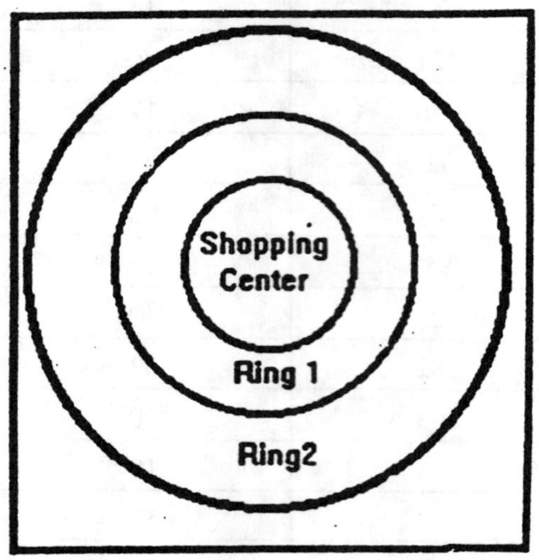

Fig. 7
Conceptual visual image of the shopping center in figure 6

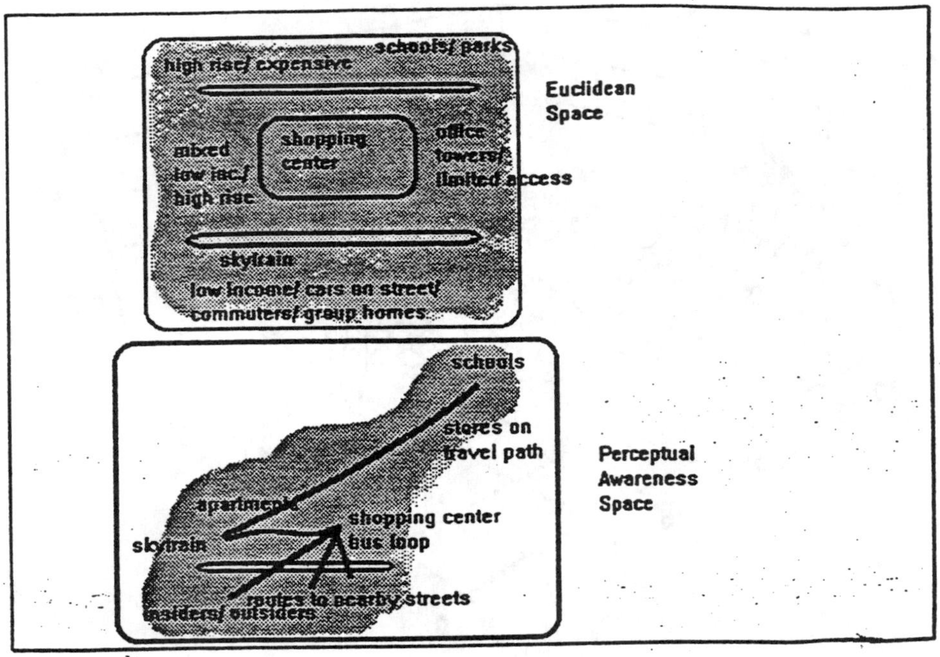

Fig. 8
Euclidean vs. perceptual awareness space

A cognitive connections or connectivity model reflects "known" connections between places. In such a model, an area *unknown* to potential offenders is excluded, regardless of its euclidean connection to known areas. Potential targets in areas unknown to an offender will always remain untouched by that offender. Building such a cognitive model for analytic purposes must be based on research from environmental psychology that explores what people learn about some particular area and why they learn it (Brantingham and Brantingham 1993b; Macdonald and Gifford 1989), but even preliminary attempts have shown great promise (Beavon et al. 1994; Brantingham and Brantingham 1993b).

This cognitive transformation, the underlying expected travel paths, actually observed and expected connections between areas, produces a distribution of LQCs and actual volume of motor vehicle thefts that identifies a hot spot for this crime.[8] A three-dimensional contour plot of the LQCs for Burnaby vehicle theft is shown in figure 9. The smaller city segment around the shopping mall shows as a series of peaks surrounding a lower area in the right-hand corner of the plot.

8. Figure 8 is a cognitive activity map based on reported observations. It is not a product of a research project, but rather, a reasonable subject for a follow-up cognitive mapping study. Its purpose is to show the value of topology, LQCs and event locations.

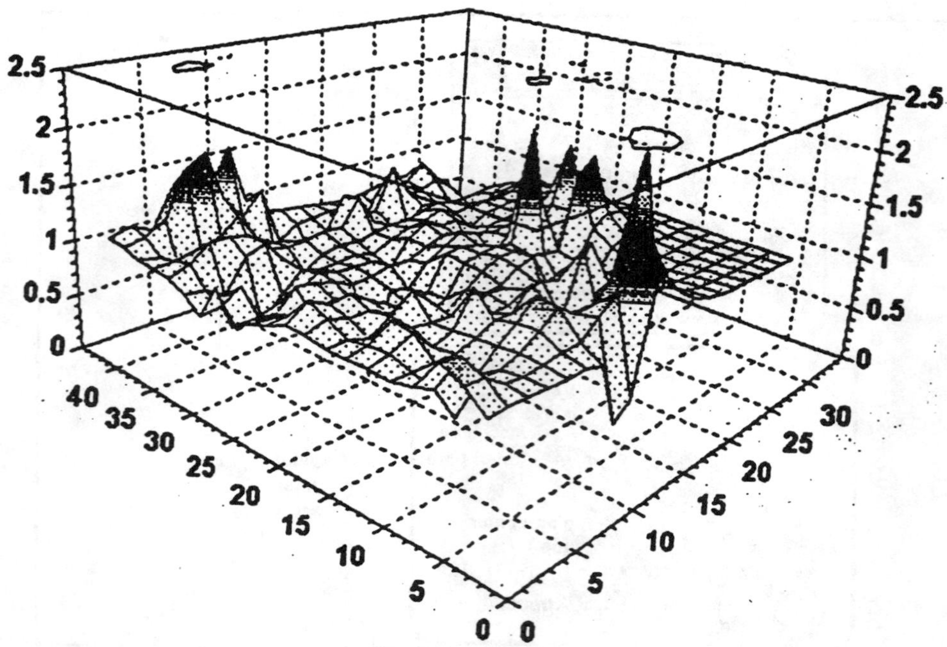

Fig. 9
Contour plot: vehicle theft location quotients

Basically, this hypothetical transformation is a transformation similar to figure 2. While done in only two dimensions, it shows what might happen when a simple connections model is transformed into a "known" connections model. The distribution of motor vehicle thefts is reasonable in this conceptual transformation of space into known space. A cluster or hot spot for auto thefts is reasonable on this simple version of the backcloth to crime.

CONCLUSION

To end this paper on a circular note, there are probably obvious reasons behind any cluster of crime. Through topological expansion, contraction, twisting, and shaping, it is possible to produce a homeomorphic space where the points representing the crime location no longer appear clustered. In essence, the boundary problem is eliminated when reasonable expectations of how the backcloth is shaped (even using a minimal few of the uncountable number of dimensions in the backcloth) actually eliminate the perception of a cluster. That is, the cluster disappears when the transformation restricts the space. It has the same effect as the change in scale shown in figure 1. We must actually move, conceptually, both into, and out and away from, clusters, viewing them at many levels of aggregation, in order to perceive and understand them. When our viewpoint is situated within a cluster, and we view it from a homeomorphic perceptual space, the cluster disappears. When we move away from the cluster, it reappears. Researchers must simultaneously become spatial insiders and outsiders in order to understand spatial patterns. We must be able to move away from our learned focus on euclidean geometry and start to see time and space in multiple, flexible dimensions. We must begin to use types of mathematics that come closer to expressing space as we experience it. Location quotients constitute one easy technique by which crime analysts can begin to make these analytic transformations in order to understand the spatial patterns of crime in particular locales.

REFERENCES

Barker, R.R. (1968). *Ecological Psychology*. Stanford: Stanford University Press.

Barr, R., and K. Pease (1990). Crime placement, displacement and deflection. *Crime and Justice: A Review of Research* 12:277–318.

Beavon, D.J.K., P.L. Brantingham and P.J. Brantingham (1994). The influence of street networks on the patterning of property offenses. Pp. 115–148 in Ronald V. Clarke (ed.), *Crime Prevention Studies*: vol. 2. Monsey, N.Y.: Criminal Justice Press.

Block, C.R. (1990). Hot spots and isocrimes in law enforcement decision making. Paper presented at conference on Police and Community Responses to Drugs, University of Illinois at Chicago.

Block, C.R. (1993). Hot-Spot Area Analysis with STAC. Chicago: Workshop on Crime Analysis Through Computer Mapping.

Boggs, S.L. (1965). Urban crime patterns. *American Sociological Review* 30:899–908.

Brantingham P.J., D.A. Dyreson and P.L. Brantingham (1976). Crime seen through a cone of resolution. *American Behavioral Scientist* 20:261–273.

Brantingham, P.L., and P.J. Brantingham (1975). Residential burglary and urban form. *Urban Studies* 12:273–284.

——— (1978a). A topological technique for regionalization. *Environment and Behavior* 10:335–353.

——— (1978b). A theoretical model of crime site selection. Pp. 105–118 in M.D. Krohn and R.L. Akers (eds.), *Crime, Law and Sanctions*. Beverly Hills: Sage Publications, Inc.

——— (1981). Mobility, notoriety and crime: A study in the crime patterns of urban nodal points. *Journal of Environmental Systems* 11:89–99.

——— (1991). *Environmental Criminology* (2nd ed.). Prospect Heights, Ill.: Waveland Press.

——— (1993a). Environment, routine and situation: Toward a pattern theory of crime. *Advances in Criminological Theory* 5:259–294.

——— (1993b). Nodes and paths. *Journal of Environmental Psychology* 13:3–28.

——— (1994). Crime analysis using location quotients. Pp. 83–94 in D. Zahm and P. Cromwell (eds.), *Proceedings of the International Seminar on Environmental Criminology and Crime Analysis*. Tallahassee, Fla.: Florida Statistical Analysis Center, Florida Criminal Justice Institute.

——— (1994). La concentration spatiale relative de la criminalité et son analyse: Vers un renouvellement de la criminologie environmentale. *Criminologie* 27:81–97.

Brantingham, P.L., P.J. Brantingham and A. Verma (1992). Crime analysis through point set and algebraic topology. American Society of Criminology meetings, New Orleans.

Brantingham, P.L., P.J. Brantingham and P. Wong (1990). Malls and crime: A first look. *Security Journal* 1:175–181.

Canter, D., and P. Larkin (1993). The environmental range of serial rapists. *Journal of Environmental Psychology* 13:63–70.

Capone, D., and N. Nichols (1976). Urban structure and criminal mobility. *American Behavioral Scientist* 20:199–201.

Carroll, J., and F. Weaver (1986). Shoplifters' perceptions of crime opportunities: A process-tracing study. Pp. 19–38 in D. Cornish and R. Clarke (eds.), *The Reasoning Criminal.* New York: Springer-Verlag.

Clarke, R.V. (1980). Situational crime prevention: theory and practice. *British Journal of Criminology* 20:136–147.

——— (1992). *Situational Crime Prevention: Successful Case Studies.* New York: Harrow and Heston.

Clarke, R.V., and D.B. Cornish (1985). Modeling offenders' decisions: A framework for research and policy. *Crime and Justice: An Annual Review of Research* 6:147–185.

Cohen, L.E., and M. Felson (1979). Social change and crime rate trends: A routine activity approach. *American Sociological Review* 44:588–608.

Costanzo, C.M., W.C. Halperin and N. Gale (1986). Criminal mobility and the directional component in journeys to crime. Pp. 73–95 in R.M. Figlio, S. Hakim and G.F. Rengert (eds.), *Metropolitan Crime Patterns.* Monsey, N.Y.: Criminal Justice Press.

Cromwell, P.F., J.N. Olson and D.W. Avary (1991). *Breaking and Entering: An Ethnographic Analysis of Burglary.* Newbury Park, Calif.: Sage Publications.

Cromwell, P.F., and D. Zahm (1991). Mitigating traffic to control crime: The impact on property crime of street closings and barricades. Paper presented at American Society of Criminology annual meetings, San Francisco.

Eck, J., and W. Spelman (1992). Thefts from vehicles in shipyard parking lots. Pp. 164–173 in R.V. Clarke (ed.), *Situational Crime Prevention: Successful Case Studies.* New York: Harrow and Heston.

Feeney, F. (1986). Robbers as Decision Makers. Pp. 53–71 in D. Cornish and R. Clarke (eds.), *The Reasoning Criminal.* New York: Springer-Verlag.

Felson, M. (1983). Ecology of crime. Pp. 665–670 in S.H. Kadish (ed.), *Encyclopedia of Crime and Justice, Vol. 2.* New York: The Free Press.

——— (1986). Predicting crime at any point on the city map. Pp. 127–136 in R.M. Figlio, S. Hakim and G.F. Rengert (eds.), *Metropolitan Crime Patterns.* Monsey, N.Y.: Criminal Justice Press.

——— (1987). Routine activities and crime prevention in the developing metropolis. *Criminology* 25:911–931.

——— (1993). *Crime and Everyday Life: Insight and Implications for Society.* Thousand Oaks, Calif.: Pine Forge Press.

Harries, K.D. (1991). Alternative denominators in conventional crime rates. Pp. 147–167 in P.J. Brantingham and P.L. Brantingham (eds.), *Environmental Criminology.* Prospect Heights, Ill.: Waveland Press.

Heelan, P.A. (1983). *Space Perception and the Philosophy of Science.* Berkeley: University of California Press.

LeBeau, J. (1993). The Temporal Ecology of Crime: Comparing Temporal Rhythms over Spatial Units. Chicago: Workshop on Crime Analysis Through Computer Mapping.

Lenz, R. (1986). Geography and temporal changes among robberies in Milwaukee. Pp. 97–116 in R. Figlio, S. Hakim and G. Rengert (eds.), *Metropolitan Crime Patterns.* Monsey, N.Y.: Criminal Justice Press.

Macdonald, J.E., and R. Gifford (1989). Territorial cues and defensible space theory: The burglar's point of view. *Journal of Environmental Psychology* 9:193–205.

Piaget, J., and B. Inhelder (1948). *The Child's Conception of Space*. New York: Norton.

Poyner, B. (1992). Situational crime prevention in two parking facilities. Pp. 174–184 in R.V. Clarke (ed.), *Situational Crime Prevention: Successful Case Studies*. New York: Harrow and Heston.

Rand, A. (1986). Mobility triangles. Pp. 117–126 in R.M. Figlio, S. Hakim and G.F. Rengert (eds.), *Metropolitan Crime Patterns*. Monsey, N.Y.: Criminal Justice Press.

Rengert, G.F. (1988). The location of facilities and crime. *Journal of Security of Administration* 11(2):12–16.

——— (1992). The journey to crime: Conceptual foundations and policy implications. Pp. 109–117 in D.J. Evans, N.R. Fyfe and D.T. Herbert (eds.), *Crime, Policing and Place: Essays in Environmental Criminology*. London: Routledge.

Rhodes, W.M., and C. Conly (1991). Crime and mobility: an empirical study. Pp. 167–188 in P.J. Brantingham and P.L. Brantingham (eds.), *Environmental Criminology*. Prospect Heights, Ill.: Waveland Press.

Ripley, B.D. (1988). *Statistical Inference for Spatial Processes*. Cambridge: Cambridge University Press.

Rossmo, D.K. (1993). Multivariate Spatial Profiles as a Tool in Crime Investigation. Chicago: Workshop on Crime Analysis Through Computer Mapping.

Sherman, L.W., P.R. Gartin and M.E. Buerger (1989). Hot spots of predatory crime: routine activities and the criminology of place. *Criminology* 27:27–55.

Timms, D.W.G. (1965). The spatial distribution of deviants in Luton, England. *Australian and New Zealand Journal of Criminology* 1:38–52.

——— (1971). *The Urban Mosaic: Towards a Theory of Residential Differentiation*. Cambridge: Cambridge University Press.

Turner, S. (1969). Delinquency and distance. Pp. 11–26 in T. Sellin and M.E. Wolfgang (eds.), *Delinquency: Selected Studies*. New York: John Wiley and Sons.

Chapter 11

State of the Statistical Art: Point-Pattern Analysis

Philip Canter
Baltimore County Police Department

INTRODUCTION

The purpose of this paper is to present an overview of how point-pattern analysis can be used by police departments to identify and analyze crime. Crime locations identified as points over a geographic area can provide clues, just as fingerprints or other tangible evidence can link a suspect to a crime. Police analysts examine the location and distribution of crime to identify areas targeted for intervention. Attributes associated with each point can assist in determining an intervention strategy. Subsequent examination of the target area at a geographic level can be used to assess the effectiveness and consequences of an intervention strategy.

There is a growing interest among police analysts in examining the geographic distribution of incidents that appear as individual points on a map. Traditionally, incidents have been aggregated to some geographic area, typically a beat or reporting area, which is usually delimited by streets or some linear barrier to interarea movement like a stream or railroad. Reports identifying "active" locations are largely based on the number of incidents occurring within a reporting area or beat, usually without consideration of the relatively few events occurring in areas contiguous to the identified active area. It is also possible to completely miss an "active" area if events tend to cluster geographically, but when aggregated to a reporting area or beat, result in a low total.

Assuming that crime locations, rather than reporting area frequencies, are used to identify active areas, then the question becomes, When does a point pattern appear? Is it two points within two blocks or three points within four blocks? Identifying geographic crime patterns through visual inspection is subjective. One police analyst may feel that a series of points constitutes a pattern, while another may feel the pattern is randomly distributed. Any tool that assists in the identification of point patterns based on probability models is helpful.

DEFINITION AND ASSUMPTIONS OF POINT-PATTERN ANALYSIS

The phrase "point-pattern analysis" indicates that we are interested in the distribution of points over a geographic area, and that upon further examination, the distribution of these points will provide information about factors influencing the location of these events. Two questions are of particular interest: When does a set of points constitute a cluster, and what are the reasons influencing or causing this point pattern to occur?

The underlying assumption of point-pattern analysis is that event locations occur at random. Consequently, the chance of a location being victimized is equally shared among other locations within the study area, and the location of an event does not influence victimization in other locations. This is referred to by Boots and Getis (1988) as a *homogeneous planar surface*.

In actuality, it is uncommon to find a completely homogeneous study area where the interaction of points does not exist. For example, areas containing an empirically confirmed point cluster may simply reflect the location of crime within a high-density residential area, such as an apartment complex. Also, point clusters may form by offenders' avoiding areas having an active crime prevention program and targeting adjoining areas that are easier to victimize.

In the process of discussing how point patterns can be influenced by a non-homogeneous surface, one begins to explore and question the possibility of other factors that might influence point patterns. It may be true that a particular set of points is clustered due to their location within an apartment complex, but what attributes associated with that apartment complex are influencing the occurrence of crime? Is it due to a lack of propinquity, caused by a transient population, some stress factors, or a gang operating within the complex? If offenders are victimizing a neighborhood because it does not participate in a crime prevention program, what does this say about the success of an adjoining area that has an active crime prevention program?

Although the assumptions underlying uniformity conditions are violated, subsequent analysis of the point-pattern distribution should lead investigators to question other factors influencing the distribution of events. Point-pattern analysis is a useful technique for exploring, describing and, in some cases, explaining crime.

MICROCOMPUTER PROGRAMS AVAILABLE FOR POINT-PATTERN ANALYSIS

Several computer programs are available that can be used to empirically identify areas where crime, identified by point locations, tends to cluster. Point locations are expressed geographically by a coordinate system that relates to a vertical and a horizontal axis. On a flat surface, this coordinate system is in the form of a Cartesian grid expressed as *x* and *y* coordinates. State plane coordinates, which appear on highway maps or map atlases, typically use a Cartesian coordinate system. The coordinates originate at a specific location and are numbered depending on direction and distance from the origin point. In a Cartesian grid, the distance between two pairs of *x-y* coordinates can be computed easily using the Pythagorean theorem. Because the earth's surface curves, points are expressed as longitude and latitude in degrees, minutes and seconds, or decimal degrees. The distance between two pairs of points identified by longitude-latitude can be computed using a trigonometric formula. However, computer programs used to identify point clusters are based on a Cartesian grid system. For this reason, point locations expressed as longitude-latitude must be converted to state plane coordinates or another Cartesian grid system.

Point patterns can be identified two ways: graphically and statistically. Crime data assigned *x* and *y* coordinates can be plotted quickly on a graph and visually inspected. Such graphic applications are easier to use than statistical applications, but they are more subjective when identifying point patterns.[1] Statistical techniques use proximity measures or frequencies relative to a probability distribution. A null hypothesis posits that the point pattern resembles "complete spatial randomness." Methods include cluster analysis, nearest-neighbor analysis and quadrat analysis.[2]

1. There is an excellent discussion of mapping techniques using graphing methods in *Geographic Factors in Policing* (1990), chapter 3, titled "Mapping: A Helpful Tool," prepared for the Police Executive Research Forum by Keith Harries.

2. See Boots and Getis (1988) regarding measures of point dispersions.

USING GRAPHS TO IDENTIFY POINT PATTERNS

Baltimore County police analysts initially relied on scatterplots, based on state plane coordinates assigned to point locations, to assist in the identification of point patterns. Figure 1 shows a scatterplot of motor vehicle thefts in western Baltimore County reported in 1992. Baltimore County has been experiencing an increase in motor vehicle thefts over the last several years, far exceeding national and suburban area rates. Most motor vehicle thefts occur in the western part of Baltimore County. The police precinct used in this example usually has the highest number of motor vehicle thefts in Baltimore County. Points defined by *x* and *y* coordinates clearly define precinct boundaries (Liberty Road to the north, Baltimore National Pike to the south, Baltimore City line to the east, and Howard-Carroll counties to the west). The blank areas shaped as an inverted *L* close to the city line and north of Baltimore National Pike correspond to interstate highways (I-70 and I-695). The western part of the precinct has few auto thefts because the area is largely rural. Darker areas formed by point clusters are either commercial or high-density land uses. The scatterplot clearly shows a high concentration of motor vehicle thefts in the southeast part of the precinct. This area is densely developed with apartment complexes and commercial centers.

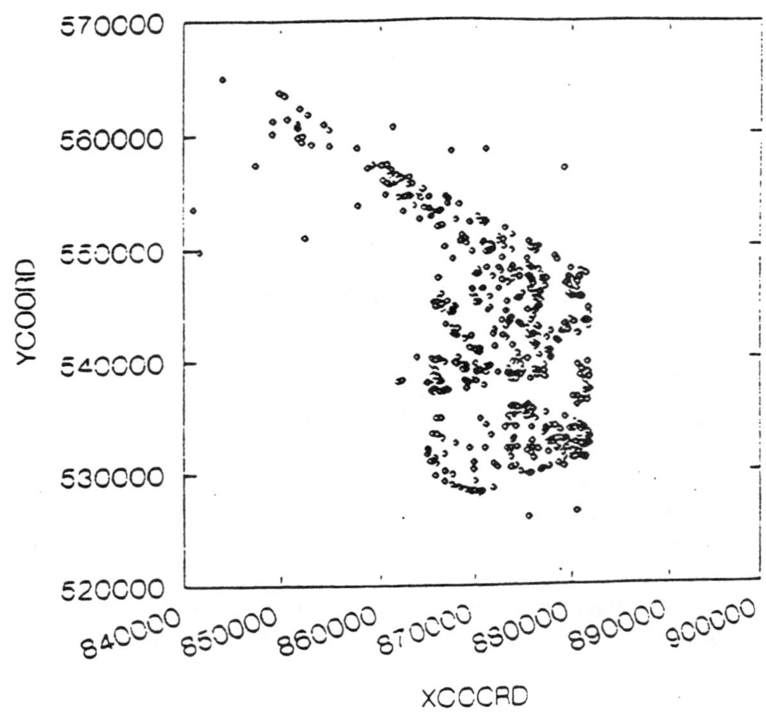

Fig. 1
Scatter plot of motor vehicle thefts in Woodlawn precinct

The scatterplot shown in figure 1, which was produced using SYGRAPH, is a quick and fairly easy technique for identifying criminally active areas. Prior to SYGRAPH, police analysts in Baltimore County graphed coordinates from a map atlas using LOTUS 1-2-3. This method was a fairly quick and easy way to identify point patterns using a microcomputer. Later, analysts purchased SYSTAT and began to explore some of the graphing methods available in the SYGRAPH program.

In addition to scatterplots, analysts have also found contour plots to be helpful in identifying point clusters. Contour plots with closely spaced lines indicate a higher density of points. Figure 2 is a contour map constructed from the *x* and *y* coordinates used in the scatterplot shown in figure 1. Closely spaced lines such as the ones shown in the middle and toward the southeast corners of the precinct indicate a higher density of points or motor vehicle thefts. Both of these areas correspond to high-density commercial uses in the precinct. The contour lines shown in the middle of the precinct correspond to a regional shopping center and various community shopping centers located in close proximity to the regional center. The contour map is a quick way to discern point patterns needed to identify active areas. The contour map also shows the extent of influence motor vehicle thefts have within the precinct.

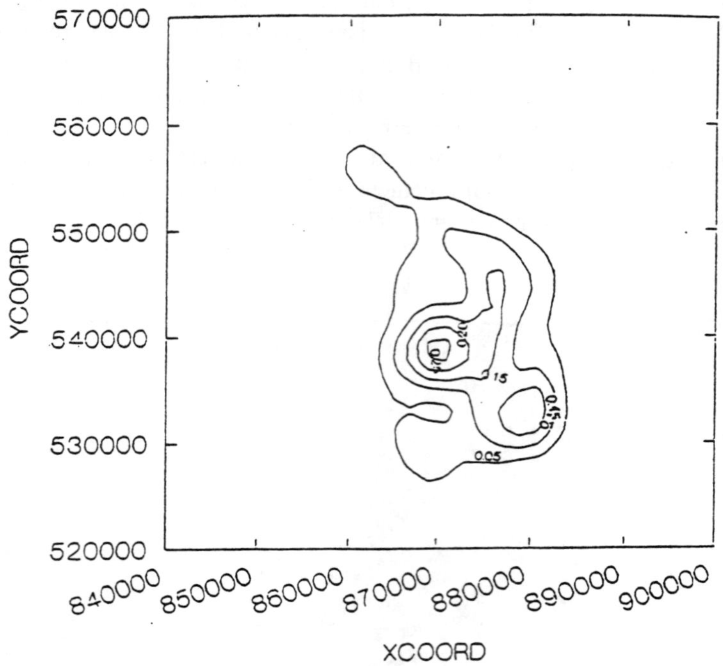

Fig. 2
Contour map of motor vehicle thefts in Baltimore County

Contour lines can also be smoothed and shaded to portray point clusters in a grid-like fashion (figure 3). Contour lines can be smoothed and shaded in SYGRAPH to identify criminally active areas. The darkest area shows a high concentration of motor vehicle thefts located at a regional shopping center and corresponds to the closely spaced contour lines shown in figure 2. The darker areas identify locations corresponding to a high number of motor vehicle thefts and are generally associated with higher residential and commercial densities. This technique can assist police analysts in identifying where resources should be deployed in response to a particular problem. The *x* and *y* coordinates shown for each axis can be related back to a map for geographic reference.

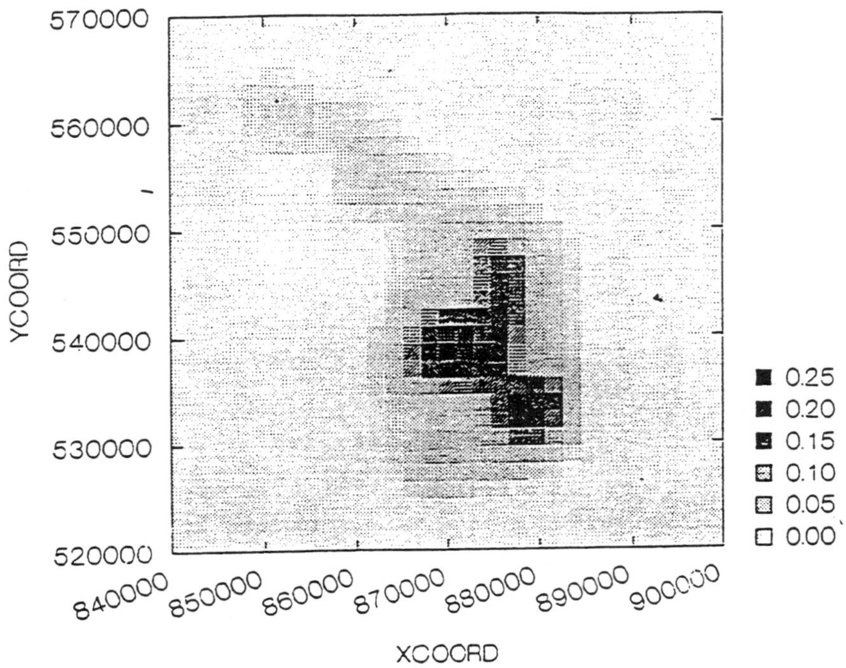

Fig. 3
Contour plot of motor vehicle thefts, with shading

Another useful technique in identifying geographic patterns is a three-dimensional graph, where the *Z*-axis denotes the number of events. This was used in an examination of aggravated assault cases on the lower west side of Baltimore County (figure 4). This three-dimensional graph shows the location of aggravated assaults reported in 1992 for communities in southwest Baltimore County. The area of interest primarily consists of apartment complexes and medium-density residential development. This graph was produced by determining the number of assaults, shown on the *Z*-axis as "count," for point locations identified by *x* and *y* coordinates. A three-dimensional graph is useful for examining the location of events as well as the number of events for a given location. The dots superimposed over the surface graph show the location of assaults, while the surface height considers the number of assaults reported for particular locations. This graph shows that points tend to cluster geographically, but there are some locations that had a high number of cases, as indicated by the peaks shown on the graph. The two small inclines in the front and middle of the graph were due to assaults occurring in apartment complexes. Areas of the graph with steep surfaces, such as the back and right of the graph, were due to assaults occurring at bars located in the study area. The three-dimensional graph was produced using SYGRAPH.

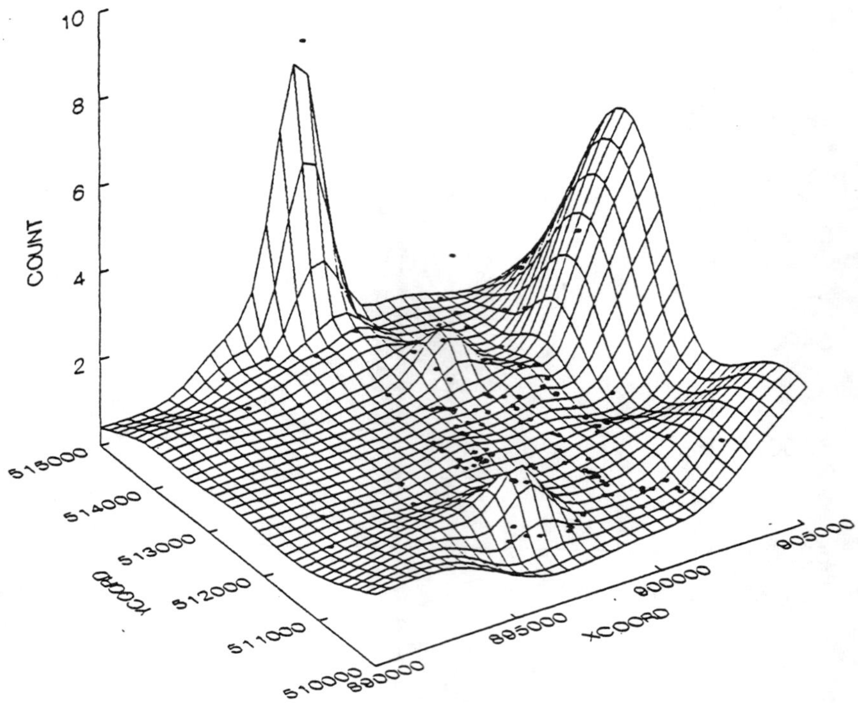

Fig. 4
Three-dimensional graph

Thiessen diagrams or Voronoi tessellations also have been used to explore market areas associated with drug activity. The Voronoi tessellation shown in figure 5 was developed from point data showing the location of cocaine arrests for a three-month period in eastern Baltimore County. The irregularly shaped polygons are formed when point locations are not equidistant from each other. The areas within each polygon represent hypothetical locations that are closest to a polygon's point (assuming each hypothetical point location has equal access to a polygon's point), and thus can be interpreted as market areas associated with locations where arrests for cocaine sales and possession occurred. Analysts are exploring the use of Voronoi tessellations to determine if drug activity and respective market areas could assist in identifying locations where drugs are being sold. The Voronoi tessellation was constructed by SYGRAPH.

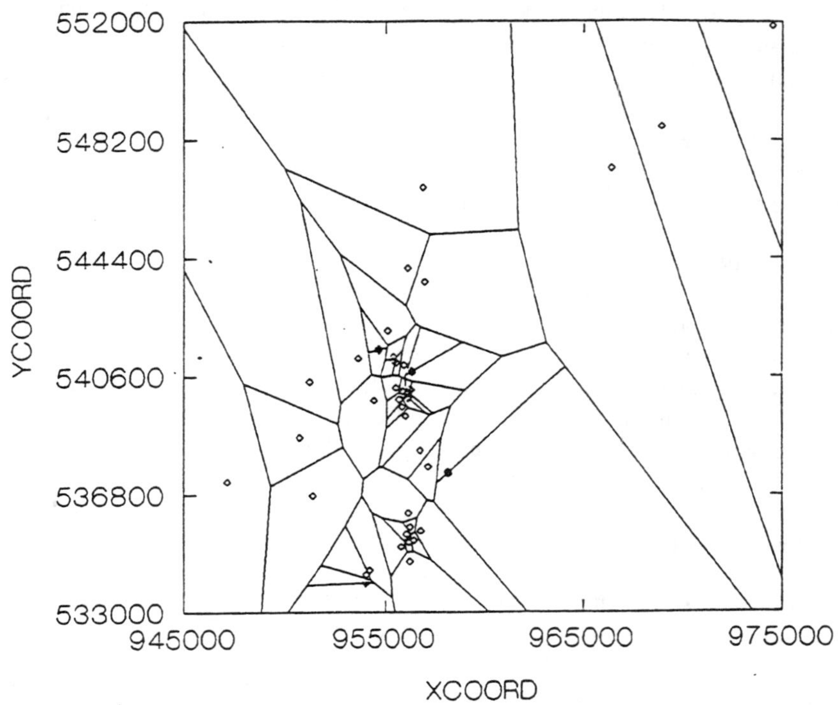

Fig. 5
The Voronoi tessellation

STATISTICAL METHODS USED TO IDENTIFY POINT PATTERNS

There are a number of micro-based computer programs that use statistical methods to identify point patterns. The following methods were selected because of their relative ease of use and their proven practicality from a crime analysis perspective. All require the use of Cartesian coordinates as input.

One technique used by Baltimore County police analysts to identify point clusters is a statistical program that uses *K*-means and hierarchal trees. The *K*-means technique in SYSTAT's CLUSTER program partitions groups consisting of points having distances with the lowest within-sum-of-squares. Depending on the number of clusters selected, output appears as groups consisting of points that maximize between-cluster variation. The CLUSTER program in SYSTAT has been used to identify geographic point clusters, as well as clusters based on case attributes. Most recently, this technique was used in Baltimore County to determine if a series of rapes involving unknown offenders had similar characteristics and thus could be ascribed to the same suspect. Clustering algorithms are, by nature, memory-intensive. Consequently, the use of microcomputer-based clustering packages may not work for a large number of points and may require a mini- or mainframe-based statistical package.

Another technique used to empirically determine if points cluster along a segment is a one-dimension nearest-neighbor analysis. Baltimore County analysts used a one-dimension nearest-neighbor analysis to determine if robberies occurring along a major highway had a tendency to cluster. Once robbery locations were geocoded in MapInfo, the resulting latitude-longitude coordinates were converted to state plane coordinates and put into a LOTUS 1-2-3 spreadsheet. The distance from one point to all other points along the roadway was computed using the Pythagorean theorem in each cell of the spreadsheet. The @MIN function was used to identify the closest distance from one robbery location to the next closest robbery location within the distance matrix. This study concluded that robberies did not tend to cluster along the roadway.

An interesting application currently being explored by police analysts in Baltimore County uses clustering techniques for epidemiologic analysis. Recently, the U.S. Department of Health and Human Services in Atlanta published a program called Cluster 3.1, which contains several clustering programs. Many of these techniques involve assigning points to boundary areas and then using the aggregate total to determine if observations cluster over time or space. The Remsa method developed by Aldrich (1981) uses the person, place and time model to determine if events are clustered within subgroups of a study area or within temporal and geographic areas. Attributes relating to crime or victimization data can be examined together with a crime's location or time of occurrence.

A powerful and fairly inexpensive micro-based geographic information system (GIS) called IDRISI is available from Clark University (Eastman 1992). IDRISI's spatial techniques in the statistical analysis ring include procedures to perform spatial trend analysis, spatial autocorrelation, mean centers of point distributions, and quadrat analysis. These procedures can be used to explore relationships between attribute data, diffusion patterns and point-pattern analyses. As a geographic information system, IDRISI can overlay information collected for different boundaries to form a composite layer. For example, as part of Baltimore County's Substance Abuse Tracking System, various county agencies contribute databases collected at different geographic levels to ensure confidentiality. Sources include Drug Awareness Warning Network data collected by zip code, treatment data collected by census tract, and drug-related school expulsions collected by district. Police analysts are interested in merging data collected at different levels to form a composite layer used to identify drug markets.

The ability to link point data to other boundary layers such as census block groups or tracts has enabled police analysts to explore relationships between demographic, socioeconomic and land-use data relative to crime and calls for police service. The department's goal is to develop models that not only help to explain crime, but also allow police resources to be used in a proactive manner. Such a model was developed in Baltimore County to identify areas where spousal assault cases may be occurring, but are underreported to police. At that time, residuals produced from a regression model were mapped and manually tested for autocorrelation using Dacey's Contiguity Test. This was done to determine whether the spatial independence assumption of variables used in a model had been violated. IDRISI, however, can quickly compute a Moran's I to test for spatial autocorrelation. Additionally, similar methods can be used to determine whether spatial autocorrelation exists for any variable. Finding a variable such as crime to be spatially autocorrelated should lead us to ask, "Why does crime tend to be higher for a group of contiguous areas?"

SPATIAL AND TEMPORAL ANALYSIS OF CRIME (STAC)

All of these computer applications offer interesting possibilities in analyzing point patterns. We can't lose sight, however, of the human element involved in manipulating data for subsequent analysis. Many of the procedures just described require data translations or point aggregations to boundary areas. Few crime analysts will take the time to perform the kinds of analyses just described. The time and effort required to prepare data for input would be too laborious. These procedures must be easy to use if they are to become effective analytical tools.

One program that has been successfully used by police analysts in Baltimore County is a public domain program called Spatial and Temporal Analysis of Crime, or STAC, produced under the guidance of Dr. Carolyn R. Block of the Illinois Criminal Justice Information Authority. Over the past four years, police analysts in Baltimore County have used STAC to identify point clusters or "hot spots." The direct interface between Baltimore County's computer mapping program, MapInfo, and STAC allows police analysts to quickly identify active areas.

The benefits of STAC to Baltimore County police have been well documented. For example, standard deviational ellipses produced by STAC of drug-related indicators, such as arrests and phone complaints, are used to identify drug markets. In addition, STAC has been used to identify motor vehicle theft areas (figure 6), highway robbery locations and, most recently, purse-snatching areas. Figure 6 shows standard deviational ellipses computed by STAC for motor vehicle thefts in western Baltimore County reported in 1992. It's interesting to compare the "hot areas" identified by STAC to the point patterns appearing in figure 1. Note that the higher density of points seen in a scatterplot (figure 1)

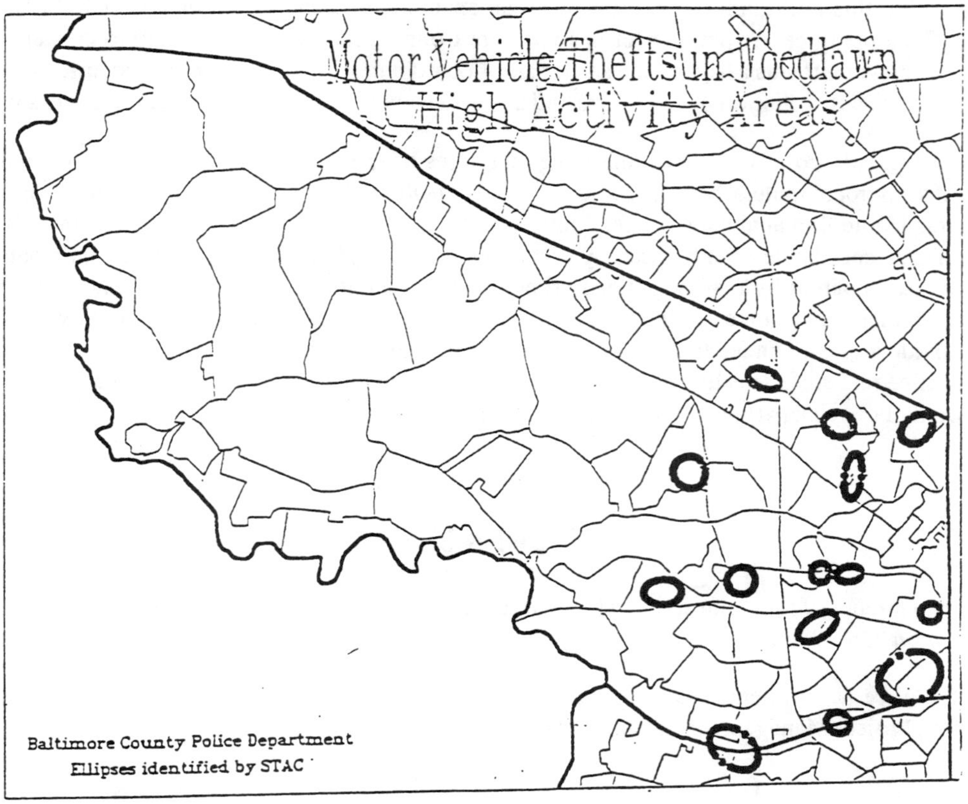

Fig. 6
Motor vehicle thefts in Woodlawn high-activity areas

appears to conform to the "hot area" ellipses. Analysts in Baltimore County have found STAC to be a useful and quick technique for identifying criminally active areas. Departments capable of producing scatterplots can easily use the same data as input to STAC to identify active areas.

CONCLUDING REMARKS: ISSUES REGARDING POINT PATTERNS AND CRIME ANALYSIS

Concluding remarks will briefly cover some issues associated with the use of crime data and point-pattern analysis. Specifically, these issues concern the examination of point data over different geographic boundaries and mapping scales.

One problem associated with point-pattern analysis is the inability to readily exchange point-related information with neighboring jurisdictions. Crime does not respect political boundaries, so it is important that police departments know what is going on in neighboring jurisdictions and vice versa. There may be one or two cases in a community contiguous to a neighboring jurisdiction, yet on the other side of the political boundary, there may be a cluster of related cases. Police departments cannot continue to examine crime only within their respective jurisdictions.

Another issue concerns the definition of the geographic area under study. Although a point is defined by a set of coordinates, the location of an event will likely fall within a two- or perhaps three-dimensional object, such as a parcel of land or an apartment building. A closer examination may reveal that the actual distribution of events displays a specific pattern within this multidimensional space. As an example, in a study of motor vehicle thefts reported to have occurred in a shopping center parking lot in Baltimore County, the thefts were found to cluster around a bus stop. Each motor vehicle theft was assigned the same pair of coordinates, since these events occurred at the same address; however, the actual distribution of cases revealed a relationship between the events and the bus stop.

Police analysts typically collect and examine large quantities of crime data, which preclude manual plotting of point locations. As microcomputers have become more affordable and powerful, computer-mapping applications have become a practical tool in analyzing crime. Points are assigned coordinates so that they can be plotted by computer on a map. These coordinates can be used by other computer programs to identify geographic patterns, which may not be otherwise apparent by mapping. Each crime location identified as a point on a map can be associated with hundreds of characteristics linked to the area containing that point. Points clustering in areas with similar characteristics can provide a greater understanding of criminal events. Ultimately, this should contribute toward a reduction in crime, as police resources are allocated more effectively. Such reductions have been noted in areas targeted by the Baltimore County Police Department—areas identified using point-pattern analysis.

REFERENCES

Aldrich, T., and N. Garcia (1981). Pattern of Melanoma Incidence in Miami, Florida. *Journal of the National Medical Association* 73:887–88.

Baltimore County Police Department (1990). *Spouse Abuse Study 1989*. Baltimore County, Md.: Planning and Budget Division, Project Management and Analysis, Operations Analysis Unit.

Boots, Barry N., and Arthur Getis (1988). *Point-Pattern Analysis*. Scientific Geography Series, vol. 8. Beverly Hills: Sage Publications.

Eastman, J. Ronald (1992). *IDRISI*, Version 4. Worcester, Mass.: Clark University, Graduate School of Geography.

Garson, David G., and Robert S. Biggs (1992). *Analytic Mapping and Geographic Databases*. Sage university paper series on quantitative applications in social sciences, series no. 07-087. Newbury Park, Calif.: Sage.

Harries, Keith (1990). *Geographic Factors in Policing*. Washington, D.C.: Police Executive Research Forum.

Illinois Criminal Justice Information Authority (1988). *Spatial and Temporal Analysis of Crime*. Chicago: Statistical Analysis Center, 120 S. Riverside Plaza.

Mapping Information Systems Corporation (1992). *MapInfo Desktop Mapping Software*. Troy, N.Y.: MapInfo Corporation, 200 Broadway.

U.S. Department of Health and Human Services (1993). *Cluster 3.1*. Atlanta: Public Health Service, Agency for Toxic Substances and Disease Registry.

Wilkinson, Leland (1990). *SYGRAPH: The System for Graphics*. Evanston, Ill.: SYSTAT, Inc.

——— (1990). *SYSTAT: The System for Statistics*. Evanston, Ill.: SYSTAT, Inc.

Chapter 12

Keeping It Simple

Michel R. Moore
Los Angeles Police Department

"To protect and to serve" has been the motto of the Los Angeles Police Department for decades. Processing the information needed to provide service to support this motto can sometimes be difficult. With over 5.5 million citizen calls for assistance, nearly a million dispatched radio calls and over 340,000 Part I crimes recorded yearly, the department must determine how to deploy its precious 7,600 officers over 467 square miles to serve 3.5 million-plus people in the most efficient way. This challenge poses a continual dilemma subject to rapidly changing conditions.

In 1990, the department began development of crime analysis as one means to support this decision-making. Daily and systematic gathering, evaluating and reporting of crime, arrests and known offenders at the area level were initiated. Each geographic division (or "precinct") was provided with a crime analysis detail (CAD) and computer equipment to pull information from the department's central records.

Although the CADs had the ability to examine all crimes, they were to focus initial efforts on robbery. The city suffered more than 100 robberies a day. Each instance involved violence and potential for serious injury or death to an innocent person. Choosing robbery ensured each occurrence would contain the exact time of the incident and a suspect(s) description—elements that proved valuable in refining the system and producing meaningful analysis.

Through technical support, area CADs were given the ability to gather daily information. CAD personnel immediately began massaging it for clues to identify suspects and recognize patterns, series and trends. The statistical reporting function was left to the department's information systems people. The CADs were charged with looking at incoming reports and arrests for details that could be disseminated to patrol and detectives that same day.

Each CAD also began a daily download of crime and arrest information from the host mainframe building to a database representing its area. Records were enhanced by the analyst with additional information not contained in the central record management system. This added information included property descriptions, weapon detail and suspect physical oddities, including tattoo and scar information. Once these enhancements were made, the analysts would review incidents for clues and correlations. When found, the information was passed to the assigned detective. Pattern, series, known offenders, and wanted suspects were detailed in bulletins distributed to patrol watch commanders and beat officers that same day.

Database development was accomplished within a Paradox 3.5 software package utilizing scripts and programming to lessen the use of codes whenever possible. WordPerfect 5.1 supported word processing. Connectivity to the host was completed with Attachmate for DOS. A laser printer produced the alerts. A FAX network provided the means for forwarding information between CADs.

Within a short period of time, it was apparent that two system failures were occurring: spatial analysis and user proficiency. Spatial analysis at this point was entirely dependent on the ability of the analyst to present events on a paper map or, worse yet, within his or her mind. The established system could provide only a tabular review. Two hundred robbery reports occurring over the past two weeks within an area only could be analyzed based on the victim or suspect profile, not the location. Even with proficient knowledge of the area, multiple crime events could not be tracked spatially. Computer mapping was needed.

In the area of user proficiency, it was observed that the majority of the analysts did not possess a high level of computer literacy. Training was provided in the operation of computer hardware and software. However, the download, import, edit, query, and reporting of the information crossed numerous software packages. Each package required its own method of completing similar functions. For example, a simple effort to print within the word processor used steps entirely different from the database management software. Transferring records required knowledge of file names and extensions, along with structures of directories. Querying of records demanded significant knowledge of the underlying data model, linking of tables and the software's querying language. Data archiving and backup were nonexistent. Analysts possessing this level of knowledge were scarce. When found, they were often promoted to a systems position within the department or elsewhere. What was needed was the simplification of the process.

A review of the marketplace was conducted. The experience of the department was not found to be unique. While the capability of software programs had increased tremendously, user competence lagged. The graphical user interface (GUI) movement appeared to offer hope to the industry.

Reviewing GUI-based software packages meeting the functional objectives of the department's automated crime analysis system revealed hope of forming a standard method for completing like functions. However, initial applications often mirrored DOS counterparts. Developers often failed to understand what the end user really needed in the way of an interface. Consequently, in the migration to Windows, developers replicated screens used in original DOS applications. This condition usually corrected itself in later versions once the end-users provided input as the product matured.

A Microsoft Windows-based solution was sought to provide a mapping software package to integrate the other functions of crime analysis within Windows programs. Experienced systems programmers were assigned to work on the overall migration to the Windows-based packages.

A complete review of the available mapping packages determined that although one (MapInformation's MapInfo for Windows Version 2.0) was Windows-based, its native package did not do enough to simplify the querying requirements of a crime-based relational data set. A custom application development was pursued with the software company to provide a custom query interface to allow the user to "point and click" queries. Simplified data import, archiving and a blending of the ability to utilize both Paradox and MapInfo were added requirements.

The interface design provided major fields typically queried by the user and the option of all fields available within the database. For example, the user merely pointed out the crime, date, time range, premise type, suspect's hair, and eye color desired in the query. The software package then took the selections and formulated the appropriate SQL statement, including the table relationships. Query results returned in the form of maps and tabular forms that allowed additional queries to narrow or broaden the search. This effort took well over a year to complete. Some additional enhancements are still ongoing.

A substantial amount of the expended effort of the development process was explaining the end-user's perspective to the programmer for the interface design. The true challenge was in creating an interface that allowed the less experienced operator to generate complex and involved questions of crime, victims and suspects without the traditional understanding of data structure or query languages. Tremendous efforts were made to design the interface based on the end-user's needs and expertise level. An added benefit of requiring the simple interface was a more complete understanding of the needs of the end-user by the programmer. Questions posed by true users of the information were initially misunderstood by the programmer. Only by requiring the program to actually compile the query did the programmer understand the "ins and outs" of the user's needs.

Today, mapping software is operational. Results have been outstanding. The migration of the software programs to the GUI has resulted in an increase in user productivity. A survey of the department's CADs showed the less experienced users utilizing the query form of the mapper over the Paradox system. Based on these results, the department is presently preparing to migrate its Paradox program into the Windows-based version. This effort will include some redesigning of the database and responsibilities of each program based on what has been learned over the past three years.

Each step of this process has been a continual effort to make the technical ability of the evolving information age serve the needs of the end-user, who frequently is less than proficient. In research completed by IBM, it was found that law enforcement possessed five times the information it had the ability to access.[1] While this can be attributed to the antiquated manner in which information is stored, much is the direct failure to understand "how" the user needs the information. Systems must be designed around the user's ability. The concept of making people "learn the computer" if they want to have access to information has failed. What is needed are systems the end-user can access easily and directly.

The overall objective will remain to provide the CAD customer with analysis that is thorough, accurate, meaningful, and timely. As the capabilities of systems improve, the ease of use of programs will remain paramount in determining if this objective will actually be met. Analysts want, and the organization needs, applications that are simple to use and involve a quick learning curve. This challenge applies to even the more advanced users. Simplicity promotes use. Applications accompanied by thick manuals and requiring days of training will not be used. Simplification, whenever possible, is the key.

Figure 1 shows the base screen for the mapping program. All operations can be initiated via mouse, keyboard or function keystrokes in compliance with Windows GUI standards.

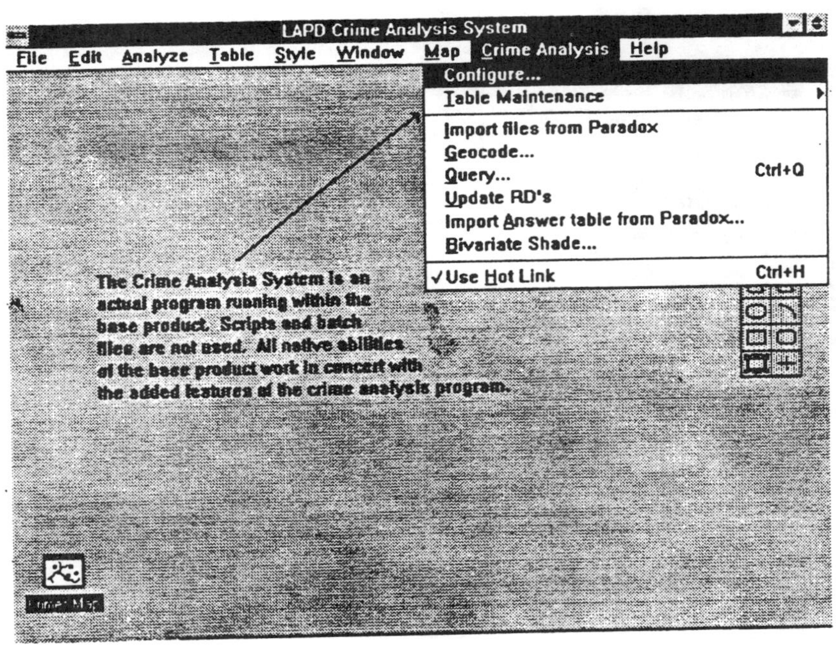

Fig. 1
Base screen, mapping program

1. IBM, Nov. 16, 1992, Fall Condex, William Schume.

Figure 2 shows the query form, which provides the major fields as "buttons." Dates and times are entered by hand.

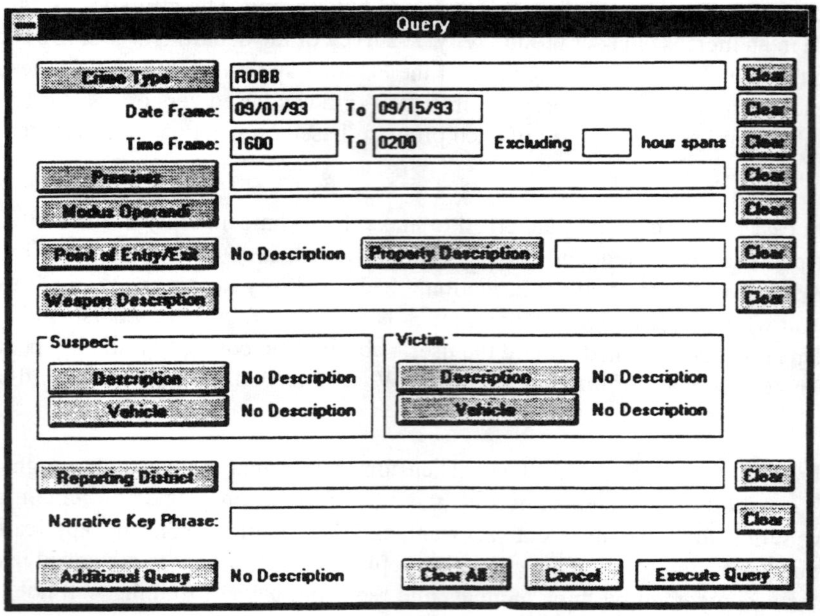

Fig. 2
Query form

The query form allows for subsets of values to be accessed in a tiered fashion (figure 3). This "walks" an analyst through a query formulation.

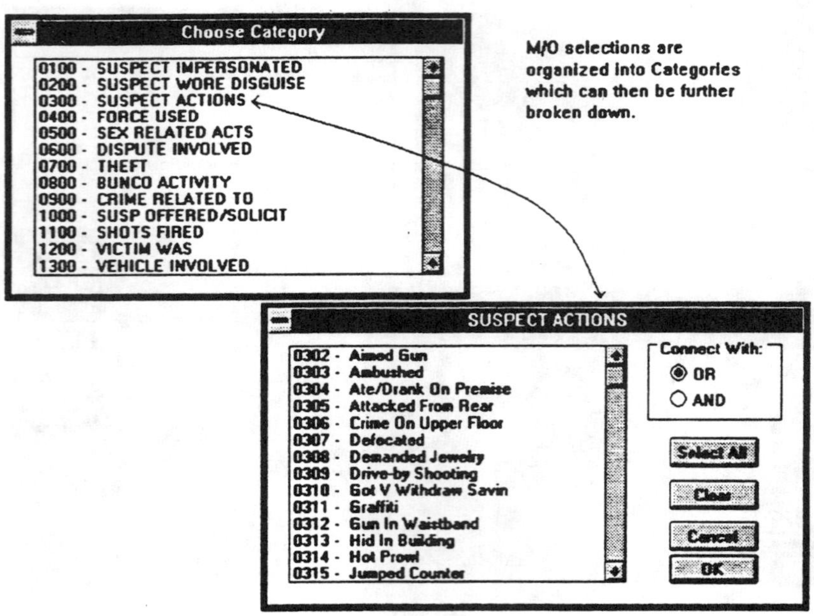

Fig. 3
Access of subsets of values

Suspect, victim and vehicle information are separate screens, containing additional information that is accessed from the master query form (figure 4).

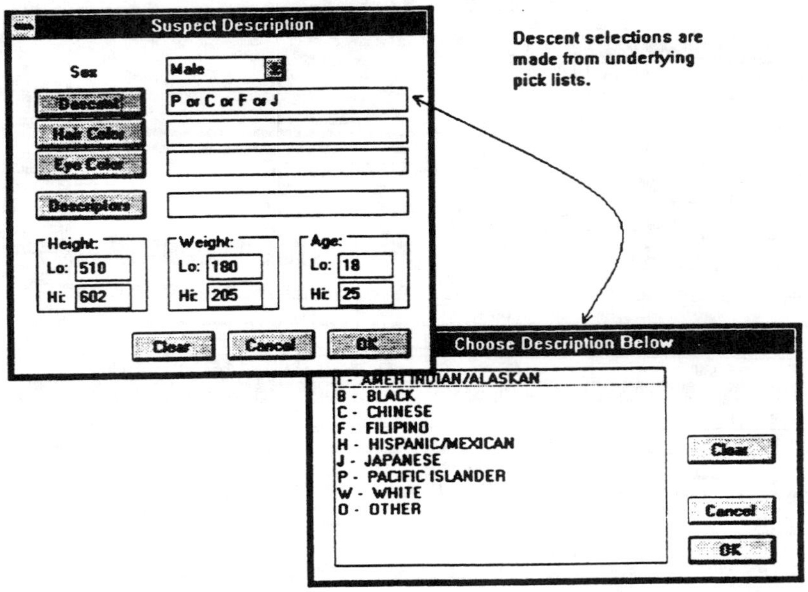

Fig. 4
Underlying pick-list organization

The query result is linked, allowing the analyst to view the corresponding suspect(s), personal descriptor(s) (scars, marks, tattoos) and property taken for each crime chosen (figure 5).

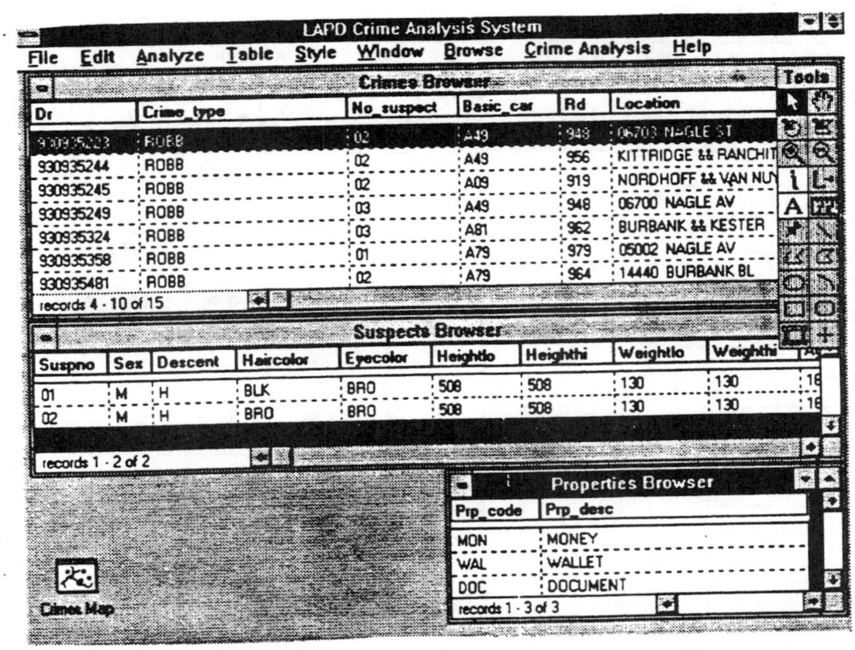

Fig. 5
Query result: suspect and property

The query results can be viewed as a map and table simultaneously, if desired (figure 6). This allows the analyst to view the location of the event and detailed descriptions at the same time.

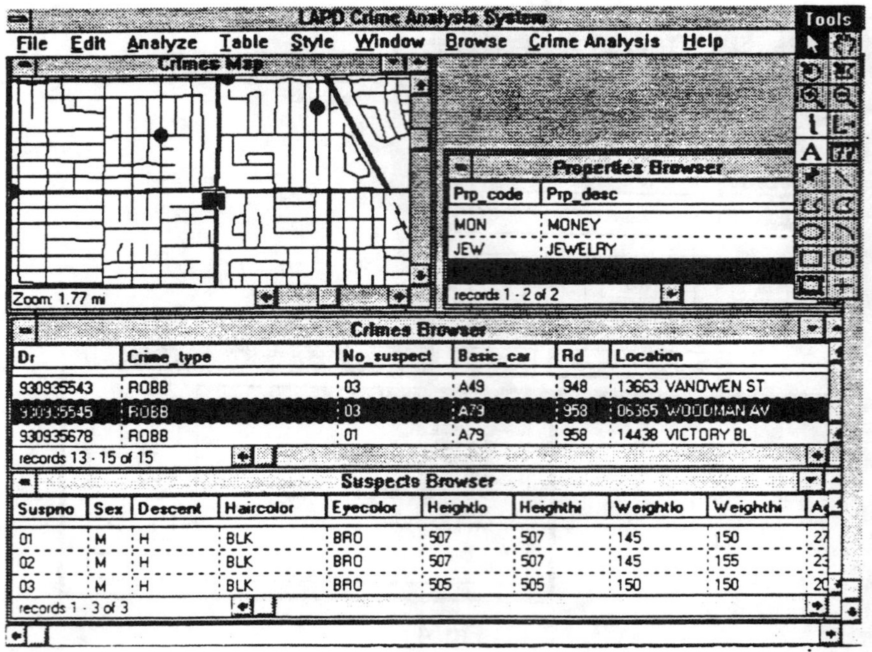

Fig. 6
Query result: map plus table

The program also will provide a quick reference of information for each point chosen, if desired (figure 7).

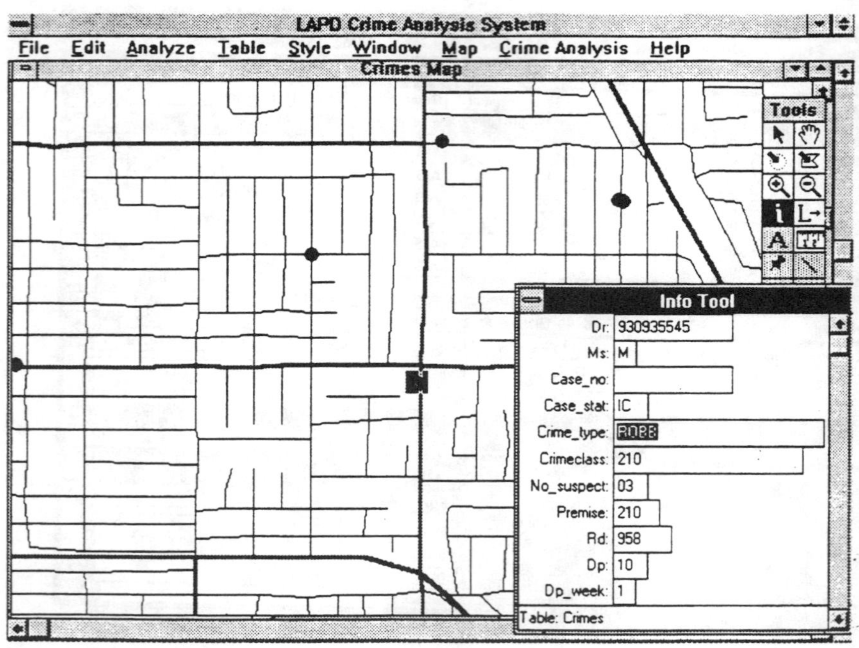

Fig. 7
Query result: quick reference

Chapter 13

A Database for the Ecological Analysis of Social Stress and Violence in Small Areas

Keith Harries
Department of Geography
University of Maryland, Baltimore County

ABSTRACT

The purpose of this research is to develop a geographic model of violent crime (aggravated assault and homicide) based on a variety of environmental stressors. The project is as yet only partially developed; hence, this report stresses procedural problems and database development rather than final results. Data are in the process of being assembled for two jurisdictions in Maryland: Baltimore City and Baltimore County. The database is relatively unique in that it spans both jurisdictions, in terms of both violence data and associated stressors. This approach is adopted under the working assumption that the boundary between jurisdictions may not have immediately recognizable functional significance; indeed, violence is a problem of the metropolitan region. However, the boundary is of at least passing interest in that various local services, including policing and land-use planning, are locally controlled. Furthermore, the eroding tax base of Baltimore City has reduced social services, tending to accentuate differences between city and county. Geographic information system (GIS) technology is utilized in order to facilitate the visualization of data layers and their juxtapositions.

INTRODUCTION

The literature of violence is replete with references to associations between violence and deprivation of various kinds, and casual observation of the media in America or a drive through virtually any inner city provides ample informal evidence of links between poverty and a host of other pathologies. Thus, the long-term intent of the research program in the process of initiation here is to penetrate beneath the broadly accepted pattern of correspondence between poverty and violence in order to develop a relatively comprehensive visualization of patterns of social stress and violence, complemented by more traditional forms of statistical analysis, and utilizing a broader-than-usual geographic frame and smaller-than-usual (and hence relatively more numerous) units of observation.

In Smith's (1986) nomenclature defining various traditions in the history of research on crime, the work proposed here falls under the rubric of "the empirical-analytical." It should be pointed out that the present work is essentially cross-sectional rather than longitudinal, an unfortunate matter of necessity rather than an intentional element of design. (This miserable flaw is shared by most ecological analyses, a fact that Byrne and Sampson [1986] found "somewhat ironic given that classical ecological theory is concerned with processes of change in urban areas.")

Violence and Stress

The theoretical perspective on which this analysis is based rests on the concept of *social stress* and the assumption, rooted in a vast body of empirical evidence, that neighborhoods with higher levels of stress are more violence-prone. In practice, correlates of violence may be viewed as derivatives of a cluster of variables or concepts such as *poverty, the underclass, socioeconomic status*, and *social pathology*. Such concepts are more or less synonymous. However, the most general, and perhaps therefore the most powerful, of these interrelated themes is stress, in that it encompasses all conditions tending to make neighborhoods more dysfunctional and at higher risk of violence. As Rose and McClain (1990:48) have noted,

> [h]igh stress can indicate the lack of access to basic economic resources and is thought to be a precipitator of a number of pathological conditions, including elevated homicide risk . . . whereas low stress indicates the opposite.

In addition to the often-used set of social variables, stress can incorporate elements of the built or physical environment, such as housing characteristics, landscape incivilities (broken glass, dumped trash, billboards) and behavioral stresses induced by severe weather or fear of crime itself.

Along with the concept of stress level as an underlying precursor of violence, an additional assumption is that neighborhoods are qualitatively different. This means that two neighborhoods with identical statistical profiles in terms of demographics and the built environment may differ significantly in their crime experiences, owing to differences in what Bursik and Grasmick (1993:4) refer to as "formal and informal networks within the neighborhood that bind the residents together as a social community," forming the basis of a theory of "systemic control." In placing emphasis on this "systemic" model of crime control centering on the concepts of neighborhood cohesion and networking, Bursik and Grasmick saw residential stability and local educational context, among other variables, as crucial indicators of neighborhood cohesion.

Recent literature on the social aspect of violence and the status of the black community reinforces the concept of relationship with social stressors (e.g., Bursik and Grasmick 1993; Jencks and Peterson 1991; Lynn and McGeary 1990; Reiss and Roth 1993; Sampson and Laub 1993; Tidwell 1993), and the reader is referred to these sources for a more comprehensive review of the literature in the general field of the ecology of crime at the neighborhood level.

Violence and the Underclass

The importance of a key stressor—poverty—in developing an understanding of violence is a recurrent theme in the literature, although various conditions nested within poverty areas, such as "measures of the density of multiunit housing" and the "prevalence of disrupted family structures," may be better correlates of neighborhood violent crime than direct measures of poverty (Reiss and Roth 1993). The term *underclass* has gained broad currency for connotation of core ghetto areas suffering multiple pathologies, including violence. Wilson (1987) used a poverty rate of 30 percent or more for urban subareas as an indication of underclass neighborhoods. Other criteria for identifying comparable areas have included neighborhoods at least one standard deviation below the national average on selected measures (Ricketts and Sawhill 1988) and 40 percent below poverty level (Jargowsky and Bane 1990). In another study of the relationship between poverty and crime, Lynn and McGeary (1990) noted that crime in poor areas tends to be more serious and constitutes a major reason for people wanting to move out of such neighborhoods. Furthermore, they argued that

> [w]e badly need better studies of neighborhoods' impact on teenage crime . . . studies that focus on the effects of very poor neighborhoods, including large public housing projects.

While analysis of the underclass is not part of this paper, it is anticipated that the distribution of violence will be reviewed at a later date in the context of the geography of the underclass in Baltimore City and County.

DEFINITION OF VIOLENT CRIME

Violence is defined for the purpose of this study as homicide and aggravated assault. These crimes were selected for their relative generic similarity (Harries 1990). Rape and robbery were excluded, although rape-murders and robbery-murders would be included in these data. It is recognized that "violence" encompasses a much broader range of behaviors than those used in this operating definition, including rape and, many would argue, suicide. Hence, the analysis discussed here should be regarded only as a reasonable approximation of the kind of violence that draws the most attention from the public and the media and is regarded in lore, law and the *National Survey of Crime Severity* (Wolfgang et al. 1985) as extremely damaging to the fabric of a community.

Note that the violence data forming the basis for this analysis record the locations of crimes without taking into account the home addresses of the offenders or victims. However, while much of the crime reported here will occur in or near the homes of both offenders and victims,[1] some study areas had quite high frequencies of incidents of violence but no recorded population. Such a situation possibly indicates the presence of a drug market, for example. Thus, analysis based on raw frequencies will yield a map differing from analysis based on rates denominated by population.[2] This point is discussed in more detail below.

QUESTIONS OF SCALE AND SCOPE

Crime studies dealing with small areas have almost always relied on the census tract (sometimes regarded as synonymous with "neighborhood") as the unit of analysis. The rationale behind this has been that tracts have generally been regarded as approximations of homogeneous neighborhoods, with a rich variety of data available from the decennial census, and a population averaging 4,000, presumably thought to be manageable or comprehensible in an analytical sense. The degree to which the census tract has been institutionalized as the only viable small-area geography was expressed in the recent report of the National Academy of Sciences, *Understanding and Preventing Violence* (Reiss and Roth 1993:129), which noted that "[t]he panel looked for evidence on violence rates for the smallest, most homogeneous areas for which data are available—census tracts."

This is a curious assertion, in that both city blocks and block groups are homogeneous (more so than tracts, by definition, since they are smaller), and any address-level crime file may be applied to any geographic base. By and large, researchers have shied away from units smaller than the tract, although data for block groups (or enumeration districts) and blocks have been available for decades.

Why has the tract become enshrined in urban ecological analysis, whether for the study of crime or for other phenomena? First, tract data have been more accessible than those for the larger-scale geographies. Printed reports with legible maps made census tract data available to anyone, whether computer-literate or not. Second, the tract is a unit everyone can understand. It has visible physical boundaries—streets, rivers, lake shores, railroads, and so on. Third, the vast array of socioeconomic data at the tract level provided something for everyone, whether the research subject was underweight births in the school of nursing, the market for new air conditioners at Carrier or Lennox, or the research arm of PepsiCo seeking profitable locations for Kentucky Fried Chicken or Taco Bell. Finally, the "comfort-

1. This distinction is often meaningless, in that arguments may escalate into violence without a definable offender or victim. These labels are sometimes applied as a consequence of who had fastest access to the most effective weapon, and the skill to use it.

2. When the population is zero, a violence frequency map will have a nonzero value, while a population-denominated rate map will have a zero value.

able" size of tracts (not too big, not too small) meant that various agencies adopted tracts as their operational geographic units, some police departments included. Thus, the tract became more and more embedded as the local geography of choice.

The block group and block share some of the attributes of the tract, notably well-defined boundaries.[3] However, census data availability declines as scale of resolution increases, owing to problems of confidentiality. This is critical, for example, on city blocks with one or a few households with specific census-measured attributes, such as race. If there is only one African-American family on a block, then all data applicable to African Americans must apply to that family, so the data are suppressed.[4] While data suppression is a thorny problem at the block level, blocks share with tracts the advantage of published maps for the entire urbanized area of each SMA. A geography seeming to combine advantages of the tract, while avoiding some of the disadvantages of the block, is the *block group*, a subdivision of a tract into multiblock parts, typically about four or five (figure 1). The chief disadvantage of the block

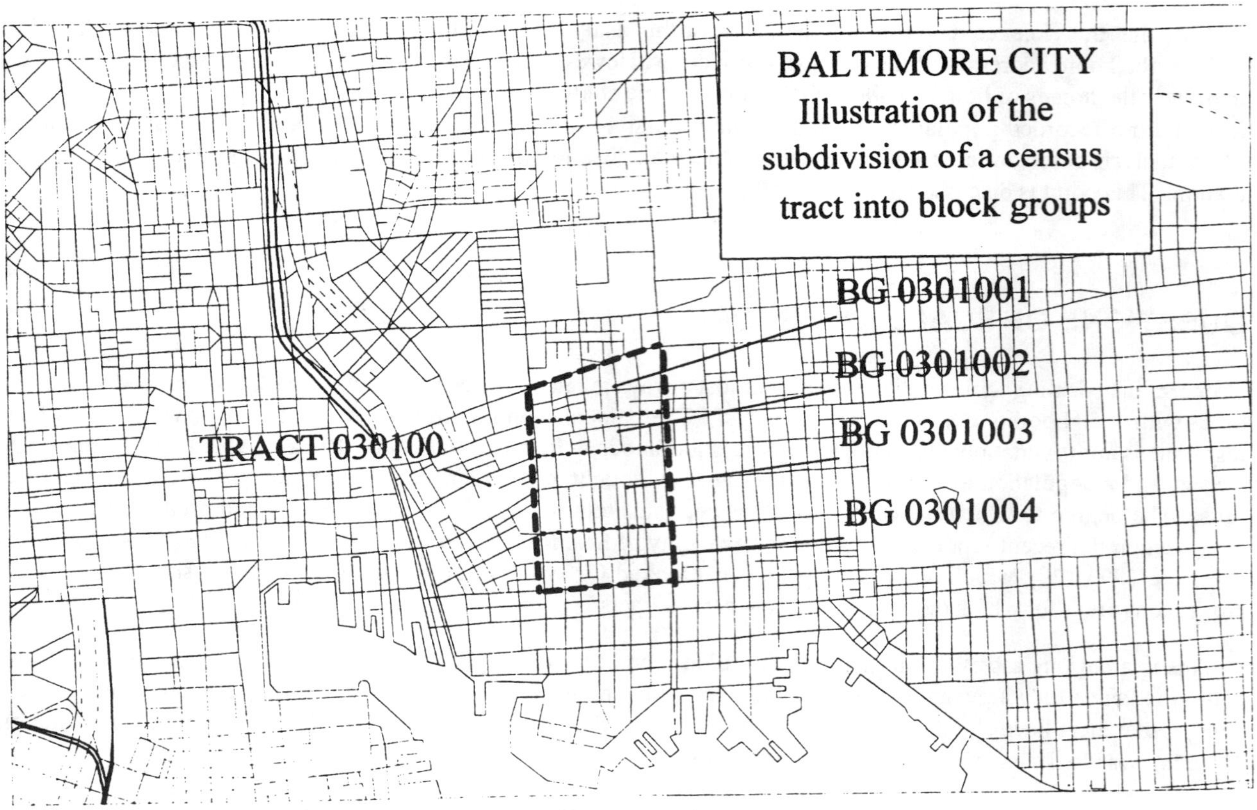

Fig. 1
Illustration drawn from inner Baltimore City of the subdivision of a selected census tract into its four component block groups

3. Block groups, as subdivisions of tracts, share their external boundaries. Internal boundaries between block groups are typically streets or other recognizable linear features (figure 1).

4. The issue is actually more complex. See "Primary and Secondary Suppression" in Jargowsky and Bane (1990), and "Ghetto Poverty: Basic Questions" in Lynn and McGeary (1990:56–57). Oddly, however, the problems presented by Jargowsky and Bane are not mentioned by Myers (1992) in his comprehensive guide to the use of census resources for local area analysis.

group is its relative obscurity. Little research has been done using this level of analysis, and it suffers the ignominy of lacking published, or readily available, maps. On the other hand, essentially the same array of socioeconomic data is available for the block group as for the tract.

The present state of information technology suggests that the barriers that previously impeded the analysis of areas smaller than tracts (principally the problem that once the researcher went below the tract level, there were, apart from any other difficulties, just too many units of observation) have now gone away. Census data are available on CD-ROM, and the advent of cheap 486-class microprocessors has made desktop mapping and analysis widely available. It is, therefore, time to rethink the scale at which local analysis is done. In particular, the analyst should give some thought to whether the census tract is the most appropriate choice. This is particularly crucial in analyses that seek to clarify relationships at the micro level.

Accordingly, the present project seeks to develop and utilize a database with the block group as the frame for census data, in combination with address-level data from noncensus sources, such as public health agencies, liquor boards and police departments. Land-use data are also being incorporated through the combination of a digital file from the Baltimore County planning agency and the conversion of a Baltimore City zoning map into digital form. Surprisingly, while land *cover* maps are readily available (from satellite imagery), land-*use* maps are more difficult to find; Baltimore City, for example, has none.

In addition to reliance on census tract data in urban ecological analyses, another weakness, historically, has been the tendency for studies to include one jurisdiction and to stop at the county or city line. There were good reasons for this, having to do with the inability of researchers to deal with large volumes of data, as well as more subtle difficulties associated with acquiring crime data from more than one police department. In addition to moving to a finer level of spatial resolution, this project includes two jurisdictions, Baltimore City and the adjacent Baltimore County, on the assumption that, with respect to violent crime, the boundary between the jurisdictions may have little functional importance. (On the other hand, it is felt that boundary phenomena are worth investigating for their own sake, so the boundary issue will not be overlooked.)

DATA RESOURCES

Data sources consisted of homicide and assault files from the Baltimore City and Baltimore County police departments for the years 1989 through 1991,[5] census data from Summary Tape File (STF) 3 on CD-ROM (Bureau of the Census 1992a, b), and a digital base map of the geography of Baltimore City and County from the Baltimore Regional Council of Governments. Other files to be incorporated later include land use, liquor licenses, fatal fires, public housing locations, injuries (intentional and unintentional), and detailed recent survey data describing the case histories of people admitted on more than one occasion to the trauma center at the University of Maryland Medical Center in Baltimore.[6]

Various problems were encountered in the course of the nominally simple process of constructing a seamless map of violence and demographic variables. Most difficult was the lack of correspondence between block group codes from the Census Bureau and codes available in the Baltimore metropolitan base map. The STF3 data tabulate block group identification in a hierarchical manner, presenting tract number and block group number as separate variables. It was possible to glue pieces together using relational database software, but the results were still unsatisfactory and it was eventually necessary to clean the codes manually. This is a critical step, of course, since lack of correspon-

5. I am indebted to Philip Canter of the Baltimore County Police Department and Michael Zotos, deputy commissioner, Baltimore City Police Department, for their generous assistance with respect to making data available.

6. This survey was a pilot for a larger study to be undertaken in the near future by the University of Maryland Violence Prevention Consortium. The objective of this interdisciplinary research is to develop interventions to reduce violence.

dence between the data codes and the base map codes implies difficulties in geocoding, or matching the "mapless" database to a map of block group geography.

Baltimore County violence data (N = 13,020) were acquired with latitude-longitude coordinates of each incident, a trouble-free way of locating incidents in which street addresses have been converted to "pure" locations. The Baltimore City data came with street addresses, some 279 (out of a possible 12,581) of which failed to geocode, a failure rate of 2.2 percent, or only 1.1 percent of the total N of 25,601 for the three-year period. This error was not random, however, as some streets or street segments (specific address ranges) repeatedly failed to geocode, resulting in some spuriously low rates when the data are mapped or otherwise manipulated.[7] Over the three-year period, reported violent crime data as defined here impacted 797 of the 832 block groups in Baltimore City (96%), and 517 of the 526 block groups in Baltimore County (98%).

PRELIMINARY VISUALIZATION AND ANALYSIS

Both spatial and statistical analyses are being used in as integrated a manner as possible in order to develop relatively comprehensive area-based interpretations of patterns of violence. Eventually, violence will be examined qualitatively as well as quantitatively, with emphasis on subcategories of events, such as handgun incidents involving young people, events with spouses or children as victims, and so forth.

In terms of substantive results, there is relatively little to report, owing to the fact that the project is in its early stages. However, the base frequency data of combined homicide and assault for 1989 to 1991 are shown as figure 2. Large variations in the areas of block groups (the units mapped) can, as with any choropleth map, make for a somewhat visually misleading map. The areas of block groups, like those of census tracts, are a function of their population. In historically densely populated neighborhoods, census tracts and block groups (which are in practice subdivisions of tracts) are small, as illustrated in central Baltimore City. In outlying areas, however, with small populations, both tracts and block groups are many times larger than their counterparts in the city. The visual effect, as shown in figure 2, is to exaggerate the importance of the county areas. This problem can be controlled to some extent by manipulating class intervals so that only the most extreme data values receive the heaviest shading, but there are limits to this kind of control. The reader is best advised to exert caution in interpreting this or any other map based on shaded areas.[8]

Figure 2 shows an area some 28 miles wide, covering on the order of 420 square miles. It is necessary to zoom in on various districts in order to gain appreciation for distributions in specific small areas. The inner city, in particular, is almost indecipherable at this scale. It can be seen, however, that the pattern of assaultive crimes is by no means a purely inner-city phenomenon, although it must be recognized that this map represents only raw totals of incidents and does not address what proportion of events were homicides vs. assaults, or proportions of assaults resulting in more serious vs. less serious injuries.

7. Streets that repeatedly failed to geocode properly (and which are thus underrepresented in maps and analyses) included (but were not entirely limited to) Eutaw Place, North Eutaw Street, West Fayette Street, West Fairmont Avenue, Ellsworth Street, Ferndale Avenue, Edgewood Street, Eagle Street, Frederick Avenue, Elgin Avenue, Eareckson Place, West Freedomway, Force Road, and North Bend Road. It is unclear whether the base map lacked certain address ranges, or whether there was systematic error in field reports. These questions await further investigation.

8. This begs the question of whether data could be represented more effectively by simply mapping points. This method works well with small N's, but is impractical when large N's would result in points' obscuring each other and covering the map as a whole. Another possibility would be to map a small random sample of all the data.

Fig. 2

Combined homicide and aggravated assault frequencies in Baltimore City and part of Baltimore County, 1989 to 1991. Underlying *N*'s are 25,601 crime incidents and 1,358 census block groups. Baltimore City is the central part of the area shown; it is nearly surrounded by Baltimore County, in a roughly horseshoe shape. Not shown is northern Baltimore County, extending to the Pennsylvania state line. The area illustrated is approximately 28 miles east-west (long dimension), or 1 inch = 2.8 miles in an 8.5-x-11-inch format. (Baltimore has roughly the same proportions as Washington, D.C.)

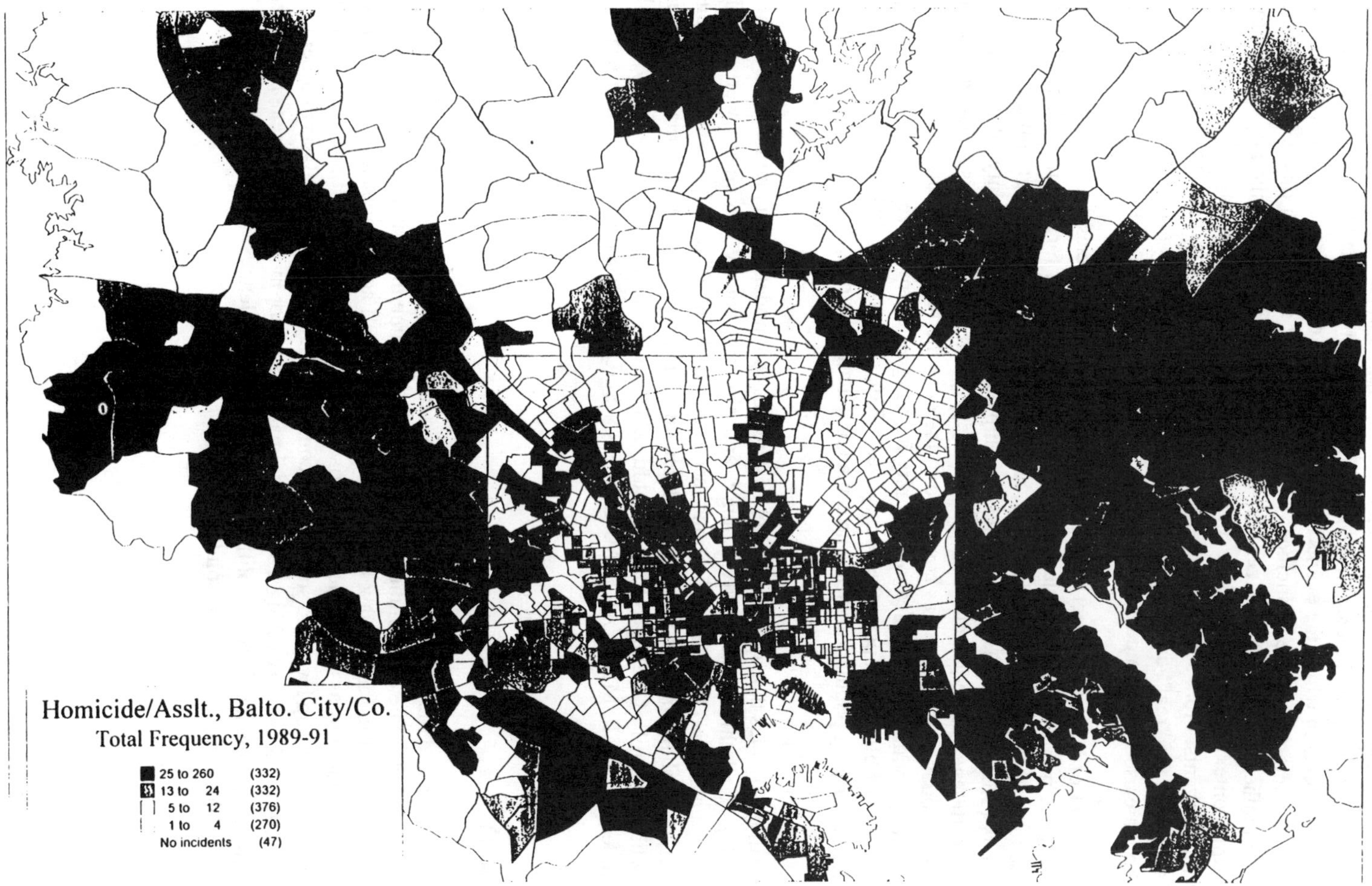

A preliminary analysis of census indicators suggests that measures of social stress prominent in other studies will be relevant here, too, although there are indications that models will differ depending on whether the city, county or an aggregation of both areas is used as the underlying frame, and on whether frequencies of events of population-adjusted rates are the dependent variables. Generally, population-adjusted rates are regarded as the "purest" measures, but it should be noted that an indeterminate number of incidents included here cannot be regarded as direct products of the population units in which the events occurred. As noted elsewhere, drug markets or random street events may have generated numerous incidents included here, but some of those locations have zero block group populations, thus creating mathematically accurate zero rates and blunting the ability of the rate concept to provide useful information. In this context, a frequency count could be seen as a measure allowing linkage between the actual urban context and violent events. From some perspectives, a model based on frequencies may be more useful than a rate model in that it addresses the "real" distribution of incidents. Given that each measure provides a somewhat different perspective, both are used as dependent variables here.

Caveats are in order with respect to the interpretation of frequencies and rates for Baltimore City and County (table 1).[9] As one might expect, population-adjusted rates are higher for Baltimore City (36.09) than for the county (33.66) (see table 1). Seemingly paradoxically, mean frequencies (per block group) are higher in the county (25.59) than in the city (15.31) (table 1). While the relationship between city and county rates is intuitively plausible, that relating to the difference in frequencies demands more explanation. The latter discrepancy is an artifact of the physical area of block groups in the county as compared to the city; the former are on average much larger compared to the latter, therefore providing the physical opportunity for a higher count of events (and a larger population). Indeed, the mean population of block groups in the county was 1,339, compared to 894 in the city. When the higher counts are adjusted for underlying population differences via computation of rates, the relative ranks of the jurisdictions are reversed.

Specifically, variables that appeared in stepwise regression models (with raw frequency of incidents as the dependent variable) at all three levels (city, county, and city and county combined) were POVERTY, NOWRKRS, FEM_CHLD, and RENTER (for definitions, see exhibit). FEM_CHLD (percentage of households with female householder, no husband present, with own children under 18) is perhaps of particular interest in that it suggests situations in which control of teenage children could be relatively difficult. A preliminary model of incident rate per 1,000 included RENTER, MHOVAL, VACANT, BRN-SOUTH, and SERVICE at all three levels.

SUMMARY

New forms of data and the availability of sophisticated tools for applications in statistical cartography offer fresh opportunities for a finer scale of resolution for the analysis of crime in urban areas. These new tools are already being exploited productively in various law enforcement agencies and academic settings. In the research under development here, homicide and assault in adjacent jurisdictions in Maryland, Baltimore City and Baltimore County are mapped at the block group level and subjected to complementary statistical analysis in order to build a model of variations in violence and stress covering a substantial part of a major metropolitan area. This research is seen as a precursor to the development of a metropolitan region archive of violence, which would in turn facilitate regional model building at the block group level of resolution.

9. See exhibit for the definitions of variables listed in table 1.

Table 1
Descriptive Statistics: Baltimore County and City, 1990
(Violence rate is per 1,000, 1989 to 1991)

Variable*	Baltimore County (*N* = 526)	Baltimore City (*N* = 832)
	Mean or Median (Values are percentages unless shown otherwise)	Mean or Median (Values are percentages unless shown otherwise)
Violence Rate	33.66 (Rate)	36.09 (Rate)
Violence Frequency	25.59	15.31
MALEPCT	46.56	46.49
BLACKPCT	10.00	55.40
YTHPCT	21.04	24.04
WHTMLPCT	8.79	4.72
BLKMLPCT	1.47	6.75
BIG_HSLD	8.19	14.01
FEM_CHLD	4.45	13.58
BRNSOUTH	9.95	15.28
FRMSOUTH	2.09	2.07
SAMEHOUS	55.76	53.44
UNEMP_M	15.76	22.35
UNEMP_F	29.75	33.27
UNEMPTOT	23.09	28.04
MANPROF	7.69	4.38
SERVICE	5.13	7.67
NOWORKRS	11.68	17.45
POVERTY	5.00	21.14
VACANT	3.85	8.89
RENTER	24.73	41.93
LONGLIVE	44.75	39.83
MHSLDINC	$42,203	$25,342
MYRBUILT	1958 (Median Year)	1942 (Median Year)
MGROSRENT	$524	$414
MHOVAL	$115,490	$54,475

*For definitions, see exhibit 1.

Exhibit 1
Key to table 1 definitions

Units of Observation: Census Block Groups, 1990	
VARIABLE	DEFINITION
VIOLENCE RATE	Rate of homicide and assault incidents, per 1,000 people, 1989 to 1991
VIOLENCE FREQUENCY	Count of homicide and assault incidents, 1989 to 1991
MALEPCT	Percentage of total population that is male
BLACKPCT	Percentage of total population that is black
YTHPCT	Percentage of total population ages 14 to 29
WHTMLPCT	Percentage of total population that are white males ages 14 to 29
BLKMLPCT	Percentage of total population that are black males ages 14 to 29
BIG_HSLD	Percentage of households with five or more people
FEM_CHLD	Percentage of households with female householder, no husband present, with own children under 18
BRNSOUTH	Percentage of area residents born in a southern state
FRMSOUTH	Percentage of area residents who moved from a southern state since 1985
SAMEHOUS	Percentage of people ages five and older in 1990 who were in the same house in 1990 as in 1985
UNEMP_M	Percentage of male population that did not work in 1989 (not adjusted for size of population of working age)
UNEMP_F	Percentage of female population that did not work in 1989 (not adjusted for size of population of working age)
UNEMPTOT	Percentage of total population that did not work in 1989 (not adjusted for size of population of working age)
MANPROF	Percentage of total population in managerial and professional occupations
SERVICE	Percentage of people in service occupations
NOWORKRS	Percentage of families with no workers in the family in 1989
POVERTY	Percentage of people below poverty level in 1989
VACANT	Percentage of housing units vacant
RENTER	Percentage of housing units renter occupied
LONGLIVE	Percentage of housing units with householders in residence since 1970 or earlier
MHSLDINC	Median household income. Statistic shown is the mean of the medians
MYRBUILT	Median year housing units were built. Statistic shown is the median of the medians
MGROSRENT	Median gross rent. Statistic shown is the mean of the medians
MHOVAL	Median home value. Statistic shown is the mean of the medians

REFERENCES

Bureau of the Census (1992a). *Census of Population and Housing, 1990: Summary Tape File 3 on CD-ROM (Maryland)* (machine-readable data files). Prepared by the Bureau of the Census. Washington, D.C.: The Bureau (producer and distributor).

——— (1992b). *Census of Population and Housing, 1990: Summary Tape File 3 on CD-ROM Technical Documentation.* Prepared by the Bureau of the Census. Washington, D.C.: The Bureau.

Bursik, R.J., Jr., and H.G. Grasmick (1993). *Neighborhoods and Crime.* New York: Lexington Books.

Byrne, J.M., and R.J. Sampson (1986). *The Social Ecology of Crime.* New York: Springer-Verlag.

Harries, K.D. (1990). *Serious Violence: Patterns of Homicide and Assault in America.* Springfield, Ill.: Charles C. Thomas.

Jargowsky, P.A., and M.J. Bane (1990). Ghetto poverty: Basic questions. Pp. 16–67 in Lynn and McGeary (eds.), *Inner-City Poverty in the United States.*

Jencks, C., and P.E. Peterson (eds.) (1991). *The Urban Underclass.* Washington, D.C.: The Brookings Institution.

Lynn, L.E., Jr., and M.G.H. McGeary (eds.) (1990). *Inner-City Poverty in the United States.* Washington, D.C.: National Academy Press.

Myers, D. (1992). *Analysis with Local Census Data.* Boston: Academic Press.

Reiss, A.J., Jr., and J.A. Roth (1993). *Understanding and Preventing Violence.* Washington, D.C.: National Academy Press.

Ricketts, E.R., and I.V. Sawhill (1988). Defining and measuring the underclass. *Journal of Policy Analysis and Management* 7:316–325.

Rose, H.M., and P.D. McClain (1990). *Race, Place and Risk: Black Homicide in Urban America.* Albany: SUNY Press.

Sampson, R.J., and J.H. Laub (1993). *Crime in the Making: Pathways and Turning Points through Life.* Cambridge, Mass.: Harvard University Press.

Smith, S.J. (1986). *Crime, Space and Society.* Cambridge: Cambridge University Press.

Tidwell, B.J. (1993). *The State of Black America, 1993.* New York: National Urban League, Inc.

Wolfgang, M.E., et al. (1985). *The National Survey of Crime Severity.* Washington, D.C.: U.S. Department of Justice.

Wilson, W.J. (1987). *The Truly Disadvantaged: The Inner City, the Underclass and Public Policy.* Chicago: University of Chicago Press.

Chapter 14

Integrating Crime Mapping With CAD and RMS

Tim Miller
San Bernardino, Calif., Sheriff's Department

INTRODUCTION

Computer automation is often used as a catchall that refers to several computer systems and many different types of software. For law enforcement, these include the following:

1. CAD (computer-aided dispatch) system,
2. RMS (records management system),
3. mapping computers and software,
4. document imaging (documents and photos),
5. word processing,
6. business management systems (accounting), and
7. integration of computers and office equipment (copiers and fax equipment, etc.).

Follow these rules when selecting your hardware and software:

1. Determine your needs.
2. Find the software that will satisfy your needs.
3. Find the hardware that the above software will run on.

However, following these basic rules may involve allowing for many different choices, which can lead to confusion. There are just too many needs and too many resolutions to those needs. In addition, many systems become obsolete before they are fully online. I will try to ease this process with the following guidelines.

Available Software Operating Systems

VAX/VMS

These systems have been common platforms for police agencies in the past. Some of the bigger agencies may have large IBM mainframes in operation.

Police agencies are still buying outdated VAX, IBM and various other mini- and mainframe systems, while many mainstream businesses are downsizing to Risc workstations and PC systems. Why is this? Well, remembering the above list of rules, we see that we have been locked into these systems because of the software. Now, however, we are seeing software companies that are switching to UNIX environments. These are very powerful work stations that run at five to 10 times the speed of the minicomputers at a cost of less than one-fifth the amount of those systems and are geared to a graphical environment.

CAD/RMS

CAD is a sound choice to form the basis of your system. This is the most critical application for the safety of all citizens and police personnel. There are many systems available on a variety of platforms. The size of your project will dictate the need for UNIX work stations, minisystems or PCs.

First, we must again follow the rules. Look at your needs—determine how many dispatchers you will have and how many remote sites you will support. The difficult part will be isolating the data that you want to track. The data will consist of fields such as type of call, date, time, call taker, dispatcher, patrol unit, and so on.

Without a doubt, the system you buy will not have everything that you need, and herein lies the main problem. In your planning, allowances must be made for change and expansion. Remember that computer systems and your needs are constantly changing. The smaller the hardware (PCs or UNIX workstations vs. the minisystems), the better. Remember that after installing your system, you must allow for change over the next three to five years. If you can have a representative (programmer) on-site to fine-tune the software to your needs, you will be much happier with the results. If you cannot afford the programmer, you will have the company charging you money and travel time for each change and enhancement.

PCs have been difficult to use in large departments because of the multiuser environment and the single-user operating systems. Here are a few guidelines for purchasing a CAD, RMS and mapping system:

1. Each CAD and RMS system is nothing more than a database with the ability to communicate through your radio systems and networks.
2. Determine your needs (number of users and remote sites that need to be networked, etc.).
3. Place terminals throughout your department, including substations, if necessary.
4. Find the software that will suit your needs and run on a UNIX workstation or PC system.
5. Choose a windowing system that will allow your dispatchers, police officers and general employees to see pictures of locations, suspects and maps.

Integrating the Mapping System With a CAD System

When integrating the mapping system, do the address matching on the CAD system. The process requires that a list of each block, with the left and right address ranges, including *X* and *Y* coordinates (latitude and longitude or state plane) and other related layers (reporting districts, cities, etc.), reside on the CAD system. These must be integrated into the database. Then you must install an algorithm to calculate the distance between the address ranges and generate the latitude and longitude coordinates, offsetting 40 feet from the centerline of the street. This may sound complicated, but it is a straightforward process that has been done many times. These steps will require your call takers to verify the address at the time of the call, thus eliminating the need for address matching when transferring the data to the mapping software.

Police Report Number System

Thought must be given to the way you use your police report numbers and what they tell you. Each report number must give you the file number to track each report for future reference. As an example, exhibit 1 shows a very informative report number and breaks down each component, so that you can decide which sections will apply to your department's needs.

Exhibit 1
Report number example

Report Number: 092-00364-1471-061

A. The first number indicates the retention (the amount of time I need to keep a copy of this report): 0 = forever, for homicides and missing persons; 4 = four years, for felonies; 1 = one year, for misdemeanors.

B. The second and third numbers represent the year.

C. The fourth through the eighth numbers are the sequential number for a station or department for the year (each year you will start at 00001 and sequentially increase them throughout the year).

D. The ninth and 10th numbers represent the station.

E. The 11th number represents the city within the station's jurisdiction.

F. The 12th number represents the reporting district within that city.

G. The last three numbers are very important (the 13th, 14th and 15th). They represent the crime code.

The states and the federal government designed their code system for their statistical needs. Police departments find it necessary to group crimes by code number for easy analysis; however, the state and federal codes make that difficult. Several police departments are using a three-digit code system for tracking their crimes. This system is very informative and is entered by the street officer while asking for the report number for a crime report. For instance, the 061 number in exhibit 1 indicates a residential night burglary with forced entry. All of the 06 series are residential burglaries, with subgroups 061, 062 and 063 night-entry burglaries, and so on. All of this makes for easy analysis and integration into your mapping software. It also eliminates the confusion of a tremendous amount of penal codes.

Maintenance of Map Files

Thought must be given to the design and upkeep of your digitized maps. The ideal solution is to have a planning or engineering department maintain your street file. The reporting districts should follow existing streets or landmarks. Parcels should be created for each house, so that dispatchers can display floor plans to drug houses and large buildings for responding police or emergency units.

Probably the toughest problem you will face at this time is guessing which hardware and operating system will last the longest and have the most software available for them. In summary, my suggestions for you are listed below.

1. Hardware—PC or workstation platforms (Pentium or Risc processors).
2. Operating system—Windows NT or, if necessary, UNIX with a system that is compatible with Windows NT (keep your options open). Choose VAX if you have to, but remember that 1992 saw DEC lose almost $2 billion because VAX systems have almost stopped selling. Also, the VMS operating system is proprietary. In fact, just about any minisystem is proprietary.

Software and Language

Relational databases are very powerful, but they require a lot of processing speed. The Pentium and Risc processors can provide the speed necessary to run these databases. Many agencies are using systems that were developed by vendors with little or no experience in law enforcement. Their knowledge was generally gained by hiring former law enforcement personnel or using police agencies as beta test sites. The databases they developed were for the mainframe and minicomputer systems. They were text-based systems that were programmed in Basic. Basic is an old programming language that has many problems. Some of these vendors started using COBOL, FORTRAN and C programming to enhance and speed up their systems. However they change and enhance their systems, they will not completely satisfy our needs. The vendors will constantly be asking for more money to change and enhance their systems.

The more we can use software that is within the mainstream of business and home applications, the less it will cost us to maintain and update these systems. There are databases that are now powerful enough to customize to our needs and that work on PCs and workstations. As an example, you could use FoxPro on the PCs or Oracle on the PCs and workstations. These databases have the capabilities that we need to develop input and query screens for a records management system. With Windows NT or UNIX, the ability to connect to many different devices and systems is enhanced enough for our needs. This combination will allow your department to have in-house programmers and alleviate costly changes to proprietary systems.

A flow chart is essential. The CAD/RMS system, whether it is purchased or developed in-house, must be organized so that you can look at a picture of how your input screens store the data and what reports use those fields. That way you will know what effect a design change will have on your system.

The Human Factor

Integrator

Systems integrators can be difficult and priceless, depending on the group that you choose. You must find a knowledgeable vendor who will supply you with the hardware and software. This vendor should be on-site or within close proximity to your department. They must coordinate the interaction between the software and hardware supplier. If you have problems, you will find that vendors point their fingers at each other and claim that it is the other vendor's fault and not theirs. An integrator insulates you from these problems and gets your system up and running in a more timely manner.

Coordinator

Picking the right person for the job is often difficult. That person must have an open mind and be very flexible. Some of these administrators tend to protect their systems more than necessary. It is commendable to protect your data, but if police personnel cannot get to the data, the system is of no value. That person must delegate the workload to trusted personnel in order for a system of this magnitude to function. Above all, he or she must constantly ask one question and apply the answer to each and every decision made for this project. The question is, Is this best for the department and its personnel? After applying that question, personal preference for software and hardware must not influence the decision. (If you have a MAC at home, you do not buy a MAC for work just because you are used to it and like it.) I have seen people buy systems for large departments because "it looks good and it is cheap."

All CAD, RMS and mapping vendors can be difficult at times. The bigger proprietary systems are the hardest to deal with in terms of money and enhancements. For example, our CAD vendor was asked to connect a scanner to the system for scanning in our crime information. Over the phone, the president of the company assured me that it would be less than $15,000, and he even followed it up with a written quote. However, when we met with the representatives of the company, the price had climbed to $75,000. They claimed that they had to write a driver for $15,000, and the rest was to integrate it into the system. We had to cancel the project. *Later research found that another company already had a driver available for $2,000.* If the scanning device would have been connected to a PC, it would have cost us the price of the scanner ($2,000).

THE FUTURE

Where are these computer systems going to take us? What can we expect in the near future, so that we can buy the right systems for our departments?

First and foremost, we must take a look at how we will input the data. Right now, the solutions are limited, with only a few choices. We either type in the data after extracting it out of the crime reports, or we use scanners to scan in the suspect descriptors and method of operation and then type in some of the data out of the reports. Whichever method you choose, you will be faced with the fact that all of your police personnel are being overwhelmed with paperwork.

We must work toward two goals:

1. Gather as much information as possible. The more we get, the more chance of catching the criminals.
2. Unburden the patrol officer. When an officer arrests someone, the first thing he or she must do is search through a penal code book that is several inches thick in order to determine the exact crime type to charge the suspect. Then the officer must decide what forms must be filled out and what notifications must be made. These forms and required notifications are constantly changing, and to burden officers with more paperwork would be detrimental to their performance.

The "catch-22" is that we need more information to catch the criminals, but if we ask the officers to enter more data, they are too tied up to catch the criminals. As a patrol officer, I can remember being in a patrol car with my head down writing reports. Is this safe? I don't think so.

Imagine a police officer in a patrol car dictating a report to the mobile digital terminal. The terminal converts words to text, spell-checks and grammar-checks the report. While dictating the report, the officer never looks down and constantly looks for criminal activity, thereby protecting the citizens and him- or herself. This is called voice recognition, which is used in computer systems today and has been tested in Florida in patrol cars. This method needs some refinement and at this time requires large amounts of storage. But this is the future for law enforcement. And this is what we should be keeping in mind when choosing a system.

Pen computing (writing on a computer tablet) is the other method you might consider for your personnel. However, the technology is very poor at this time, and again, your patrol officer will be gazing down while writing the report. When the officer identifies the type of crime that the report will be about, the terminal should identify the forms necessary to fill out and automatically send the pertinent data from the report to the proper personnel. This will entail the integration of a document-imaging system. This is nothing more than a database of your reports. The computer should keep a permanent copy of your final report and transfer a copy to the detectives and supervisors for approval and court filings.

After the report is dictated into the computer system, the data pertinent to crime analysis are extracted automatically from the report and transferred to crime analysis. The crime analysis system should automatically transfer the data to the mapping software, which should start analyzing the data immediately. Patterns and hot spots should automatically be identified by the system with suggestions on beat changes, according to the amount and location of calls vs. the travel time. With the input of the department's schedulers, the mapping software will know who is working that shift and what their particular qualifications are. The software can then suggest possible beat assignments, where and what time crimes are occurring in those areas, and where and when they might occur in the future.

The mobile digital terminals we choose will have an effect on how we display data in the patrol car. Most agencies have chosen text-only terminals. This has been cost-effective and productive, but it does not allow for the expansion that is necessary for law enforcement.

Why do we need graphics terminals? They will allow us to show our patrol officers maps of their patrol area. Imagine getting an emergency call at a location of which you never heard. That sounds familiar! You pull over, take out your map book and try to look up the street and find the right map page. Once you find those, then you cannot find the street in the grid. All the while, the dispatcher is asking for your estimated time of arrival. You advise the dispatcher that you cannot find the street, and he or she advises you that they are also looking up the street. Is there a better way? Yes. Why not display a map of the area on the car's terminal, showing the location of the victim's house and the location of the patrol car? This requires that you have a mapping system in the car. This can be done with the present technology. Your department will have to install a satellite tracking system to monitor your patrol cars.

As a call is dispatched and the car's terminal displays the victim's location and the patrol car's location, it can also display the recent crimes around the area and, perhaps, a floor plan of the residence or business. Certainly it should display the layout of apartment complexes, condominiums, mobile-home parks, malls, and so on.

Recently, I purchased a car with a heads-up display. It was annoying to see my speed on the windshield at first, but after I got used to the display, I came to depend on it. Imagine being in pursuit, the suspect weaving in and out of traffic at high speeds. The dispatcher is asking you for information, speed, direction of travel, vehicle description, and so on. This oftentimes leads to confusion; both you and additional cars are trying to transmit at the same time, while the dispatcher is asking for information, and your watch commander is stressed trying to determine whether this pursuit should continue in lieu of safety. The officer must look away from the suspect and road to check speed and gauges to determine the condition and speed of the car. Why not display that information on the windshield? I can tell you that it does not get in the way and it is effective as a safety tool. If the military can use it in their planes, we can use it in our cars. Keep in mind that with a satellite system you will not need to get that information (speed, direction and so on) from the unit, because it will be displayed to the dispatchers on their terminals.

This technology is within your grasp. You just have to make some of the right decisions to make sure that it becomes a reality within your department.

Standardization is the key to communication with other departments, but it is limited to the way you track your data. An example might be the three-digit crime codes. Beyond that, do what is best for your department, and don't let your engineering or planning departments tell you what's best for you. Contact other departments and ask them about their problems, and whether they can suggest a solution to them.

Visual information can do more for your department than anything. We do not have time to search through stacks of paperwork when we are so understaffed and the crime rate continues to rise. Insist on graphs and charting capabilities, so that you can see results at a glance. Maps are important to law enforcement. They will tell us more in a few minutes than we could learn in a lifetime. The presentation of our crime data in the form of maps and graphs will enhance our abilities to fight crime dramatically. The text-only terminals of the past should be dead and gone.

MAPPING SOFTWARE

Street and Map Files

You must first develop a street file. This entails starting with the DIME or TIGER files from the Census Bureau. The DIME file is from the 1980 census, and the TIGER file is from the 1990 census. In some cases, the TIGER file is not much of an improvement over the DIME file. However, I would recommend you start with the TIGER file.

Next, you must determine how you will enhance your TIGER file, and then who in your department will maintain it. My recommendation is to have your planning or engineering department maintain it. This can be at the county or city level, with each benefiting department helping pay for the cost of the file's maintenance. They must update your reporting districts and beats in a timely manner. Communication between departments is vital, and they must be responsive to your needs.

The file must update two systems: the first is your CAD (computer-aided dispatch) system, and the second is the mapping software you use for crime analysis. We receive biannual updates to our street file. Both our CAD and mapping software are updated at the same time, which allows us to address-match our data on the CAD system. The address-matching on the CAD system allows for immediate downloading into our mapping software for quick analysis. The software used to update the street file does not have to be the same as the software used to do the crime analysis. However, they must be able to use a compatible street file format.

The list of geographic data that may be pertinent to your needs varies depending on the geography in your area. We are in California, so we are concerned with fault lines, waterways and so on. Our geographic file contains the following geographic layers:

1. county,
2. cities,
3. beats,
4. reporting districts,
5. freeways,
6. highways,
7. local streets,
8. waterways,
9. fault lines,
10. railroads,
11. ambulance zones,
12. fire demand zones, and
13. fire station areas.

Criteria for Mapping Software

What should my crime analysis mapping software do for me? First, let's look at our needs:

1. ease of use (pull-down menus in language we understand; no formulas),
2. display of hot spots,
3. summary and list reports, and
4. compatibility with street file formats.

Look for the following things in mapping software:

1. Easy customization. Quick changes need to be made for emergency operations centers, as well as the normal changes for crimes, calls for service, parolees, sex registrants, accidents, citations, and so on.

2. Platform compatibility (PCs, Risc workstations, etc.). We are interested in software that can be used on several platforms. For instance, if we can afford a Risc workstation for our headquarters and PCs for our stations, we want software that will work across those and other platforms. The operating system that will allow us to use these different platforms will be Microsoft's Windows NT. Our mapping software is both DOS- and Windows-compatible. The mapping company has committed to develop a Windows NT version for us. Since Windows NT is just being released, it will take some time to determine who will support this operating system. It is the only operating system that will allow us to transcend the hardware platforms.

3. AVL (automatic vehicle location) system. Make sure your software has the capability to track vehicles from the CAD consul. Automated vehicle tracking is going to be a big part of our future. There are many benefits to AVL, including quicker response times and safety for your officers. Your officers will not have to look up calls in a map book if the location is displayed on their car's terminal, or if the dispatcher sees the location of their car and the location of the call and can direct them appropriately.

4. Versatile analysis capabilities. Automated functions are what we will be using now and in the future. For instance, we determined what we would like our mapping software to analyze. We wanted to overcome the boundary problems we face when using reporting districts for finding our hot spots. Suppose the burglars are committing their crimes across bordering reporting districts. We might not see it as a hot spot, because the crimes are divided between two districts. We asked our mapping vendor to give us the capability to find patterns without using predefined boundaries. We determined how we would use this new tool, and the vendor implemented it. The process is to select the crimes and time frame to be analyzed, then select the radius and threshold level. For example, we might select burglaries for the month of January and February for 1993 between 1700 and 2400 hours. Then we would select the threshold (10 crimes) and radius (.5 mile). The resulting map would indicate any half-mile radius with more than 10 burglaries that occurred within the designated time frame. These areas are represented by symbols of our choosing, and the actual amount of crimes is shown in the center of the symbol. We plan to enhance the analysis tools that our users can apply to their data and automate the process as much as possible.

5. Efficient mapping systems. We are facing cutbacks in personnel, as well as rising crime rates. The number of parolees (repeat offenders) is expected to double or triple in the next five years. To combat this, we must become more efficient. At times, this puts management personnel in a compromising position: save money on the budget and yet become more efficient—almost impossible! You must spend some money to purchase the systems that will enhance your efficiency, and next you must add personnel to run the systems that you purchased.

Try to find mapping software that is easy to use. The vendor must be very flexible, allowing you to determine your needs and how you want the mapping software to be used. Menus must use plain English and easy-to-use pull-down menus. The process must follow three basic steps—select crimes and areas, find the hot spots and give summary and individually listed crime reports. The custom analysis tools must go beyond these three basic steps with formulas that are applied to your data in a manner that is easy for the users, similar to our ability to find the hot spots within a radius. The easier the software is to use and the more automated it is, the fewer personnel you will need to run it. In fact, we are using clerks and, occasionally, police personnel to run the mapping software.

6. Vendor that works with you. Our vendor has responded to our needs without question. When we chose our vendor, we tested several different mapping systems, each of which had different capabilities. What became important to us was to have software that suited our needs. Most of the vendors refused to customize the software; some even argued with us. Our vendor simply said, "What do you want?" We advised them as to how we wanted the interface to look and what tools we needed. After the first release of the software, we found that we needed some changes and that we had left out some functionality. The vendor responded by saying that even though the new options were not in the contract, they would include them anyway. They were honest enough to say that they were minor changes and were not very costly to them. The result was a system that is easy to use and works well in the police environment.

Mapping Software of the Future

We want to add many more options to the mapping software. For instance, we want to be able to enter a list of our patrol personnel and their qualifications, and have the software determine where the crimes are occurring and how best to schedule and automatically deploy our personnel. The software would customize the beats on the fly, according to the number of personnel working that shift and the crime patterns.

In addition, we want to add options to use formulas to determine when and where crimes will occur in the future. Of course, these formulas would be hidden behind pull-down menu choices.

Problem-oriented policing is being used to isolate problem locations and coordinate teams to avert future crimes. In San Bernardino, we identify locations that we have responded to more than four or five times, to determine the reasons for the crime calls. The mapping software quickly identifies these locations, and we can identify the types of calls. We determine the response necessary to alleviate further problems at the location. Child services or counselors take care of domestic problems, while gang intervention teams handle gang disputes.

FOR MORE INFORMATION

For more information, the following is a list of the vendors that we are using at the present time:

1. CAD: P.R.C.,
2. RMS: Tiburon, and
3. mapping: Strategic Mapping Systems (Atlas GIS).

We are using the mapping software as the central point for our crime analysis. Strategic Mapping Systems has been unusual, to say the least. They have been reasonable when we have requested changes to the software, and their software is very powerful. They are about to release a Windows version of their software, which we believe is going to be a large part of our future. I would highly recommend this company to any department that has a need for mapping software, and particularly mapping in crime analysis units.

I am retired from the Los Angeles Sheriff's Department, where I was a criminal intelligence detective. I have a background in crime analysis and have worked with many different CAD, RMS and mapping software vendors. I have worked in live emergency operation centers during critical emergencies and have worked with many crime analysis units throughout the United States, Canada and Europe. Please do not hesitate to contact me at the address and phone number below if you would like more information.

Timothy J. Miller
Crime Mapping Coordinator
San Bernardino Sheriff's Department
655 E. Third St.
San Bernardino, CA 92415
(909) 387-3479

Chapter 15

Geocoding of Crime Incidents Using the 1990 TIGER File: The Chicago Example

Richard Block
Loyola University, Chicago

An accurate digitized map of a police jurisdiction and accurate and complete entry of address information on police records are crucial to computerized spatial analysis of crime patterns. In a jurisdiction as large as Chicago, geocoding must be quick, mostly automated and accurate. The TIGER file, created for the 1990 census, seemed to be that map.[1] Unfortunately, when I began spatial analysis of crime two years ago, I found that the TIGER file was replete with errors and did not represent a law enforcement view of the city.

After two years of work to amend the TIGER file to correct errors and reflect a law enforcement perspective, and to create a program to define street extensions and correct for common errors in data entry, we now are able to achieve a first-pass geocoding hit rate of 98 percent. The general tactic used to achieve this very high success rate was to permanently correct errors and omissions in mapping (by alteration of the TIGER file) and spelling and proper street extensions (in a FoxPro program), as they were detected. The operative assumption was that if one crime occurred at a specific address, a second was also likely to occur there. Rather than manually geocode incidents at the same address, the decision was made to systematically accumulate a map that would be useful for crime analysis. This decision made for very slow going at first, but very rapid and accurate geocoding as corrections accumulated.

The following outline summarizes the problems that were found in geocoding Chicago crime incidents, and the tactics used to overcome them.

1. The streets underlying the city boundaries in the TIGER file are very inaccurate. About one-half of the street segments are wrong or nonexistent. Many of these street segments simply did not exist. Anyone living on the Chicago side of Harlem Avenue, represented in the TIGER file by the dotted line on the western border of map 1, would have been missed in the 1990 census, as incidents occurring there were missed in my initial geocoding of crime. Occasionally, parts of suburbs were included in Chicago (as was my Evanston house), or parts of Chicago were included in suburbs.

   The TIGER file is accurate only to 120 feet. While this may not be crucial in the city's interior, on its border, 120 feet will define a location as in or out of the city. To overcome this problem, in the MapInfo file, the city's boundary was eliminated and each street segment on the city's boundary was checked for accuracy. Many additions and changes were required.

1. Technically, geocoding was not done with the TIGER file, but with a MapInfo map of Chicago that was based upon the pre-1990 census TIGER file.

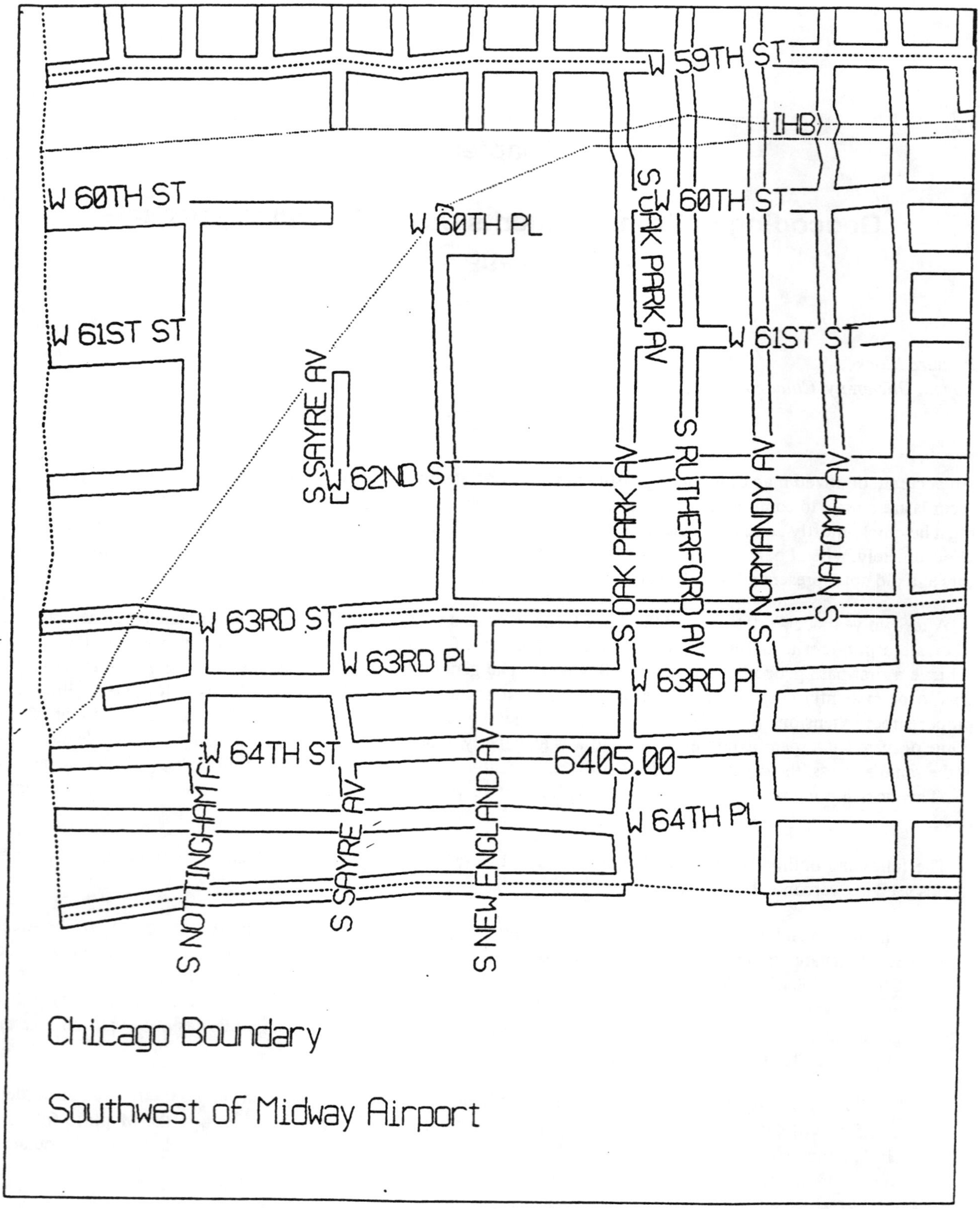

Map 1
Missing street segments in the TIGER file

2. The TIGER file contains many unnamed street segments. This problem was especially difficult because the unnamed streets were not randomly distributed. In Chicago, many streets were unnamed on the Gold Coast and the Southeast Side, where many north-south streets were unnamed for several miles, including (for those who know the area south of the University of Chicago) Ellis, University, Drexel, Harper, and many others. For the 1990 census, this meant that less-automated techniques had to be used to make sure surveys were received. Their success is not fully documented. For spatial analysis of crime, this means that there is an initial bias in coding occurrences of crime. Those areas with many unnamed streets are underrepresented (map 2).

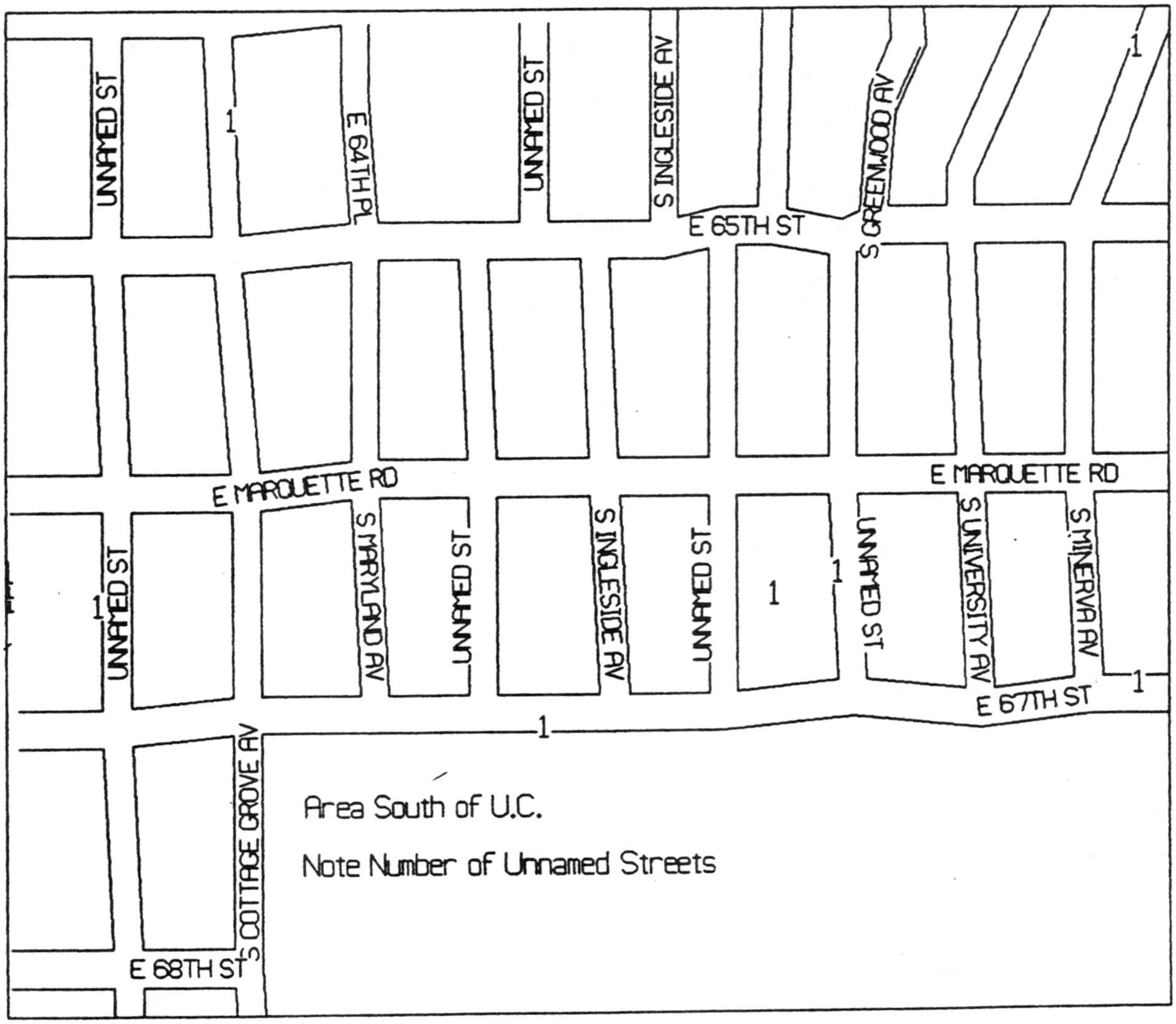

Map 2
Unnamed street segments in the TIGER file

A related, though less important, problem is caused by new or realigned streets. While not a major concern in Chicago, portions of downtown Chicago and the area around O'Hare have been substantially rebuilt in the last decade.

Overcoming these problems required a very substantial time investment. After initial automated geocoding, incidents that failed to geocode were sorted by street name, direction and address. This sorting served as a marker for missing or inaccurate street segments. After consulting paper maps, street segments were added or corrected on the electronic TIGER-based map.

3. Named streets were sometimes misnamed in the TIGER file. For example, Lake Shore Drive was sometimes designated as US 41 (correct, but not useful) and sometimes as US 14. Streets in an entire neighborhood, Hegwisch, were either unnamed or misnamed, and almost all lacked address ranges. This indicates an almost complete lack of quality control by the census in that area.

   The solution to these problems was similar to that of point two.

4. Many blocks have incorrect or missing address ranges. Some blocks simply have no addresses on them; others have more addresses than exist; others have address ranges that are obviously incorrect. Some have address ranges on the wrong side of the street. All these range problems result in an inaccurate placement of events.[2]

   Because an incident may be automatically geocoded but inaccurately placed, there is no obvious solution to these address range problems, except to correct them as they are found.

5. Many streets are accurately represented in the TIGER files as having no address ranges. These include expressways and streets running through parks (favorite spots for crime). For police purposes in rectangular-grid Chicago, it is useful to assign address ranges to these streets, although for the census it is not. Similarly, the police will invent street continuations or locations that do not exist if these addresses help in accurately locating a crime scene (for example, 4400 N. Lakefront). Each of these addresses must somehow be geocoded into a file of incidents.

   Those that are recurrent, such as 4400 N. Lakefront or 3500 S. Dan Ryan Expressway, can be added to the electronic map to allow for automated geocoding. Some locations that may occur only once, such as a railroad track, will have to be geocoded by using a pointing device. However, this is a very time-consuming technique that should be minimized. In the last file of 1,800 homicides that were geocoded, 10 were of this type.

6. Prior to the advent of automated geocoding, there was little need for completely accurate entry of the address of an incident. Slight errors in spelling, incorrectly identifying an avenue as a parkway, or using a name variation (for example, the many variations of "Dr. Martin Luther King Jr. Drive") cause few problems for the officer working a beat. Nor do multiple identifications of the same street (for example, Marquette Road in map 2 is also known as 66th Street). However, the computer lacks the flexibility of an officer. Street names in the incident file must be very nearly accurate. Furthermore, in order for an address to be automatically geocoded, the address must be of the same form as that used in the TIGER file. For example, incidents occurring on "Lake Park Ave" must be coded as occurring on "Lk Park Ave."[3]

   These spelling and extension differences are major problems for automated geocoding. Rather than instruct police and data entry personnel to record the address more accurately, a FoxPro program was written that adds street extensions to all street names and rewrites names when necessary to reflect the TIGER file name. This program was very time-consuming to write, but it is crucial to successful automated geocoding. Just as map corrections are cumulative, so is this program. As incidents occur that should be successfully geocoded but are not, additional commands are added to the program to add street extensions or correct spellings.

---

2. The census method used to identify address ranges is prone to error and makes address corrections very difficult. Basically, it involves standing on a hypothetical street corner, looking down the street, determining whether odd or even are on your left or right and whether address numbers go up or down from where you stand, and, in Chicago, repeating this exercise 56,000 times.

3. The use of nonexact "close" algorithms in MapInfo and FoxPro was found to be inaccurate, especially where the same syllable appears first in several street names (for example, "Lake" in Lake Street, Lake Park Avenue, Lake Shore Drive, and Lakewood Avenue).

The Chicago Homicide Project and the CAPS evaluation were able to overcome many of the problems of the TIGER file through progressive correction. Assuming that the addresses of homicides in one year are representative of addresses in the other years, the TIGER file was modified to correct city boundaries, unnamed streets and inaccurate address ranges as these problems were discovered in geocoding of specific incidents. The file was also modified to reflect the police view of the city's grid. The first 900 incidents that were geocoded required more than two months. Project staff are now able to geocode by address and locate by tract 50,000 incidents (about one month's total) in a week.

Chapter 16

DMAP in Jersey City: Implementing a Technological Revolution

Charles Bellucci
Jersey City, N.J., Police Department

The Jersey City Police Department, in cooperation with Rutgers University, School of Criminal Justice, Center for Crime Prevention Studies, participated in the Drug Market Analysis Program (DMAP) grant sponsored by the National Institute of Justice, for a three-year period beginning in January 1990. The purpose of the grant was to analyze street-level drug activity and develop and test strategies to combat select locations throughout the city. While the DMAP program was quite extensive in scope, this report references only the technical aspect. Therefore, information regarding the entire program will not be found in this paper.

Prior to 1990, the Jersey City Police Department (JCPD) had been developing a computer-aided dispatch (CAD) system, which ultimately went "on line" in June 1991. The CAD software development stage coincided ideally with the designing of the DMAP information system. By determining DMAP's needs, the JCPD Planning Unit, along with Rutgers University's research team, was able to recommend a satisfactory technical configuration.

The configuration utilized the CAD system's two minicomputers (located at police headquarters), which acted as host servers for seven 386SX PCs, one at each of the four police districts located throughout the city, two at the Narcotic Unit, and one at the Center for Crime Prevention Studies. The minicomputers were capable of storing data files in an MSDOS format, which ensured compatibility with the remote PCs. All PCs were remotely linked to the minicomputers via 9600-baud modems utilizing dedicated telephone lines, except for Rutgers, which used a 2400-baud call-guard dial-up modem with a password and callback feature for security reasons (see figure 1).

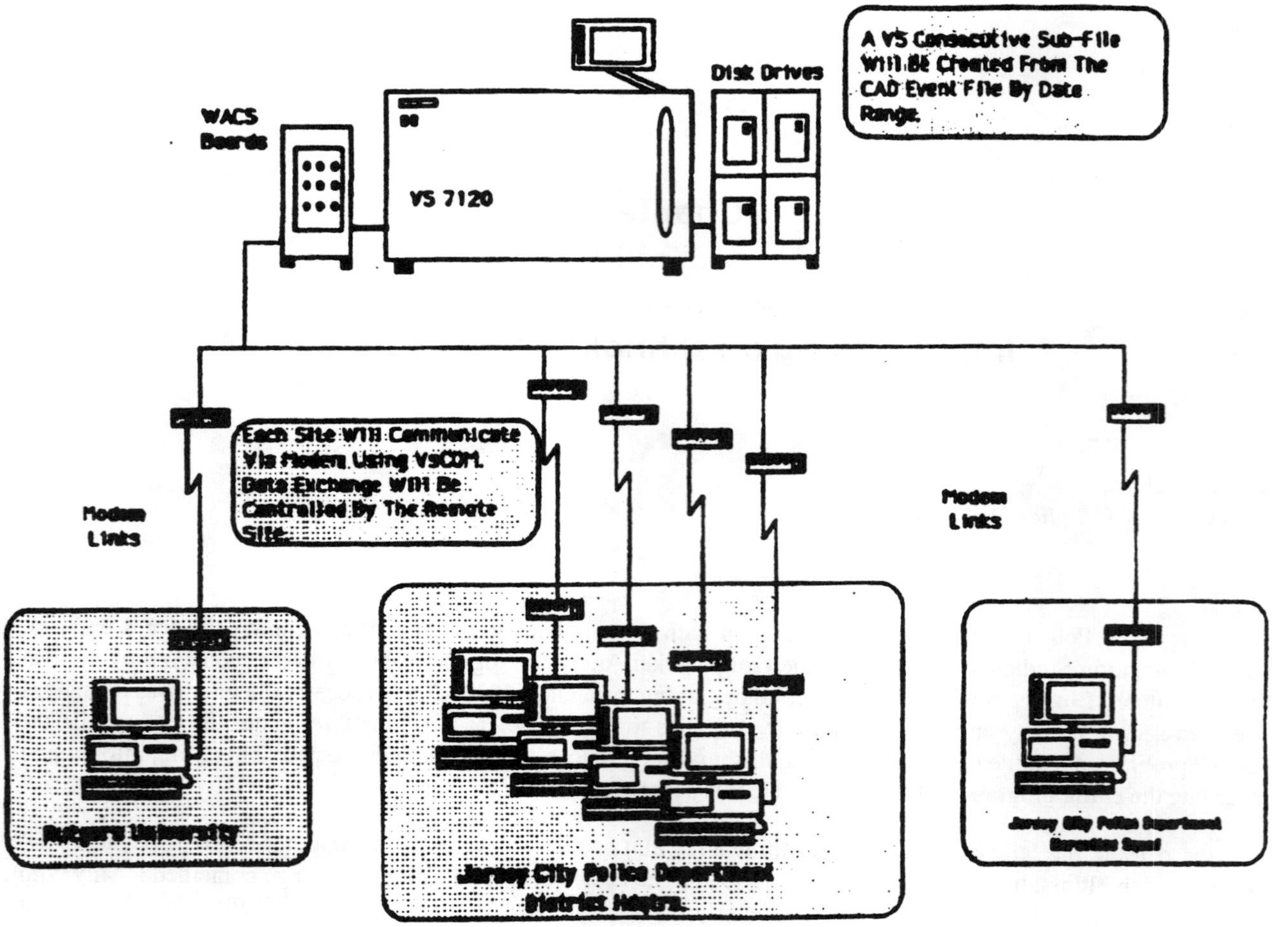

Fig. 1
Jersey City Police Department VS to PC data transfer

The software selected for DMAP consisted of FoxPro for database management and MapInfo for geographic data analysis. FoxPro was chosen for its speed, especially when indexing large databases (one database was 30 megabytes and contained tens of thousands of records). Additionally, it was compatible with the department's local area network (LAN), which used DBase and Clipper for investigation and arrest data. MapInfo was chosen because of its ease of use, and also because it, too, was compatible with the LAN databases (see map 1).

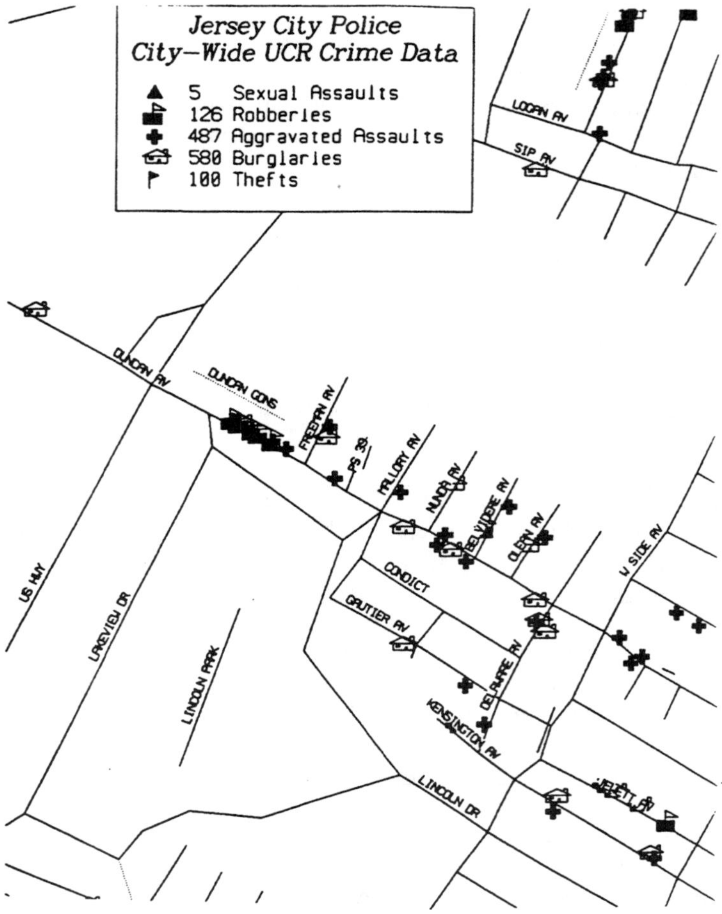

Map 1
Example of a Jersey City DMAP map

One of the first major problems encountered concerned MapInfo's geographic data files. While MapInfo correctly states that its maps are 85 percent accurate (or better), there is no way of telling what information is inaccurate without checking all the data. One way of finding inaccurate location information is to create a database with all the street addresses and intersections within your jurisdiction, then geocode the database in MapInfo. The resultant unmatched locations can then be checked and corrected. This is very time-consuming, but it pays off in the end. Before the JCPD did this, we checked with other city agencies and were fortunate enough to find several databases being used, one at Traffic Engineering and another at the Department of Urban Research and Design.

Early in the data-gathering stage, it became apparent that the LAN's investigation and arrest data would present a problem for geocoding in MapInfo. The Electronic Data Processing (EDP) Unit keyed this information into the LAN directly from hard-copy reports. Since EDP's original needs for these data concerned only UCR requirements, exact location information was not a priority. Therefore, location information was not standardized, nor was it even considered important. Location information could be found in these databases in a variety of forms. For example, Police Headquarters could be entered just as that, or as PDHQ, HQ, 8 Erie, 8 Erie St, 8 Erie Street, 2nd Fl. 8 Erie, rear of 8 Erie, Erie/Bay, Erie and Bay, Erie & Bay, and even PD ERIE ST. Add to this similar street names such as Stegman St, Stegman Ct and Stegman Pl.

Any data analyst can readily see the difficulties a geographic mapping system would have trying to assign coordinate locations to data fields represented in this manner. Multiply the above examples by 700 or so streets, 100,000 or so addresses, and literally thousands of commonplace names in Jersey City, and the problem is magnified immensely.

To overcome this problem, a series of programs were written by the Police Planning Unit. The programs parsed out location information and attempted to match the parsed-out data with a master street-name file or a commonplace-name file. Locations that were unable to be corrected ultimately had to be reviewed one at a time and manually adjusted. Needless to say, this was a very time-consuming and tedious task.

Initially, positive location coordinates were successful in about 40 percent of the cases. After running through the "cleaning programs," the match rate reached up to 85 percent. Finally, after manually manipulating the data, over 90 percent of the data were geocoded. At times, a 96 percent match rate was possible.

It was obvious that geocode matching could not continue in this fashion, because of the exorbitant amount of personnel hours expended in accomplishing a 96 percent match rate. A training program was begun to impress upon EDP personnel the importance of entering location data in a correct and standardized way. Afterward, the geocode match rate improved substantially, but not to the level hoped.

CAD data were quite another story. After correcting MapInfo's geographic databases, the final product was used to create the CAD geofile. This resulted in a 98 percent match rate, since the two databases were exactly the same. The 2 percent errors occurred when the Communications Bureau's call takers "forced" location information into the system, even though the CAD geofile indicated that the address was not valid.

The one problem that plagued the Planning Unit throughout the DMAP grant period was the timeliness of providing investigation and arrest data to all users. EDP was responsible for keying the data into the LAN after receiving the hard copies from the various divisions and units throughout the department. The hard copies were prepared by these units and then reviewed by clerical personnel before being delivered via departmental mail to EDP. This process took about five days. It took another two days for EDP to key the information into the LAN.

The data at this point were already seven days behind. However, because of the design of the LAN's databases, it was difficult to download data for DMAP on a daily basis. There was no way to prevent duplication of records during the process. No control number was assigned to the individual records. In order to be assured of collecting all relevant data without duplication, Planning had to wait until the 10th of each month before downloading the prior month's data. This resulted in DMAP's being a month behind at times. The new records management system being installed in the two minicomputers will alleviate this delay. It will also eliminate the need for correcting location data, since the address data on the minicomputers is validated via a geofile in the same manner as CAD data.

Once all the databases were installed on the system, narcotic investigators could easily search for information by one of 22 different criteria (or any combination of the 22). Among some of the choices were names (first, last, AKA, nickname), age, race, D.O.B., tattoos, associates, drug type, locations (arrest site, crime site, arrestee's home), date, time, and several others. This was accomplished in FoxPro by following a user-friendly menu system. Searches in MapInfo were not as extensive, but they were adequate for the investigators' needs and just as easy to use.

While many minor problems were encountered, they were not difficult to overcome. The aforementioned problems were by far the hardest to surmount, but the most difficult of all was training for personnel involved in the DMAP grant. No matter how successful the technology, it cannot compensate for lack of training. Rutgers University staff provided excellent training for the Jersey City police personnel, which resulted in a successful outcome for the DMAP program relative to this technology.

Chapter 17

How to Develop a Tactical Early Warning System on a Small-City Budget

Ray Sanford
Crime Analyst
Vacaville, Calif., Police Department

WHAT IS AN EARLY WARNING SYSTEM?

My definition of an early warning system for law enforcement is a system that provides an alert to patrol officers about specific crime trends *before* they have noticed the problem themselves. Patrol sergeants and seasoned veteran patrol officers know when crime is on the upswing in their area. However, because they are on duty only about eight to 10 hours a day, they are able to observe crime only during their shift. New patrol officers may not have enough experience in their beat to recognize the changing crime patterns. New policing methods, such as community-based policing, are placing additional responsibility on beat officers to be aware of what is happening in their beats so they can take corrective action.

This is the reason, I believe, that crime analyst positions were originally conceived—to help patrol. We should be able to see what crimes are occurring and keep patrol briefed on what is happening in every patrol area in the city or county we serve. However, I found I was unable to do this when using traditional crime analysis methods. My solution has been to develop a tactical early warning system where I track specific crimes daily, looking for statistical changes that indicate that a crime series is starting, and *then* I distribute a bulletin to patrol alerting them to this fact.

WHAT'S WRONG WITH TRADITIONAL CRIME ANALYSIS?

Traditional crime analysis methods are too slow to provide near real-time tactical information for patrol officers' needs. What I mean by "traditional crime analysis" is obtaining police reports and then analyzing them in various ways, looking for crime patterns and series. We analyze crime using methods such as studying modus operandi (MO), looking for patterns or similarities between cases. We use time-series analysis methods to find the most likely time period in which crimes such as burglary are occurring, when the victims can give us only a time spread. We use spatial analysis methods to look for geographical patterns, such as crime clusters. We look at suspect descriptions, checking for similarities. We study victimology in certain crimes, looking for some common thread running through all the cases, so we can link them together. All of these studies can, and do, provide useful data. However, in order to use these tools, it is necessary for crime analysts to review all incoming crime reports to gather the data and then store the data for retrieval when needed. Since *every* report within a particular crime category is *potentially* linked to every other case, this becomes a very time-consuming task, especially in smaller departments with only one crime analyst.

I think most crime analysts have made a mistake by diving right into research, trying to identify crime patterns and series as soon as possible. State or federal grants may dictate this approach by requiring *daily* reports to patrol. Most of the crime analysis manuals I have read guide us toward this approach. By using traditional crime analysis methods, however, most of us run into some major problems.

In addition, "overalerting" patrol is a concern. Officers have told me that endless bulletins coming from crime analysis only cause them to be frustrated; they are "running from call to call" and cannot do anything about the crimes, anyhow. I also believe one of the causes of stress and morale problems among police officers is that they are in a constant crime mode. Crime *never* stops, and no matter how many people they arrest and how hard they work, the next shift brings new calls. I understand that a few years ago, the U.S. Postal Service noticed low morale among their sorters and had a consultant study the problem. The story goes that the consultant found that at the end of the sorting table was a giant stack of mailbags. The sorters were expected to sort about 1,000 bags a day. But as they worked, other workers threw new bags on the pile, so that by the end of the day, the pile was exactly the same size as when they started. The consultant identified this never-ending work as the cause for the workers' low morale, and recommended bagging the mail in different colored bags, such as 1,000 blue bags and 1,000 green bags. As the workers sorted the mail, the blue bags begin to decrease, so they could see some progress being made. The other incoming mail was placed in green bags. Morale picked up, and productivity increased, too.

I think police officers suffer from this never-ending work problem, and I think by "overalerting" them, all crime analysis does is add to their frustration. However, if we alert them only when a particular crime is above normal, and then tell them when that crime has returned to normal, we allow them some "closure" on that issue and help them to feel some accomplishment, especially if they have conducted some kind of special patrol or other tactic to end the crime series. The low threshold in Vacaville's early warning system does just that. It tells patrol when something (possibly our special patrol tactics) has had a positive impact on the problem by driving that crime below normal, at least for a little while.

Another problem is that reports being processed through the system do not get to crime analysis with enough speed. It can take as much as two weeks for reports to be written, reviewed, possibly returned to the officer for correction, revised, reviewed again, approved, forwarded to the records section, copied, and finally forwarded to crime analysis. You *cannot* do tactical crime analysis with two-week-old data! However, you *can* produce useful information for detectives and administration. I believe this is one reason crime analysis units tend to become used primarily for strategic analysis of data (such as preparing statistical reports) and for helping investigations clear cases after a suspect is arrested (matching recovered property with stolen property, and so on). These functions are very necessary for the proper functioning of a law enforcement agency, and crime analysis will always be involved in assisting with these functions.

However, if we stop here, patrol is left without adequate information to allow them to become *proactive*, which we all would like. Beat officers working under some of the new programs, such as community-based policing, are told they are *responsible* for handling everything within their beat, including crime apprehension, suppression and prevention. They have no way of keeping track of what crimes are occurring within their beat 24 hours a day. If we cannot provide this information, then who can?

I attended a crime analysis conference a few years ago, and one of the speakers was an old sergeant with 30 years' experience, who told us that "fighting crime is like mowing the grass; they will not let you kill it; all you can do is mow it down when it gets too high." I believe this is a very true statement. All crime is *never* going to go away, no matter what any of us do and no matter how many officers we hire. And if this is true, then for whatever specific crime you are studying, there is an underlying body of crimes that is *normal.* If we jump right into traditional crime analysis, we haven't established what levels of crime are "normal" in each area under study. If we do not know what is normal, then we will not know when that crime is "too high." We then spin our wheels trying to kill crime when it just is not possible.

BIRTH OF THE VACAVILLE EARLY WARNING SYSTEM

A foundation of the Vacaville early warning system is the use of civilian volunteers, usually retired senior citizens, to compile and enter data. In order to obtain the most reliable and accurate historical information available, my volunteers and I started our research by counting every burglary (auto, commercial and residential) that was reported during every seven-day period for the previous year, by the patrol beat of occurrence. I decided to use beats, in order to break down data into the most useful form for patrol officers. Our city is divided into six beats, with each officer assigned to a beat. Beats are further divided into reporting districts, which are useful for analysis but not very useful for patrol officers, who are responsible for patrolling the entire beat. Since I was using a complete count of the data, I did not have to worry about sample size and the corresponding error.

We entered this information into a spreadsheet and obtained the weekly mean average and standard deviation figures for each beat. For each beat and for the city as a whole, I established a high threshold by adding the standard deviation to the mean average, and a low threshold by subtracting the standard deviation from the mean average. I chose one standard deviation because it is easily calculated by a spreadsheet (or scientific hand calculator) and is easily explained to people without formal statistical training, using the bell curve. Since 68 percent of the burglaries would fall within the normal range and 16 percent would fall below normal, I would be alerting patrol officers about above-normal burglaries only about 16 percent of the time. Figure 1 is a printout of my spreadsheet, showing low threshold, high threshold, mean average, and standard deviation columns for all the crimes I am now tracking.

A tactical early warning system requires data no older than 24 hours. I reviewed all available information and discovered that I was not using a really powerful information resource: dispatch. Crime analysts shy away from dispatch information because it provides very limited information concerning the data elements we have been taught to track. However, the following *is* available: incident type (nature), date reported, time reported, location of the incident, disposition of the call, and the dispatcher's notes.

As I reviewed dispatch data, I discovered that the "nature codes" used in my computer-aided dispatch (CAD) system were not necessarily designed for gathering crime statistics, but were designed to set service levels for patrol units by separating calls into priority levels for response purposes. I found that auto burglary, commercial burglary and residential burglary were all lumped together as burglary, and there was no way to separate them for analysis. I also found that other codes, such as illegal entry, grand theft, petty theft, and trespass, needed to be looked at, since all of these may actually be burglaries for statistical purposes. We may be able to prove in a legal sense only that the suspect trespassed into someone's house. For our purpose, I now classify them all as burglaries. It was essential to fix this problem before I could proceed any further. By working with the dispatch supervisor, we were able to develop a new set of nature codes for all incidents, which provided me with the additional details I needed for analysis and also provided for proper prioritization of calls to meet the needs of the dispatchers.

I was now ready to begin checking every day to see if the number of crimes in each beat was "normal," "above normal" or "below normal." To do this, I review the daily log produced by CAD, which shows the number of incidents reported in each beat for the last 24 hours. (Refer to the daily log example, figure 2, for this discussion.) If your agency is not using CAD, you will have to refer to the dispatch cards or manual logbook. I highlight on the log every crime that I am tracking, and then I review each incident to obtain any further notes the dispatchers may have made that would be helpful. I filter out all unfounded and most of the civil and family calls, because they rarely indicate someone who is committing serial crimes.

JAN - JUN	LOW	HIGH	AVG	SDEV
BEAT 1				
AUTO BURGS	0	7	3.4	3.5
CMCL BURGS	0	2	0.8	1.1
RES BURGS	1	6	3.6	2.7
TOTAL BURGS	3	13	7.8	4.9
SEX CRIME	0	0	0.0	0.0
ROBBERY	0	1	0.3	0.5
VANDALISM	2	6	4.0	2.0
VEHICLE THEFT	0	1	0.4	0.6
BEAT 2				
AUTO BURGS	1	5	2.9	2.3
CMCL BURGS	0	2	0.8	1.0
RES BURGS	1	5	2.8	2.1
TOTAL BURGS	3	9	6.4	3.1
SEX CRIME	0	1	0.2	0.4
ROBBERY	0	0	0.1	0.3
VANDALISM	0	7	3.3	3.3
VEHICLE THEFT	0	2	0.9	0.8
BEAT 3				
AUTO BURGS	0	3	1.4	1.1
CMCL BURGS	0	2	0.9	1.0
RES BURGS	1	4	2.1	1.5
TOTAL BURGS	2	7	4.4	2.2
SEX CRIME	0	1	0.2	0.4
ROBBERY	0	1	0.3	0.7
VANDALISM	0	2	1.3	1.0
VEHICLE THEFT	0	1	0.6	0.8
BEAT 4				
AUTO BURGS	0	3	1.4	1.4
CMCL BURGS	0	1	0.4	0.6
RES BURGS	1	6	3.3	2.4
TOTAL BURGS	2	8	5.2	3.1
SEX CRIME	0	1	0.5	0.5
ROBBERY	0	1	0.3	0.5
VANDALISM	3	7	5.1	2.4
VEHICLE THEFT	0	2	1.1	1.1
BEAT 5				
AUTO BURGS	0	4	2.1	2.[illegible]
CMCL BURGS	0	1	0.7	0.7
RES BURGS	0	2	0.9	0.9
TOTAL BURGS	1	6	3.7	2.5
SEX CRIME	0	1	0.2	0.6
ROBBERY	0	1	0.2	0.4
VANDALISM	0	4	2.2	1.8
VEHICLE THEFT	0	1	0.4	0.5
BEAT 6				
AUTO BURGS	1	3	1.9	1.2
CMCL BURGS	0	2	1.0	0.9
RES BURGS	1	5	2.7	2.0
TOTAL BURGS	3	8	5.6	2.6
SEX CRIME	0	1	0.2	0.4
ROBBERY	0	0	0.0	0.0
VANDALISM	1	4	2.4	1.4
VEHICLE THEFT	0	1	0.6	0.7
CITYWIDE TOTALS				
AUTO BURGS	8	19	13.2	5.6
CMCL BURGS	2	7	4.6	2.4
RES BURGS	10	20	15.3	5.0
ALL BURGS	24	43	33.1	9.5
SEX CRIME	0	3	1.1	1.4
ROBBERY	0	2	1.2	1.1
VANDALISM	11	26	18.4	7.7
VEHICLE THEFT	1	7	4.0	2.6

Fig. 1
Spreadsheet showing early-warning statistics

Fig. 2
Daily log example

INCIDENTS	BEAT	DATE	TIME	ADDRESS	NATURE	REPORT	RD	DISP	PRI
[illegible]	2	08/07/93	00:12:07	178 REVERE CT	DISTURB PEACE (AUTO)		328	02	M3
3047267	2	08/07/93	00:38:08	RUBY DR/YOUNGSDALE DR	SUSPICIOUS VEHICLE		328	01	36
3047275	2	08/07/93	01:31:45	1501 ALAMO DR	DVI (IN PROGRESS)	93-06535	318	06	32
3047282	2	08/07/93	02:42:52	130 LA PAZ ST	DISTURB PEACE-FIGHT	93-06536	316	06	SB
3047293	2	08/07/93	04:39:21	1267 BALSAM WY	MAL MISCHIEF (JUST OCCURRED)	93-06537	106	06	32
3047297	2	08/07/93	05:39:45	359 MARNA DR	FURNISH TRANSPORTATION		321	02	35
3047314	2	08/07/93	10:00:21	485 BURLINGTON DR	BATTERY (REPORT)	93-06542	319	06	22
3047320	2	08/07/93	11:12:52	1809 BROOKWOOD DR	ALARM (BURGLARY - AUDIBLE)		320	02	22
3047364	2	08/07/93	16:56:44	2100 PEABODY RD	TRAFFIC HAZARD		702	00	K1
3047363	2	08/07/93	17:46:13	MARSHALL RD/PEABODY RD	RECKLESS DRIVING (JUST OCCUR)		309	01	K1
3047368	2	08/07/93	17:51:43	3560 NUT TREE RD	ADW (REPORT)	93-06553	331	06	22
3047376	2	08/07/93	20:05:45	1495 ALAMO DR	DVI (IN PROGRESS)		318	02	22
3047378	2	08/07/93	20:25:54	1495 ALAMO DR	DVI (IN PROGRESS)	93-06555	318	06	35
3047385	2	08/07/93	21:20:09	ALAMO DR/MARSHALL RD	DISTURB PEACE (MUSIC)		316	01	34
3047414	2	08/07/93	22:11:03	190 REVERE CT	DISTURB PEACE (MUSIC)		328	02	34
3047396	2	08/07/93	22:21:51	1467 ALAMO DR	WELFARE CHECK		318	02	M3
BEAT 2									
3047257	4	08/07/93	00:12:23	167 RANDALL AV	PROWLER		329	01	32
3047259	4	08/07/93	00:27:10	125 KEARNEY WY	THREATS	93-06532	330	06	36
3047277	4	08/07/93	01:35:04	6200 VANDEN RD	THEFT-PETTY (RES JUST OCC)		338	02	BOL
3047296	4	08/07/93	05:20:28	348 ROYAL OAKS DR	PROWLER		326	02	35
3047298	4	08/07/93	06:10:32	340 RIVERDALE CT	PROWLER		330	02	32
3047303	4	08/07/93	07:31:10	242 OAK VALLEY CT	ALARM (BURGLARY - AUDIBLE)		338	02	13
3047309	4	08/07/93	08:44:22	440 EDWIN DR	KIDNAP (REPORT)	93-06540	329	06	16
3047365	4	08/07/93	17:42:47	107 GREG CT	BURGLARY (RES-REPORT)	93-06552	322	06	K1
3047393	4	08/07/93	22:09:09	135 WOODBURY CI	DVI (IN PROGRESS)		327	02	34
3047402	4	08/07/93	23:36:16	160 LONGVIEW CT	DISTURB PEACE (PARTY)		327	02	34
3047406	4	08/07/93	23:01:55	528 GREGORY DR	FOLLOW UP		322	06	K1
BEAT 4									
3047258	6	08/06/93	23:54:06	159 AEGEAN WY	DISTURB PEACE (OTHER)		325	02	36
3047263	6	08/07/93	00:42:40	301 NUT TREE RD	FOLLOW UP		333	00	23
3047265	6	08/07/93	00:47:17	301 NUT TREE RD	FOLLOW UP		333	02	23
3047268	6	08/07/93	00:53:34	292 NUT TREE RD	ALARM (BURGLARY - AUDIBLE)		334	02	23
3047271	6	08/07/93	01:11:01	301 NUT TREE RD	FOLLOW UP		333	06	23
3047285	6	08/07/93	01:47:37	199 AEGEAN WY	ANNOYING PHONE CALLS	93-06534	325	06	S11
3047283	6	08/07/93	02:16:49	352 NUT TREE RD	SUSPICIOUS VEHICLE		334	01	35
3047295	6	08/07/93	03:11:43	1000 NUT TREE RD	MENTAL		340	02	11
3047290	6	08/07/93	04:19:44	199 AEGEAN WY	ANNOYING PHONE CALLS	93-06534	325	06	S11
3047294	6	08/07/93	04:58:36	400 ORANGE DR	MEAL BREAK (CODE 7)		334	02	32
3047312	6	08/07/93	09:55:47	195 LASSEN CI	FOLLOW UP		334	06	T1
3047319	6	08/07/93	10:27:42	320 ORANGE DR	BURGLARY (AUTO-JUST OCCURRED)	93-06546	334	06	16
3047323	6	08/07/93	11:20:01	111 NUT TREE RD	MISSING CHILD		333	02	S1
3047324	6	08/07/93	11:26:56	281 ARROWHEAD DR	FOLLOW UP		324	02	22
3047328	6	08/07/93	11:53:26	555 ELMIRA RD	DISTURB PEACE (MUSIC)		325	02	16
3047336	6	08/07/93	13:41:36	281 ARROWHEAD DR	FOLLOW UP		324	02	22
3047356	6	08/07/93	16:16:16	NOTRE DAME DR/ANGUS WY	DISTURB PEACE (MUSIC)		340	01	22
3047358	6	08/07/93	17:12:00	320 ORANGE DR	TFC COLLISION (AMBULANCE SENT)		334	06	M3
3047362	6	08/07/93	17:17:54	761 NOTRE DAME DR	DISTURB PEACE (MUSIC)		340	02	K1
3047369	6	08/07/93	18:12:21	274 NUT TREE RD	SHOPLIFTER IN CUSTODY	93-06551	334	07	35
3047373	6	08/07/93	18:37:05	761 NOTRE DAME DR	DISTURB PEACE (MUSIC)		340	02	SB

After I have identified all of the legitimate crimes, I then enter my mapping program, obtain the *x* and *y* coordinates for each crime location, and write them down right on the daily log. (I have found this is actually faster than having the map "auto-place" the crimes later.) At this point, I enter the following data into the database illustrated below:

Early Warning Information From CAD				
CRIME:	XCOORD:	YCOORD:		
CASE:	DATE RPTD:		TIMERPTD:	
ADDRESS:				
BEAT:	DISTRICT:	MAPKEY:		
NOTES:				

When this information has been entered, I ask the database to count all the crimes that have occurred during the last seven days, by beat and by crime type. (If you are using Q&A, here is the command to use with Intelligent Assistant: COUNT FORMS BY BEAT BY CRIME TYPE WITH DATE REPORTED < = 08/07/93 AND > = 08/07/93-6.)

I then enter the figures produced by the database into my spreadsheet, and I check these figures against the previous year's high thresholds to see if any of the crimes I am tracking in each beat are above normal. I also check to see if the citywide high threshold has been exceeded. As I enter the data into the spreadsheet, it recalculates the current year's mean average, standard deviation, and high and low thresholds. This will be used next year.

If everything is at or below normal, then I am done for the day and can spend time working on other projects. This part takes about one hour. If I find a crime is above normal, then I prepare a crime bulletin, which takes several more hours.

A sample graph called "Citywide Burglary Series 1" and a set of crime bulletins are found in figures 3 to 6. Beginning on May 21, I distributed an early-warning crime bulletin declaring a citywide burglary series, because we had exceeded the citywide high threshold. Actually, I had begun alerting some beat officers on May 10 that burglaries within their beats were high, and 10 arrests were made, but the crimes continued to escalate. Patrol got busy working on this problem, and two days later more arrests started. Between May 23 and May 28, patrol made 14 more arrests. On May 28, burglary returned to normal citywide, and as you can see by studying the graph, continued down. On June 2, it dipped below the low threshold, indicating an abnormally low number of burglaries being reported. I cannot prove this effect was caused by the arrests, but I believe we had a direct impact.

FOR LAW ENFORCEMENT USE ONLY

TARGET	CASE	DATE REPORTED	TIME REPORTED	ADDRESS	NOTES
AUTO	93-04055	05/14/93	1744	372 VINE ST	OUTBOARD MOTOR TAKEN FROM BACK OF MOTORHOME.
AUTO	93-04127	05/17/93	1615	1130 EAST MONTE VISTA AV	REAR OF BIG O TIRES - PARTS REMOVED FROM VEHICLE.
AUTO	93-04206	05/20/93	0754	113 EL CERRITO WY	
AUTO	93-04208	05/20/93	0846	447 SHANNON DR	
AUTO	93-04219	05/20/93	1051	106 SILVEY ACRES DR	
AUTO	93-04248	05/20/93	1904	826 DERRY CI	
AUTO		05/20/93	2038	131 EL CERRITO WY	OCCURRED BETWEEN 1800-2000
CMCL		05/17/93	1958	148 VALLEY DR	(TRESPASS) 5 TO 6 JUVENILES CLIMBING FENCE INTO SCHOOL YARD. SOME WERE HMJ.

VALLEY AREA

BEAT 2: 5 Auto Burgs have been reported in Beat 2 during the last 7 days. 2 have been reported in the last 24 hours. This is above normal and may be linked to other series occurring around the city. Below are the known details for all burgs reported during the last 7 days. A map of the auto burgs is attached.

TARGET	CASE	DATE REPORTED	TIME REPORTED	ADDRESS	NOTES
AUTO	93-04074	05/15/93	0954	1900 GLENCREST DR	
AUTO	93-04109	05/17/93	0519	954 SARDONYX WY	HAD JUST OCCURRED - NEIGHBOR HEARD AUTO ALARM. PASSENGER FRONT WINDOW BROKEN. STEREO TAKEN.
AUTO	93-04133	05/17/93	2035	742 PEREGRINE WY	
AUTO	93-04209	05/20/93	0849	190 REVERE CT	
AUTO	93-04214	05/20/93	0943	1213 REPUBLIC WY	
CMCL	93-04184	05/19/93	1004	100 PADAN SCHOOL RD	LITTLE OAK CHILD CARE
RES		05/14/93	1750	1921 ALETHA LN	GLENWOOD ESTATE CONDOS - [redacted], 13 YEARS, TOOK BIKE FROM GARAGE ACCORDING TO 15 YEAR OLD RP.
RES	93-04075	05/15/93	0955	1636 AMAPOLA ST	ITEMS TAKEN FROM GARAGE OF VACANT RENTAL HOUSE.

BEAT 4: Beat 4 is experiencing a Residental Burglary series. 7 Residential burglaries have been reported during the last 7 days; 3 within the last 24 hours. These appear to be linked to the Auto Burg series occurring in Beat 2 due geographical clustering of the crimes. Below are the details of all burglary crimes reported during the last 7 days. There is a map showing the location of all Residential burglaries during the last 7 days.

TARGET	CASE	DATE REPORTED	TIME REPORTED	ADDRESS	NOTES
RES	93-04112	05/17/93	0832	173 COLUMBIA DR	
RES	93-04130	05/17/93	1745	178 WOODBURY CI	(TRESPASS)
RES		05/19/93	1007	607 PRINCETON CT	THEFT FROM GARAGE.
RES		05/19/93	1307	112 DOVER WY	THEFT OF 38 COLT SPECIAL - (IL) IS [redacted]
RES	93-04216	05/20/93	1035	6080 VANDEN RD	CABINETS TAKEN - LINKED TO 93-4217 (VANDALISM) - CITATIONS ISSUED.
RES	93-04247	05/20/93	1853	141 WOODBURY CI	4-PLEX APTS
RES	93-04250	05/20/93	1950	2321 MARSHALL RD	

BEAT 6: Beat 6 remains at or below normal for burglary.

Fig. 3
Sample early-warning crime bulletin

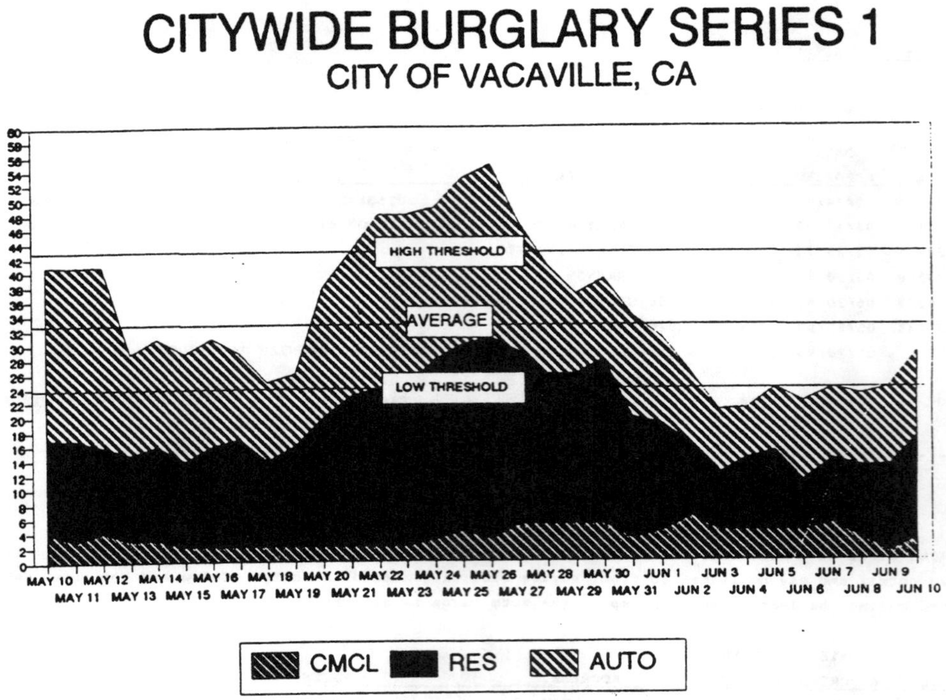

Fig. 4
Crime bulletin: burglary

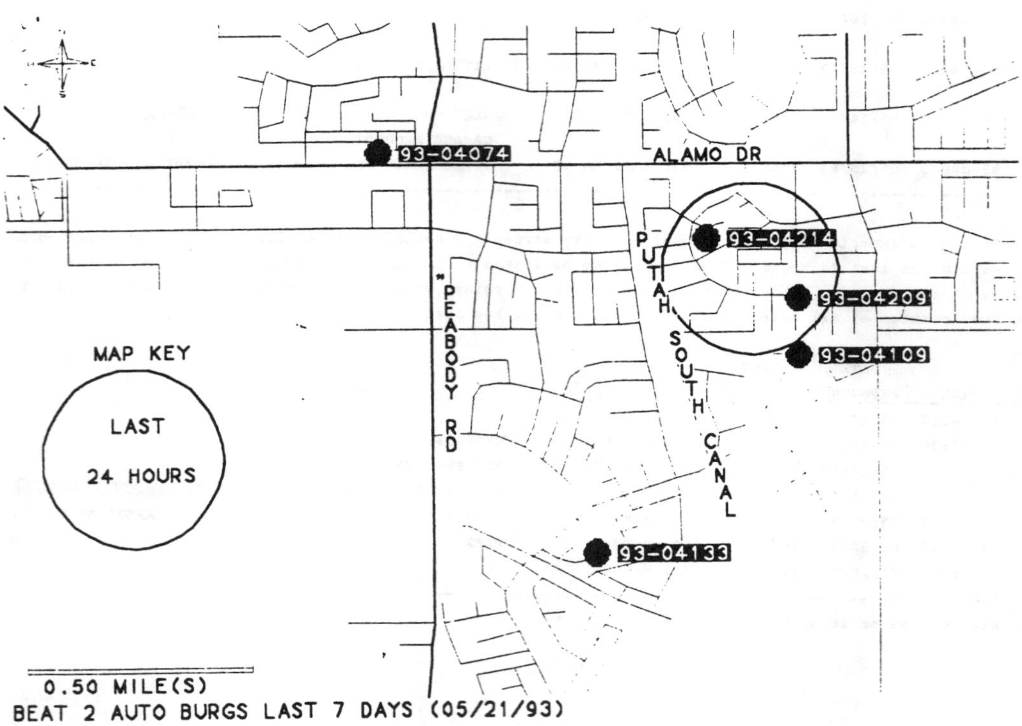

Fig. 5
Crime bulletin: auto burglary, beat 2

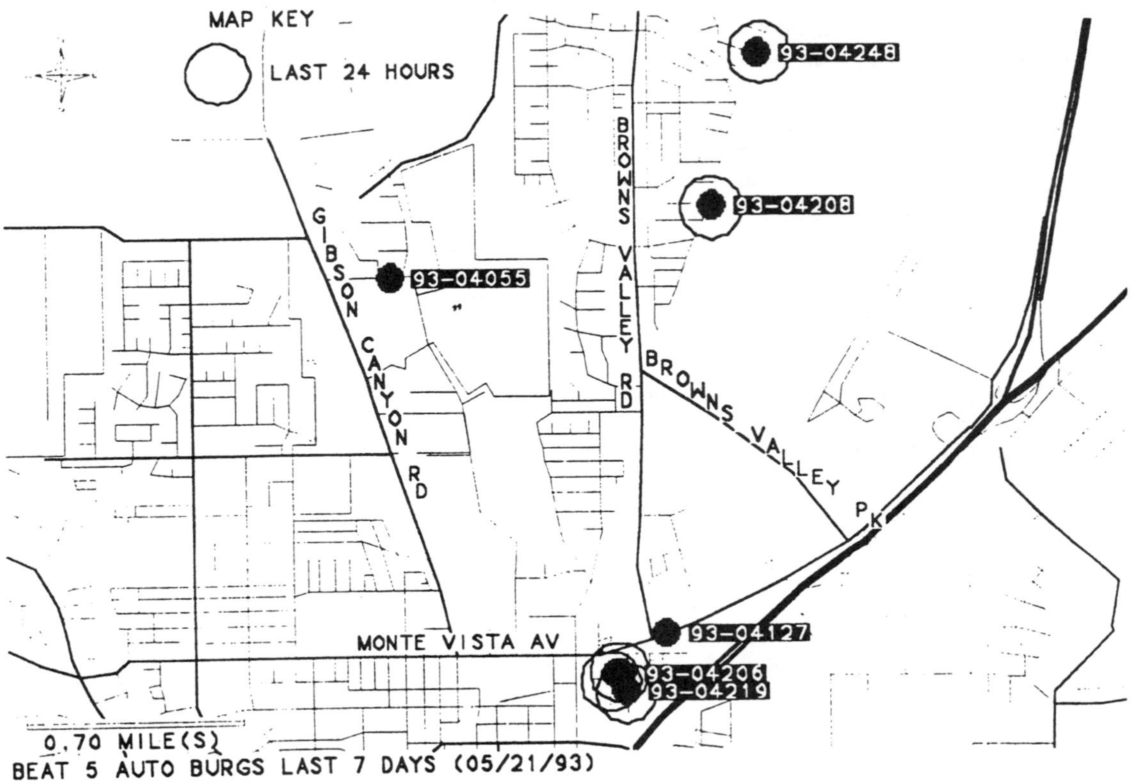

Fig. 6
Crime bulletin: auto burglary, beat 5

WHAT EQUIPMENT IS NEEDED?

To fully implement this system, you will need an IBM PC or 100-percent compatible clone. I recommend at least a 386, 33 megahertz computer with a 125-meg hard drive, six megs of RAM, a VGA screen or SVGA screen, a math coprocessor, and a mouse. The cost should be less than $1,600.

You will also need a printer, and I suggest getting a laser printer. A color printer would be nice for maps but is not essential. A dot matrix printer will print the maps, but the quality is not as good. A laser printer will cost about $800, but it is worth the extra money.

WHAT SOFTWARE IS NEEDED?

You will need mapping software. Maps provide the fastest way for patrol officers to see where crimes are occurring, and computer mapping allows you to produce new maps every day during a series, if needed. Manual pin maps become outdated rapidly and are difficult to maintain. I use "Streets on a Disk" because it is the least expensive ($225), produces high-quality laser maps, and comes with latitude-longitude and *x-y* coordinates already calculated when you buy the county map for your area (an additional $90). All of the mapping companies (including the most expensive) use TIGER files, which are produced by the federal government, so their accuracy is about the same. Some of the more expensive mapping systems offer additional features, which should be carefully examined before making your selection.

You will also need a word processing program to prepare bulletins and a database in which to enter the crimes. I use Q&A because it is a combined database and word processor, is easy to learn and use, and allows for moving database information easily into the word processor. However, there are many other word processors and database programs that will work equally well. Q&A costs about $250.

You will also need a spreadsheet program to store each day's figures for the year. I use QuattroPro because it can store very large spreadsheets and prepares nice-looking graphs. However, there are many spreadsheets on the market that will work equally well. Just be sure you can calculate the mean average and standard deviation for a row of numbers, and that it has sufficient capacity to hold a year's worth of data. QuattroPro costs about $350.

So, for about $3,300, you will have all of the equipment and software needed to operate your early warning system.

If you have any questions regarding this system, please do not hesitate to call me at (707) 449-5607, or write to

Vacaville Police Department
630 Merchant St.
Vacaville, CA 95688

ATTN: Ray Sanford, Crime Analyst

Chapter 18

Computer Mapping and Baltimore County's Crime Analysis Unit

Philip Canter
Baltimore County Police Department

Baltimore County's Crime Analysis Unit formally began in the late 1970s, with the purpose of determining when and where police resources should be deployed in response to spatial and temporal trends in crime. To identify spatial patterns, crime analysts relied on large 2,000-scale wall maps and pushpins. Base maps consisted of Maryland State Highway Administration metroseries maps, which contained all roads in Baltimore County. To mount one wall map of Baltimore County required 12 metroseries maps and 70 square feet. Four of these wall maps were located throughout the unit, with each map dedicated to a particular crime, such as breaking and entering or robbery. Each police precinct was subdivided into reporting areas delimited by streets or other geographic points of reference, such as railroad tracks or power lines. There are over 1,200 reporting areas in Baltimore County. The temporal component was captured by the color of a pin, with white indicating daylight and black indicating nighttime offenses. The size of the pin pertained to the kind of modus operandi, such as breaking-and-entering cases involving the use of pillowcases.

A large amount of an analyst's time was spent on determining where pins should be placed on a map. Due to the large volume of crime, pins were often placed in the middle of a reporting area, which likely approximated the incident's address. Any point clusters formed by pins falling along reporting area boundaries were likely missed. Eventually, the emphasis shifted away from the pins and more toward the number of offenses by reporting area. As a result, some patterns were missed, because point clusters are based on frequency as well as proximity to other offense locations. At the time, nearly all crime data were collected and processed from written reports.

By the mid-1980s, three events moved the Baltimore County Crime Analysis Unit into an automated environment. The first was implementation of a mainframe-based records management system. Although designed to collect and summarize incident and arrest reports for purposes of reporting Uniform Crime Report statistics, additional data elements, such as the address of an offense location, were now available. Furthermore, these data could now be downloaded from a mainframe system to a microcomputer and subsequently imported as a database file. As a result, crime locations could be identified by address, along with any attributive data needed by the analysts to identify and relate trends to geography or offenders.

A second development was the drop in microcomputer costs, coupled with an increase in processing power and storage capacity. Microcomputers were not only becoming affordable, but they were also capable of processing large quantities of data. Databases maintained by the Crime Analysis Unit in a microcomputer environment could now be merged with data maintained at the mainframe level. As a result, incident-based data collected by the Crime Analysis Unit could now be plotted as a point based on an address—provided that the address could be geographically located relative to state plane coordinates or longitude and latitude. Associating a crime location with a coordinate system could be done manually by approximating an address to state plane coordinates using a map atlas, or the procedure could be automated by using a computer-mapping program capable of geocoding locations based on a digital map file. The latter option was preferred, given the savings in time and effort, but it required an accurate digital map file of the county.

The final event leading to implementation of a computer-mapping system for crime analysis involved development of an accurate digital map file for Baltimore County. Baltimore County's old 911 CAD geofile was outdated, causing a number of problems, including police cars' being dispatched to wrong call locations. The Baltimore Region Metropolitan Planning Organization (MPO) had been maintaining a digital map file based on the 1980 census GBF/DME file. This agency was contracted to update its digital file to include new subdivision activity added since the 1980 census. Since this same 911 geofile was also to be used for geographically tracking police cars via an automated vehicle locator (AVL) system, it was important that the file be geographically accurate. Once the geofile had been updated by the MPO, the digital maps were sent to a firm in California (ETAK) for adjustment. All of the ingredients needed to migrate to a computer-mapping environment were now in place.

Baltimore County police analysts had seen MapInfo and felt that the program, if used in combination with our statistical software, could be useful in identifying geographic patterns and trends. The test came when analysts were able to address-match several thousand points relating to drug arrest data using the same 911 geofile as a map file in MapInfo. These maps were included in a grant application to demonstrate how computer mapping could be used to identify drug markets. As a result, Baltimore County received a Bureau of Justice Assistance grant through the state of Maryland for over $100,000, and Baltimore County's Substance Abuse Tracking System was born. This grant allowed the department to buy the hardware and software needed to track and identify drug markets in Baltimore County.

The department was soon demonstrating computer-mapping technology to other county and state agencies. With the coordination of Baltimore County's Office of Planning and Zoning, 14 county agencies bought MapInfo for computer mapping. As a group, these agencies entered into a site license agreement with the MPO to provide quarterly updates to MapInfo map files. There were several advantages to this arrangement, notwithstanding map files' being updated quarterly to account for development and changes in land use at a very reasonable price. In addition, other county agencies now used the same computer-mapping system to assign coordinates to point locations. As a result, the police department has access to geocoded information collected by other county agencies, such as school enrollment data, demographic information, land use, and subdivision activity. This relationship has been critical to the success of the department's scanning functions. For example, we are currently examining drug markets relative to census block group data downloaded from CD ROM, located in the health department, and land-use information collected from Baltimore County's Office of Planning and Zoning. We want to use these data in conjunction with calls-for-service data downloaded from the 911 CAD system to help identify latent drug markets, areas where drug activity is occurring but not being reported. This same information is also being examined for purposes of developing models estimating the impact that changes in land use will have on demand for police resources.

From an application's perspective, computer mapping with point-pattern analysis is an effective tool for analyzing crime. There are numerous examples describing how Baltimore County police use computer mapping and point-pattern analysis, but the following describe some of the more successful applications.

We successfully used computer mapping in conjunction with a statistical examination of case characteristics to explore geographic and behavioral attributes associated with a series of robberies in Baltimore County. This information was used to develop a profile of shotgun robbers who had committed over 70 robberies in Baltimore County and Baltimore City. Based on data collected from police departments in Baltimore City and County, analysts knew when these robberies occurred and where they were likely to occur again within a particular time period and by day of week. Within two weeks of developing this profile, these suspects were apprehended while attempting to rob a savings and loan in Baltimore County. It was an example of how police departments in two jurisdictions, Baltimore City and Baltimore County, could work together to share geographically based data.

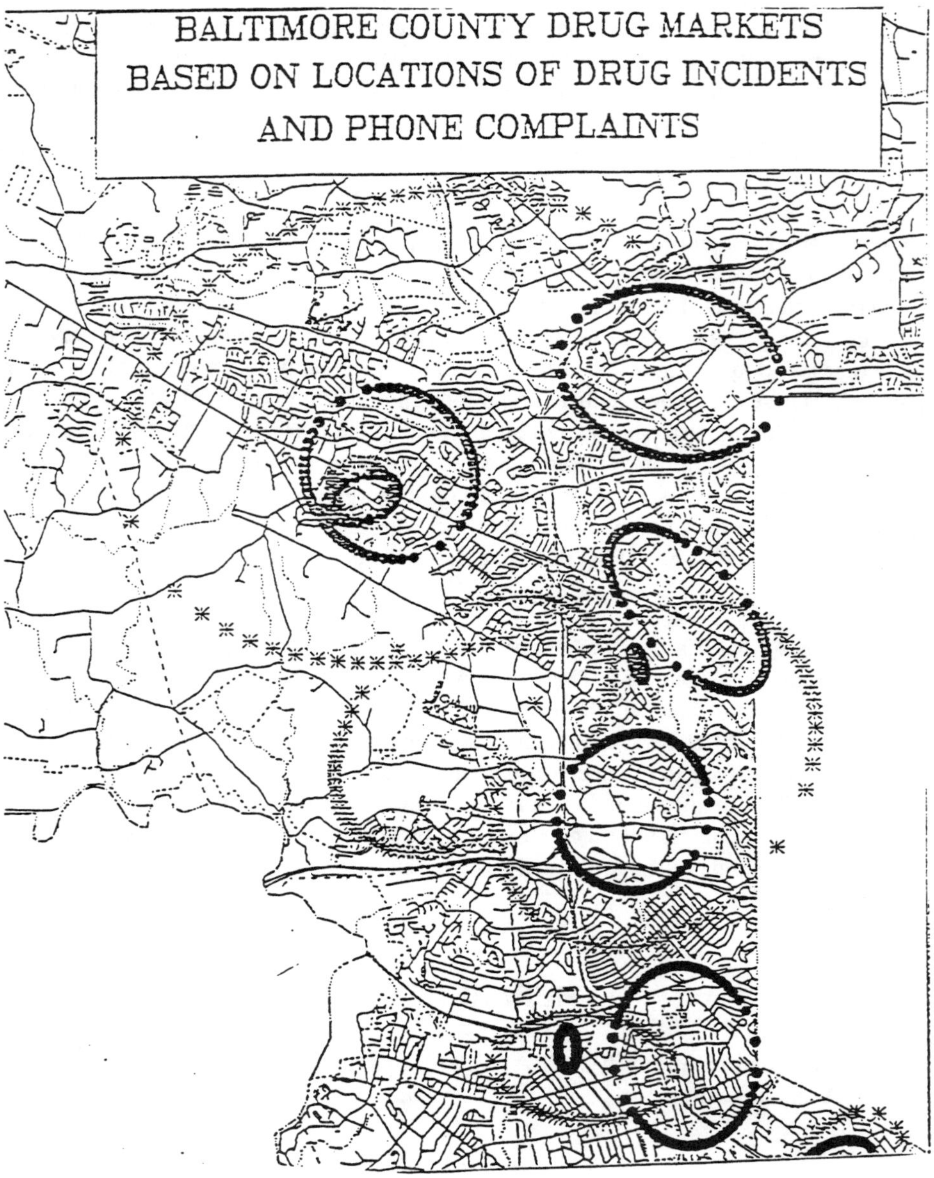

Fig. 1
Baltimore County drug markets based on locations of drug incidents and phone complaints

Analysts have used proximity measures to examine the distribution of crime locations along a highway. Baltimore County's robberies have been increasing steadily over the last five years. Robberies increased 25 percent in 1991 over 1990, and 7.2 percent in 1992 relative to 1991. Highway robberies make up a large percentage of Baltimore County cases. One major roadway in Baltimore County consistently has the highest number of highway robberies, likely due to the large amount of commercial uses in the form of ribbons and centers along the arterial. Analysts were interested in determining whether robbery locations along this highway were randomly distributed. Robberies found to empirically cluster along this roadway were examined to determine factors that may be influencing the location of cases. Using a one-dimension nearest-neighbor analysis, police analysts concluded that cases did not cluster and that the location of cases was probably influenced by opportunity factors.

Baltimore County's Substance Abuse Tracking System is largely based on computer mapping. Data are provided by a number of agencies, but at this time the primary indicators of a drug market are point-specific data pertaining to calls for service, phone complaints and drug arrests. Once points denoting drug activity are geocoded in MapInfo, the STAC (Spatial and Temporal Analysis of Crime) procedure is executed to identify point clusters or "hot spots" (ICJIA 1988). Ellipses are developed for each set of points, representing calls for service, phone complaints or drug arrests. Figure 1 shows standard deviational ellipses produced by STAC for drug incidents (dark dots) and phone complaints (light asterisks).

Analysts map both variables to determine if areas generating phone complaints coincide with drug incidents. Most of the time, there is a real congruence among phone complaints and drug incidents, indicating that the problem has been likely addressed through arrests. There are occasions, however, when phone complaints are generated in an area that has no known drug activity. This will be reflected in an ellipse formed around calls for service or phone complaints that does not correspond to a drug-arrest ellipse. This indicates that drug activity may be occurring that is not known to the department. These areas are identified on a monthly basis and are evaluated by a steering committee, which is responsible for developing strategies aimed at eliminating the market. Police strategies include undercover operations, buy-bust and sweeps, while prevention-side strategies include community outreach programs and treatment centers. Following each strategy is a heavy dose of community policing and high-visibility patrols. Analysts continue to monitor these areas to look for the D.R.U.E. effect (displacement, reduction, unchanged, or elimination) of drug activity. Analysts have noticed each type of effect after various strategies have been used to counter a market area.

Baltimore County's Crime Analysis Unit has evolved over the last several years in response to greater demand and limited resources needed to analyze crime. The Crime Analysis Unit is in the process of going through some significant changes in the way crime data will be processed into information. The unit now has the capability to download files directly from the 911 CAD system, resulting in near real-time data describing the type and location of an offense. We have set up a network to connect various units with crime analysis so that data of common interest can be shared readily. This will help in coordinating strategies among various police units within the department. The unit has come a long way from pin maps, but much remains to be done in the way data are processed into meaningful information. Computer mapping and point-pattern analysis are a start.

REFERENCE

Illinois Criminal Justice Information Authority (ICJIA) (1988). Spatial and Temporal Analysis of Crime. Chicago: ICJIA, Statistical Analysis Center.

Chapter 19

Crime Mapping and the Drug Market Analysis Program (DMAP)[1]

Michael D. Maltz
Departments of Criminal Justice and Information and Decision Sciences
University of Illinois at Chicago

INTRODUCTION

I thought that it would be instructive to give some of the history of the Drug Market Analysis Program that was initiated by the National Institute of Justice in 1986. In particular, I will concentrate on the role that crime mapping played in it, seen from my standpoint, first, as the director of a National Institute of Justice (NIJ)-sponsored crime-mapping project that included participants from the Chicago Police Department, the Chicago Alliance for Neighborhood Safety, Northwestern University, and the University of Illinois at Chicago (UIC); and second, as a member of the Project Advisory Team for NIJ's Drug Market Analysis Program (DMAP).

CRIME MAPPING IN CHICAGO

The project's birth was neither short nor easy. In late 1984, I was approached by a colleague in the School of Engineering, one who lived in the neighborhood of UIC and was active in a local community organization. Although the area had been undergoing gentrification for some time, the crime rate was not insignificant, and he was interested in doing something about it. One of his areas of expertise was spatial pattern recognition, and he was familiar with the use of such techniques by NASA to forecast crop distributions. He felt that the same techniques could be used on crime data, which also vary chronologically and spatially, so that crime could be forecast.

My response to him was that these methods would not be very useful, and I still feel this way despite the fact that some employ them in analyzing crime data. My feeling was (and is) that such techniques would let us know only that crimes occur on weekend evenings in the poorer inner-city neighborhoods, and that they vary according to the weather.[2] Forecasting where a crime might take place would require looking through all of the crime data to see if it was possible to tie specific crimes to specific individuals, and then attempting to infer patterns of those individuals'

1. The opinions expressed in this paper are my own and do not reflect the policies or opinions of the National Institute of Justice, the University of Illinois at Chicago, or any of the other agencies or organizations mentioned herein.

2. Of course, this pattern information has its uses, in terms of the police's setting general deployment patterns based on time of day, day of week, location, and weather. But in terms of my colleague's expectations of using such techniques for tactical purposes, it left a lot to be desired.

behaviors based on their past activity. In other words, the general problem called *crime* had to be parsed into specific problems called *crime patterns* in order to be able to forecast activity. Otherwise, what would result would be so general as to be relatively useless from a crime-control standpoint.

My metaphor for the difference between what standard statistical methods can do and what a map can do is seen in figures 1 and 2. Suppose that between 10:30 and 11 p.m. on a Friday night, four calls for service are received by a police department, all within a mile of each other: a street robbery, an attempted break-in, a smash-and-grab, and a gang fight (figure 1)—in other words, a mini-crime wave.

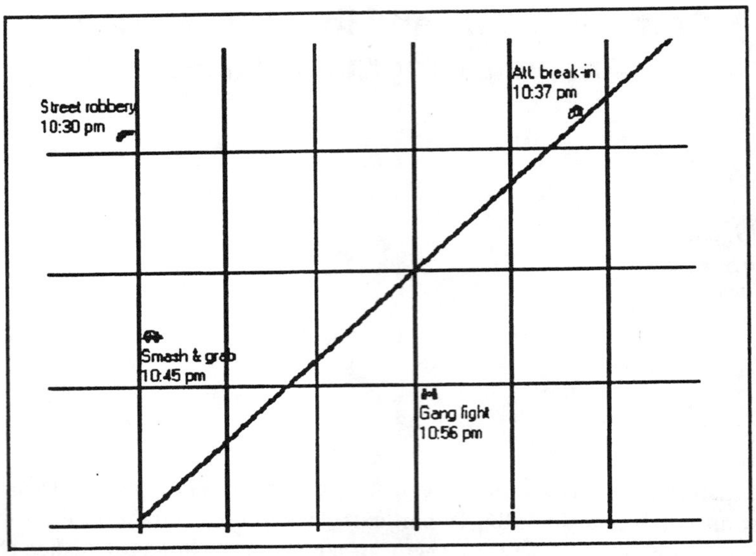

Fig. 1
A "crime wave"

In most police departments, these incidents would be handled by four different officers, especially if they occurred in different beats or different districts. Follow-ups would be handled by different units as well: violent crimes, gang crimes, property crimes. It is likely that no one would tie them together.

Suppose, however, that there is a high school right in the center of this activity and that a high school basketball game between two traditional rivals let out at 10:15 (figure 2). A map showing this event, providing both the social and the geographical context of activity, permits an analyst to relate these four calls for service to each other in ways that computer algorithms cannot.

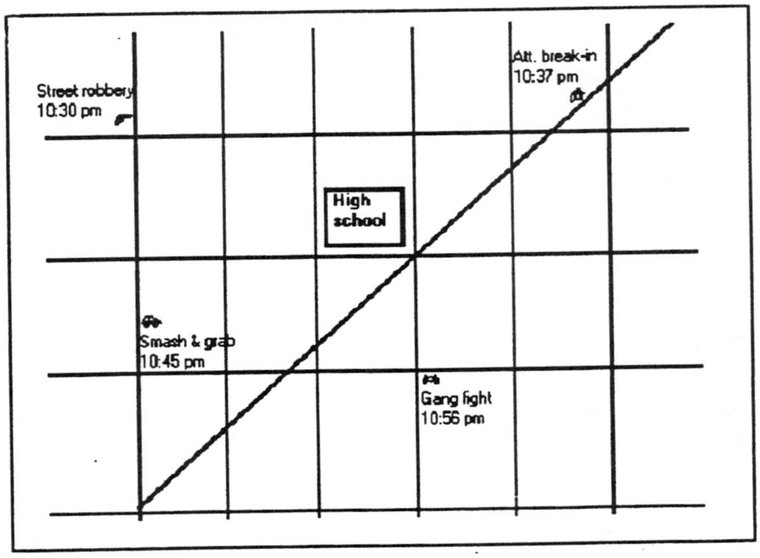

Fig. 2
Context of the "crime wave"

I therefore decided to look into computer mapping as a method of analysis. Personal computers were just beginning to catch on—the first commercially successful personal computer, the Apple II, was only about five years old, and the IBM PC had just come out—and their graphics capabilities and ease of programming made them promising as platforms for computerized mapping. We decided to write a proposal to NIJ to develop and test mapping software to be used for automated crime mapping.

A year earlier, in 1983, Dennis Nowicki, then the deputy superintendent of administrative services of the Chicago Police Department,[3] had created a research advisory committee, consisting of faculty from a number of local universities, to assist him in planning research for the department. It was through his auspices that we were able to obtain the agreement of the Chicago Police Department to develop and test it in cooperation with them and the community group with which my colleague was affiliated, and we sent off a grant application to NIJ in the spring of 1985. Unfortunately (or perhaps fortunately), the project was not funded.

In the fall of 1985, Dennis Nowicki found out that Warren Friedman, then as now director of the Chicago Alliance for Neighborhood Safety, and Andrew Gordon, then on the sociology faculty of Northwestern University and now at the University of Washington, had approached the CPD for access to crime data, for the express purpose of mapping it. They had been using Apple computers to do so, but they were upgrading to the Macintosh because of its greater capabilities. Moreover, they were able to use a commercial software package called Business Filevision to map areas and events with relative ease. I got in touch with them, and we decided to pool our efforts and approach NIJ again; this time we were successful, and our project, "Mapping Crime in Its Community Setting" (Maltz, Gordon and Friedman 1991), began in November 1986.

THE PROJECT'S FINDINGS

The project ran for about two years and was quite successful, more than we had anticipated at the outset, primarily due to the dedication and efforts of Mathias Casey, the commander of the district in which we implemented the project (District 25), and his analysis officer, Marc Buslik. In particular, we found the following:

3. Nowicki is now chief of police in Charlotte, N.C.

Calls for Service

Calls for service are very useful in tactical planning and in community-oriented policing. In the past, they had not been used at all, primarily because of their great number—in 1987, the CPD had over 3 million calls for service, generating over 2 million radio dispatches. But mapping makes them more amenable to rational assessment; when the 113,000 calls for service in District 25 are spread over the district's 12 beats, it averages out to a little over one call per hour.

Proactive Management

In most police departments, middle managers don't have the information available to them to manage effectively. Although all of the activity under their jurisdiction is reported on forms that are entered into computers, the lags between writing the report and having it appear on the computer are often a matter of days. This effectively precludes a commander from making timely deployment decisions. The system we developed for the district commander of District 25 permitted him to gain access to the previous day's activity—and just as important, to prior days' activity, so that he could spot patterns—in a very timely manner. We called this procedure "proactive management," because the commander was able to take command and deploy resources in ways that were not possible without the timely access to data that the system afforded.

Institutional Memory

An automated mapping system helps to reduce the compartmentalization in police departments, by serving as the "institutional memory." A patrol officer may feel that he or she knows his or her beat pretty well, but in actuality, that is not the case. In order to cover a beat over 24 hours, five officers are needed over a year's time, and each may have a different impression about the beat's nature, depending upon whether his or her tour of duty is on weekdays or weekends, at night or during the day, and so on. Furthermore, if the department practices cross-beat dispatching (as virtually every police department does), then half of the incidents in a beat may be handled by an out-of-beat officer; moreover, half of the incidents handled by the beat officer are outside his or her assigned beat. Thus, no single person in the police department knows what's going on in a particular area—no one "owns" it.

In addition, as a rule, patrol officers and detectives don't talk to each other about activity, and in fact may keep information from each other for competitive reasons. Therefore, *the only place where a person can get an overview of all activity on a beat is the map.*[4]

Cognitive Data Analysis

To get back to the original impetus for this project, pattern recognition, we found that mapping was invaluable in spotting patterns. We did not, however, use automated methods to do so. What we found was that we could do a lot better with "cognitive data analysis" than with standard statistical methods. In other words, we put all the information on the maps and allowed the officers to determine what type of patterns might be there. This is also in keeping with Tufte's (1983, 1990) suggestions for handling and displaying complex data.

4. Of course, the same data can be provided by any computer system that can give a listing of all activity on a beat, but a map can make more sense out of it because it locates the activity geographically. We found it useful to augment the map with more detailed information about the incidents portrayed on the map.

For example, suppose that an officer found a number of robberies of dry-cleaning establishments within one mile of expressway on-ramps, occurring right before closing time. Once this pattern is found, it would be possible to develop an algorithm to search crime data for it—but it would not be very helpful. This pattern might never recur, and in the meantime, the "arteries" of the computer would become clogged with this and with all other idiosyncratic crime patterns that individual offenders might follow.

This is not to say that keeping track of crime patterns in an MO file is not warranted. It is very useful, especially for keeping track of sex-crime offenders, where the same pattern might be used over a matter of decades.

THE DRUG MARKET ANALYSIS PROGRAM

The Chicago crime-mapping project was seen by NIJ as one that could contribute to its effort to provide police departments with practical tools to use to combat street drug trafficking. It was obvious to all that the then-current police practices, like buy-and-bust (Moore 1977), were ineffective in stopping drug activity. Another approach that appeared promising, one in keeping with the burgeoning problem-oriented policing movement, was to look on the drug business as a business—that is, as an enterprise that needs a distribution network, customers, advertising, stability of location, supplies, support services, security, and so on, in order to do business and make a profit. Different markets might have different vulnerabilities, depending on the nature of the product, the customers and the location. In particular, since drug markets generally rely on stability of location to ensure that their customers know where to buy their products, a map-based means of analyzing the markets seemed very appropriate.

Craig Uchida of NIJ, who was involved in developing the Drug Market Analysis Program (with the appropriate acronym of DMAP), invited CPD Officer Marc Buslik to Washington to describe our crime-mapping project to prospective applicants for DMAP funding. Police departments from five cities were selected to implement the DMAP concept: Hartford, Conn.; Jersey City, N.J.; Pittsburgh; Kansas City, Mo.; and San Diego. All but Kansas City decided to include mapping in their development of the DMAP concept.

A program advisory team was established for DMAP to advise and to help identify problem areas and share information. It consisted of Alan H. Andrews, then chief of police of Peoria and now retired; Stephen Mastrofski of Pennsylvania State University, who has done a great deal of research on problem-oriented policing; Albert J. Reiss Jr. of Yale University, who has been involved in policing research for over 30 years; and myself. As a result, those of us on the advisory committee have tracked the efforts of the five cities for a number of years. Since San Diego and Jersey City are well represented here, I would like to give you a brief summary of what we found in the other cities.

Hartford focused on choropleth maps and on animating them, showing how drug market activity in general varied geographically over time. However, we had reservations that these averaged maps would be useful only for administrative purposes, but not for tactical purposes—our feeling was that it would be best if individual incidents were plotted, allowing the officers to see each of them. And after they began to use the individually mapped incidents, it turned out that they preferred seeing the individual incidents on the maps; the lieutenant running the sweeps was able to develop useful and innovative tactics. However, the lack of support of this project from some of the units in the department and, more importantly, from the rest of the city agencies, made this project much less successful than it could have been.

Kansas City did not use maps; they became interested in the relative efficacy of different tactics used to close down drug houses, the most common type of sales location in Kansas City. They found that police actions seemed to have little effect on subsequent activity at the same locations.

Pittsburgh found that the maps gave them a whole new way of looking at street drug activity. One of their first map-based applications was just to plot drug-related calls and activity. They were very pleased that this resulted in their finding a drug hot spot that they didn't know existed. Another application they tried was to look at activity before and after suppression actions taken against drug markets. Using maps, they were able to see just how much displacement occurred after closing down hot spots. Third, they were able to show the relationship between drug complaints and gun-related complaints. They found that when drug markets moved, so did gun-related complaints.

The maps were also useful in providing very graphic evidence that helped to target so-called nuisance bars that were the scenes of many drug and disturbance calls for service, and to begin proceedings to close them. It was much easier to convince the state liquor control board to initiate such proceedings using the maps. This effort did not always meet with complete success, because of the legal difficulties involved in closing these establishments. It did, however, have a beneficial effect on those businesses against which proceedings were started.

CONCLUSION

The ways that maps have been used in these and other applications also confirm my belief that detailed maps are better than summary maps or statistics in finding patterns in data. As Tufte (1990:37) says:

> Simplicity of reading derives from the context of detailed and complex information, properly arranged. A most unconventional design strategy is revealed: *to clarify, add detail.*

Standard statistical analyses hide too much from the analyst. To quote Tufte (1990:50) again:

> High-density designs also allow viewers to select, to narrate, to recast and personalize data for their own uses. The control of information is given over to *viewers*, not editors, designers or decorators [or, I would add, programmers and statisticians]. Data-thin, forgetful displays move viewers toward ignorance and passivity, and at the same time diminish the credibility of the source. Thin data rightly prompts suspicions: "What are they leaving out? Is that really everything they know? What are they hiding? Is that all they did?"

I also feel that the direction that mapping should take is to develop methods to show events in time as well as in space. My example of the high school game provides the rationale for this belief: the sequencing of the time of completion of the game and the time of occurrence of the calls for service provides the connection among the seemingly disparate events.

Another addition that police departments should work for is embodied in this example as well: to try to include the community "social calendar" in the map as well. Adding to the mapping information system the times when events start and end, and including the schedules of transit vehicles as well, will provide the police with an "early warning system" for when people are likely to be on the street and vulnerable to crime. This is especially the case during the evening and nighttime hours, when many social events occur, when people are more reluctant to leave home because of fear, and when train and bus schedules are more likely to be followed. The addition of time and social activity to such maps will, I feel, help to make computer mapping live up to its full promise as a means of reducing crime and fear in our cities.

One of the most important lessons from this effort is that police departments and research organizations, when they work together as a team, can do some really good work. The more the two entities understand what the other does and work cooperatively with each other, the better the results. Fortunately, in the computer-mapping field, there seems to be a strong basis for continuing cooperative efforts.

REFERENCES

Maltz, Michael D., Andrew C. Gordon and Warren Friedman (1991). *Mapping Crime in Its Community Setting: Event Geography Analysis.* New York: Springer-Verlag.

Moore, Mark H. (1977). *Buy and Bust: The Effective Regulation of an Illicit Market in Heroin.* Lexington, Mass.: D.C. Heath.

Tufte, Edward (1983). *The Visual Display of Quantitative Information.* Cheshire, Conn.: Graphics Press.

——— (1990). *Envisioning Information.* Cheshire, Conn.: Graphics Press.

Chapter 20

The Chicago Area Four GeoArchive: An Information Foundation for Community Policing

Sgt. Ronald F. Rewers
Case Management Supervisor
Chicago Police Department

Lynn A. Green
Research Analyst
Illinois Criminal Justice Information Authority

INTRODUCTION

The concept of crime analysis introduced by August Vollmer in the early 1900s and moved by O.W. Wilson into the 1960s is now being guided into the 21st century by the Chicago Police Department (CPD). Detectives in CPD Area Four are using the Chicago Early Warning System geoarchive as an information foundation for law enforcement and community decision making and problem solving. This paper will describe Chicago's geoarchive, show how it builds on the concepts of Vollmer and Wilson, and outline how this geographic database was constructed and is being maintained.

THE CONCEPT OF CRIME ANALYSIS

August Vollmer

The concept of crime analysis can be traced back to the early 1900s, when August Vollmer introduced the English technique of systematic classification of known offender modus operandi (MO). In addition, Vollmer pioneered the idea of a nationwide standardized crime classification and reporting system, which evolved into the Uniform Crime Reporting System. He has also been cited as the originator of the modern police records system, the beat analysis based on examination of recorded calls for service, and the concept of pin or spot mapping to visually identify areas where crime and service calls are concentrated. In his essay entitled *The Police Beat*, Vollmer offered the following statement regarding the use of crime analysis to support police operations:

> On the assumption of regularity of crime and similar occurrences, it is possible to tabulate these occurrences by areas within a city, and this determines the points [that] have the greatest danger of such crimes and what points have the least danger (Vollmer 1933:1–2).

O.W. Wilson

The term *crime analysis* was first used by O.W. Wilson in his book *Police Administration* (Wilson 1963:103). Wilson identified crime analysis as an essential police function and recommended that a crime analysis section be created within the planning and research divisions of large police departments. The crime analysis section was envisioned as being responsible for the systematic examination of

> daily reports of serious crimes in order to determine the location, time, special characteristics, similarities to other criminal events, and various significant facts that may help to identify either a criminal or the existence of a pattern of criminal activity (Wilson 1963:103).

Formal crime analysis units were established as a vital part of large police departments in the late 1960s. The crime analysis units were primarily responsible for using crime data to detect criminal modus operandi, discover crime patterns within geographical areas, and look for an association between known offenders and crimes. The following paragraphs will compare this traditional method of crime analysis used for policy decisions at centrally located units with the development of an information foundation—the geoarchive for problem solving at the neighborhood level.

The Early Warning System Project

The original concept for the Early Warning System Project (officially begun in March of 1991 as a collaboration between the Illinois Criminal Justice Information Authority and the Chicago Police Department) arose from extensive research into both homicide syndromes (the Chicago Homicide Project) and geographic statistics (the Spatial and Temporal Analysis of Crime program [STAC]). Analysis of street gang homicide in Chicago reveals specific patterns or spurts of violence over time, area of the city, and type of victim (Block and Block 1992).

The project identifies geographical areas that are at a high risk for street gang-related crimes, specifically violent crimes and other incidents that lead to street gang violence. But in order to identify and target community areas at risk, a vast amount of information is required—not only from law enforcement, but also from other city agencies and the community. The Early Warning System project has assembled data from CPD (such as incidents, victims and offenders) and data from the community (such as locations of abandoned buildings, liquor license addresses and street gang territories) and organized them into an automated database called the geoarchive. Computer-assisted methods (STAC) are used to summarize the data and find hot-spot areas for use in crime analysis and local decision making.

THE GEOARCHIVE

The Early Warning System (EWS) project in Chicago Police Department Area Four is supported by a geographic information system (GIS) called a geoarchive. Characteristics of the geoarchive are address-based data, information about both law enforcement and the community, and analysis that is used at the community level.

The geoarchive functions as an automated institutionalized memory that stores different types of events and places as they change over time for access by the law enforcement officer. The flow chart (figure 1) describes the input sources, information flow and analysis distribution. The geoarchive uses Vollmer's (1933:1–2) 100-year-old vision of crime analysis to determine areas of the city that have the greatest danger of crimes and those that have the least danger, but takes it into the 21st century.

Fig. 1
Early warning system

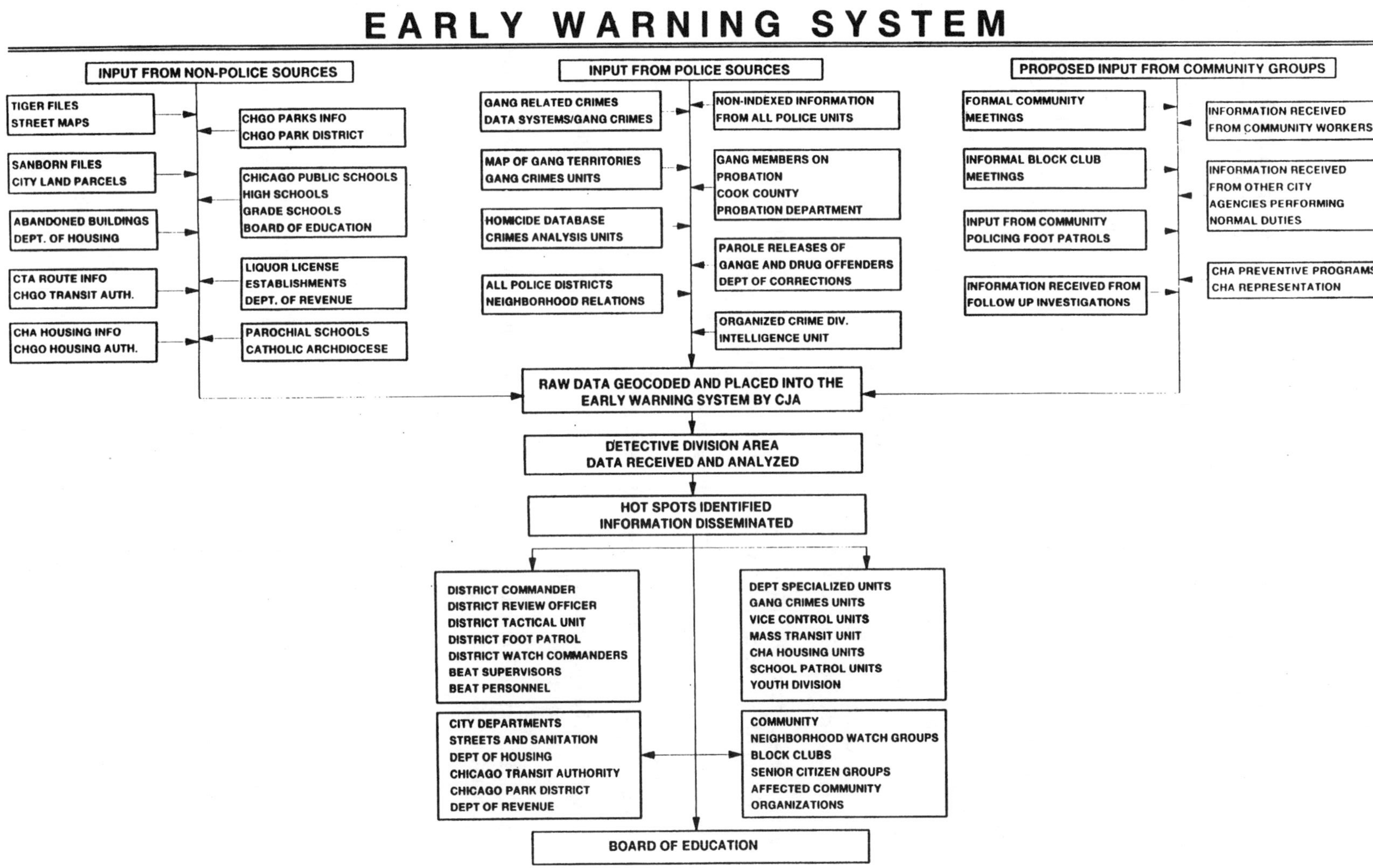

Law Enforcement Data

Source Data

The law enforcement data in the geoarchive are supplied by CPD from the Case Reporting Information and Management Evaluation System (CRIMES) file. The CRIMES file contains information about every incident that has been assigned an RD number, which indicates that investigation has determined that the offense actually occurred. CRIMES contains information from both case and supplementary reports. These reports are entered into the CRIMES file by remote terminal operators at the detective division, area level.

The following are CRIMES source files from which the data for the geoarchive are downloaded:

1. General file—contains 273 fields designed to capture data pertaining to a particular incident. These are fields relating to case type, beat, type of offense, weapon, method codes, crime analysis unit codes, address of occurrence, method assigned, and so on. Vice incidents and traffic incidents are not part of the general file.
2. Vice file—contains 165 fields designed to capture data pertaining to a particular vice incident. According to Bobrowski (1990:25), the vast majority of street gang vice cases involve street-level distribution of narcotics by the gang members.
3. Victim file—contains 75 fields designed to capture data pertaining to the victims of a particular incident. Each victim file record is linked with the incident by RD number.
4. Offender file—contains 99 fields designed to capture data pertaining to perpetrators of a particular incident. Each offender file record is linked with the incident by RD number.

The following files may eventually be added to the geoarchive:

1. Calls-for-service data—taken from radio dispatch cards. These data consist of information recorded by the radio dispatcher when a beat car is assigned to an incident, whether or not an RD number will later be issued.
2. Cook County Probation Department—information collected pertaining to street gang members sentenced to probation by the courts.
3. Illinois Department of Corrections—database of all Illinois prison releasees. This information contains data relative to nicknames, gang affiliation, addresses, and the crime of which the individual was convicted.

Geoarchive Data

The geoarchive data sets differ from the CPD source data sets. Since the EWS project focuses on street gang-motivated violence, data were selected on the basis of codes flagging a record as gang-related and extracted on a monthly basis from the CRIMES file on CPD's mainframe by data division analysts. A street gang-motivated general offense is defined by CPD as an incident motivated by one or more gang situations, including retaliation, recruitment, representing, turf violation, affiliation (or prestige), street fight, personal conflict, and extortion. CPD defines vice street gang crime as any offense related to the street-level distribution of narcotics by street gang members (Bobrowski 1992:32).

The law enforcement data were further streamlined by Area Four detectives and ICJIA staff to include only valuable information in the incident, victim and offender databases and to exclude the fields unnecessary (unused or empty), such as date and detective assigned, and time of data entry. The geoarchive version of the data is described in *The Early Warning System GeoArchive Codebook: Area Four Project* (Green and Whitaker 1994).

On a monthly basis, the Early Warning System project receives updates of five databases of street gang-motivated information: general incidents, vice incidents, general offenders, vice offenders, and victims of general incidents. Each update includes all street gang-motivated data from the first of the year to the date of downloading, including any updates or additions of supplementary case report information.

After these source files are verified and validated, the remaining data are geocoded and introduced into the geoarchive. For a general review of verification and validation processes, see *The GeoArchive Handbook: A Guide for Developing a Geographic Database as an Information Foundation for Community Policing* (Block et al. 1994).

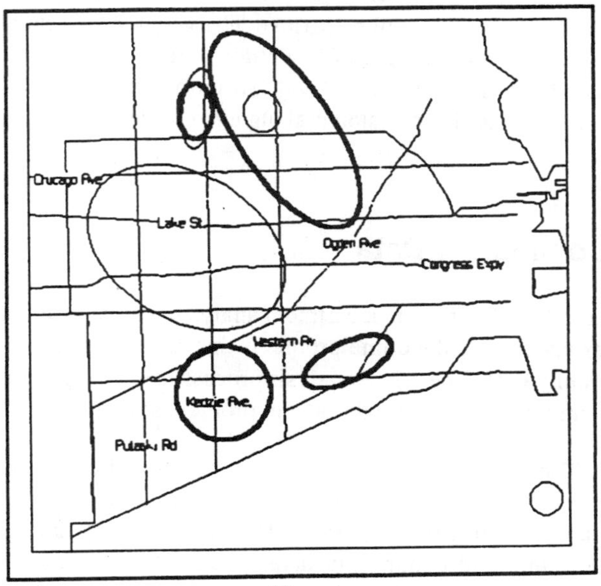

Map 1
Hot-spot areas: violent and drug incidents, CPD Area Four

The general and vice incident files contain detailed information about the characteristics of an incident, date and time of occurrence, address and type of location, gang affiliation, and number of offenders and victims involved. Map 1 shows an analysis of hot-spot areas of violent incidents (thick ellipses) and vice incidents (thin ellipses) in CPD Area Four. Three unique crime problems are illustrated—the neighborhood along the southern boundary has a violent crime problem, the neighborhood in the center has a drug problem, and the neighborhood to the north has both.

The general and vice offender files and general victim files contain specific information on the age, race, gender, and address of all offenders and victims involved in an incident. In the EWS/Area Four project, victim and offender information is linked to the incident data by the record division identification number. As a result, we are able to analyze the relationship between the address of the offenders and the victims involved in different types of street gang incidents. In map 2, the thick-lined hot-spot areas of victims' addresses and the thinner-lined hot-spot areas of offenders' addresses coincide for violent street gang-related crimes.

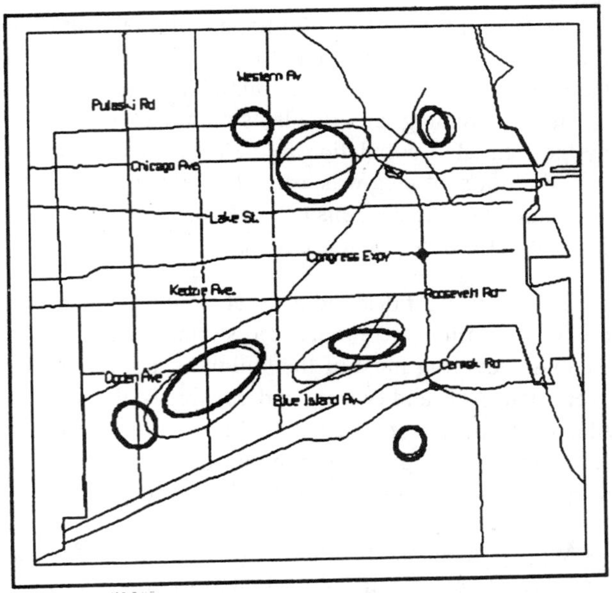

Map 2
Hot-spot areas: locations of victim addresses and offender addresses in CPD Area Four: violent street gang incidents

Data files were created to weigh the severity of an incident by the number of victims or offenders involved, by linking information in the incident file to the victim and offender files. In these files, the incident address is geocoded instead of the victim's or offender's address.

In addition to point files of crime, the geoarchive contains boundary files of CPD jurisdictional boundaries. These files illustrate how CPD has divided Chicago and Area Four into patrol beats and districts. Map 3 is a map of police beats in CPD District 10.

Much of this law enforcement information is in police department information systems, but may not be known or available to every police officer. The geoarchive acts as an institutionalized memory for law enforcement, holding not only a vast amount of law enforcement information, but also community information that is not normally available to the neighborhood-level law enforcement official. The law enforcement data and the community data can be used together for decision making and problem solving.

Community Data

Traditionally, police department analysis consisted of identification of MO patterns for solving crime. In order to better understand the crime problems that law enforcement and the community face today, crime analysts require community data. The crime analysis process using the geoarchive explores the usefulness of community data and the role community factors might play in problem solving.

The community data come from a variety of city, state and federal agencies. The geoarchive contains a street map obtained from the Census Bureau, necessary to map the crime and community data. These TIGER files are corrected and edited on a continuing basis. (For more detail, see R. Block, "Geocoding of Crime Incidents Using the 1990 TIGER File," elsewhere in this volume.)

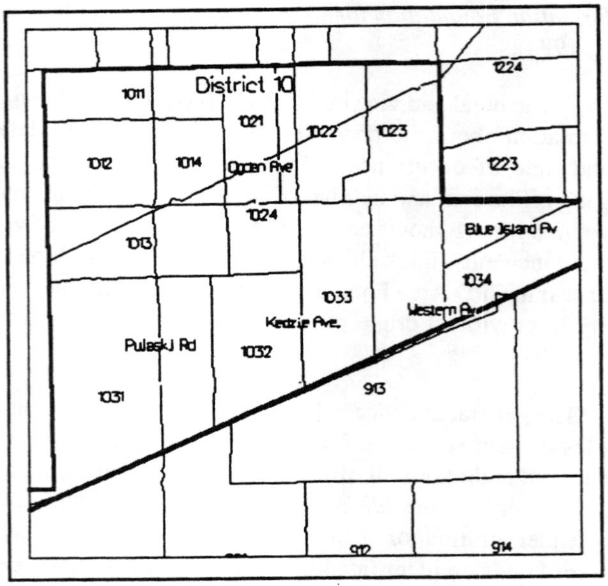

Map 3
Beats in CPD District 10

The geoarchive also contains Census Bureau demographic data. Every census record contains the latitude and longitude of a central point (centroid) of the area (block or other area defined by the census), which makes it easy to link the census information with other law enforcement or community data. For example, in map 4, the rate of Part I incidents per 100,000 residents was calculated by dividing total incidents within a hot-spot area by the estimated population in the area. The population within a hot-spot area was estimated by aggregating the populations of all the census blocks with centroids that fell within the hot-spot area boundary.

One of the most detailed data sets in the geoarchive is the Sanborn file—a computerized structure and land-use database covering most of the buildings and real estate parcels located within the Chicago city limits. It describes every parcel of land (vacant and occupied), the use, the type of building, and its condition. If we were to map this file, it would blanket Chicago. Fields of information were therefore copied to files that would be more useful for analyzing crime. Databases of religious institutions, retail and warehouse spaces, residential corridors, locations of abandoned buildings, and medical buildings were generated.

Another abandoned building file was derived from a file of demolition court cases in Chicago Police Department Area Four. Analysis of hot-spot areas of abandoned buildings and hot-spot areas of vice crime in map 5 illustrates that there is not a direct spatial correlation between the two.

Other community information includes locations of establishments that sell liquor, including liquor stores, restaurants and taverns; locations of high schools and public grammar schools; street gang territory boundaries; public housing; boundaries of public parks; boundaries of community areas; and the location of elevated train routes and stops. Map 6 shows public housing and public parks located in CPD Area Four.

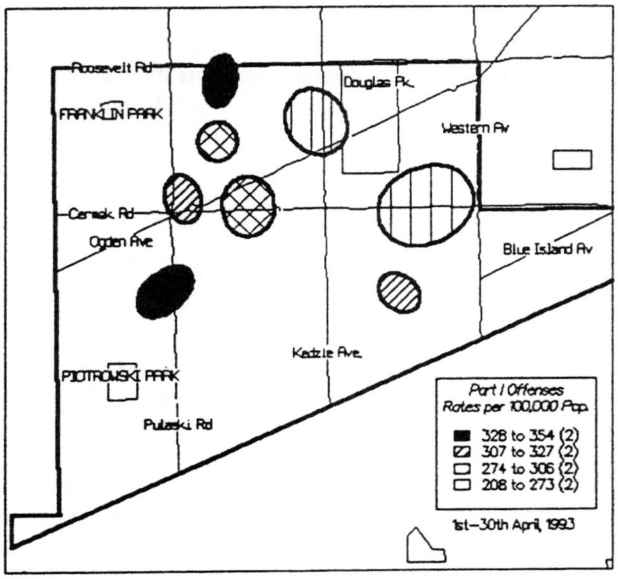

Map 4
Part I offenses: hot-spot areas and rates per 100,000, CPD District 10

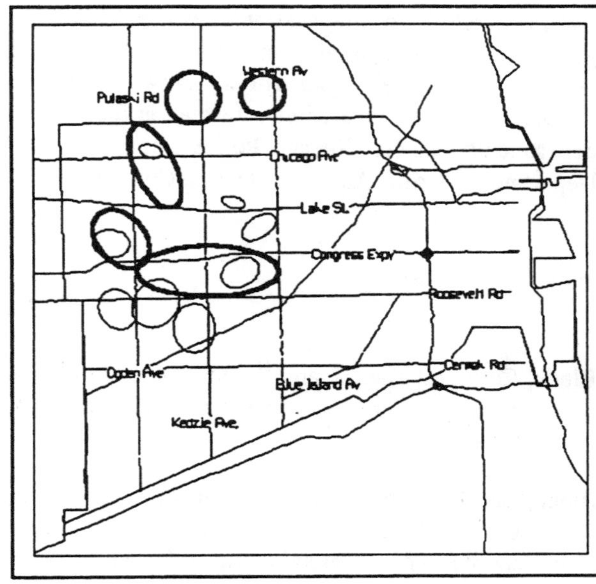

Map 5
Hot-spot areas: abandoned buildings and drug incidents

Street gang territory boundary information was collected from street officers assigned to the gang crime unit and tactical officers in Area Four districts, and continues to be developed with input from community sources.

Detectives in CPD Area Four distribute geoarchive analysis to neighborhood-level law enforcement officials. For example, map 5 (above) shows how community data were used together with law enforcement data for problem identification. Hot-spot areas (densest concentrations) are identified, and the information is disseminated to beat personnel and tactical units at role call.

These geoarchive data are accessible to those who most require it. Questions asked by the neighborhood officer can be answered in his or her district and used to help make more informed and quicker practical problem-solving decisions than ever before.

CONCLUSION

The original concept of crime analysis was that it would be conducted in a centrally located division within the police department, and crime data would be moved down to the street-level officer. The geoarchive is designed so that all the data can be updated, maintained, mapped, and analyzed by police analysts within the district.

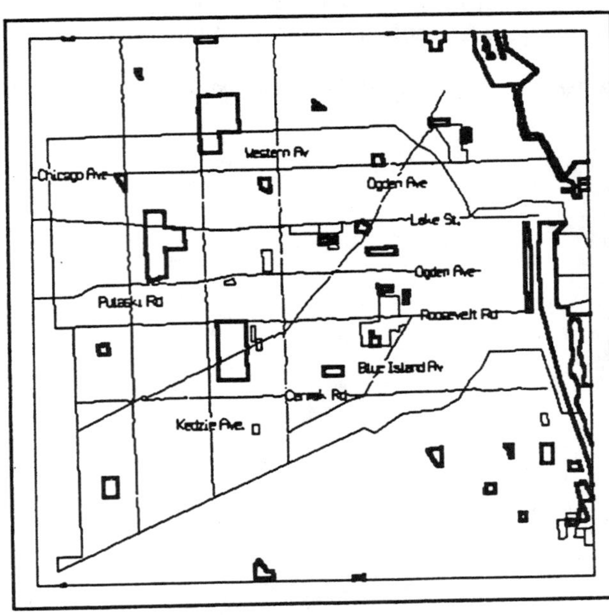

Map 6
Public housing and public parks, CPD Area Four

Transferability of the geoarchive concept to other jurisdictions was considered throughout its development. The project is organized and documented so that not only can district personnel use it in daily decision making and problem solving, but the system will also serve as a prototype for application in other police departments throughout the nation. Today, the geoarchive information foundation is serving in this prototypical capacity for two Illinois police departments—in the Chicago Police Department's Crime Analysis Technology project, and in the Joliet Police Department's Crime Analysis Through Computer-Mapping project.

REFERENCES

Block, Carolyn Rebecca, and Richard Block (1992). Homicide syndromes and vulnerability: Violence in Chicago's community area over 25 years. *Studies in Crime Prevention*, vol. 1. Oslo/Stockholm: Scandinavian University Press.

Block, Carolyn Rebecca, Richard Block, Lynn M. Higgins, and Lynn A. Green (1994). *The GeoArchive Handbook: A Guide for Developing a Geographic Database as an Information Foundation for Community Policing.* Chicago: Illinois Criminal Justice Information Authority.

Bobrowski, Lawrence J. (1988). Collecting, organizing and reporting street gang crime. Presented at the American Society of Criminology meetings. Chicago Police Department, Special Functions Group.

Green, Lynn A., and Robert Bennett Whitaker (1994). *The Early Warning System GeoArchive Codebook: Area Four Project.* Chicago: Illinois Criminal Justice Information Authority.

Vollmer, August (1933). Remarks at the 1932 annual conference of the International Association of Chiefs of Police, in Portland, Ore. Published in *The Police Yearbook: Official Proceedings of the 40th IACP Annual Conference.* Alexandria, Va.: International Association of Chiefs of Police.

Wilson, O.W. (1963). *PoliceAdministration.* New York: MacGraw-Hill, Inc.

Chapter 21

Mapping Software and Its Value to Law Enforcement

Mark Stallo
Dallas Police Department

Across the country, many police departments are moving toward community-based or problem-oriented policing. Community-based policing is predicated on the concept that the police department should interact more closely with a community to solve problems and improve the quality of life. In order for this to work effectively, police departments and citizens need to share crime and police-related information. Unfortunately, many police departments only track or plot crime as it relates to traditional police boundaries. Some police departments have transformed their boundaries to accommodate the use of census or other demographic data. In other words, many police departments must evaluate crime statistics on a citywide basis or by artificial beats or reporting areas. A solution to this problem can come from a variety of mapping software programs. This software can be adapted to customize neighborhoods, crime watch groups and other more community-oriented boundaries.

Many benefits can be derived by using mapping software. Mapping provides the ability to display data in a variety of geographical forms, which makes identifying trends and patterns much easier. The data can be displayed by points in relation to boundaries, thematically and so on. Simply stated, it makes use of the old adage "a picture is worth a thousand words." The type of data is limited only by one's imagination. Today, data can be transferred from many sources into a database-compatible format, which can be read into most mapping software. The greatest expense with most mapping software involves the time required by personnel to become knowledgeable with the program. This process can range from a few weeks for basic usage to several months for more advanced applications. Nevertheless, the underlying assumption is that individuals will use the software on a regular basis to keep their skills at an optimal level.

The emphasis of this article is to demonstrate how to combine police-related information with other data, such as census tracts, for more effective decision making. As police departments and the citizens they serve become more familiar with each other and the specific problems related to individual neighborhoods, community-based policing will become more effective. Many times, information related to community activities and potential community problems (drug houses, bootleg houses and so on) is not analyzed together by the police department and citizens. This analysis can be most effective when the police accept and use current community input to analyze ongoing community problems. Examining all information related to the community (number of churches, schools and hospitals) can be directly linked with criminal activity, including crime, vice information and demography data.

By working with crime watch groups and neighborhood associations, the police department and the citizens can make informed decisions. All relative information about a neighborhood can be analyzed before a plan of action is developed. This article will explain that, by linking relationships within a community and using computer mapping software, a neighborhood can improve its access to information and increase its capability to improve the quality of life. Nevertheless, it is critical that the data related to this neighborhood be timely. Analysis is useless if the data being evaluated are several weeks old.

Initially, most would conclude that a mapping software package is useful for displaying dots or squares on a map, showing various occurrences of crime, calls for service or arrests. Often, the map covers a small neighborhood, showing these crimes or calls in close proximity to each other. Although this can be useful, there are many more procedures for analyzing and displaying the data. For example, Dallas police officers have always suspected that violent crimes resulted near drug-trafficking areas. Yet this was difficult to demonstrate until the violent crimes were mapped over suspected drug house locations. A very strong correlation was shown (see map 1). This type of information, in conjunction with other intelligence information such as bootleg houses, vacant buildings and so on, assists the police command staff in deciding where to deploy police personnel and conduct covert operations.

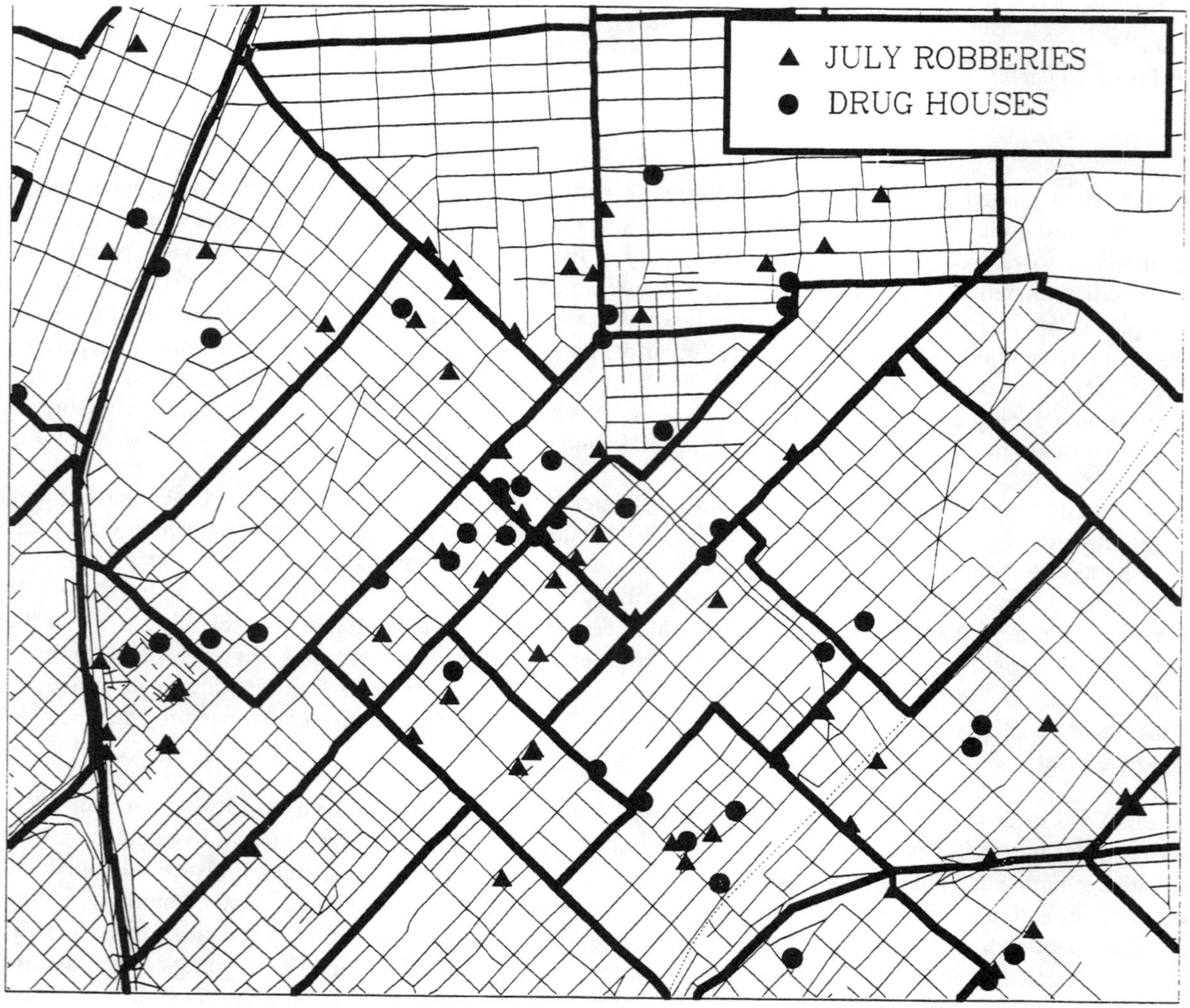

Map 1
Correlation between crime and drug house locations

Mapping software enables all of the neighborhood problems to be observed at one time. Furthermore, as these community problems are resolved, the impact of this action can be measured by reviewing recent occurrences of crimes or calls on a neighborhood map. This opens a dialogue with the citizens about their insight into the police department's approach to making their community a better place. The need for open communication with citizens and increased community involvement is paramount to community policing. Mapping specific calls, crimes or arrest data brings the message home, thus motivating local citizens to get involved.

There is a wide variety of information that has already been developed and that can assist police agencies in better serving their communities. For example, the Census Bureau has published extensive information related to populations in every community across the country. This information is at the census-block level, which is a very small geographical boundary. (There are 310 census tracts and approximately 20,000 census blocks within the city of Dallas.) Also, there is significant information on the tract level, which is a conglomerate of census blocks. This information can assist police departments with understanding the population by race, income, occupancy information, and the value of housing in neighborhoods. This can be invaluable in customizing a plan to improve a neighborhood. Crime and other related police functions are the major components missing when an analysis of a neighborhood is conducted. This problem can be corrected by associating as much data as possible with neighborhood boundaries. The integration of police data, demographic data and other information can improve the planning process.

The boundary function of most mapping software is equally important for analysis purposes. For years, police departments have divided their cities by reporting areas (districts), beats, sectors, and divisions (bureaus or precincts). These boundaries are assigned a number, and the entire police operation is driven by these boundary names. Beats and car assignments are designed by these boundaries; however, very few people know where the boundaries are located without seeing them mapped and displayed on paper. Often, police boundaries are ranked by crime volume, without regard for how close each boundary is located to another. Today, a computerized map provides a means for displaying a variety of layers of boundaries, from the smallest to the largest, as they relate to the city. For example, other frequently used boundaries, such as census blocks and tracts, crime watch boundaries, council districts, and public housing, can be layered to show a specific correlation. The data displayed can be linked to existing data about geographical areas, such as crime to census data.

A variety of significant factors makes these boundaries extremely useful. For instance, by using a boundary, the map contained within it can be developed into a separate map. Data within a boundary can be counted, singled out for display or analyzed in several ways. In addition, many police departments are only able to report crime by designated police boundaries. This occurs because many departments have not perceived a need to produce statistics by communities or other nonpolice boundaries. A mapping package provides the ability to report crime in a flexible manner.

Data read by mapping systems can be in a variety of formats. Police-related information ranges from crimes, calls for service, arrests, known offenders, and suspected drug house locations, to several other categories. By using base boundary data, such as the name of a boundary, data can be collected into one database, as it relates to any specific boundary. The police data can also be added to other list data, such as population, property value and other census data. Furthermore, it can be determined if a crime victim and/or suspect(s) fit the general profile of the inhabitants of the neighborhood. Did the complainant come to shop, buy drugs or attend an event? In addition, any data with an address can be associated to a boundary.

Once the data have been added to the system, several options exist for using the data. Data can be searched in multiple ways. The data that are displayed on the computer screen can also be counted and interpreted. If a crime pattern is visually observed, the computer can provide a report of the incidents that are displayed on the screen. There are numerous types of data searches. A typical search might be to find a certain type of crime that occurred in a particular time frame, with a similar method of operation and similar suspect descriptions. This analysis can be handled outside of a mapping program or within. Either method will create the search. Distance searches can be more efficiently covered within mapping software. Diameter searches or what you see is what you get (WYSIWYG) on the computer screen can also be conducted within mapping software.

Throughout the previous paragraphs, several concepts have been covered. Sample uses of a mapping system can be used to explain these concepts. The use of tabular data that is related to a boundary, such as the number of murders or the number of disturbance calls by reporting area or beat, is a basic but important function. Tabular data can be related to the boundary within the mapping program. The data are then displayed by a colored or shaded thematic map, which gives a quick overview of the density of crimes or calls within any type of geographic area as compared to other similar geographic areas (map 2). Another key factor in examining boundary data is the use of population data. For example, if a black male is the victim of a crime in a predominantly white or Hispanic neighborhood, what brought the black complainant to the neighborhood? This type of analysis helps to pinpoint community problems.

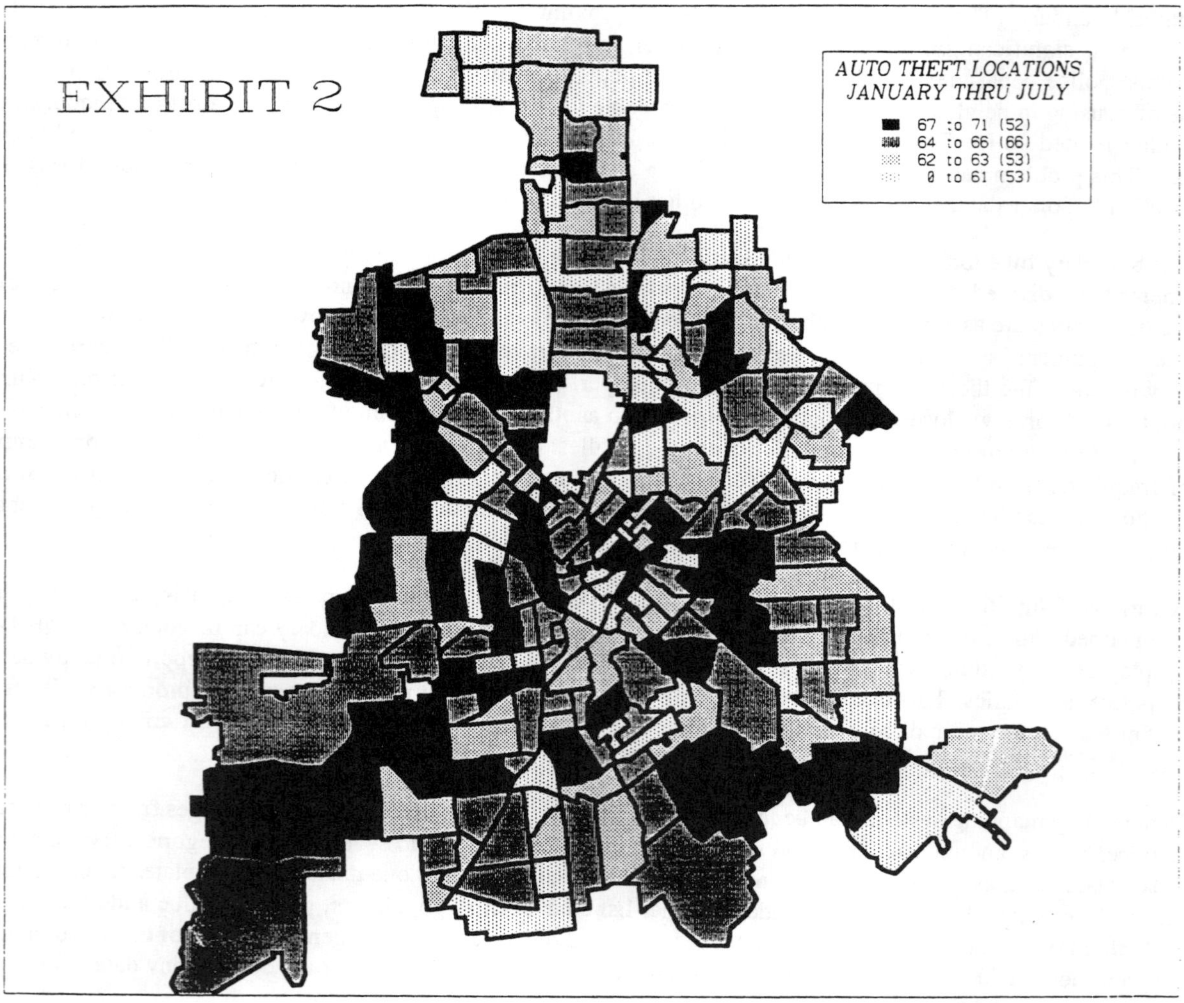

Map 2
Auto theft frequency: Dallas police districts

Mapping software can be a very useful tool within the law enforcement field. Many useful mapping software packages are on the market today. The prices and functions of these packages vary widely. Prices range from $1,000 to many times this amount. Some packages can perform very exact engineering functions, while others are designed for the purpose of displaying information. Many of the mapping softwares can interact with a variety of other software, such as spreadsheets and databases, which broaden their function. Some softwares can read data only from within a standard programming environment, while others can read data from unlimited sources. Use of this technology provides versatility and produces the capability to perform a wide variety of studies. Therefore, it is important to consider a police department's current and future needs before purchasing mapping software. Many times, it may be practical to purchase a relatively inexpensive program while the more complicated package is being developed.

Mapping software operates on several platforms, including the mainframe environment, UNIX, Macintosh, Windows, and DOS. These softwares have a wide array of uses, but all contain three basic components: maps, boundaries and data. One other very important distinction must be made. Maps can be displayed in multiple formats; however, this article has been limited to vector (line map) and raster (pictorial map) capabilities. Mapping brings about tremendous opportunities for observing data. The most effective method of explaining how data can be displayed is to outline a few examples of the major functions of typical mapping software.

There are other more general uses of mapping software, such as designing parade routes or drawing landmarks inside of the map for a special event. It is also possible to import building designs and display building plans, floor by floor. This is useful for tactical operations or when evaluating offenses inside multilevel buildings. In some areas of the country, agencies have the ability to link the streets (vector images) to a map of the underlying terrain (raster images), which opens a wide variety of applications, such as crime scene search, auto accident reconstruction and emergency preparedness. The future of mapping in law enforcement is wide open and bounded only by one's imagination.

Chapter 22

Geographic Analysis to Support Community Policing: An Information Foundation for the Future

Douglas Hicks
Sgt. Jim Wilson
Crime Analysis Section
Systems Development Division
Minneapolis Police Department

INTRODUCTION

The challenge presented to us was to illustrate the variety of mapping products and community sources of data that we use to support community crime prevention and control decisions, and to speak to what the future may hold. We have selected a variety of products to share with you here. We have also developed many more crime analysis tools to assist investigators with serial offenses, cases with unknown suspects and complex matrix comparisons of cases.

MPD CRIME ANALYSIS MAPPING ENVIRONMENT

Minneapolis has had a geographic information system for about 15 years that is capable of incorporating data from a variety of sources. This system has been used to provide a clear picture of crime and other related data to the public. The base geographic information system has been customized by Geographic Software Specialists, Inc., to make it easy for personnel inexperienced with computers to swiftly produce complex products. Our system is set up to use individually selected crime categories or defined map legends and predefined report structures, such that for any crime type and any level of geographic zoom one can get consistent output reports. Our geographic crime information system has been built to free us from the overwhelming complexity of GIS programming, and to allow us to perform the jobs we need easily.

The MPD currently has its primary data in a Unisys mainframe. Data are transferred each morning to the GIS system for crime analysis. For all practical purposes, the only data not transferred to the GIS are the case narratives, and they are available to the GIS via a data server. The information in the GIS is current with offense and arrest data available since January 1990.

The MPD crime analysis section receives many requests from investigators, beat patrol officers, community crime prevention/SAFE (our community policing arm), precinct commanders, city council members, and so on. To individually satisfy these requests would be very time-consuming and impossible to accomplish, given the current crime analysis staffing. To solve this problem, the crime analysis mapping tool has a batch processing option that allows us to specify the requested mapping and report output configuration and date range. When activated, it produces literally hundreds of maps and reports a week to supply the information needs of our department. To meet the public's need, one output report is designed to contain only public-level information.

Our crime analysis mapping computer (a Hewlett Packard/Apollo 433s) is centrally located. Maps are printed on a Tektronix RGB color screen copy device, allowing us to make an image every 35 seconds.

The MPD information system has evolved and moved from the mainframe to a PC network. This move has given us great flexibility. The new system allows for maps to be produced from any system report that has case number reference. It also allows users anywhere on the PC network to view mapping products stored in a central file. Users can select the map image they want to see, view it, zoom in or out to the level they desire, manually select groups of cases, and generate printed reports to summarize the selected cases. This feature has put spatial crime analysis at the fingertips of literally hundreds of users in our department.

COMMUNITY AND MAPPING DATA

Below are examples of "community data" that have been developed and used to deal with crime problems in Minneapolis. I will discuss them grouped by the city department using the product. Many of these products were created by the city's Public Works Engineering and Design Office, since they have been the longest user of the GIS and are a central repository of many different types of data and talents. Most of these products were originally in color and are not as impressive in black and white. I hope you can use your imagination to add color to the images.

MPD Community Crime Prevention/Safe (CCP/SAFE)

CCP/SAFE responds to livability issues in our city's neighborhoods. It teams civilians with sworn officers to resolve community problems and to establish block watch groups. Minneapolis has 84 neighborhoods, many of which have very active resident associations. The crime analysis section supplies crime information weekly to CCP staff by neighborhood and supplies maps monthly or on demand.

CCP/SAFE uses the neighborhood maps and information to keep themselves aware of crime patterns, to produce articles for neighborhood newspapers (figure 1) and to generate crime alerts (figure 2). They also produce summaries for block captains.

SOUTHEAST JUNE 1993

COMMUNITY POLICING

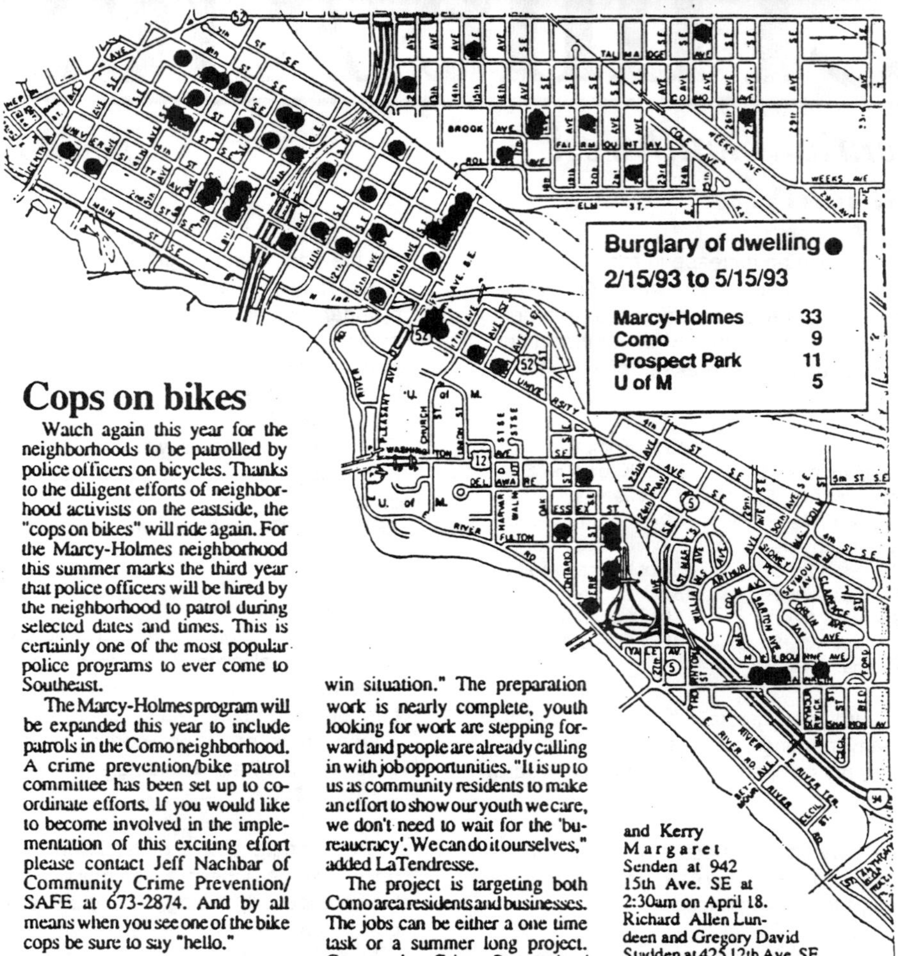

Cops on bikes

Watch again this year for the neighborhoods to be patrolled by police officers on bicycles. Thanks to the diligent efforts of neighborhood activists on the eastside, the "cops on bikes" will ride again. For the Marcy-Holmes neighborhood this summer marks the third year that police officers will be hired by the neighborhood to patrol during selected dates and times. This is certainly one of the most popular police programs to ever come to Southeast.

The Marcy-Holmes program will be expanded this year to include patrols in the Como neighborhood. A crime prevention/bike patrol committee has been set up to coordinate efforts. If you would like to become involved in the implementation of this exciting effort please contact Jeff Nachbar of Community Crime Prevention/SAFE at 673-2874. And by all means when you see one of the bike cops be sure to say "hello."

Como youth project

Parents, neighbors and youth who live around Van Cleve Park have been getting together over the past few months to help find more productive activities for our youth to be involved in. Sparked by recent events and concerns about vandalism and other problems they all came together to discuss their common ground. Out of these meetings came the Como Youth Employment Project.

"It is really quite simple," said block leader Sue LaTendresse, "We have lots of people in the neighborhood who could use help with jobs around the house and yard. Plus we have youth with time on their hands who could use a few extra bucks. All we need to do is get them together. The project is a win-win situation." The preparation work is nearly complete, youth looking for work are stepping forward and people are already calling in with job opportunities. "It is up to us as community residents to make an effort to show our youth we care, we don't need to wait for the 'bureaucracy'. We can do it ourselves," added LaTendresse.

The project is targeting both Como area residents and businesses. The jobs can be either a one time task or a summer long project. Community Crime Prevention/SAFE will be helping implement the program with Como area volunteers. If you have a task or chore that you could use help with, are a youth or have a youth looking for summer employment, or would be willing to help mentor a youth worker, call Candice or Don at Van Cleve Park, 348-8131. They will take your name, address, phone number, then someone will get back to you to work out the details.

Noisy party tags

Minneapolis Police issued 10 tickets in Southeast from April 18 to May 15 for violation of the city's noisy party ordinance. Those who got tags were:

Albert John Born, Christopher Alan Wunsch, Jason Scott Bump, Todd Michael Burkhardt, Joseph Moran Ray and Kerry Margaret Senden at 942 15th Ave. SE at 2:30am on April 18.

Richard Allen Lundeen and Gregory David Stadden at 425 12th Ave. SE at 4:00 am on April 18.

Bradley Mark Lewis, Christopher Kit Hagen and Jonathan Louis Scherling at 1112 14th Ave SE at 12:30 am on April 24.

Jennifer Lynne Burgy and Jennifer Ann Kellimer at 1018 University Ave. SE at 11:50 p.m. on April 24.

Arne Magnar Rimmereide and Alan Edward Sneve at 608 Erie St. SE at 1:20 am on April 25.

Patrick John Tepe, Matthew Gilbert Jelinek, Jon Rinde Florence and Kurt Allen Benoer at 814 Essex St. SE at 2:00 am on May 1.

Stephen Anderson II, William Marcell Grape and Jonathan Way at 1203 8th St. SE at 2:18 am on May 8.

Michael Scott Armstrong and Lynn Ann Schnathorst at 1815 University Ave. SE at 3:39 am on May 14.

Eric Joel Wulff at 1109 17th Ave SE at 11:20 pm on May 14.

Alan Mitchell Delaney and Devang Bhaktakumar Shah at 2625 Cole Ave. SE at 12:15 am on May 15.

Fig. 1

Map for a neighborhood newspaper

Crime Alert

Attention Southwest Residents!

June 14, 1993

There has been an increase in reported garage burglaries throughout southwest Minneapolis. Listed are the approximate addresses in order of occurrence, starting on June 8 through the present. (Most occurred on the weekend of June 11, 12, 13.)

54xx Newton Ave. S.
58xx Pleasant Ave. S.
59xx Pillsbury Ave. S.
39xx Thomas Ave. S.
52xx Washburn Ave. S.
52xx Vincent Ave. S.
50xx Thomas Ave. S.
51xx Sheridan Ave. S.
59xx Newton Ave. S.
51xx Thomas Ave. S.
57xx Knox Ave. S.
58xx Knox Ave. S.
57xx James Ave. S.
50xx Upton Ave. S.
52xx James Ave. S.
56xx Morgan Ave. S.
57xx Logan Ave. S.
58xx Logan Ave. S.
48xx Grand Ave. S.

These burglaries are taking place during late night, early morning hours. Most times, entry was gained by prying open service doors with a screw driver.

There is very little suspect information. In one case, two men were seen near a garage that was later found to be burglarized.

Here are some suggestions on securing your garage's overhead door, service door, and windows:

Overhead door:
- If you have a service door, install a padlock 1/4 inch above a roller in the overhead door's track when the door is in a closed position.
- If you do not have a service door, install an electric garage door opener.

Service door:
- If the door is panelled or hollow-core, reinforce it.
- If the door doesn't contain glass, use a medium- or heavy-duty single or double cylinder deadbolt lock.
- If the door contains glass, use a medium- or heavy-duty double cylinder deadbolt lock or reinforce or cover the glass.
- Install a maximum-security strike plate secured with 3-inch screws.

Garage windows:
- Cover your windows with curtains or reflective plastic so people can't see what you keep in your garage.
- Place a grille or bars over windows to secure permanently.

What else can I do?

Lighting can often deter nighttime burglaries. Consider installing motion detector lights. These lights are activated by motion and will automatically turn on if someone walks up to your garage. These lights are most commonly placed on garages. They are available at hardware stores for about $20.

- Put your neighborhood watch force to work (or get one started). Keep a watchful eye out on your block, especially during dark hours, when these burglaries are occurring.
- Call 911 if you see suspicious behavior! Someone prying at doors or appearing to be casing garages, for example, are things the police should know about. Call 911!

For additional information on crime prevention, improving garage security, neighborhood watch, Operation Identification, or free home security checks, call Jim Long (673-2819) or Officer T.J. Johnson (673-2820).

CRIME PREVENTION
COMMUNITY CRIME PREVENTION/SAFE
217 South Third Street
Minneapolis, MN 55401-2139
(612) 673-3015
"Community and Police Working Together"
FAX (612) 673-2512

CA-5
JL/6.14.93

Fig. 2
Example of a crime alert

STEVENS AREA MANAGERS & OWNERS ASSOCIATION

1820 Stevens Avenue So., Suite D, Minneapolis, MN 55403 • 612 / 870-0901

October 12,1990

Honorable Judge Rob Lynn
Hennepin County District Court
Minneapolis, Minnesota 55487

Re: Plea bargain case of Arnell Rucker
Case number MP9008223180 COCAINE/Narcotics Violation

HONORABLE JUDGE ROB LYNN:

Enclosed please find a **COMMUNITY IMPACT STATEMENT** comprised of letters composed by the citizens who live and work in the Stevens Park neighborhood. Collectively, we are requesting that you impose stricter sentencing than the maximum guidelines suggest. You will understand from our letters that Stevens Square has come as far as it can in terms of organizational cohesiveness through the work of our coalitions and task forces.

The following letters speak for themselves. While it is true that we are recognized as one of the best organized neighborhoods in the inner city through our own sheer determination, police support, internal community resources and outside agencies- we feel we are now at the mercy of your court. As we prepare this first DRUG-FREE ZONE courtwatch for Stevens Park please show us and the rest of Minneapolis on October 24th when we appear in your court for Rucker's sentencing that our judicial system will prevail on the side of law and order.

Respectfully yours,
Mahryam Daniels
Mahryam Daniels, chair
SAMOA Drug Task Force

cc:

The Hon. Mayor Don Fraser
Council Member Brian Coyle
Chief of Police John Laux
Inspector Willow, 5th Precinct
Officer Tom Sawina, CCP/SAFE
SAMOA Board of Directors
SSCO Board of Directors
Carl Doss, Prosecuting Attorney
Nancy Hansen, Probation Officer
Joanne Guillery, Volunteers of America
Jean Bulau, Hennepin County Prevention Center
Mark Brunswick, Star-Tribune police reporter
Gary Hill, editor, KSTP Television

STEVENS SQUARE

There is a great past in our future.

Fig. 3
Community impact statement (cover page)

Specific crime problems demand specific strategies. Crime impact statements have been utilized to impress authorities with the negative impact of crime on individuals or businesses. Figure 3 is page one of an 80-page document presented at the sentencing hearing of a drug dealer. The community spirit captured in this document may have influenced the judges, who gave the defendant the maximum penalty he was allowed—a sentence that exceeded the guidelines. After the sentencing, the defendant remarked that he felt he had been victimized by the community.

The MPD geographic crime information system has a site center report (figure 4) that can be utilized very effectively in community impact statements or when dealing with problematic establishments and their clients. This report centers on the problem location and calculates the crime per spatial area in six 1/10-mile bands around the location. The report graphically depicts the distance-decay pattern in two ways: with darker bands for higher crime concentrations per area, and with a bar graph illustrating the 95 percent confidence interval for each band. Gaps in the confidence levels reflect significant differences, and overlaps reflect no significant difference. The distribution also makes it clear if the center is a focus of criminal activity or if the activity is evenly distributed around the selected area.

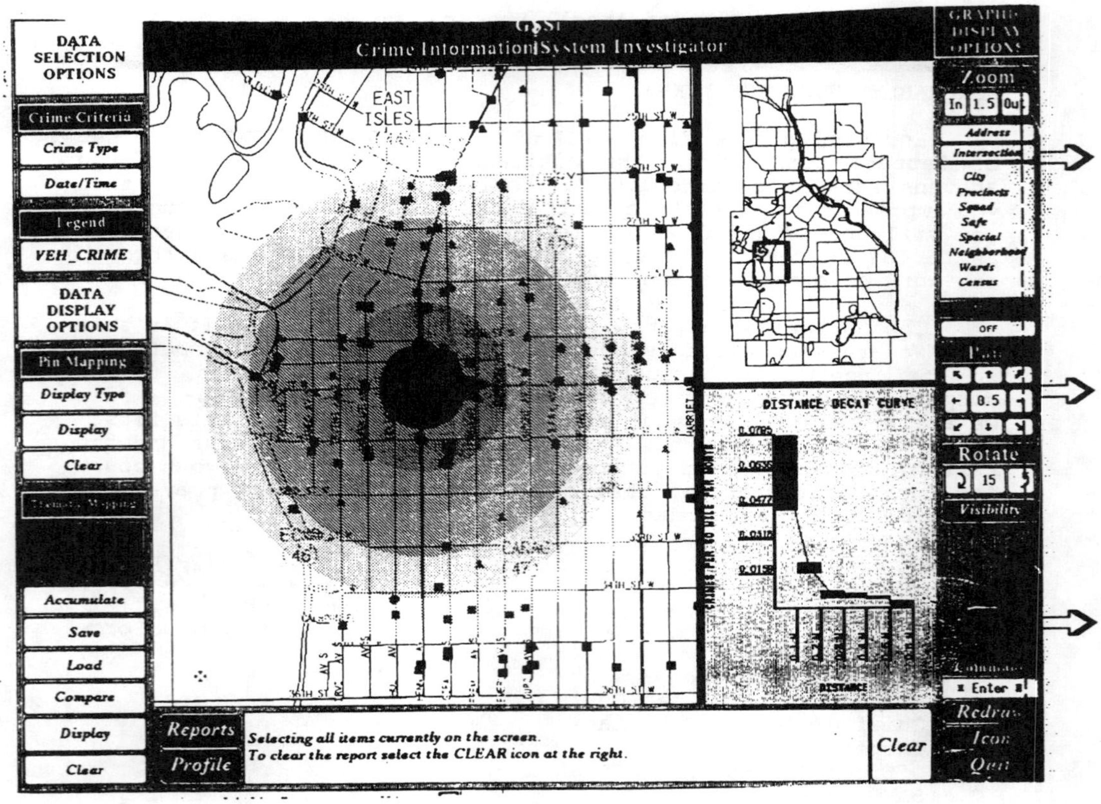

Fig. 4
Site center report

CCP/SAFE organizes McGruff safe houses to give children safe places to run to if they are on their way home from school and at risk of being victimized. Figure 5 shows the distribution of the residences of children in kindergarten through sixth grade, and a shaded 660-foot circle around existing McGruff safe houses. This map was used to pinpoint areas that needed safe house families and in the recruiting of new safe homes.

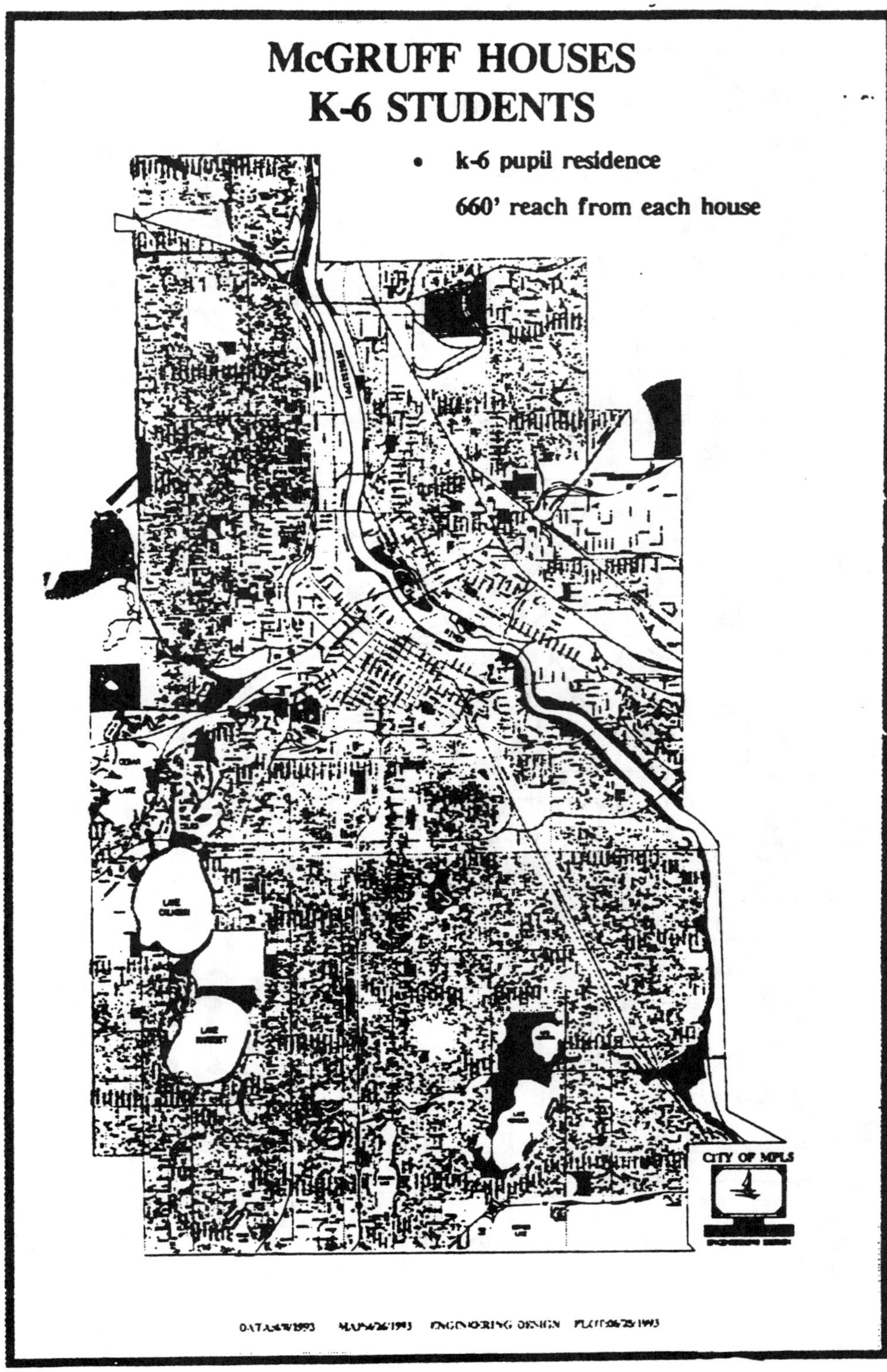

Fig. 5
Analysis for "safe house" location placement

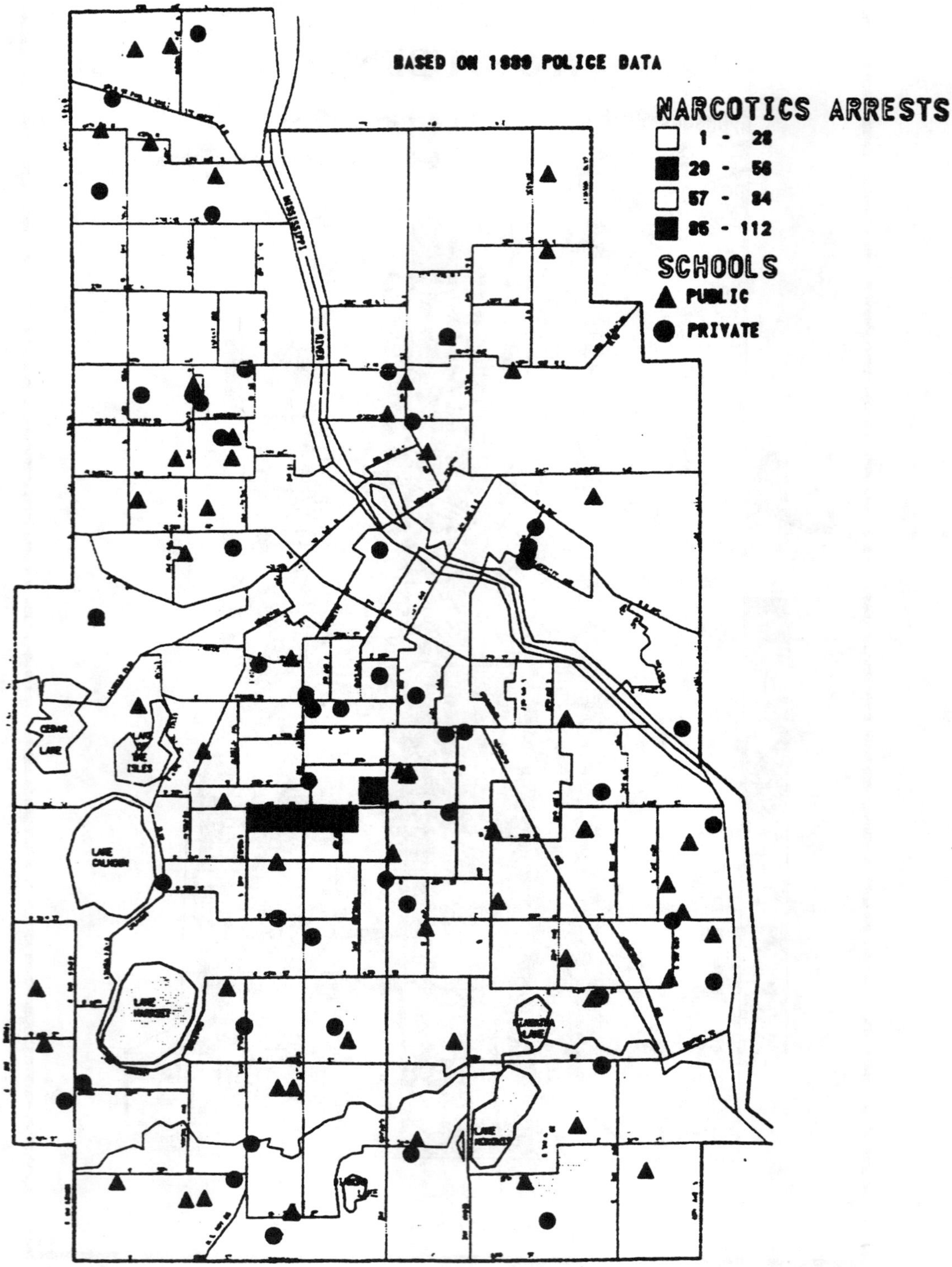

Fig. 6
Map for school board transportation

School Board Transportation Studies

The school board used school locations and narcotic arrest locations (figure 6) to negotiate additional funding for bussing to transport students who may be subjected to additional risks walking to school near narcotic activity areas.

MPD Narcotics Division

The narcotics division used a map (figure 7) combining areas shaded by density of the number of complaints by citizens about narcotic dealing and arrest sites to illustrate a close correlation in defense of its narcotic law enforcement efforts.

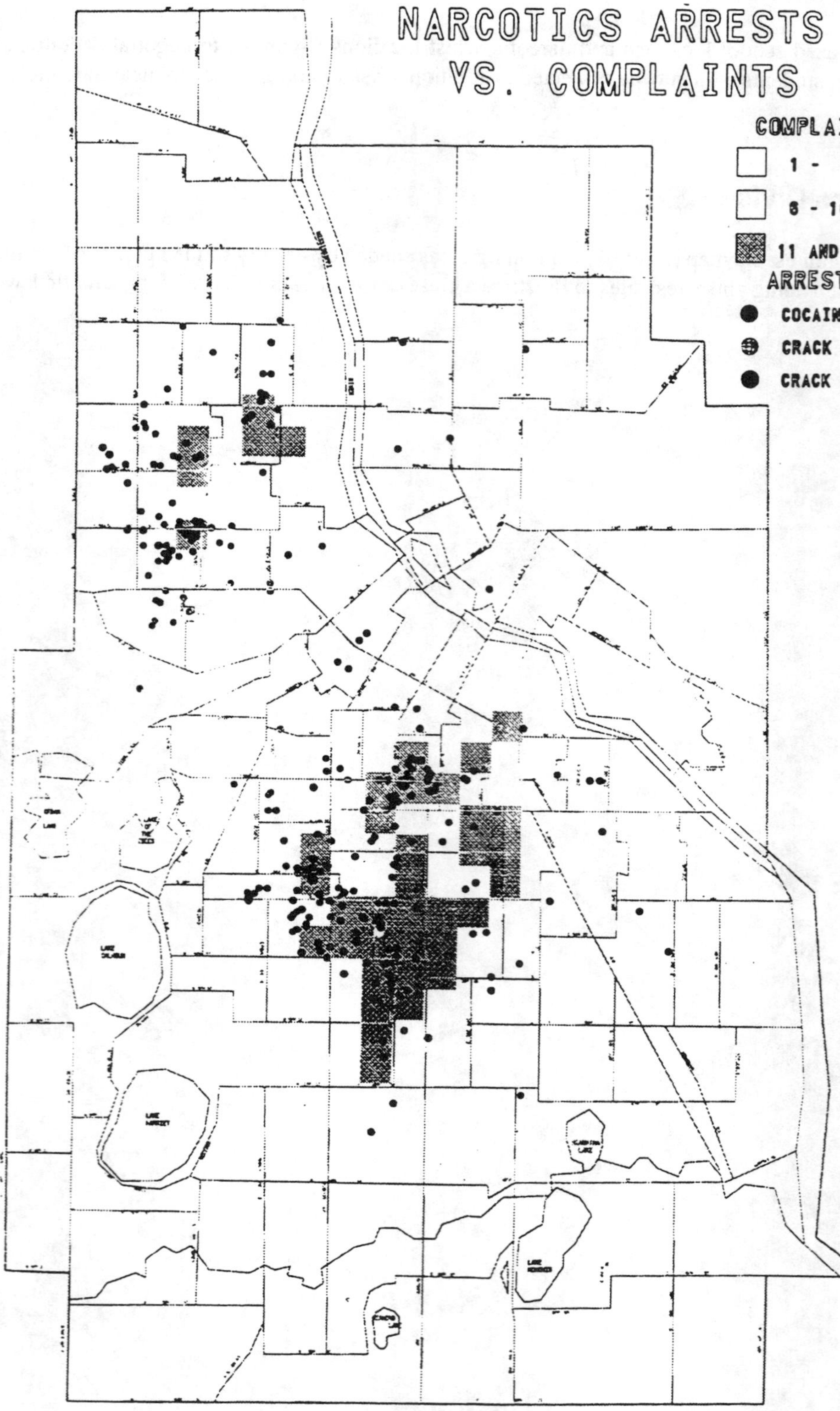

Fig. 7
Map for narcotics division

Minneapolis Public Housing Authority and the State Legislature

The Minneapolis Public Housing Authority and the state legislature have explored the impact of dispersing public housing and consequently reducing the magnifying impact of poverty, lack of opportunity and crime that frequently is associated with concentrated public housing.[1] Minnesota state Rep. Myron Orfield has been very active in the spatial analysis of crime, income, public housing, jobs, and so on. Figure 8 shows a dot map pattern of crime; figure 9, the thematic distribution of the same crime; and figure 10, the population distribution. We have worked closely with Rep. Orfield to make old archive data available for analysis. His contribution gives us a 10-year perspective on the distribution of crime in Minneapolis.

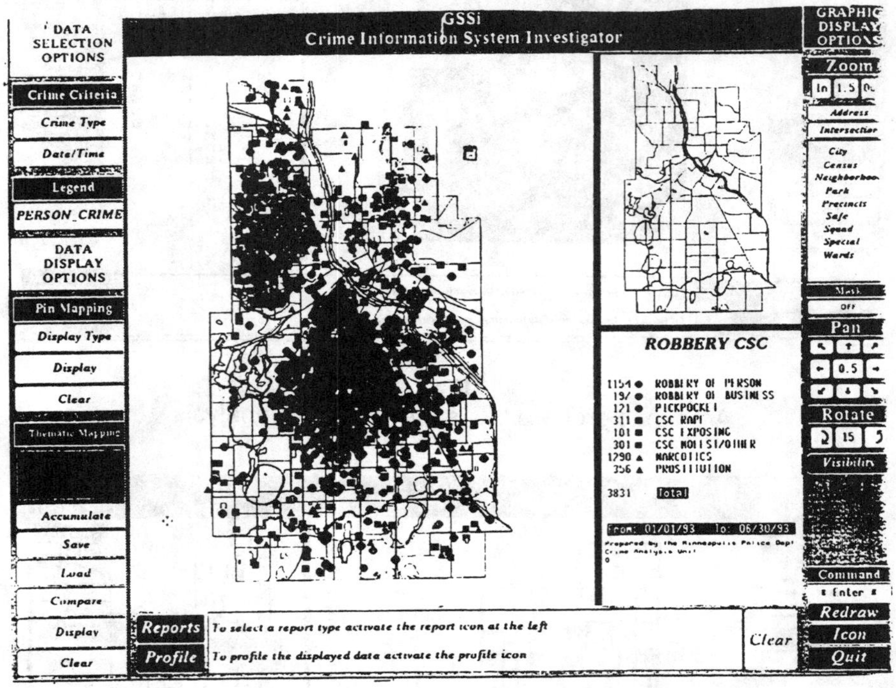

Fig. 8
Dot map prepared for state legislative analysis

1. Minnesota state Rep. Orfield may be contacted at 521 State Office Building, St. Paul, MN 55155, phone (612) 296-9281.

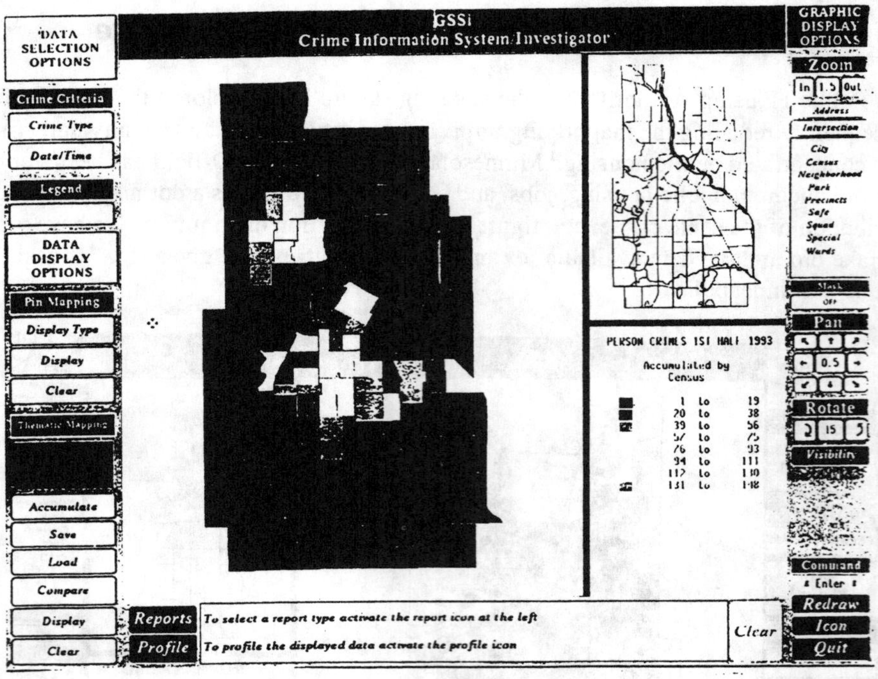

Fig. 9
Area map prepared for state legislative analysis

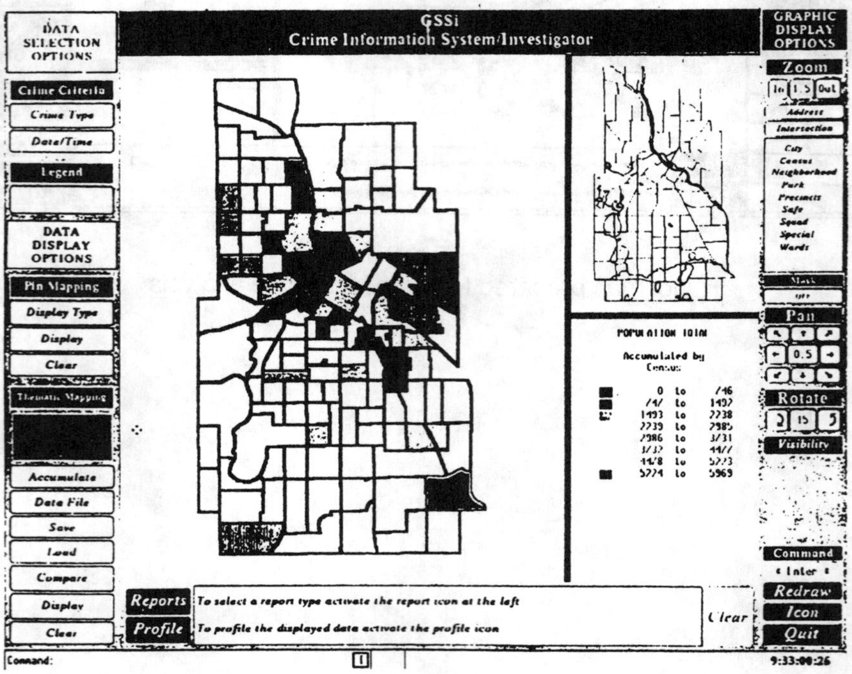

Fig. 10
Population map prepared for state legislative analysis

THE FUTURE

"Communication" will be critical to successful law enforcement, whether the communication is to and from a community or among law enforcement agencies. Mapping tools will help us communicate clearly. Communication among law enforcement agencies and the willingness to share data and ideas will improve policing and the technological tools we are using. We need to recognize that what is the future for one department may be the past or present of another. Our examples and ideas may be the catalyst that helps another agency move to new levels of effectiveness. Some of the things I see in the future for Minneapolis and generally are the following:

Electronic Kiosks

Electronic kiosks would be located in strategic places throughout the city, providing activity information, maps to events and special places, and crime data. These would be especially helpful to conventioneers and tourists.

Default Hotel Television Programming

Default programming kicks in immediately when the TV is turned on, and is available now in many hotels. Traditional programming includes information about the hotel, including safety tips, current special events and places in the host city, and information about the movie lineup. I would like to see maps showing the hotel location, other major place locations (such as sports centers, convention halls, entertainment centers, historic sites) and recent crimes surrounding each site. If there is a particular crime problem in an area, the guest should be warned. Naturally, this idea will receive resistance from the tourist and convention bureaus and will require their involvement and creative data display to implement.

Public Access TV

Minneapolis has public access channels as part of the cable television contract. One channel allows for user interactivity, in that a user may call a given phone number when tuned to that specific channel, and then, by entering numbers on his or her phone that correspond with a table of contents displayed on the TV, leaf through various products. We are actively pursuing the display-of-crime maps for the major crimes of interest to the public: burglary, criminal sexual conduct offenses involving strangers, robbery of person and purse snatches, motor vehicle theft, and theft from auto.

Several concerns have been raised about this project: the fear it may cause, how to balance the crime perspective with information about what is good in the neighborhood, and the lack of similar information from surrounding communities. Some worry it will create sufficient fear to drive people from the city. These concerns should be counterbalanced by the public's right to know and the benefits that can be derived from the public's knowing their risks and taking appropriate safety actions. Fear could be moderated by using the crime location quotient (CLQ) described by Paul Brantingham. The CLQ could be calculated for each area, thereby letting residents know how one area compared to the city as a whole.

The ideal implementation for Minneapolis may be neighborhood-level maps and summaries, since there are many organized neighborhoods. Existing neighborhood organizations could provide balancing information about the benefits of living in the particular area, when their organization meets, and how to get involved. CCP/SAFE could provide crime prevention tips for each particular crime type.

Geographic Expansion of Crime Analysis

We need to expand crime analysis from a particular jurisdiction to the broad metropolitan level. We are all aware that criminals do not abide by jurisdictional boundaries and that some crimes and criminals are highly mobile. We have developed the capability to link motor vehicle theft sites with their corresponding recovery sites (figure 11). Our current implementation is limited to Minneapolis proper. We will be exploring the capability of expanding this function to our larger metropolitan area. The benefits are obvious—to visualize concentrations of theft and concentrations of recovery will allow investigators to focus on offenders and operations in the appropriate areas.

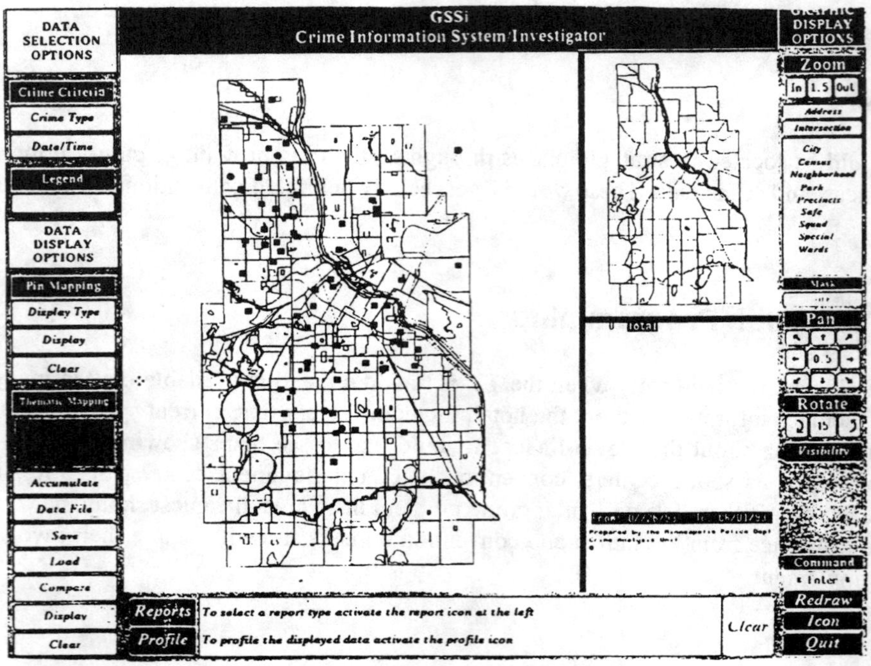

Fig. 11
Linking motor vehicle theft and recovery sites

Private Service Bureaus for Crime Analysis

With government guidelines declaring that crime data (with limits) are public data, it is very feasible that a private security company could purchase data from public law enforcement agencies, process it for patterns, and sell the refined analysis back to the public agencies. Benefits could be derived from merging the information from many jurisdictions to accomplish a more cohesive picture of crime patterns.

Integration of Census, Land Use, Citizen Complaints, Housing Turnover Rates, and so on, With Crime Data

We are currently incorporating some census data into our mapping system and are working to expand the variety of information used for comparison. The data are being used by our city in a neighborhood-by-neighborhood, citizen-directed revitalization effort. This information would be very helpful for crime-prevention-through-environmental-design efforts.

Increased Citizen Involvement in the Analysis of Complex Issues, Including Crime

As citizens become more computer literate and experienced with sophisticated programs that are available over the counter, we will see increased challenges to our municipal analytical abilities and resources.

Information Sharing

Information sharing will stimulate greater interagency cooperation for use and acquisition of highly technical resources. Crime analysis and intelligence analysis will become more closely coordinated.

Crime Analysis/Market Analysis

Crime analysis will provide the same function to law enforcement as market analysis provides to business.

Chapter 23

Spatial Analysis in the Evaluation of the "CAPS" Community Policing Program in Chicago

Richard Block
Loyola University, Chicago

THE EVALUATION OF CHICAGO'S COMMUNITY AREA POLICE STRATEGY

The multifaceted evaluation of Chicago's Community Policing Program (CAPS), currently under way, is one of the most elaborate assessments yet developed. The evaluation, as implemented by a team headed by Wesley Skogan of Northwestern University and funded by the Illinois Criminal Justice Information Authority and the McArthur Foundation, includes assessment of crime levels and perceptions of crime and disorder in the five experimental districts and matching control districts. It includes pre- and post-community policing training surveys of police and a process evaluation of the department's implementation of the program. The evaluation also entails pre- and post-community policing implementation telephone interviews with community residents about disorder, fear of crime and victimization, and observation of community groups and beat meetings. (The program began in May 1993, in five of 26 police districts.)

The most unique aspect of the evaluation is an operationalization of Skogan's concepts of community disorder and decline (Skogan 1990). Skogan holds that the physical appearance of a community and the perceived civility or incivility of its residents are strongly related to neighborhood perception of crime, fear of crime, and community decline. Based upon these concepts, in March and April 1993, observers recorded characteristics of every building and general conditions in 1,500 randomly chosen residential blocks. Included in these observations were abandoned cars, taverns, schools, bus stops, broken windows, graffiti, gang presence, security measures, police presence, and so on. These observations will be repeated in September 1993.

The analysis also includes the spatial distribution of crime, based on census units (tracts and block groups) and the social and population characteristics of these census units, and hot-spot area analysis to assess crime risk and dispersion or displacement of crime to non-CAPS areas. Spatial analysis tasks in the CAPS evaluation program encompass geocoding of each of the 1,500 face blocks included in the assessment, adding census information for each block, geocoding to exact address the approximately 50,000 incidents known to the police each month, and adding census tract and block group identification to each incident.[1]

As of this writing (Dec. 8, 1993), police-recorded incidents for the first half of 1993 have been geocoded. There are approximately 50,000 incidents per month citywide. We are consistently geocoding about 97 percent of the inci-

1. Geocoding involves electronically adding the longitude and latitude of a crime location, census tract or block to a database of previously collected information.

dents. The anticipated geocoding "hit rate" of 98 percent is well beyond that usually achieved, and primarily results from long experience, efficient algorithms developed for geocoding Chicago's crime distribution, and correction and modification of the TIGER file for Chicago to more accurately reflect a police perspective (see Block, elsewhere in this volume). Once census information is added to CAPS block information and crimes are aggregated to census block groups or tracts, both traditional methods of geographic analysis, such as regression or point-pattern analysis, and the techniques discussed here can be applied.

Maps 1 and 2 are examples of the data gathered for spatial analysis of the CAPS observation blocks. In these maps, the five CAPS experimental districts have a broader outline. Random blocks were chosen throughout the city, but blocks in the experimental districts were oversampled. Census data (based on block group), observational data and crime data can be analyzed for each CAP face block. In map 1, the distribution of percentage of female-headed households is depicted. Percentage of female-headed households is generally taken as a surrogate measure for both poverty and informal social control. Among the face blocks, the greatest concentration of female-headed households is in the northern sections of District 10, and the lowest percentage of female-headed households is in parts of districts 24 and 22.

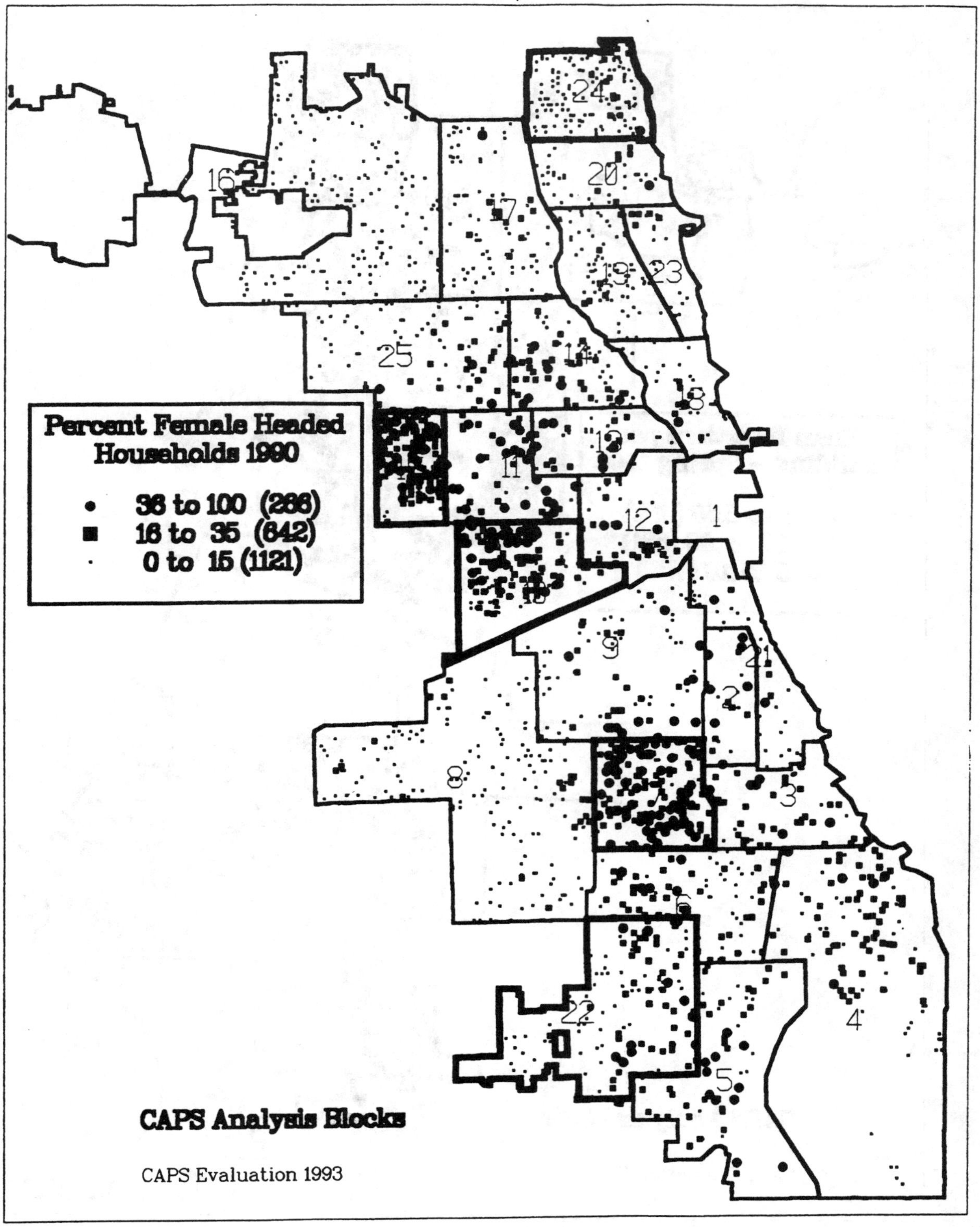

Map 1

CAPS map example: percentage of female-headed households

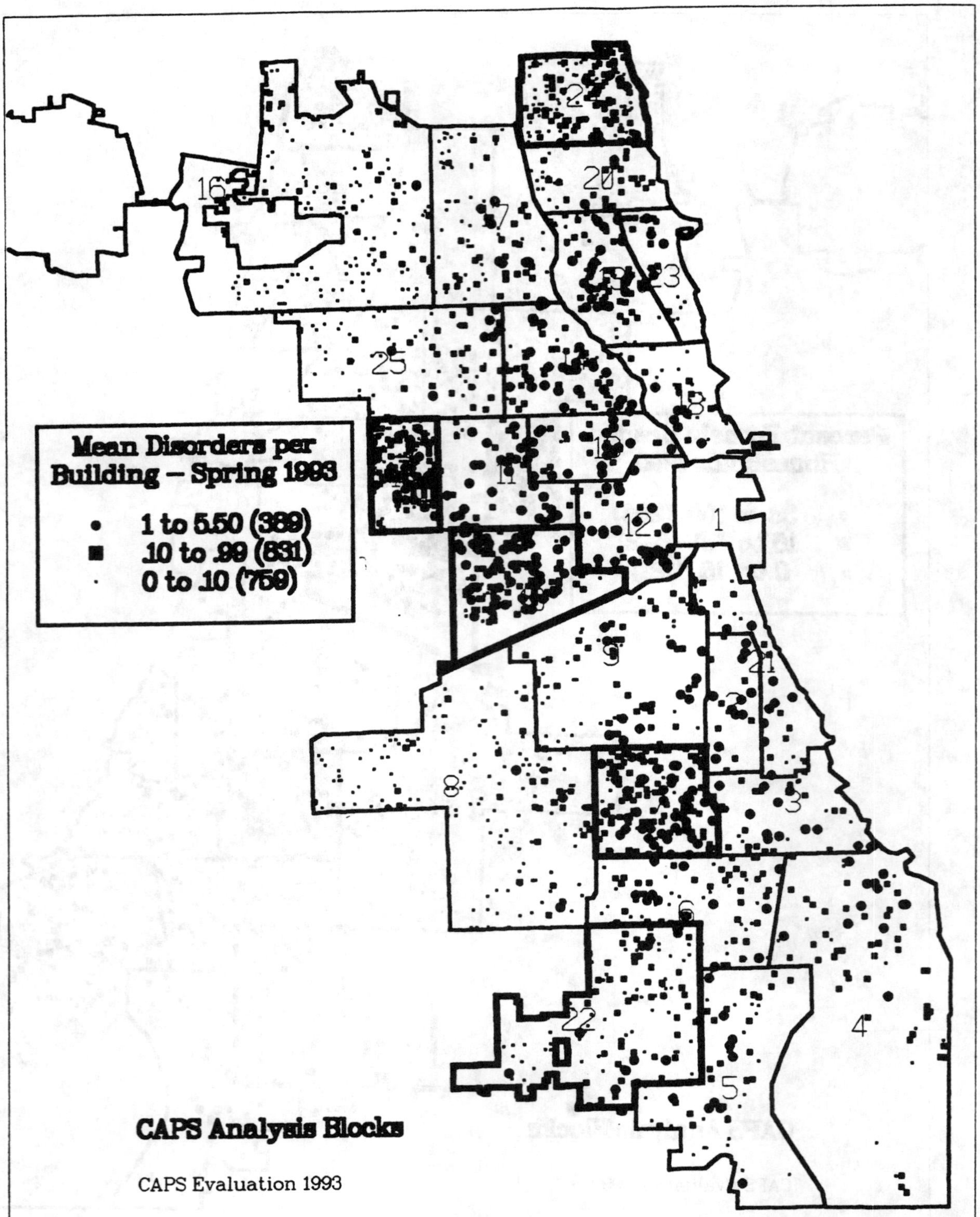

Map 2
CAPS map example: disorders per building

In Skogan's perspective, the appearance of disorder (broken windows, graffiti) is as great a producer of fear and the perception of criminal activity as victimization. In map 2, face blocks are divided into those with less than .10 disorder per building, from .10 to .99 disorder per building, and with 1.00 or greater disorders per building. Almost all observed residential blocks in police District 15 had a high or medium level of building disorder. The lowest levels of residential disorder were in District 22 and the western part of District 24.

HOT-SPOT AREA ANALYSIS OF DISTRICTS 20 AND 24

In addition to these geocoding tasks, we are beginning to analyze the clustering of specific crime types in CAPS districts. The STAC program for hot-spot area identification developed by ICJIA is being used for this analysis (Block 1990). These hot-spot area patterns will be examined for changes by police watch and day of the week, and combined with census and housing data to derive population and community characteristic rates of crime within and outside hot-spot areas. This analysis should prove useful both for the CAPS evaluation and the CAPS program itself.

Map 3 is an analysis of hot-spot areas for three crime groups—burglary, drug-related crimes and personal violence—occurring in March 1993, in District 24 (CAPS) and District 20 (not a CAPS district). These three crime groups have different spatial meanings. Burglaries (excluding theft from a motor vehicle) occur at nonmobile locations—a home or business. A point clearly indicates the location of an incident. Personal violence may occur anywhere. Particular bars or train stops may be attractors of personal violence. Drug crimes as recorded by the Chicago police rarely occur without an arrest. Thus, drug hot spots reflect both occurrence and law enforcement practice.

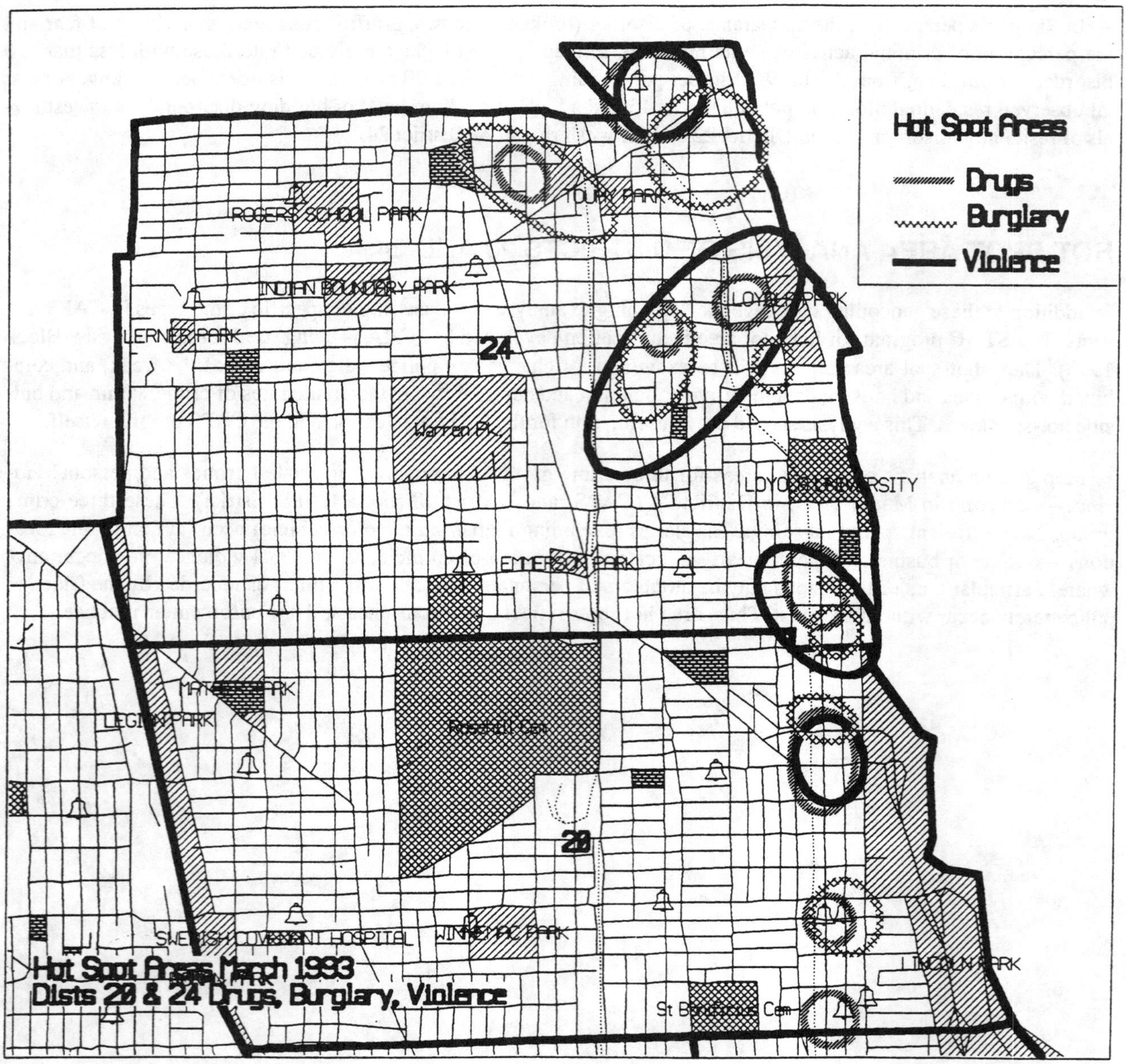

Map 3
Hot-spot areas of drugs, burglary and violence

What do the hot-spot ellipses mean? They are statistically derived, and they represent a remarkable spatial coincidence of the three forms of crime and a coincidence with "common knowledge." Hot-spot areas of one crime type usually overlap those of another. Each burglary hot spot is related to a drug hot spot, although often at a slight distance. Most of the hot-spot areas are associated with the Howard elevated rapid transit line. The northeast hot-spot area is at the end of the line. This station, which demarcated "dry" Evanston from "wet" Chicago, was one of the examples given by Chicago school sociologists of the high levels of disorder in areas near transportation breaks in the 1920s and 1930s. Thus, it is an area that has had a high level of crime for many years.

The line of hot-spot areas to the south of Loyola University also has a relatively long history of disorder. This line of hot-spot areas is also centered on rapid transit stops, but it is not transportation alone that explains high crime levels. These blocks are highly transient, with a number of large residential hotels. Many of the other apartments are "Four Plus Ones," a uniquely cheap construction technique of the 1960s that is no longer permitted.

The hot-spot area in central Roger's Park is of great concern to the police and residents. It is relatively new, is particularly destructive of the business district, and shapes many people's conception of the entire community. The small hot-spot areas of drug crime concentration are a particular concern for community policing. Each is related to one or two specific businesses or apartments.

It is not enough to simply know where incident hot-spot areas are. They obviously differ in size and population. Therefore, the analysis continues, looking at density of incidents per square mile, per 100,000 population, and per 100,000 households, and comparing the results to the remainder of districts 20 and 24. As expected (table 1), incidents are much more densely concentrated in hot-spot areas than outside of them.

Table 1
Incident Density Inside and Outside of Hot-Spot Areas, Police Districts 20 and 24, March 1993

	Population	Households	Square Miles	Incidents	Per Square Mile	Per 100,000 Population	Per 100,000 Households
Burglary							
In Hot Areas	26,852	13,448	.5292	94	177.63	350.07	698.99
Outside of Areas	215,338	98,415	8.9678	208	23.19	96.59	211.35
Personal Violence							
In Hot Areas	36,357	18,929	.7250	219	302.07	602.36	1156.95
Outside of Areas	205,833	92,934	8.7720	507	57.80	246.32	545.55
Drug Crimes							
In Hot Areas	18,651	10,061	.3640	70	192.31	375.31	695.76
Outside of Areas	223,539	101,802	9.1330	56	6.13	25.05	55.01

In March 1993, a household within a hot-spot area was about three times as likely to be burglarized as a household outside any burglary hot-spot area (699 vs. 211 per 100,000 households). The hottest burglary hot-spot area had a rate of 118 per 100,000 households, implying that as many as 1 percent of the households were burglarized in that month. This area (the second burglary hot spot from the bottom) not only coincides with hot-spot areas of drug offenses and personal violence, but also is at the end of Lake Shore Drive, allowing quick departure following the crime.

There were about 2.5 times as many incidents of personal violence per 100,000 resident population within hot-spot areas than outside of them. The risk was greatest in the northeast hot-spot area (919 per 100,000 population). As noted above, this is an area that has long been noted for its violence.

Probably reflecting both enforcement practices and the actual occurrence of drug crimes, the difference in risk within and outside of drug hot-spot areas is very large. Fifty-six percent of all drug crimes occurred in a drug hot-spot area. These areas include only 3.8 percent of the total area and 7.7 percent of the total population of the two districts. There were 192 incidents per square mile within the hot-spot areas, and only six outside of the areas. In the hottest area, located close to an elevated station on decaying Morse Avenue, the number of incidents per square mile was more than 100 times higher than outside of the hot-spot areas. This specific area was well known as a trouble spot by community residents and was the first area analyzed by the Loyola Community Safety Project.

CONCLUSION

The CAPS program began in May 1993. Spatial analysis of its success will integrate pre-CAPS and post-CAPS assessments of community security and civility, order and disorder, in observation blocks. It will continue the analysis of changing crime patterns using hot-spot area analysis to describe dispersion, displacement and, we hope, decline in crime levels.

REFERENCES

Block, Carolyn Rebecca (1990). Hot spots and isocrimes in law enforcement decision-making. Paper presented at conference on Police and Community Responses to Drugs. University of Illinois at Chicago.

Skogan, Wesley (1990). *Disorder and Decline: Crime and the Spiral of Decay in American Neighborhoods*. New York: Free Press.

Chapter 24

Use of Mapping to Support Community-Level Police Decision Making[1]

Jonathan Lewin
Research and Development Division
Chicago Police Department

Kevin Morison
Research and Development Division
Chicago Police Department

INTRODUCTION

The city of Chicago's police department is implementing its Chicago Alternative Policing Strategy (CAPS) in prototype districts. Each district will be equipped with computer equipment to provide mapping and crime analysis capabilities. This paper explores the use of mapping technology to provide community-level support in police decision making at both the district and citywide levels. As an example, we use the analysis of motor vehicle theft.

PROGRAM GOAL: ENHANCE POLICE CAPACITY TO REDUCE MOTOR VEHICLE THEFTS IN CHICAGO

Chicago currently accounts for nearly two-thirds of the reported motor vehicle thefts in Illinois and over 80 percent of Illinois vehicle theft arrests. The goal of this program is to enhance the Chicago Police Department's capacity to reduce motor vehicle thefts and further increase the apprehension of vehicle theft offenders. This goal will be accomplished through the use of computerized crime analysis and mapping technology to identify hot-spot areas of vehicle theft activity and to support the development of effective enforcement and prevention strategies.

This type of strategic approach to reducing motor vehicle thefts has proven effective in other jurisdictions. In Baltimore County, Maryland, for example, auto thefts were increasing at an alarming rate, having nearly doubled during the 1980s. The county's vehicle theft rate of 800 per 100,000 population was 21 percent higher than the national rate. In an effort to attack the problem, the Baltimore County Police Department began using computer-based mapping techniques to more accurately identify specific problem areas for vehicle thefts. Maps showing these hot-spot areas were produced with the Spatial and Temporal Analysis of Crime (STAC) program developed by the Illinois Criminal

1. This analysis was developed by the Research and Development Division, Bureau of Staff Services, Barbara B. McDonald, director for the Auto Theft Section, Detective Division, Bureau of Investigative Services.

Justice Information Authority. Neighborhoods experiencing a high number of auto thefts were identified by this system, and Baltimore County's Auto Theft Squad targeted those areas for undercover operations and other intensified enforcement activities. This approach produced almost immediate results: in 1992, Baltimore County reported a 28 percent drop in motor vehicle thefts in the targeted areas (ICJIA 1993).

Implementing a similar strategy in Chicago could have a significant impact on the motor vehicle theft problem, not only in the city, but also statewide. During the 11-year period from 1981 to 1991, 64 percent of all motor vehicle thefts in Illinois took place in Chicago. If the state is to have an impact on the auto theft problem, it must address the problem in Chicago.

COMPUTERIZED THEFT ANALYSIS AND MAPPING

For the Chicago Police Department to be more effective in combating motor vehicle theft, it must have a more timely and useful system for collecting, analyzing and sharing information about vehicle thefts. The current paper-driven environment is too slow, inefficient and prone to fragmentation. In its place, a computerized crime analysis system, with a sophisticated crime mapping component, is needed. Only then will the police department and the community gain the necessary advantage over increasingly mobile and sophisticated auto thieves.

The department is already moving in this strategic direction. The Area 4 detective division, in conjunction with the Authority, is currently using STAC to develop an automated early warning system to track and monitor street gang-related violence on the city's West Side. A similar crime analysis system (with mapping capabilities) is also being installed in the five prototype police districts (007, 010, 015, 022, and 024) that are currently part of the Chicago Alternative Policing Strategy (CAPS). Also, through the department's District and Area Automation project, an automated crime-mapping capability was recently installed in two districts (002 and 025).

This Strategic Motor Vehicle Theft Reduction Program will apply crime analysis technology to the city's remaining 18 police districts, as well as the department's Auto Theft Section, in a concerted attack on motor vehicle theft throughout Chicago. The department is implementing, in each of these police districts, an automated crime analysis and mapping system targeting vehicle theft in that specific geographic area. This integrated approach is expected to accomplish the following:

1. Enhance the decision-making capabilities of department commanders in deploying their resources more effectively.
2. Perhaps more importantly, strengthen the investigative capabilities of both auto theft detectives and district patrol officers in targeting hot spots for motor vehicle thefts and recoveries.

Both of these goals are critical for reducing the number of motor vehicle thefts in Chicago, as well as increasing the apprehension of offenders. Two critical problems are addressed by this program: the high number of motor vehicle thefts that occur each year in Chicago, and the department's lack of an efficient and technologically advanced system for collecting and analyzing vehicle theft information that would enhance enforcement and prevention activities.

MOTOR VEHICLE THEFT IN CHICAGO

With a population of nearly 2.8 million, Chicago is home to about 24 percent of the Illinois population, but it accounts for nearly two-thirds of the state's motor vehicle thefts. If Chicago were a state, it would have ranked 11th in the number of vehicle thefts in 1991, according to the FBI's Uniform Crime Reports. When analyzing the motor vehicle theft problem in Chicago, several factors must be considered:

1. Motor vehicle theft in Illinois is predominantly a Chicago problem. Chicago has traditionally accounted for nearly two-thirds of all motor vehicle thefts occurring in Illinois. Between 1986 and 1990, Chicago experienced 65 percent of the auto thefts in the state. In 1991, Chicago accounted for 63 percent of the motor vehicle thefts reported in Illinois.

2. Chicago's rate of motor vehicle theft exceeds state and national averages by wide margins. In 1991, Chicago's motor vehicle theft rate was 1,714 per 100,000 population, compared with a national rate of 659 and an Illinois rate of 655. High levels of vehicle theft are found in practically all of the city's 25 police districts.

3. The Chicago Police Department makes the vast majority of the arrests for motor vehicle theft in Illinois. In 1991, the state recorded 10,839 arrests for motor vehicle theft. Chicago police reported 82 percent of this total, some 8,899 arrests. Still, only a small percentage of motor vehicle offenses (in Chicago and statewide) are cleared by arrest or otherwise. In 1991, less than 14 percent of the motor vehicle thefts reported in Chicago were cleared. Over the five-year period from 1988 to 1992, arrests for motor vehicle theft in Chicago averaged 19 percent of the total number of offenses reported during that period.

4. Like offenses and arrests, most vehicle recoveries occur in Chicago, with many involving vehicles stolen outside of the city. In 1991, the department reported a total of 44,740 vehicle recoveries. Of this total, 35,092 were reported stolen in Chicago; 6,585 were immediate theft and recoveries; 2,405 were reported stolen outside of Chicago but within the state; and 658 were reported stolen outside Illinois.

Continuing a Downward Trend

As these data indicate, the motor vehicle theft problem in Illinois is driven by the motor vehicle theft problem in Chicago. In 1991 and 1992, however, auto thefts did decrease by 9 percent in Chicago. This decline of 4,122 vehicle thefts since 1990, at $5,000 per vehicle average value, would equate to a savings of more than $20 million (IMVTPC 1993:21). While the two-year trend is a positive development, it is uncertain if it will continue. The national trend from 1981 to 1983 also showed a decrease, before it spiraled up again over the next eight years.

For Chicago not to repeat this pattern, it must develop new capabilities to provide police personnel with location-specific data regarding hot-spot areas for auto thefts and recoveries. This will require the collection, analysis and sharing of pertinent data, on a real-time basis, for use by patrol officers, detectives, their supervisors, and, in some cases, officers from surrounding law enforcement agencies.

The department currently has a limited capacity to accomplish this type of sophisticated data analysis with respect to motor vehicle theft. The department collects a large amount of data concerning this problem, but because of the volume of information involved, the lack of computer integration and a shortage of personnel, current procedures and systems do not always provide timely and usable information to the officers on the street. To effectively address the problem of auto theft, the department must provide these officers, as well as department managers who have vehicle theft enforcement responsibilities, with information that depicts both local (district) and citywide auto theft and recovery patterns. Hot-spot locations, the types of vehicles being stolen, the time of day, and other pertinent information all need to be collected and made readily available in a format that allows for quick and accurate analysis.

Neither vehicle thefts nor vehicle recoveries are distributed evenly across the city. Both are concentrated in certain areas. Figure 1 shows the seven densest clusters (hot-spot areas) of vehicle recoveries in Chicago, for June, July and August 1993. Although there are some hot-spot areas on the near South Side, a large cluster of recovery hot-spot areas is on the West Side, specifically District 11. District 11 also had 550 vehicles recovered within its boundaries during this three-month period, many more than the next highest district, which had 403 recoveries. Vehicles stolen from around the city end up in District 11 (figure 2). Conversely, when a vehicle is stolen in District 11, it is likely to be recovered there (figure 3). As part of the initial analysis of vehicle recovery patterns, we looked at the recovered vehicles in one District 11 hot-spot area (figure 4). This recovery hot spot, in the Pilsen neighborhood, had at least one stolen vehicle recovered from most of the blocks. The "steals" (figure 5) and recoveries (figure 6) are scattered throughout the district. Note the heavy concentration in the Pilsen neighborhood, at the southeast corner. In just one beat of District 11 (figure 7), numerous vehicles were stolen, and others recovered.

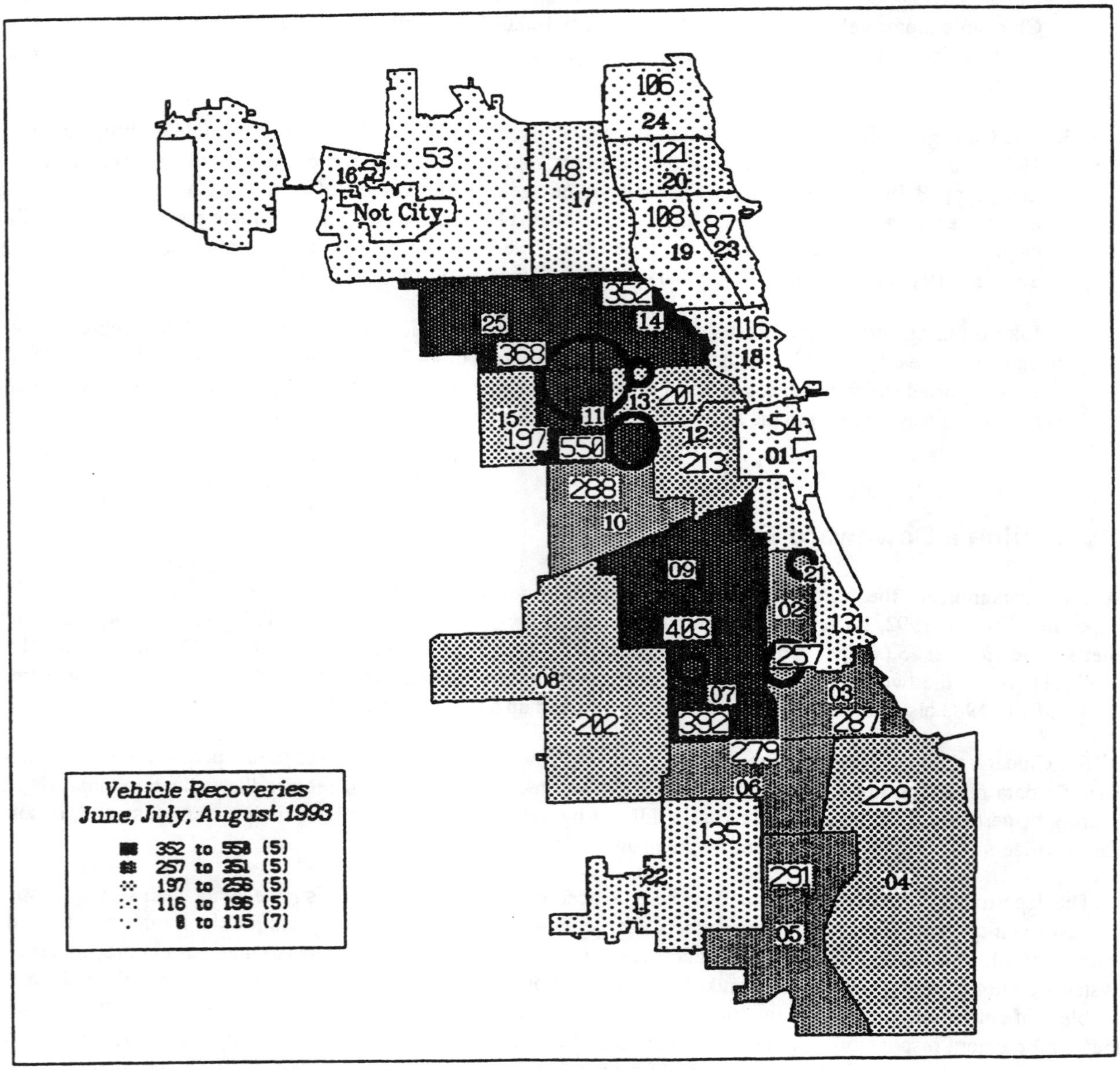

Fig. 1
Locations where stolen vehicles were recovered: hot-spot areas, June to August 1993

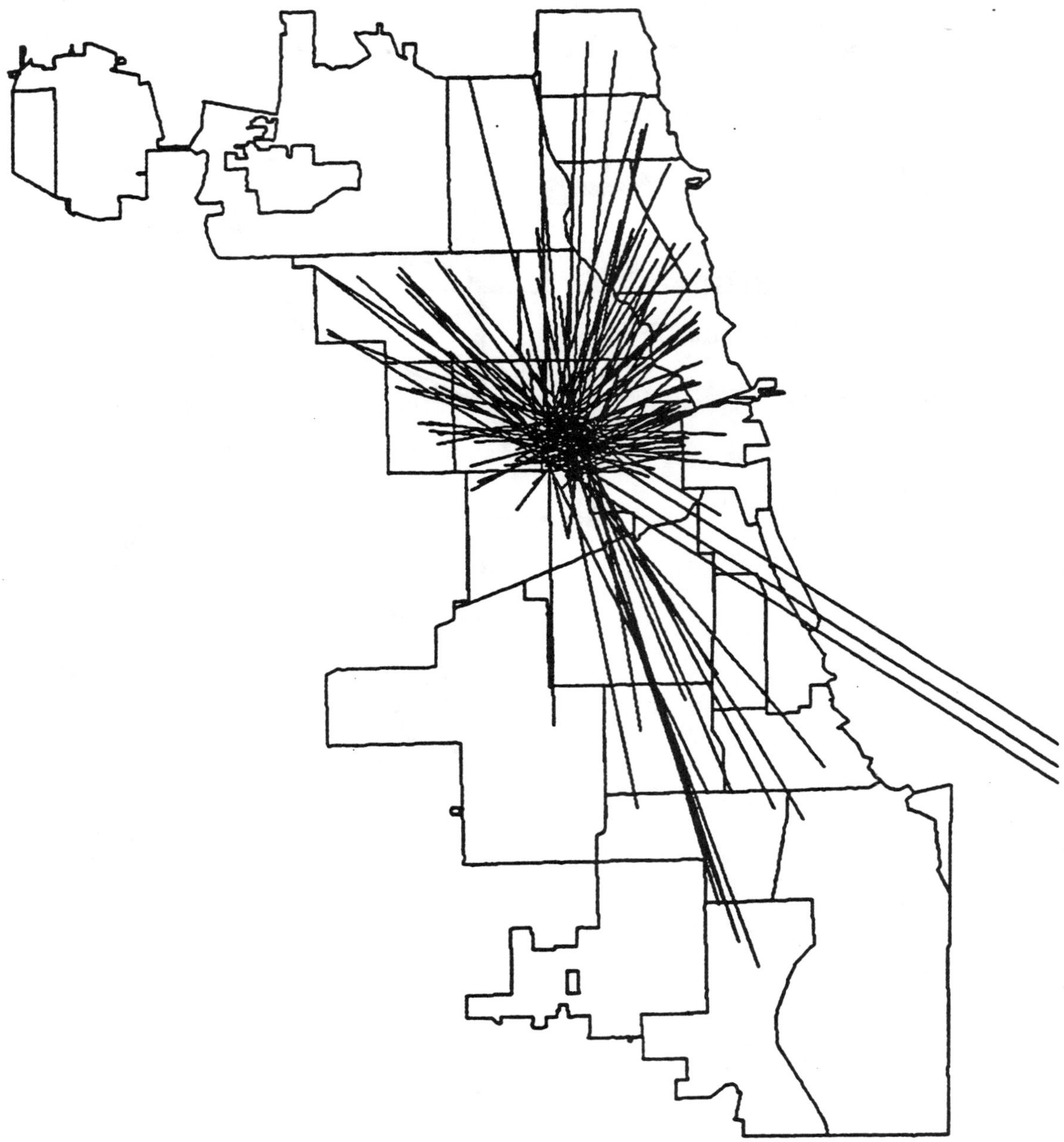

Fig. 2
Points of origin for stolen vehicles recovered in District 11

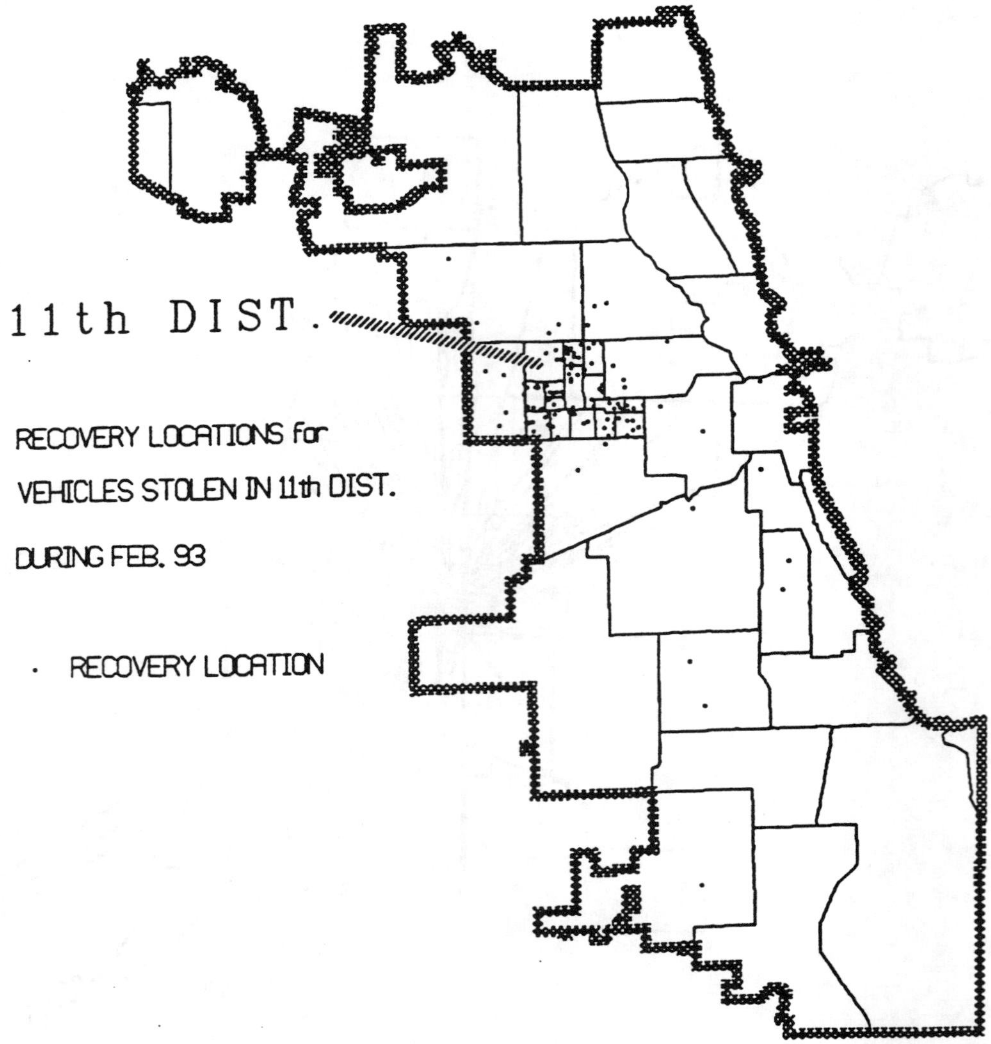

Fig. 3
Recovery locations for vehicles stolen in District 11

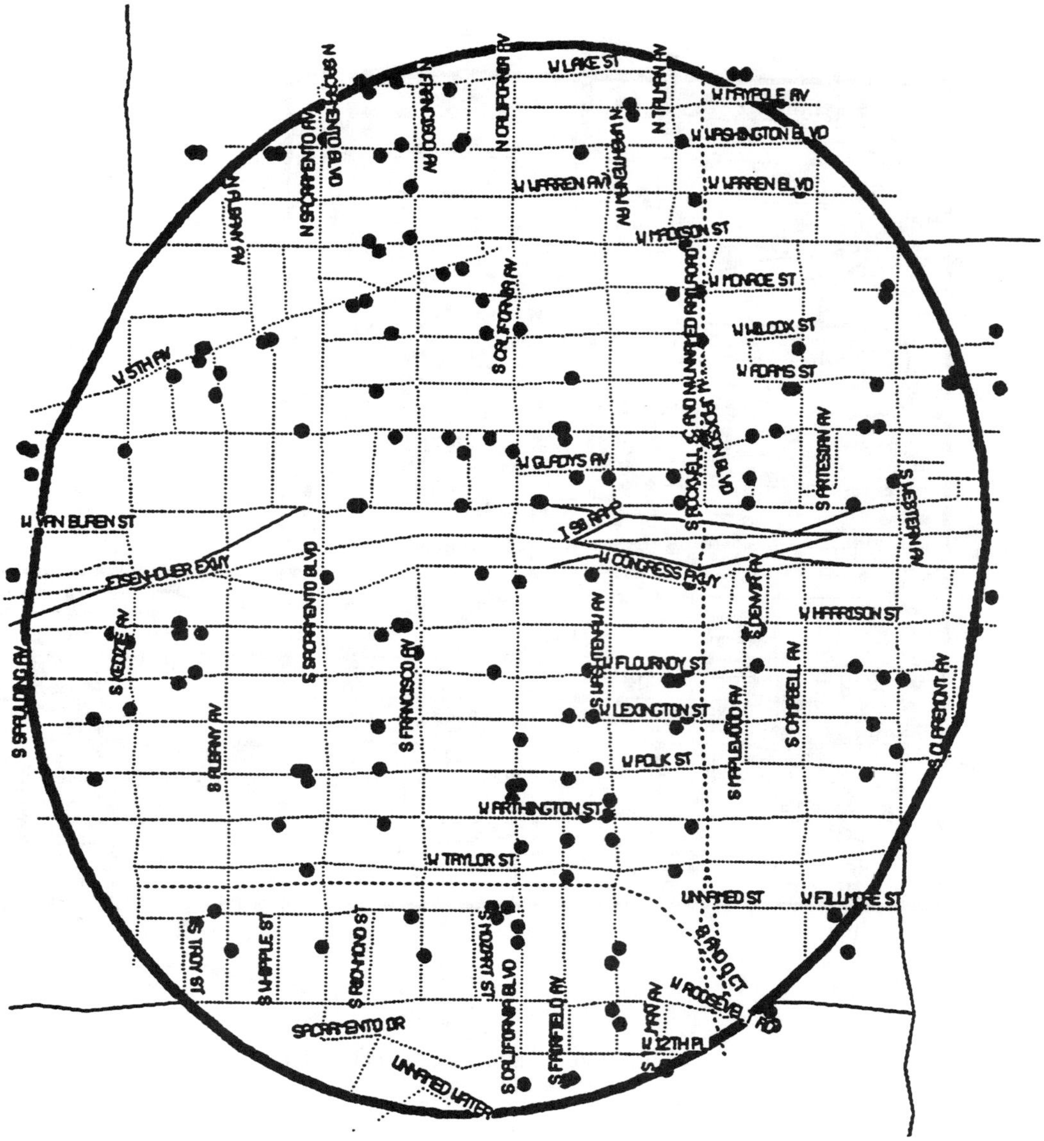

Fig. 4
Detail of a District 11 hot-spot area: Pilsen

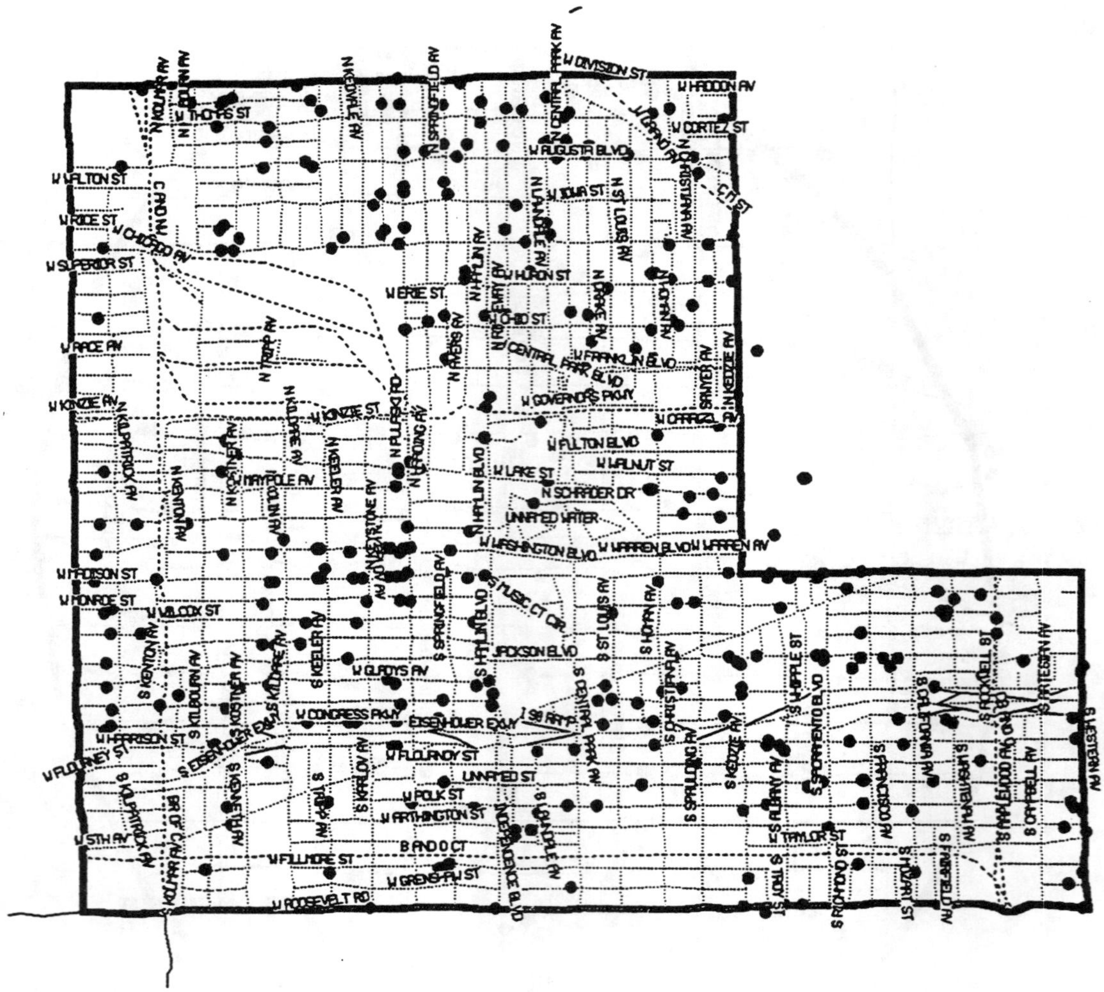

Fig. 5
Stolen vehicle locations, District 11

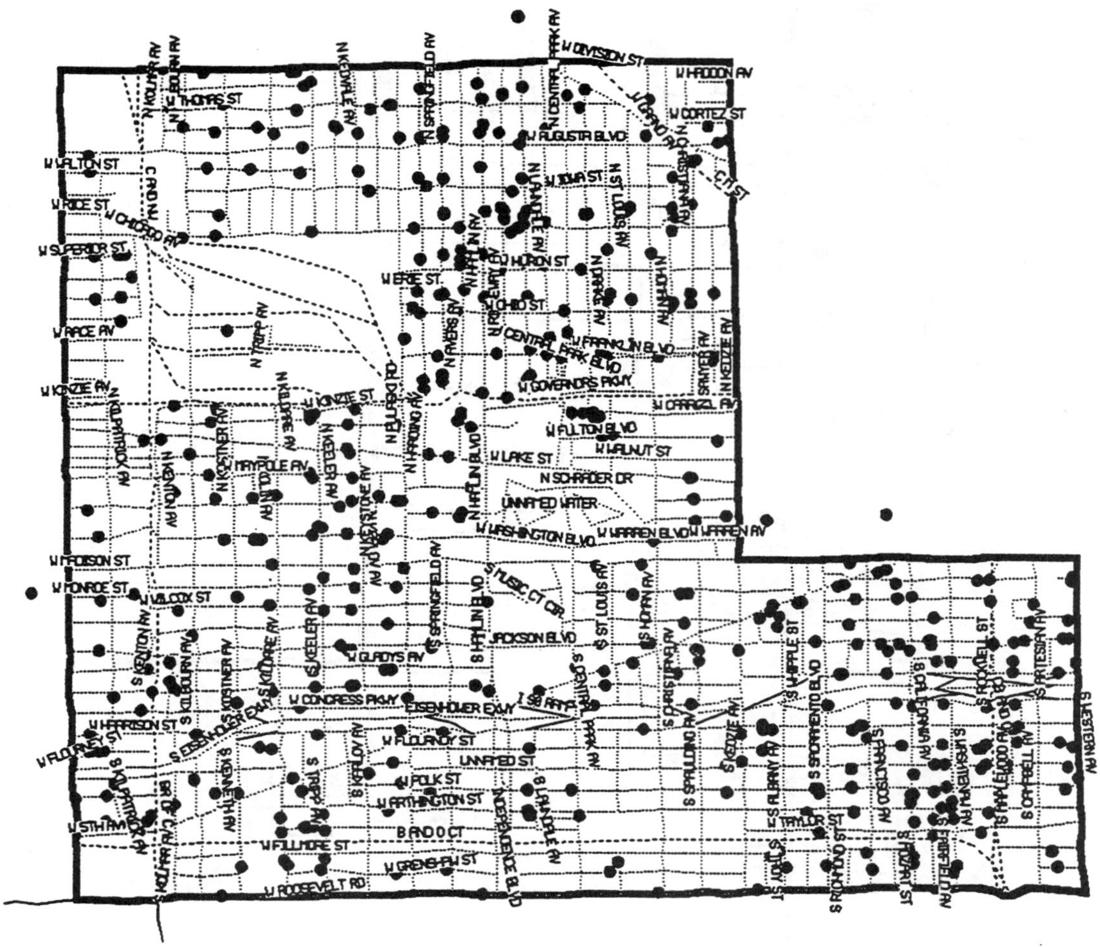

Fig. 6
Locations of recovered stolen vehicles, District 11

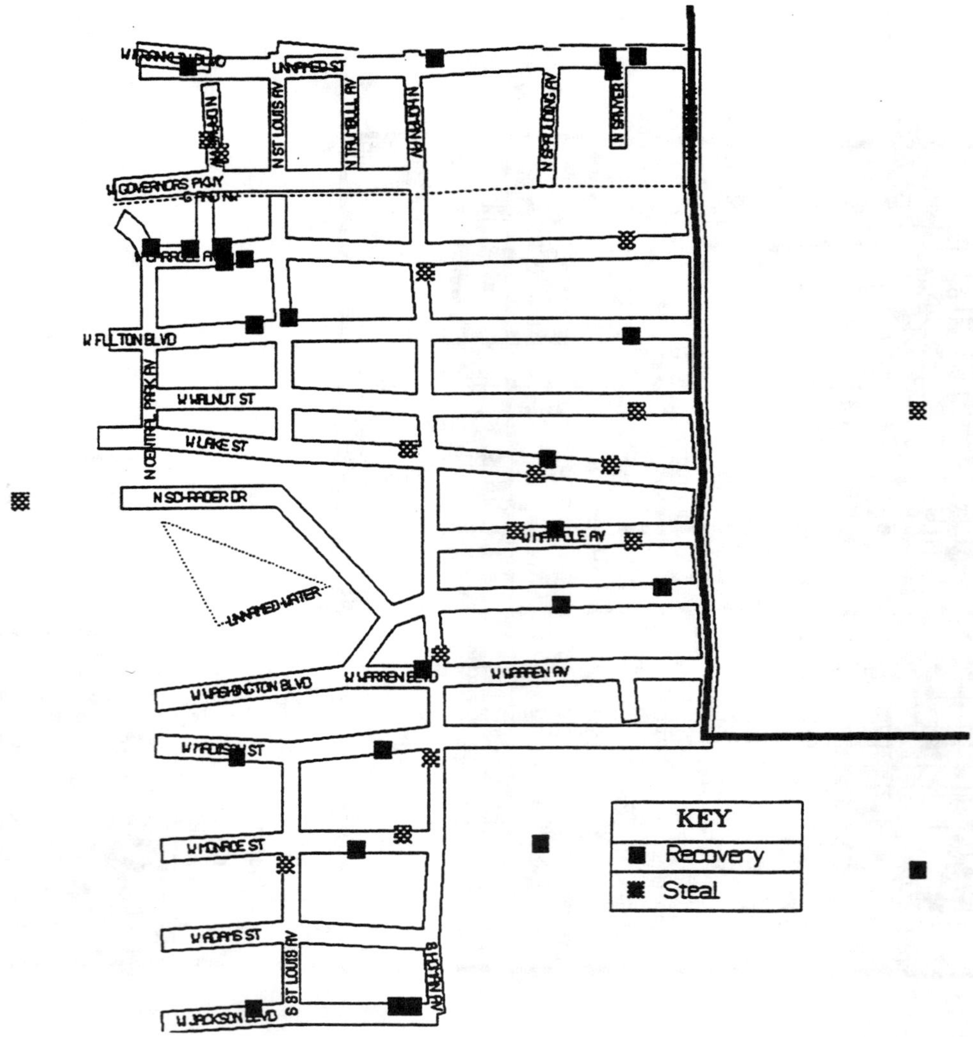

Fig. 7
Vehicle steal and recovery locations: beat 11

Vehicle Theft Analysis Capabilities, Before the Theft Reduction Program

A brief examination of the current system will reveal some of its shortcomings and the need for improvements. The Auto Theft Section is responsible for ensuring accurate identification data on all vehicle theft case reports (CPD-11.412). The section also provides follow-up investigation of vehicle thefts where circumstances indicate organized crime activity; where an arrestee is a known professional auto thief or has an extensive history of involvement in auto theft or stripping; where an arrest involves the theft of more than one vehicle or false, forged or altered ownership or registration documents; or whenever the circumstances of an incident dictate the need for an in-depth investigation, which may entail working with other law enforcement agencies.

In addition to these duties, the section has four data entry operators (DEOs) who enter vehicle theft and recovery information into CRIMES, the department's Case Reporting Information and Management Evaluation System. CRIMES contains select data from the original case report. Data entered into this system serve as the basis for the department's Illinois Uniform Crime Reports (I-UCR), and can be a valuable investigative tool when used in conjunction with the Random Access Management Information System (RAMIS II), a database analysis tool, and with data from the arrest/identification system, which contains information on people arrested. Data entered into the mainframe system are analyzed, and crime patterns are periodically prepared for distribution to the districts. Because of the volume of reported vehicle thefts and recoveries, however, the Auto Theft Section is currently experiencing a 24- to 48-hour delay in entering theft data and a 72-hour delay in entering recovery data. These delays inhibit the development of timely crime patterns for auto theft, impact statistical arrest data and slow down monthly I-UCR reporting.

In addition, one officer from the Auto Theft Section is responsible for preparing and disseminating auto theft crime analysis pattern reports, designed to identify existing emerging crime conditions occurring both within a specific area and citywide. These patterns are based upon computer data obtained from RAMIS II, but because of the delays in entering data into CRIMES, the data from RAMIS II are not timely. In preparing crime analysis patterns, the officer reviews computer data on thefts and recoveries occurring in the city to determine if there is an emerging auto theft problem. The officer then manually pulls the appropriate case reports to determine their accuracy in terms of location (address, beat number), time, types of vehicles, parts being stripped from the vehicles, and so on. Because of the volume of information that must be reviewed, the officer usually focuses on obvious locations around high schools, parking garages and shopping centers. During the first five months of 1993, the unit issued just 13 crime analysis patterns citywide. On a monthly basis, the officer also submits to each district commander and tactical lieutenant a computer printout of all autos stolen and recovered within that district during the previous month.

One other source of information available to the district officer is the department's criminal activity report, which is prepared on a daily basis by the district review officers. It lists select information on all Part I crimes (including those cleared by arrest) that occurred during the previous 24-hour period. Officers on the third watch are given a copy of the report for placement in the beat car's *Field Reporting Manual/Beat Book*, where it is kept for seven days before it is destroyed. Officers' schedules (days off, vacation), watches and beat assignments (if not the same each day) limit their ability to recognize emerging patterns using this 24-hour report.

A common problem with all of these reports—the crime analysis patterns, the monthly reports to district commanders and the criminal activity reports—is that they are little more than simple listings of offenses and other activities. They do not organize and present data in a visually compelling format (such as a hot-spot area map) that would make it easy for officers and supervisors to detect patterns. In addition, the information is not timely enough to allow for the development of strong enforcement responses. Thus, these reports are currently underutilized, and the department's ability to strategically respond to motor vehicle theft is not as efficient as it could be.

Problems in efficiently collecting and analyzing auto theft information are not limited to the districts, but impede the capacity of the department's Auto Theft Section as well. Auto thieves do not confine themselves to geographic boundaries. Vehicles stolen in one district are often recovered in another district. If the commander of the Auto Theft Section is to effectively deploy the section's limited resources to target major theft operations, then he or she must have a better way to pinpoint hot spots and determine if and how they may relate to one another. As in the districts, a computerized motor vehicle theft crime mapping system would not only provide more information to the administrator, but would also make Auto Theft Section detectives and district patrol officers more productive in investigating this serious crime.

The goal of the Strategic Motor Vehicle Theft Reduction Program is, therefore, to enhance the police department's capacity to reduce motor vehicle thefts and to increase the apprehension of offenders. To achieve this goal, the department is establishing an automated crime analysis and mapping system that will track and monitor vehicle thefts and recoveries in a timely manner. This computer system will be backed up by a specialized training program for officers and detectives. This training will focus on how to use the new technology in developing effective motor vehicle theft enforcement and prevention strategies. This integrated approach of technology and crime mapping, backed up by training, will not only enhance the management capabilities of department command personnel to effectively deploy resources, but it will also help make auto theft detectives and district personnel more effective in investigating motor vehicle theft and arresting offenders.

MOTOR VEHICLE THEFT CRIME ANALYSIS THROUGH COMPUTER MAPPING

While crime analysis experts have long advocated the geographic analysis of crime, law enforcement applications of this tool have, until recently, been limited. The Chicago Police Department's Strategic Motor Vehicle Theft Reduction Program is a major enhancement of the department's crime analysis and mapping capability, and the first effort of its magnitude to specifically target the problem of motor vehicle theft. A brief examination of the department's use of different crime analysis and mapping techniques will help illustrate the significance of the new program. The program becomes even more significant in light of other important developments in the department, most importantly the strategic shift to a community-based approach to policing.

Limitations of Pin Mapping

Like many other law enforcement agencies, the Chicago Police Department has for several years used manual crime maps. These police "pin maps" are essentially regular maps on which pins or other markers are placed to indicate the location of different crimes.

Because of their inherent limitations, however, pin maps have never been fully integrated into the department's crime analysis system. Pin maps display location and activity information only at a given time; consequently, they cannot easily identify changes or shifts in crime hot-spot areas. To update pin maps is tedious and time-consuming, and it is extremely difficult to quickly and accurately reproduce the results of a pin map and provide a visual handout to the people who could benefit from the information the most—auto theft detectives and patrol officers.

Early Applications of Automated Crime Mapping

In 1988, the department, working with a group of Chicago universities and community groups, implemented a basic computerized crime mapping system in the 25th District (and its corresponding area detection division). The goal of the program was to cooperatively develop a dynamic, versatile mapping system that would utilize the demonstrated skills and resources of police and community or university groups to identify crime analysis techniques, develop appropriate retrieval mechanisms and, at the same time, involve the community in crime prevention strategies (Maltz, Gordon and Friedman 1991). Funded by a federal grant (National Institute of Justice Grant 86-IJ-CX-0074), the program used microcomputers and rudimentary mapping software to collect and analyze basic crime information. Crime analysis officers could then manually draw crime maps and geocode crime locations by hand. A separate, manual process of examining each crime location and visually plotting this information on a hand-drawn map was required. In this early system, databases of crime information were not centralized or integrated with the mapping component, and the 25th District system had no access to data stored on the department's mainframe.

Despite these technical limitations and the underpowered and outdated equipment used in the project, clear benefits were realized, including benefits in the area of motor vehicle theft. Using the system, police in the 25th District were able to pinpoint an important pattern that had previously eluded them, in the occurrence and recovery of stolen vehicles. Many of the vehicles were stolen from a small area on one beat and recovered in a small area on another beat. Officers increased surveillance of the two areas, and they eventually cleared several cases and broke up a major theft ring in the area.

Perhaps even more important, the project helped prove some of the underlying theoretical bases of crime mapping. Specifically, the project demonstrated the benefits of computer-based cognitive data analysis, which simulates the manner in which an individual filters data through his or her own experiences to infer patterns in the data or to generate hypotheses or conclusions. Cognitive data analysis proved useful in identifying patterns of criminal activity among a variety of available data.

Area 4 Early Warning System

Taking advantage of what had been learned from previous systems, as well as dramatic technological advancements in computerized crime mapping, the department began work on an automated early warning system for street gang violence crisis areas in police Area 4 on Chicago's West Side. This highly sophisticated system is being developed by the Illinois Criminal Justice Information Authority in conjunction with the department, several criminal justice educators and community leaders. The system will link computerized mapping technology with vast amounts of data, not just about crime, but also about the characteristics of a neighborhood, its residents and the problems that give rise to crime there.

Using the Authority's STAC program, a geographic analysis tool that runs with a computerized mapping system such as MapInfo, department analysts can identify clusters of crime incidents on a map, draw those incidents on a map and (importantly) draw boundaries around the densest areas of activity. Crime trends can be more easily identified, and then plotted against known street gang territories and the locations of parks, schools, public housing facilities, transit stations, liquor stores and taverns, abandoned buildings, vacant lots, and other neighborhood features that can affect crime patterns. This information, along with population and other demographic data, is available in the system's geoarchive (a database of geographically represented information).

The Early Warning System project relies on more advanced techniques than were available to the 25th District in 1988. MapInfo, an advanced computerized mapping application for DOS-based personal computers, is the mapping component. Paradox is the relational database component. These software elements, along with STAC, run on Intel 386-based DOS PCs, which are linked to the centralized information databases in the department's mainframe computer. While this project is focusing exclusively on street gang-related violence, it is demonstrating the efficacy of this approach to crime analysis for any type of crime, including motor vehicle theft. Many important strategies for the use of geographic-based crime information have been, and are still being, developed through the Area 4 project, which is a continuing effort.

However, downloading and analyzing data in the Area 4 project is still a multistep process that is not entirely integrated. Case report data from the department's mainframe are downloaded to a computer in Area 4, and crime locations are then geocoded using MapInfo. Information stored in the department's mainframe, gathered through paper reports collected in the field and later entered by data entry operators (DEOs), often contain incomplete address information, making the geocoding process time-consuming and inaccurate. Centralized data from case reports are available on the mainframe only after delays associated with the entry by DEOs, which occur at each of the five police areas in the city. The data must be downloaded to the PC, pulled into Paradox, reformatted, prepared for geocoding, exported, pulled into MapInfo, geocoded, and corrected. By the time this process is completed, timeliness, and thus usefulness, of information becomes a consideration.

Crime Analysis and the Chicago Alternative Policing Strategy

At the same time it is making these and other technological advancements, the police department is implementing major strategic changes, which themselves have implications for information technology and crime analysis. The department has implemented its vision of community-based policing—known as the Chicago Alternative Police Strategy (CAPS)—in five prototype police districts throughout the city (007, 010, 015, 022, 024).

A critical component of CAPS (and one that makes it unique among community policing programs) is the development and use of crime analysis and mapping technology to upgrade the base of information available to officers at the district level. This community policing crime analysis system will provide a mechanism for collecting and analyzing, at the local level, information about crime and other problems of neighborhood disorder. Because motor vehicle theft is one of the more frequently reported crimes, often with highly localized offense and arrest patterns, it is particularly well-suited to this type of decentralized crime analysis and decision support system.

Under the CAPS initiative, advanced computer networks were installed in each of the five prototype districts and in the offices of the department's Research and Development Division in July 1993. These networks consist of five workstations and one server, a laser printer and associated software to provide mapping, database and word processing functions. In addition, each network was connected to the department's mainframe computer. From this platform, a proactive, strategic response to various crime problems (including vehicle theft) may be formulated in a dynamic, flexible manner at the district level.

More recently, the Research and Development Division has proposed to the Authority that key features of the Area 4 early warning system be incorporated into the CAPS crime analysis systems in the prototype districts. These districts represent an ideal environment to test the concept of developing a strategic response to crime through decentralized analysis of data about different types of crime and their connection with other neighborhood problems and trends.

THE STRATEGIC MOTOR VEHICLE THEFT REDUCTION PROGRAM

Chicago's New Records Management System

By December 1993, the test phase of the department's new Records Management System (RMS) will be completed, and by the summer of 1994, Phase I will be on-line. The new RMS replaces several current stand-alone department information services, such as the CRIMES case report system, the "Hot Desk" (local wanted people and vehicles), the arrest system, and many currently manual processes. The new RMS will centralize, through the use of relational databases, currently scattered information that may be located across many different, isolated systems. This will create an integrated environment with a much more flexible and easy-to-use query system.

This flexibility and ease of use in a centralized system will strengthen the processing power and problem-solving capabilities of the various decentralized information systems being installed at the district level, including the Area 4 early warning system, the CAPS crime analysis system in the prototype districts, and the extension of that system to strategically reduce auto theft in all 25 police districts.

Citywide Analysis of Motor Vehicle Theft Data

Under this new Strategic Motor Vehicle Theft Reduction Program, the Chicago Police Department is installing in 18 police districts, and in the department's Auto Theft Section, crime analysis and mapping networks similar to those being used as part of the prototype implementation of the Chicago Alternative Policing Strategy (CAPS). This will extend the crime analysis procedures and capacities developed for the prototype CAPS districts to specifically address motor vehicle theft and related crimes throughout the city.

The Strategic Motor Vehicle Theft Reduction Program is currently working toward implementation of the following:

1. Providing a source of intelligence for analyzing auto theft incidents and related information, such as recoveries, types of steals and other information at the district level.

2. Providing an integrated set of applications allowing access to accurate, timely crime information for distribution to beat officers, tactical officers, auto theft detectives, and area detectives.

3. Generating useful maps, tables, data summaries, and other easy-to-use reports in a timely and flexible manner. These maps and other products will significantly enhance the ability of street officers, detectives and their supervisors to accurately identify auto theft problems and to develop creative solutions.

4. In keeping with the concepts embodied by CAPS, establishing better lines of communication between the department and members of the community. This is being done by compiling, analyzing and sharing with the community information about auto theft that will be useful in individual target-hardening as well as in formulating broader citizen awareness and prevention campaigns against vehicle theft.

5. Developing a centralized automated database of vehicle theft information for use by the Auto Theft Section in developing citywide tactical responses to auto thefts and related crimes. This system will allow the department to more easily target areas for specialized activities, such as undercover operations, targeted enhanced patrols and neighborhood problem solving. Recognizing that motor vehicle theft is a regional problem, the department will use the system to provide information across districts and, in some cases, to surrounding suburbs if a motor vehicle theft pattern begins to affect their jurisdictions.

6. Providing training, support and enhancements, and a path for future enhancements and additions to the system.

7. Providing additional vehicle theft training for department members, including roll-call training conducted by Auto Theft Section personnel, the issuance of up-to-date training bulletins, and the production of two roll-call training videos.

8. Providing enhanced connectivity to the department's new records management system, thereby allowing more points of access to the database of centralized auto theft and related crime information.

The hardware and software configurations for this program should not only provide for the timely and efficient collection and analysis of motor vehicle data at the district level, but should also promote the easy collection and analysis of citywide vehicle theft data and the sharing of such information across police districts. They should be compatible with the hardware and software configurations being installed in the prototype CAPS districts. In each of the 18 districts, a total of three machines (two workstations and one server) will be installed. The workstations will be used by the district review officer for data entry, report generation and map preparation, and they may also be used by all district personnel for rapid database inquiries or ad hoc map generation and serve as an access point to the department's mainframe computer, for nonmapping inquiries against other databases and for Hot Desk (wanted vehicles) and state (motor vehicle registration, driver's license) inquiries. The server will be used for routine network administration tasks, such as backing up the database and performing user maintenance. The server also functions as an additional workstation when the volume of activity warrants it.

At the Auto Theft Section, a total of three machines (two workstations and one server) are being installed. One workstation will be dedicated to a DEO for entry of auto theft-related case report data into the mainframe computer and central auto theft databases. One workstation will be used for inquiry, report generation, statistical analysis, and map generation functions by auto theft detectives. The server will be used for routine network administration tasks, such as backing up databases and performing user maintenance. It can also provide general access functions when needed.

Training

A comprehensive, yet economical, training program, backed up by command accountability for achieving results in reducing motor vehicle thefts, is being developed to support the new program. One police officer, known as a key mapping trainer, has been detailed to receive extensive MapInfo and STAC training at the Illinois Criminal Justice Information Authority. This key trainer is responsible for training personnel in each of the five prototype CAPS districts. The key trainer, assisted by two training consultants, will train each review officer at the remaining 20 non-CAPS districts, as well as key personnel in the Auto Theft Section. The district review officer, who is responsible for reviewing all case reports, will now also review and analyze all auto theft-related information, including entry of key elements of auto theft cases into a localized database and mapping and analysis of this information. The review officer will also be involved in helping to train other district personnel (tactical units, beat officers and so on) in using the system. In addition, specialists from the Auto Theft Section, trained by the key mapping trainer, will provide roll-call training in the districts on the use of information resources in the reduction of auto thefts and related crimes in the districts, which will increase the motivation, skills, knowledge, and ability of police officers to prevent auto thefts and to increase offender apprehensions and vehicle recoveries.

A *Trainer's Guide* and a *User's Guide* will be produced by the Research and Development Division to support the ongoing training of district personnel. To further enhance officer skills in these areas, the Auto Theft Section, in co-operation with the Training Division, will also publish up-to-date training bulletins and produce two videos on these subjects. Using the Video Information System and Training Aid (VISTA), a department cable television roll-call training program, videos can be shown at 35 roll-call sites, 16 times per week.

Operational Procedures

Each district will be the clearinghouse for auto theft-related information within its boundaries. On a daily basis, each district will upload to a mainframe location a file containing its daily activity. The Auto Theft Section will then download one daily activity file per district from the mainframe and merge them into its own central auto theft database. This will be an automated process. In this manner, the Auto Theft Section will be a central repository for citywide auto theft information and will be able to identify trends and patterns that may cross district boundaries or extend into neighboring law enforcement agencies. Should this occur, a crime analysis pattern will be developed and submitted to the appropriate district(s). If the pattern extends beyond the city limits, other local law enforcement agencies will be notified. Eventually, this process will become more integrated. In 1995 (projected), a fiber optic network will be installed linking all department facilities. This network will eliminate the necessity of using the mainframe for file distribution. Initially, however, the mainframe provides the only common link among all districts and the Auto Theft Section.

Unlike the Area 4 project, which relies on mainframe data requiring extensive downloading, exporting, reformatting, and general "cleaning," the data required for district crime analysis activities will be corrected for mapping at the time they are entered at the district level, and will be in a prescreened format, ready for immediate district mapping. No exporting, reformatting or address field corrections will be necessary. In the Area 4 project, a separate "job" must be created to support each area of data analysis. This job is then submitted to the mainframe system. Under the Strategic Motor Vehicle Theft Reduction Program, this entire process will be eliminated. On-line, real-time queries will easily and quickly select data for immediate mapping through an integrated (mapping and database) process. This will encourage analysis in entire new directions that are not possible or practical now at Area 4 simply due to the overhead required to support each area of inquiry.

District review officers will continue to enter select information about all motor vehicle thefts and related incidents (recoveries, thefts from autos and so on) into local databases maintained at each district. Review officers are already familiar with the process of entering Part I crime information in a local database for the district criminal activity report. This concept is being expanded on to include more detailed motor vehicle theft information. Since this information is entered locally, it will be in an error-check format ready for immediate mapping. No downloading process will be necessary. While some of the district data will duplicate data entered by the Auto Theft Section into the mainframe system, the district data will be more detailed. District-level review officers will generate maps outlining concentrations of auto thefts and related crimes, by watch and day. Individual beat maps will be prepared and distributed at each roll call by the review officer.

Currently, approximately 35 percent of vehicle theft-related case reports are taken by the department's Communication Operations Section Alternate Response (Call-Back) Unit, located at police headquarters. Under the new system, information taken by this unit will be submitted to the review office in each district on a daily basis, for entry into its local database. As a result, each district will have the full range of activity within its boundaries available, in a decentralized, accessible database. This database, to be maintained at the district level, will then be accessible using any workstation connected to the district network, for rapid inquiry access, report generation and mapping operations.

Vehicle theft case reports will continue to be forwarded from the district and Call Back Unit to the Auto Theft Section, where unit personnel check the case reports for accuracy and completeness (license identifiers, addresses, beats, and so on) and then enter the vehicle information into the mainframe. Reports are then forwarded to the Field Inquiry Section, where data are entered into LEADS, NCIC and so on. Because the Auto Theft Section's new crime analysis network will be connected to the department's mainframe, any of their workstations can be used for data entry or inquiry against the mainframe database or the local database.

SUMMARY

The Chicago Strategic Motor Vehicle Theft Reduction Program is an innovative citywide program pioneering the large-scale use of crime analysis and mapping technology to strategically fight motor vehicle theft. It combines sophisticated computer technology (including, for the first time, fully automated crime mapping of motor vehicle theft trends) with a foundation of training and support. We hope that this project will empower district-level personnel with the timely, accurate information needed to strategically respond to vehicle theft and related crimes. In addition, the ability of the Auto Theft Section to develop citywide antitheft priorities and strategies will be enhanced. With this new program, Auto Theft Section personnel will be able to more easily identify citywide trends and crime patterns crossing district boundaries. This will promote more effective and proactive enforcement and prevention strategies. As a result, we expect that the number of motor vehicles stolen in Chicago (and therefore in the state as a whole) will be reduced and that recoveries will be increased.

REFERENCES

IMVTPC (Illinois Motor Vehicle Theft Prevention Council) (March 1993). Statewide Strategy. Chicago: Illinois Motor Vehicle Theft Prevention Council.

ICJIA (Illinois Criminal Justice Information Authority) (1993). *STACNews.* Winter 1993.

Maltz, Michael D., Andrew C. Gordon and Warren Friedman (1991). *Mapping Crime in Its Community Setting: Event Geography Analysis.* New York: Springer-Verlag.

Chapter 25

The Usefulness of Maps for Area and Place Research: An Example From a Study of Retail Drug Dealing

John E. Eck
Crime Control Institute[1]

INTRODUCTION

That maps can be helpful for researchers as well as crime control and prevention practitioners was an underlying principal of the Drug Market Analysis Project (DMAP) of the National Institute of Justice. One of the five police agencies awarded DMAP grants was the San Diego Police Department. This department had two DMAP goals. The first was to implement a comprehensive mapping system to support the antidrug efforts of the police department, primarily the narcotics unit and the patrol division. The second goal was to conduct research into drug markets in order to learn more about drug dealing patterns and to inform policy. In this paper, I will describe a research effort under the second goal. The purpose of this presentation is to address a particular question: When are maps useful for learning about crime patterns, and when are they less useful?

A MODEL OF RETAIL DRUG DEALING

Even in areas with a great deal of drug dealing, most places do not show evidence of drug dealing. This raises two related questions. Do drug dealers select dealing places on the basis of site characteristics? Or are drug dealers indifferent to the characteristics of places and do they just happen to choose whatever is available? I was interested in testing the hypothesis that dealers select specific locations to help achieve two purposes: first, to maximize the profits from selling drugs, and second, to protect themselves, assets and profits from being ripped off by criminals or seized by the police.

Based on a rational choice perspective (Cornish and Clarke 1986), routine activity theory (Felson 1994) and environmental criminology (Brantingham and Brantingham 1981), I developed the segmented model of the geography of retail drug dealing. The segmented model describes the geography of drug dealing as the outcome of the routine decisions of three participants: drug dealers; drug users/customers; and managers of apartment buildings, retail estab-

1. The research reported here is part of a larger study of drug dealing in San Diego funded by the National Institute of Justice under grant number 90-IJ-CX-K006 through the San Diego Police Department. Opinions expressed in this paper are those of the author and not necessarily those of the Crime Control Institute, the Police Executive Research Forum, the San Diego Police Department, or the National Institute of Justice. For details on the model of drug dealing used, the research designs and the data, see Eck (1994). At the time of this writing, John Eck was the associate director for research at the Police Executive Research Forum.

lishments, parks, and other locations. Each of these participants engages in rational decision making to achieve his or her goals while keeping costs and risks as low as practical.

The segmented model claims that these actors pair off in two separate markets—the drug market and the place market. Dealers and customers operate in the drug market, while dealers and place managers operate in the place market. Each set of actors in a market pair has conflicting as well as compatible goals. Though these two markets are not completely independent, the segmented model predicts that each market affects the geographic distribution of drug retailing at two geographic levels: area and place. We will next examine each segment separately and describe the goals of the participants.

The segmented model contains two parts. The first part, or segment, describes how the decisions of drug dealers and drug purchasers interact to create drug areas. Retail drug dealing will take place in areas where both the customer and the dealer feel comfortable. These areas will be close to places familiar to dealers, thus providing quick and well-known escape routes and the protection of friends against other offenders. These areas will also be close to places with which customers are familiar, to provide assurances of security. If customers and dealers do not live in the same vicinity, then the most likely reason for them to have overlapping areas of familiarity is that customers enter the dealers' area while going to and from shopping, work, recreation, school, or other routine activities. This description of the creation of drug dealing areas is similar to the "geometry of crime" sketched by Brantingham and Brantingham (1981), except that retail drug sellers are relatively immobile.

The first part of the segmented model only explains the creation of drug areas. The second segment describes how drug places are created within these areas through the interactions of drug dealers and people who control locations. The segmented model claims that drug dealers will seek places that provide security but also permit customer access. How a dealer balances these conflicting objectives will depend on a variety of factors—the risks of arrests and ripoffs, the willingness of customers to visit isolated and heavily defended places, and the revenue that can be gained from the drugs being sold. Regardless of the type of place selected for selling drugs, the dealer will want to be left alone by the person or organization who has control over the place. Inattentive place management will be attractive to dealers in drug areas. Places with managers who screen tenants, strictly enforce leases, check the conditions of their property, and are willing to invoke their legal authority over the way their property is used will be unattractive to dealers.

The segmented model assumes that most place managers probably prefer not to have drug dealers using their sites (though some landlords may profit from renting to drug dealers). The drug market imposes higher costs on the place market. Drug dealers increase the wear and tear on places because of the visitors they will draw to the place. Because of the increased traffic through the place, drug dealing will produce noise and incivilities that will reduce the attractiveness of the place to others—renters in apartments, park users in recreation areas, and shoppers in legitimate retail places, for example. Finally, drug dealers and users will also present a perceived crime threat to others who use the place. Thus, if place managers can find an inexpensive way to keep drug dealers out, they will use it.

In short, both the drug dealer and the place manager participate in markets that force them to weigh security and profit. The drug dealer will undertake a limited search for places that offer good security with access to customers. The place manager will want to control a site that has few costs and a reasonable return. The physical features most strongly associated with drug dealing will be those features that the place manager can afford to do least about, either because of the expense of making the changes or because these same features serve some important other function. There will be situations where place managers and drug dealers reach an accommodation that benefits both. Such accommodations will be more common when place management is expensive relative to what the manager can afford or the place market has disincentives to attentive place management. Since attentive place management will be more difficult in some places relative to others, the distribution of difficult-to-manage places will describe the geography of dealing places within an area favorable to the drug trade.

Both of these processes must support drug dealing for the creation of a drug dealing area. If an area is conducive to the retail drug trade, but all place managers take steps to prevent drug dealing at their locations, little dealing will take place. The drug trade that does exist will be highly secretive and be among close acquaintances. If an area is not favorable to drug dealing, inattentive place management will not be related to drug dealing. Instead, the dealing that takes place will be isolated, unrelated to the routine activities of the area, and carefully hidden from the scrutiny of place managers.

STUDY DESIGN

Data from the San Diego Police Department was used to identify all of the persistent drug dealing places in a five-beat area in San Diego. These beats were selected because retail drug dealing is quite widespread in this area. Any census block with at least one drug dealing place in it was called a drug dealing block. All 132 dealing blocks in the area were studied to examine the first part of the segmented model—the association between drug dealing and routine activities in the drug market area. To examine place characteristics, a case-control study design was used (Schlesselman 1982). A probability sample of 189 drug dealing places was selected from the known drug dealing locations. Another probability sample of places without any evidence of drug dealing—non-dealing places—was selected for comparison purposes. For more details on the study design and data collection procedures, see Eck (1984).

DRUG AREAS

Maps are particularly useful for studying areas. The arterial routes cutting through the area are shown in figure 1, along with the beat boundaries. In figure 2, the drug dealing blocks are shown in three shades. Darker blocks have four or more drug dealing places (DDPs). Medium-shaded blocks have two or three DDPs. Lightly shaded blocks have a single dealing place. One can see quite readily that the dealing blocks are almost all along major arterial routes, and the blocks with the greatest density of dealing are all adjacent to arterials. In the corridor formed by the parallel arterials of University and El Cajon, there is a substantial concentration of drug dealing.

The land use of this area is shown in figure 3. Here we see that along the routes where the most drug dealing takes place, the area is zoned commercial. Immediately adjacent to these commercial strips along the thoroughfares are multifamily apartment-zoned areas.

These maps provide evidence supporting the first part of the segmented model. Drug dealing areas are near areas used by many people as part of their routine activities. Based on these maps, one might also come to believe that apartment complexes are associated with drug dealing.

DRUG PLACES

Maps can provide interesting patterns that are larger than the smallest mappable feature. In figure 2, we mapped blocks, so we can see patterns larger than blocks. If we had mapped drug places, we could have seen patterns larger than the place level. But in neither case could we have seen patterns the size of the feature mapped (blocks or places) or smaller.

The second part of the segmented model cannot be tested using maps because it deals with features (places) that are the smallest size that can be mapped. Thus, any place pattern would show a characteristic of the area, but not of the places.

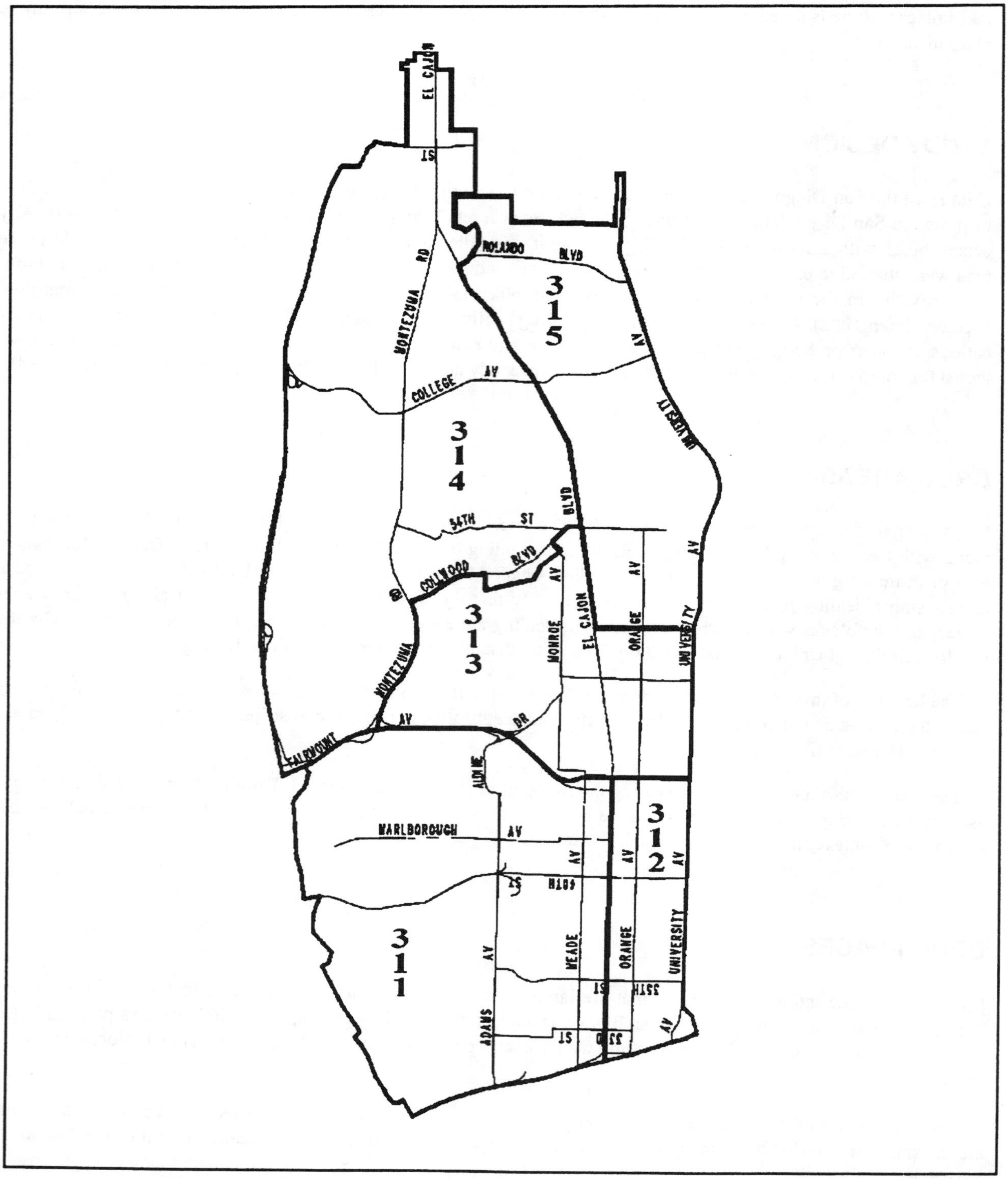

Fig. 1
Beats and arterial routes

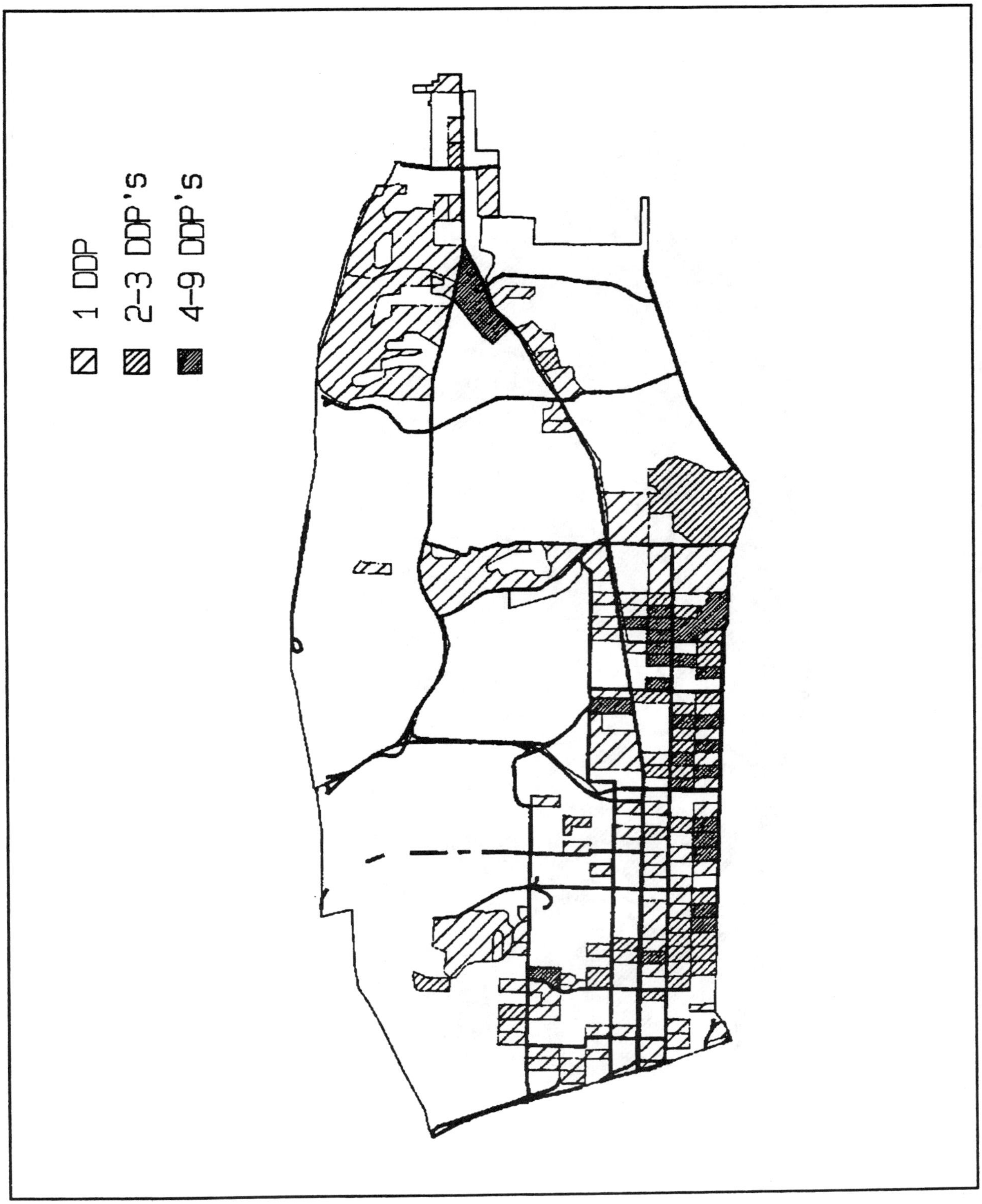

Fig. 2
Drug dealing blocks and arterial routes

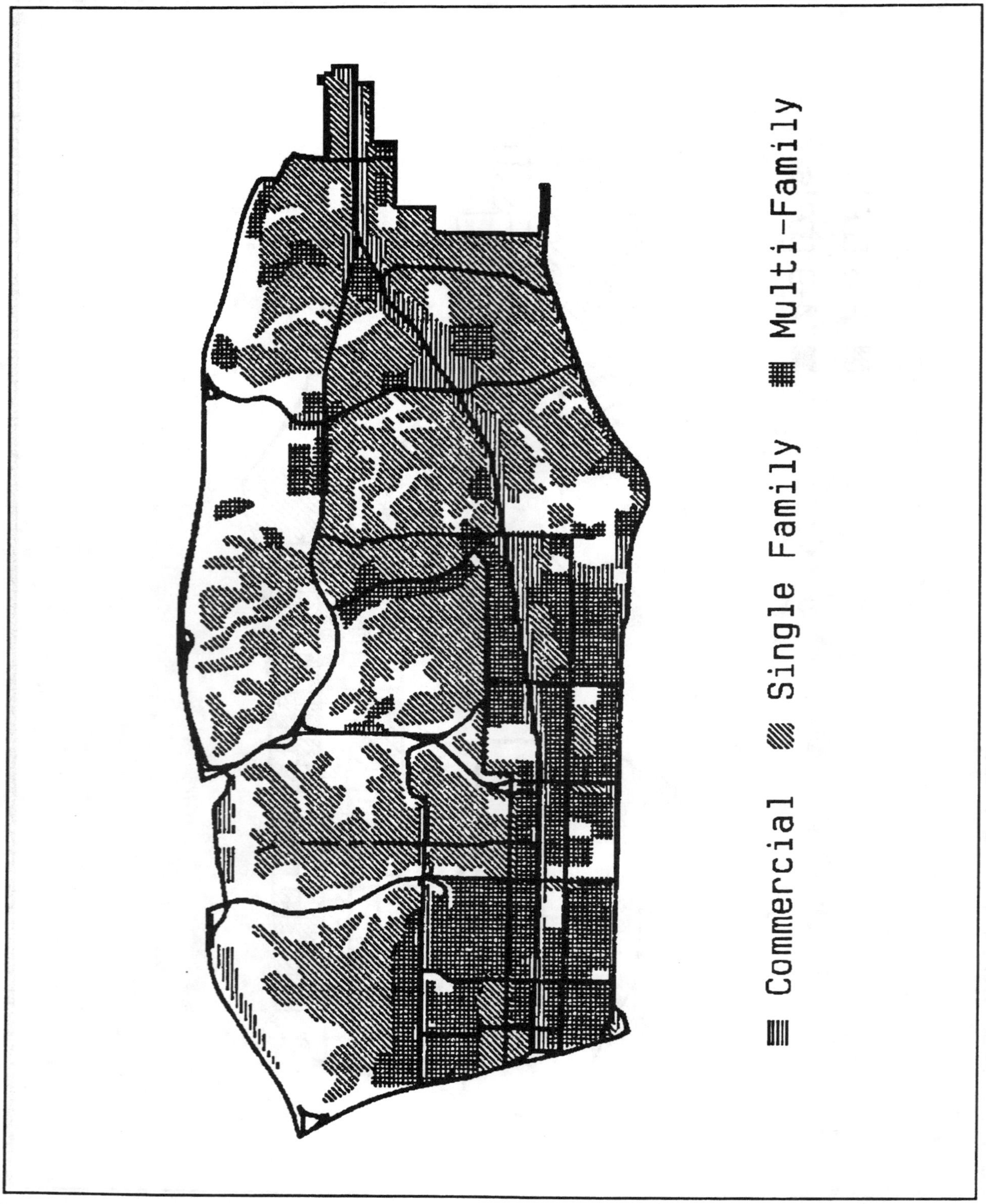

Fig. 3
Zoning patterns and arterial routes

To examine places, we need to use other analysis procedures. In the tables that follow, I use data from the case-control study, weighted to account for the number of dwelling units at risk, to show the relationship between drug dealing and different types of buildings.

Table 1
Structure Type and Drug Dealing

	Proportion of Sample With Attribute			
	Dealing (189)	Non-Dealing (181)	Odds Ratio	95% Confidence Interval
Apartments	.608 (115)	.770 (139)	.4642	0.2951–0.7301
Duplexes	.063 (12)	.072 (13)	0.8709	0.3868–1.9052
Single-Family Homes	.153 (29)	.106 (19)	1.5342	0.8276–2.8443
Commercial Sites	.175 (33)	.052 (9)	3.8484	1.8080–8.1916

Four types of buildings are compared in table 1: apartment buildings, duplexes, single-family homes, and commercial sites. Because the data come from a case-control design, correlation coefficients and normal measures of association will be biased (Loftin and McDowall 1986). Instead, I use odds ratios, which provide an unbiased estimate of the relative risk when the outcome is rare in the population (Schlesselman 1982). An odds ratio of one is an indicator of no association. An odds ratio greater than one is an indicator of a positive association, and an odds ratio less than one but greater than zero is an indicator of a negative association.

Despite the apparent association between apartments and drug dealing at the area level (figures 2 and 3), apartment units are underrepresented as drug dealing places in table 1. The negative relationship between apartments and drug dealing is significant. Judging from the lack of significance at the .05 level, duplexes and single-family homes do not seem to be related to drug dealing. Commercial establishments are associated with drug dealing, judging from the significant odds ratio. It appears that the reason dealers are found so often in apartment buildings is that there are so many apartment units available.

Table 2
Apartment Size and Drug Dealing

	Proportion of Sample With Attribute			
	Dealing (112)	Non-Dealing (47)	Odds Ratio	95% Confidence Interval
Small (3–8 units)	.536 (60)	.289 (14)	2.8383	1.3651–5.0901
Medium (9–15 units)	.241 (27)	.194 (9)	1.3161	0.5669–3.0557
Large (16–40 units)	.223 (25)	.517 (24)	0.2690	0.1303–0.5551

Table 2 shows the estimated odds ratios for apartment building sizes and drug dealing. Apartments in small buildings are significantly associated with drug dealing. Apartments in medium-size buildings have little association with drug dealing, and this association is not significant. Large apartment buildings are significantly negatively associated with drug dealing.

Smaller apartment buildings may be more vulnerable to drug dealers. With fewer units to rent, a landlord of a small building will face greater hardship if he or she evicts a tenant than will a landlord of a larger building. Small-time landlords, according to San Diego police detectives who work with them, are less knowledgeable about property management practices and their legal powers than are landlords of larger complexes. This evidence is supportive of the second segment of the model.

THE UTILITY OF MAPS

Using as an example data from a study of drug dealing, we see that maps can shed light on some aspects of the geography of crime. Studies of areas will benefit the most from the use of maps. However, maps cannot provide information about the characteristics of places. The segmented model of drug dealing requires information at the area and the place level. Maps were very useful for examining this model at the area level. But inferences from area maps to place characteristics can be misleading. Based on the maps, one might believe that apartment complexes were associated with drug dealing. Though much drug dealing goes on in apartment buildings, it is because there are a large number of apartment buildings. When one looks at place-level data, one finds that commercial places may be selected by dealers, even though these places are not as common as apartments. Within the category of apartments, it is the smaller complexes, with fewer apartment units at risk, that seem to be disproportionately selected for drug dealing sites, relative to larger complexes.

REFERENCES

Brantingham, Patricia L., and Paul J. Brantingham (1981). Notes on the geometry of crime. Pp. 27–54 in Paul J. Brantingham and Patricia L. Brantingham (eds.), *Environmental Criminology*. Beverly Hills: Sage.

Cornish, Derek, and Ronald Clarke (eds.) (1986). *The Reasoning Criminal: Rational Choice Perspectives on Offending*. New York: Springer-Verlag.

Eck, John E. (1994). *Drug Markets and Drug Places: A Case-Control Study of the Spatial Structure of Illicit Drug Dealing*. Unpublished doctoral dissertation. University of Maryland, College Park.

Felson, Marcus (1994). *Crime and Everyday Life: Insight and Implications for Society*. Thousand Oaks, Calif.: Pine Forge Press.

Loftin, Colin, and David McDowall (1988). The analysis of case-control studies in criminology. *Journal of Quantitative Criminology* 4:85–98.

Schlesselman, James J. (1982). *Case-Control Studies: Design, Conduct, Analysis*. Oxford: Oxford University Press.

Appendix

STAC and the Innovations in State and Local Government Program[1]

Carolyn Rebecca Block
Illinois Criminal Justice Information Authority

The STAC/Early Warning System, a joint project of the Authority's Statistical Analysis Center and the Chicago Police Department, was recently selected from nearly 2,000 applications as one of 25 finalists in the 1992 Innovations in State and Local Government program of Harvard University's J.F. Kennedy School of Government and the Ford Foundation.

The Innovations program was developed because Kennedy School public policy analysts had observed that

> although U.S. society values private sector innovation, it placed numerous barriers in the way of public sector innovation. . . . The challenge is to identify the appropriate means of encouraging creativity within the essential framework of democratic accountability.[2]

To encourage creativity in government, the Innovations program identifies strategically innovative programs at the state and local levels of U.S. government, recognizes and publicizes them as sources of inspiration for others, and uses them as models for training programs and curricular materials that encourage innovation.

What brought STAC to the attention of the Innovations program was not only its ability to identify hot-spot areas regardless of arbitrary ward, district or census tract boundaries, but also the use of mapped information as a foundation for identifying and solving community safety problems. Up until now, most STAC users have applied STAC to describing and combating property crime. Since street gang violence tends to occur in spurts within small geographic areas, the Early Warning System uses STAC to summarize police and community information and identify a crisis situation—a potential spurt of serious violence—in time to save lives.

For more information about the Ford Foundation/J.F. Kennedy School of Government Innovations in State and Local Government program, write to Innovations, Taubman Center for State and Local Government, J.F. Kennedy School of Government at Harvard University, 79 JFK St., Cambridge, MA 02138; or call (800) 722-0074.

1. This article was originally published in the Winter 1993 (vol. 1, no. 1) issue of *STACNews*.
2. Page 16 in Alan Altshuler and Marc Zegan's "Innovation and Creativity," *Cities*, February 1990, pages 16–24.

ABOUT THE POLICE EXECUTIVE RESEARCH FORUM (PERF)

The Police Executive Research Forum (PERF) is a national professional association of chief executives of large city, county and state law enforcement agencies. PERF's objective is to improve the delivery of police services and the effectiveness of crime control through several means:

1. the exercise of strong national leadership,
2. the public debate of police and criminal issues,
3. the development of research and policy, and
4. the provision of vital management leadership services to police agencies.

PERF members are selected on the basis of their commitment to PERF's objectives and principles. PERF operates under the following tenets:

1. Research, experimentation and exchange of ideas through public discussion and debate are paths for the development of a comprehensive body of knowledge about policing.
2. Substantial and purposeful academic study is a prerequisite for acquiring, understanding and adding to that body of knowledge.
3. Maintenance of the highest standards of ethics and integrity is imperative in the improvement of policing.
4. The police must, within the limits of the law, be responsible and accountable to citizens as the ultimate source of police authority.
5. The principles embodied in the Constitution are the foundation of policing.